Verse by Verse Commentary on

1 and 2 CHRONICLES

Enduring Word Commentary Series
By David Guzik

*The grass withers, the flower fades,
but the word of our God stands forever.*
Isaiah 40:8

Commentary on 1 and 2 Chronicles

Copyright ©2021 by David Guzik

Printed in the United States of America or in the United Kingdom

Print Edition ISBN: 978-1-939466-69-3

Enduring Word

5662 Calle Real #184

Goleta, CA 93117

Electronic Mail: ewm@enduringword.com

Internet Home Page: www.enduringword.com

All rights reserved. No portion of this book may be reproduced in any form (except for quotations in reviews) without the written permission of the publisher.

Scripture references, unless noted, are from the New King James Vesion of the Bible, copyright ©1979, 1980, 1982, Thomas Nelson, Inc., Publisher.

Contents

1 Chronicles 1 – From Adam to Abraham 7
1 Chronicles 2 – Descendants of Abraham and Judah 14
1 Chronicles 3 – The Royal Line of David and the House of Jesse 19
1 Chronicles 4 to 8 – The Tribes of Israel and their Descendants 22
1 Chronicles 9 – Leaders in Jerusalem 41
1 Chronicles 10 – The Death of Saul 47
1 Chronicles 11 – David's Reign and Mighty Men 52
1 Chronicles 12 – David's Army 59
1 Chronicles 13 – The Ark of the Covenant Comes to Jerusalem 66
1 Chronicles 14 – David's Throne Is Secured at Jerusalem 72
1 Chronicles 15 – The Ark Is Brought to Jerusalem 77
1 Chronicles 16 – David's Psalm of Thanks 83
1 Chronicles 17 – A House for God and a House for David 92
1 Chronicles 18 – The Security of David's Kingdom 101
1 Chronicles 19 – War with Ammon and Syria 107
1 Chronicles 20 – Ammon is Defeated at Rabbah 113
1 Chronicles 21 – Where to Build the Temple 117
1 Chronicles 22 – David's Charge to Solomon 127
1 Chronicles 23 – New Duties for the Levites 134
1 Chronicles 24 – The Sections of the Priesthood 140
1 Chronicles 25 – Musicians for the Temple 143
1 Chronicles 26 – The Gatekeepers for the Temple 147
1 Chronicles 27 – Tribal Leaders and Officials of State 151
1 Chronicles 28 – David's Public Charge to Solomon 155
1 Chronicles 29 – The End of David's Reign 161

2 Chronicles 1 – Solomon Seeks God 168
2 Chronicles 2 – Supplies and Workers for the Temple 175
2 Chronicles 3 – The Building of the Temple 180
2 Chronicles 4 – Furnishings for the Temple and Its Court 185
2 Chronicles 5 – The Ark is brought to the Temple 189
2 Chronicles 6 – Solomon's Prayer of Dedication 194

2 Chronicles 7 – The Temple Dedicated 202
2 Chronicles 8 – Achievements of Solomon 209
2 Chronicles 9 – More Achievements of Solomon 213
2 Chronicles 10 – The Reign of Rehoboam 221
2 Chronicles 11 – The Defection of the Levites 227
2 Chronicles 12 – The Chastisement of Rehoboam and Judah 232
2 Chronicles 13 – King Abijah and a Victory for Judah 238
2 Chronicles 14 – The Reign of Asa 243
2 Chronicles 15 – Revival and Reform in Judah 247
2 Chronicles 16 – Asa's Disappointing End 255
2 Chronicles 17 – Features of Jehoshaphat's Reign 261
2 Chronicles 18 – Jehoshaphat, Ahab, and Micaiah 266
2 Chronicles 19 – Jehu's Rebuke 275
2 Chronicles 20 – Jehoshaphat's Victory 278
2 Chronicles 21 – Jehoram's Evil Reign 288
2 Chronicles 22 – The Evil Reigns of Ahaziah and Athaliah 294
2 Chronicles 23 – Jehoiada and the Crowning of Joash 300
2 Chronicles 24 – The Rise and Fall of Joash 306
2 Chronicles 25 – The Reign of Amaziah 315
2 Chronicles 26 – The Reign of Uzziah 323
2 Chronicles 27 – Jotham's Godly Reign 330
2 Chronicles 28 – The Evil Reign of Ahaz 334
2 Chronicles 29 – Hezekiah and the Cleansing of the Temple 342
2 Chronicles 30 – Hezekiah's Passover 350
2 Chronicles 31 – Provision for the Priests 358
2 Chronicles 32 – God Protects Jerusalem 365
2 Chronicles 33 – The Reigns of Manasseh and Amon 375
2 Chronicles 34 – Josiah and the Book of the Law 385
2 Chronicles 35 – Josiah's Passover 395
2 Chronicles 36 – The Fall of Jerusalem 403

Bibliography – 414
Author's Remarks – 415

1 Chronicles 1 – From Adam to Abraham

A. From Adam to Abraham.

1. (1-4) From Adam to the Sons of Noah.

Adam, Seth, Enosh, Cainan, Mahalalel, Jared, Enoch, Methuselah, Lamech, Noah, Shem, Ham, and Japheth.

> a. **Adam, Seth, Enosh**: The opening verse of the Books of Chronicles indicates something of their focus. We know that Adam and Eve actually had three sons by name (Genesis 4:1-2, 4:25) plus many other unnamed sons and daughters (Genesis 5:4). Yet in this first verse we read nothing of Cain or Abel; only of **Seth**. This indicates that the Chronicler was inspired by God to make a selective genealogy for a specific purpose.
>
>> i. The Books of 1 and 2 Chronicles were originally one book, and focus historically on King David and his dynasty after him. The actual history begins with the death of Saul, but the stage is set with these genealogical tables. The story continues until the return of the exiles from the Babylonian captivity, leading many to think that the Books were written by Ezra or at least in his time.
>>
>> ii. "Since Chronicles appears to be the work of an individual writer, who was a Levitical leader, some identification with Ezra the priest and scribe (Ezra 7:1-6) appears possible from the outset." (Payne)
>>
>> iii. We can imagine the importance of these genealogical lists for the returning exiles. The message of the continuity of God's work through the generations was important for them, as well as helping them to affirm their own place in that flow of God's work through the ages.
>>
>> iv. "The principal design of the writer appears to have been this: to point out, from the public registers, which were still preserved, what had been the state of the different families previously to the captivity, that at their return they might enter in and repossess their respective

inheritances. He enters particularly into the functions, genealogies, families, and orders of the *priests* and *Levites*; and this was peculiarly necessary after the return from the captivity, to the end that the worship of God might be conducted in the same way as before, and by the proper legitimate persons." (Clarke)

v. "These books of the CHRONICLES are not the same which are so called, 1 Kings 14:19, and elsewhere, (because some passages said to be there mentioned are not found here,) but other books, and written by other persons, and for other ends." (Poole)

vi. "It was not in fact until the fourth century A.D. that Jerome, the famous Bible translator, first applied the term 'Chronicle' to these books…. The mediating influence came from Luther, whose German title, *Die Chronika*, passed into English with Bible translations proliferated during the Reformation period." (Selman)

b. **Noah, Shem, Ham, and Japheth**: This father and his three sons – each survivors of the flood – became the basis for the nations in the post-flood world.

i. The span from Adam to Noah and his sons is common to all humanity. This first chapter is "A summary of the 'generations' of Genesis, from Adam to Edom/Esau, shows that all the nations were God's creation and therefore part of his special purpose for Israel." (Selman)

2. (5-7) The descendants of Japheth, the son of Noah.

The sons of Japheth *were* Gomer, Magog, Madai, Javan, Tubal, Meshech, and Tiras. The sons of Gomer *were* Ashkenaz, Diphath, and Togarmah. The sons of Javan *were* Elishah, Tarshishah, Kittim, and Rodanim.

a. **The sons of Japheth**: It is commonly supposed that "The seven sons of Japheth founded the people of Europe and northern Asia." (Payne)

- From **Javan** came Greek Ionia.
- From **Gomer** came the ancient Cimmerians of the Russian plains.
- From **Madai** came the Medes and Persians of Iran.
- From **Tubal** and **Meshech** came the inhabitants of the Turkish plateau.

b. **Kittim, and Rodanim**: These are respectively the islands of Cyprus and Rhodes.

3. (8-16) The descendants of Ham, the son of Noah.

The sons of Ham *were* Cush, Mizraim, Put, and Canaan. The sons of Cush *were* Seba, Havilah, Sabta, Raama, and Sabtecha. The sons of

Raama *were* Sheba and Dedan. Cush begot Nimrod; he began to be a mighty one on the earth. Mizraim begot Ludim, Anamim, Lehabim, Naphtuhim, Pathrusim, Casluhim (from whom came the Philistines and the Caphtorim). Canaan begot Sidon, his firstborn, and Heth; the Jebusite, the Amorite, and the Girgashite; the Hivite, the Arkite, and the Sinite; the Arvadite, the Zemarite, and the Hamathite.

> a. **Ham**: The descendants of Ham are the peoples who populated Africa and the Far East.
>
> b. **Cush**: Apparently, this family divided into two branches early. Some founded Babylon (notably, **Nimrod**) and others founded Ethiopia.
>
>> i. Clarke cites an early Jewish Targum regarding Nimrod, who **began to be a mighty one on the earth**: "He began to be bold in sin, a murderer of the innocent, and a rebel before the Lord."
>
> c. **Mizraim**: This is another way the Bible refers to Egypt. **Put** refers to Libya, the region of North Africa west of Egypt. **Canaan** refers to the peoples who originally settled the land we today think of as Israel and its surrounding regions.
>
>> i. **From whom came the Philistines**: "The Hamitic Philistines were 'sea peoples' before settling in Palestine, coming from the Casluhim, who were of Egyptian origin but are related to the Minoan culture of Caphtor (Crete) and the southern coast of Asia Minor." (Payne)

4. (17-27) The descendants of Shem, the son of Noah.

The sons of Shem *were* Elam, Asshur, Arphaxad, Lud, Aram, Uz, Hul, Gether, and Meshech. Arphaxad begot Shelah, and Shelah begot Eber. To Eber were born two sons: the name of one *was* Peleg, for in his days the earth was divided; and his brother's name *was* Joktan. Joktan begot Almodad, Sheleph, Hazarmaveth, Jerah, Hadoram, Uzal, Diklah, Ebal, Abimael, Sheba, Ophir, Havilah, and Jobab. All these *were* the sons of Joktan. Shem, Arphaxad, Shelah, Eber, Peleg, Reu, Serug, Nahor, Terah, and Abram, who *is* Abraham.

> a. **The sons of Shem**: From Shem came **Elam**, who was an ancestor to the Persian peoples; **Asshur**, who was the father of the Assyrians; **Lud** was father to the Lydians who lived for a time in Asia Minor; and **Aram** was father to the Arameans, who we also know as the Syrians. **Arphaxad** was the ancestor to Abram and the Hebrews.
>
>> i. Significantly, the Chronicler included the nations that held Israel in exile (such as the Persians). As the Chronicler recorded this sweeping panorama of all the nations as having a part in God's plan, it assured

Israel that *they* were still part of the Lord's plan and so were the nations that held them in exile.

b. **Uz**: Later, a region in Arabia was named after this son of Aram. Job came from the land of Uz (Job 1:1).

i. "Uz gave the name of the home of the patriarch Job (Job 1:1), who may thus have been an early Edomite descendant of Esau (cf. Lamentations 4:21)." (Payne)

ii. Some think that **Jobab** is another name for Job, but their names are actually quite different in the Hebrew. "Supposed by some to be the same as *Job*, whose book forms a part of the canon of Scripture. But in their names there is no similarity." (Clarke)

c. **And Shelah begot Eber**: "The name Eber forms the root of 'Hebrew'; but this patriarch was the ancestor not only of Abraham (v. 27), but also of a number of other unsettled people, know in ancient history as Habiru or Apiru." (Payne)

d. **Peleg, for in his days the earth was divided**: This seems to refer to the dividing of the nations at the tower of Babel described in Genesis 11:1-9.

B. The sons of Abraham and their descendants to David.

1. (28) The sons of Abraham.

The sons of Abraham *were* Isaac and Ishmael.

a. **Isaac**: This was the son of promise and the covenant, whose birth was announced in Genesis 17 and 18 and whose life is recorded in Genesis 21-27.

b. **Ishmael**: This was the son born of Hagar, blessed as a son of Abraham but not an heir to the promise or the covenant (Genesis 16 and 21).

2. (29-31) The descendants of Abraham through Ishmael.

These *are* their genealogies: The firstborn of Ishmael *was* Nebajoth; then Kedar, Adbeel, Mibsam, Mishma, Dumah, Massa, Hadad, Tema, Jetur, Naphish, and Kedemah. These *were* the sons of Ishmael.

a. **These were the sons of Ishmael**: God promised to make a great nation through **Ishmael** (Genesis 21:18). These descendants were the beginning of the fulfillment of that promise, ultimately fulfilled in the Arabic peoples.

3. (32-33) The descendants of Abraham through Keturah.

Now the sons born to Keturah, Abraham's concubine, *were* Zimran, Jokshan, Medan, Midian, Ishbak, and Shuah. The sons of Jokshan *were*

Sheba and Dedan. The sons of Midian *were* Ephah, Epher, Hanoch, Abida, and Eldaah. All these were the children of Keturah.

> a. **All these were the children of Keturah**: This was the second wife of Abraham, taken after the death of Sarah (Genesis 25:1-4).

4. (34-42) The descendants of Abraham through Issac's son Esau.

And Abraham begot Isaac. The sons of Isaac *were* Esau and Israel. The sons of Esau *were* Eliphaz, Reuel, Jeush, Jaalam, and Korah. And the sons of Eliphaz *were* Teman, Omar, Zephi, Gatam, *and* Kenaz; and *by* Timna, Amalek. The sons of Reuel *were* Nahath, Zerah, Shammah, and Mizzah. The sons of Seir *were* Lotan, Shobal, Zibeon, Anah, Dishon, Ezer, and Dishan. And the sons of Lotan *were* Hori and Homam; Lotan's sister *was* Timna. The sons of Shobal *were* Alian, Manahath, Ebal, Shephi, and Onam. The sons of Zibeon *were* Ajah and Anah. The son of Anah *was* Dishon. The sons of Dishon *were* Hamran, Eshban, Ithran, and Cheran. The sons of Ezer *were* Bilhan, Zaavan, *and* Jaakan. The sons of Dishan *were* Uz and Aran.

> a. **The sons of Isaac were Esau and Israel**: Of these two sons, only **Israel** was chosen as the son of the promise and the heir of the covenant of Abraham. Nevertheless, **the sons of Esau** were still important to God and had a place in His eternal plan.

5. (43-54) The Kings and Chiefs of Edom

Now these *were* the kings who reigned in the land of Edom before a king reigned over the children of Israel: Bela the son of Beor, and the name of his city was Dinhabah. And when Bela died, Jobab the son of Zerah of Bozrah reigned in his place. When Jobab died, Husham of the land of the Temanites reigned in his place. And when Husham died, Hadad the son of Bedad, who attacked Midian in the field of Moab, reigned in his place. The name of his city *was* Avith. When Hadad died, Samlah of Masrekah reigned in his place. And when Samlah died, Saul of Rehoboth-by-the-River reigned in his place. When Saul died, Baal-Hanan the son of Achbor reigned in his place. And when Baal-Hanan died, Hadad reigned in his place; and the name of his city was Pai. His wife's name was Mehetabel the daughter of Matred, the daughter of Mezahab. Hadad died also. And the chiefs of Edom were Chief Timnah, Chief Aliah, Chief Jetheth, Chief Aholibamah, Chief Elah, Chief Pinon, Chief Kenaz, Chief Teman, Chief Mibzar, Chief Magdiel, and Chief Iram. These *were* the chiefs of Edom.

> a. **These were the kings who reigned in the land of Edom before a king reigned over the children of Israel**: It seems that the kings of Edom came

into power *before* the kings of Israel. In this, the Chronicler reminds the reader that God's ways have their own timing and wisdom; a timing and wisdom which is sometimes apparent and sometimes not.

> i. This list of the **kings** of Edom shows that Esau was indeed a blessed man (Genesis 33:8-16, Genesis 36), though he was rejected as the inheritor of the covenant of Abraham.

b. **Bela.... Jobab.... Zerah.... Husham**: The steady repetition of the names may seem to be an irrelevant blur to the modern reader, but they have an important place in God's plan of the ages. If nothing else, they demonstrate the *reality* of prior generations and our *connection* to both them and God's broader plan – just as a walk through a graveyard can speak the same things to us.

> i. "This is an ancient graveyard. The names of past generations who were born and died, who loved and suffered, who stormed and fought through the world, are engraven on these solid slabs. But there is no inscription to record their worth or demerit. Just names, and nothing more." (Meyer)

c. **These were the chiefs of Edom**: The chapter closes without a mention of the name of God in the entire chapter. Yet, as the Chronicler mentions these men as quoting from the sacred history of Genesis, God is the unspoken main character in the entire sweeping drama.

> i. "This chapter has therefore become a panoramic view of God's dealings with humanity in both creation and redemption. God's name does not actually appear, of course, but his activity is visible everywhere to the discerning reader." (Selman)
>
> ii. We see God almost everywhere in this chapter:
> - We see God calling out for Adam, hiding in his shame.
> - We see God blessing the birth of Seth, providing a son to replace both the one murdered and the murderer.
> - We see God walking with Enoch.
> - We see God calling to Noah and shutting the door of the ark.
> - We see God speaking to the sons of Noah and making His covenant with them.
> - We see God as the Most High, dividing an inheritance to the nations (Deuteronomy 32:8).
> - We see God dividing the earth at the tower of Babel in the days of Peleg.

- We see God choosing a Babylonian, from an idol-worshipping family, named Abraham.
- We see God stopping the sacrificial knife held over a surrendered Isaac.
- We see God orchestrating the choice of Israel over his brother Esau, despite all fleshly efforts of man to do otherwise.
- We see God blessing Esau and his descendants, as He promised to do.

1 Chronicles 2 – Descendants of Abraham and Judah

A. Descendants of Abraham.

1. (1-2) The descendants of Abraham through Israel.

These *were* the sons of Israel: Reuben, Simeon, Levi, Judah, Issachar, Zebulun, Dan, Joseph, Benjamin, Naphtali, Gad, and Asher.

> a. **These were the sons of Israel**: The line of the patriarchs began with Abraham, and was passed down to Isaac (and not Ishmael) and then to Jacob/Israel (and not to Esau). Yet with the **sons of Israel**, all the sons were chosen as inheritors of the covenant.
>
> b. **Reuben, Simeon, Levi, Judah, Issachar, Zebulun, Dan, Joseph, Benjamin, Naphtali, Gad, and Asher**: These twelve sons of Israel actually became 13 tribes of Israel, because two tribes came from **Joseph** (Manasseh and Ephraim).
>
> > i. "The order of names follows Genesis 35:23-26, with one exception. Dan is expected after Benjamin, and no convincing reason has been put forward for the change (*cf.* also Exodus 1:2-4). A different order is used in the following chapters." (Selman)

2. (3-17) The descendants of Judah to the family of Jesse, the father of David.

The sons of Judah *were* Er, Onan, and Shelah. *These* three were born to him by the daughter of Shua, the Canaanitess. Er, the firstborn of Judah, was wicked in the sight of the LORD; so He killed him. And Tamar, his daughter-in-law, bore him Perez and Zerah. All the sons of Judah *were* five. The sons of Perez *were* Hezron and Hamul. The sons of Zerah *were* Zimri, Ethan, Heman, Calcol, and Dara; five of them in all. The son of Carmi *was* Achar, the troubler of Israel, who transgressed in the accursed thing. The son of Ethan *was* Azariah. Also the sons of

Hezron who were born to him *were* Jerahmeel, Ram, and Chelubai. Ram begot Amminadab, and Amminadab begot Nahshon, leader of the children of Judah; Nahshon begot Salma, and Salma begot Boaz; Boaz begot Obed, and Obed begot Jesse; Jesse begot Eliab his firstborn, Abinadab the second, Shimea the third, Nethanel the fourth, Raddai the fifth, Ozem the sixth, *and* David the seventh. Now their sisters *were* Zeruiah and Abigail. And the sons of Zeruiah *were* Abishai, Joab, and Asahel; three. Abigail bore Amasa; and the father of Amasa *was* Jether the Ishmaelite.

a. **The sons of Judah**: There were twelve sons of Israel, and thirteen tribes from those twelve sons. Yet the tribe of **Judah** received first attention from the Chronicler.

i. "*Judah* heads the tribal genealogies, and receives more extensive treatment than any other tribe. The reason for this special prominence is to be found in the central position of *David's* line (2:10-17; 3:1-24)." (Selman)

ii. "But while our Chronicler lists all twelve of the sons of Israel-Jacob, his attention quickly focuses on Judah (2:3), the description of whose tribe occupies the next two and one-half chapters." (Payne)

b. **Er, the firstborn of Judah, was wicked in the sight of the LORD; so He killed him**: This listing of the line of Judah also includes those with a darker testimony of life, including **Er**, **Onan**, **Tamar**, and **Achar** (also known as *Achan* in Joshua 7:24-26).

i. "Achan was also guilty of 'unfaithfulness', a key term in Chronicles.... This word has the nuance of depriving God of his due, and is Chronicles' favourite explanation for the disaster of the exile." (Selman)

c. **Jesse begot...David the seventh**: This section of genealogy deals with the line of Judah to David, the founder of the Davidic dynasty that ruled over Israel and Judah.

i. **Abishai**, **Joab**, **Asahel**, and **Amasa**: "The genealogies of these four warriors, made famous under their half-uncle David (cf. 2 Samuel 2:18-19; 19:13), are not drawn from 2 Samuel 2:18 and 17:25; but apart from this later passage, we would not have known that their mothers, Zeruiah and Abigail, were step-daughters of Jesse, born to David's mother by her presumably earlier marriage to Nahash." (Payne)

B. **Other descendants of the tribe of Judah.**

1. (18-24) The family of Hezron, a grandson of Judah.

Caleb the son of Hezron had children by Azubah, *his* wife, and by Jerioth. Now these were her sons: Jesher, Shobab, and Ardon. When Azubah died, Caleb took Ephrath as his wife, who bore him Hur. And Hur begot Uri, and Uri begot Bezalel. Now afterward Hezron went in to the daughter of Machir the father of Gilead, whom he married when he *was* sixty years old; and she bore him Segub. Segub begot Jair, who had twenty-three cities in the land of Gilead. (Geshur and Syria took from them the towns of Jair, with Kenath and its towns; sixty towns.) All these *belonged to* the sons of Machir the father of Gilead. After Hezron died in Caleb Ephrathah, Hezron's wife Abijah bore him Ashhur the father of Tekoa.

    a. **Caleb the son of Hezron**: This traces a side-line in the tribe of Judah, separate from the line that culminated in David.

        i. "In practice, the otherwise unknown Caleb son of Hezron is probably distinct from Caleb, a Kenizzite and son of Jephunneh, who is frequently said to have 'followed the LORD wholeheartedly' (*e.g.* Numbers 14:24; 32:12; Joshua 14:6, 13-14)." (Selman) Caleb the Kenizzite seems to be mentioned in 1 Chronicles 4:15-16.

    b. **Jesher, Shobab, and Ardon**: These obscure names connected with the tribe of Judah are listed for an important general reason. Most of the returning exiles in the general time Chronicles was written were connected to the tribe of Judah.

        i. "The land that was occupied by the Jews who had returned from the Babylonian exile consisted primarily of the tribal territories of Judah and Benjamin. Also, the people who make up Ezra's community were largely from these same two tribes (Ezra 1:5; 10:9)." (Payne)

2. (25-41) The family of Jerahmeel, a great-grandson of Judah.

The sons of Jerahmeel, the firstborn of Hezron, *were* Ram, the firstborn, and Bunah, Oren, Ozem, *and* Ahijah. Jerahmeel had another wife, whose name was Atarah; she was the mother of Onam. The sons of Ram, the firstborn of Jerahmeel, were Maaz, Jamin, and Eker. The sons of Onam were Shammai and Jada. The sons of Shammai *were* Nadab and Abishur. And the name of the wife of Abishur *was* Abihail, and she bore him Ahban and Molid. The sons of Nadab *were* Seled and Appaim; Seled died without children. The son of Appaim *was* Ishi, the son of Ishi *was* Sheshan, and Sheshan's child *was* Ahlai. The sons of Jada, the brother of Shammai, *were* Jether and Jonathan; Jether died without children. The sons of Jonathan *were* Peleth and Zaza. These were the sons of Jerahmeel. Now Sheshan had no sons, only daughters. And Sheshan had an Egyptian servant whose name *was* Jarha. Sheshan

gave his daughter to Jarha his servant as wife, and she bore him Attai. Attai begot Nathan, and Nathan begot Zabad; Zabad begot Ephlal, and Ephlal begot Obed; Obed begot Jehu, and Jehu begot Azariah; Azariah begot Helez, and Helez begot Eleasah; Eleasah begot Sismai, and Sismai begot Shallum; Shallum begot Jekamiah, and Jekamiah begot Elishama.

    a. **The sons of Jerahmeel**: This traces a side-line in the tribe of Judah, separate from the line that culminated in David.

3. (42-55) The family of Caleb, a great-grandson of Judah.

The descendants of Caleb the brother of Jerahmeel were **Mesha, his firstborn, who was the father of Ziph, and the sons of Mareshah the father of Hebron. The sons of Hebron** were **Korah, Tappuah, Rekem, and Shema. Shema begot Raham the father of Jorkoam, and Rekem begot Shammai. And the son of Shammai** was **Maon, and Maon** was **the father of Beth Zur. Ephah, Caleb's concubine, bore Haran, Moza, and Gazez; and Haran begot Gazez. And the sons of Jahdai** were **Regem, Jotham, Geshan, Pelet, Ephah, and Shaaph. Maachah, Caleb's concubine, bore Sheber and Tirhanah. She also bore Shaaph the father of Madmannah, Sheva the father of Machbenah and the father of Gibea. And the daughter of Caleb** was **Achsah. These were the descendants of Caleb: The sons of Hur, the firstborn of Ephrathah,** were **Shobal the father of Kirjath Jearim, Salma the father of Bethlehem,** and **Hareph the father of Beth Gader. And Shobal the father of Kirjath Jearim had descendants: Haroeh,** and **half of the** families of **Manuhoth. The families of Kirjath Jearim** were **the Ithrites, the Puthites, the Shumathites, and the Mishraites. From these came the Zorathites and the Eshtaolites. The sons of Salma** were **Bethlehem, the Netophathites, Atroth Beth Joab, half of the Manahethites, and the Zorites. And the families of the scribes who dwelt at Jabez** were **the Tirathites, the Shimeathites,** and **the Suchathites. These** were **the Kenites who came from Hammath, the father of the house of Rechab.**

    a. **The descendants of Caleb**: This traces another side-line in the tribe of Judah, separate from the line that culminated in David.

        i. "Caleb's 'daughter' Acsah was only a distant descendant of Caleb the son of Hezron, though she was an immediate daughter of Caleb the son of Jephunneh, the faithful spy (listed in 4:15). She is remembered as the bride of Othniel, the first of the judges (Judges 3:9-11), having been promised to him for his conquest of Debir (Joshua 15:15-19; Judges 1:11-15)." (Payne)

b. **These are the Kenites**: "The Kenites were originally a foreign people (Genesis 15:19), some of whom, by marriage or adoption, became incorporated into the tribe of Judah." (Payne)

1 Chronicles 3 – The Royal Line of David and the House of Jesse

A. The descendants of David.

1. (1-3) The wives of David and their sons.

Now these were the sons of David who were born to him in Hebron: The firstborn *was* Amnon, by Ahinoam the Jezreelitess; the second, Daniel, by Abigail the Carmelitess; the third, Absalom the son of Maacah, the daughter of Talmai, king of Geshur; the fourth, Adonijah the son of Haggith; the fifth, Shephatiah, by Abital; the sixth, Ithream, by his wife Eglah.

> a. **Now these were the sons of David**: David had several wives and seven are listed in this chapter; **Ahinoam the Jezreelitess**, **Abigail the Carmelitess**, **Maacah**, **Haggith**, **Abital**, **Eglah**, and Bathshua (verse 5). These were in addition to his *concubines* (2 Samuel 5:13).
>
>> i. **Daniel**: "In 2 Samuel 3:3, this person is called *Chileab*; he probably had two names. The Targum says, 'The second, Daniel, who was also called Chileab, because he was in every respect like to his father." (Clarke)
>
> b. **Eglah**: Most suppose that this is another name for Michal, the daughter of Saul.

2. (4-9) Sons born to David in Jerusalem.

***These* six were born to him in Hebron. There he reigned seven years and six months, and in Jerusalem he reigned thirty-three years. And these were born to him in Jerusalem: Shimea, Shobab, Nathan, and Solomon; four by Bathshua the daughter of Ammiel. Also *there* were Ibhar, Elishama, Eliphelet, Nogah, Nepheg, Japhia, Elishama, Eliada,**

and Eliphelet; nine *in all*. *These were* all the sons of David, besides the sons of the concubines, and Tamar their sister.

    a. **And in Jerusalem he reigned thirty-three years**: The reign of David can be divided into these two parts; before he made Jerusalem his capital city and after.

    b. **Bathshua**: Most suppose that this is another name for Bathsheba.

        i. "*Bathshua* is probably an alternative pronunciation for *Bathsheba*, perhaps influenced by 2:3, though *Solomon* is described unexpectedly as her fourth son (*cf.* 2 Samuel 12:24-25)." (Selman)

B. The royal line of Judah after David.

1. (10-16) The line of David until the time of Judah's exile.

Solomon's son *was* Rehoboam; Abijah *was* his son, Asa his son, Jehoshaphat his son, Joram his son, Ahaziah his son, Joash his son, Amaziah his son, Azariah his son, Jotham his son, Ahaz his son, Hezekiah his son, Manasseh his son, Amon his son, *and* Josiah his son. The sons of Josiah *were* Johanan the firstborn, the second Jehoiakim, the third Zedekiah, and the fourth Shallum. The sons of Jehoiakim *were* Jeconiah his son *and* Zedekiah his son.

    a. **Solomon's son was Rehoboam**: This section traces the descent of the line of David from Solomon to the time after the exile, when Chronicles seems to have been written.

        i. "All the Davidic kings are here, and only Athaliah, Ahab's daughter (*cf.* 2 Kings 11) is missing." (Selman)

        ii. "Josiah's firstborn son, Johanan, is not mentioned elsewhere and may have died young." (Payne)

        iii. Selman on **Shallum**, **Jehoiakim**, and **Zedekiah**: "The information here cannot be reconciled with what is said about their ages in 2 Kings 23:31, 26; 24:18, and it is easiest to assume some scribal error in connection with the numbers."

2. (17-24) The line of David after the time of Judah's exile.

And the sons of Jeconiah *were* Assir, Shealtiel his son, *and* Malchiram, Pedaiah, Shenazzar, Jecamiah, Hoshama, and Nedabiah. The sons of Pedaiah *were* Zerubbabel and Shimei. The sons of Zerubbabel *were* Meshullam, Hananiah, Shelomith their sister, and Hashubah, Ohel, Berechiah, Hasadiah, and Jushab-Hesed; five *in all*. The sons of Hananiah *were* Pelatiah and Jeshaiah, the sons of Rephaiah, the sons of Arnan, the sons of Obadiah, and the sons of Shechaniah. The son of

Shechaniah was Shemaiah. The sons of Shemaiah *were* **Hattush, Igal, Bariah, Neariah, and Shaphat; six** *in all.* **The sons of Neariah** *were* **Elioenai, Hezekiah, and Azrikam; three** *in all.* **The sons of Elioenai** *were* **Hodaviah, Eliashib, Pelaiah, Akkub, Johanan, Delaiah, and Anani; seven** *in all.*

a. **And the sons of Jeconiah**: These were the descendants of the line of David born *after* the fall of Judah. They carried on the royal line of David.

i. "Jeremiah has said (Jeremiah 22:30) that Jeconiah, or, as he calls him, *Coniah*, should be *childless*; but this must refer to his *posterity* being deprived of the throne, and indeed thus the prophet interprets it himself: *For no man of his seed shall prosper, sitting upon the throne of David, and ruling anymore in Judah.*" (Clarke)

ii. "Through this multitude of largely unknown names, the Chronicler points out that God's election purposes were still at work despite the vicissitudes of Judah's history (*e.g.* 2:3,7) and the exile (*e.g.* 3:17-24)." (Selman)

1 Chronicles 4 through 8 – The Tribes of Israel and their Descendants

"How barren to us is this register, both of incident and interest! And yet, as barren rocks and sandy deserts make integral and necessary parts of the globe; so do these genealogical tables make necessary parts of the history of providence and grace in the maintenance of truth, and the establishment of the church of Christ. Therefore, no one that fears God will either despise or lightly esteem them." (Adam Clarke)

"Here tribes, and individual men, are seen as gaining importance and value in proportion as they co-operated in the purpose of God." (G. Campbell Morgan)

A. The tribes comprising the later kingdom of Judah.

1. (4:1-23) The descendants of Judah.

The sons of Judah *were* Perez, Hezron, Carmi, Hur, and Shobal. And Reaiah the son of Shobal begot Jahath, and Jahath begot Ahumai and Lahad. These *were* the families of the Zorathites. These *were* the sons *of the father* of Etam: Jezreel, Ishma, and Idbash; and the name of their sister *was* Hazelelponi; and Penuel *was* the father of Gedor, and Ezer *was the* father of Hushah. These *were* the sons of Hur, the firstborn of Ephrathah the father of Bethlehem. And Ashhur the father of Tekoa had two wives, Helah and Naarah. Naarah bore him Ahuzzam, Hepher, Temeni, and Haahashtari. These *were* the sons of Naarah. The sons of Helah *were* Zereth, Zohar, and Ethnan; and Koz begot Anub, Zobebah, and the families of Aharhel the son of Harum. Now Jabez was more honorable than his brothers, and his mother called his name Jabez, saying, "Because I bore *him* in pain." And Jabez called on the God of Israel saying, "Oh, that You would bless me indeed, and enlarge my territory, that Your hand would be with me, and that You would keep *me* from evil, that I may not cause pain!" So God granted him what he requested. Chelub the brother of Shuhah begot Mehir, who *was* the

father of Eshton. And Eshton begot Beth-Rapha, Paseah, and Tehinnah the father of Ir-Nahash. These *were* the men of Rechah. The sons of Kenaz *were* Othniel and Seraiah. The sons of Othniel *were* Hathath, and Meonothai *who* begot Ophrah. Seraiah begot Joab the father of Ge Harashim, for they were craftsmen. The sons of Caleb the son of Jephunneh *were* Iru, Elah, and Naam. The son of Elah *was* Kenaz. The sons of Jehallelel *were* Ziph, Ziphah, Tiria, and Asarel. The sons of Ezrah *were* Jether, Mered, Epher, and Jalon. And *Mered's wife bore* Miriam, Shammai, and Ishbah the father of Eshtemoa. (His wife Jehudijah bore Jered the father of Gedor, Heber the father of Sochoh, and Jekuthiel the father of Zanoah.) And these were the sons of Bithiah the daughter of Pharaoh, whom Mered took. The sons of Hodiah's wife, the sister of Naham, *were* the fathers of Keilah the Garmite and of Eshtemoa the Maachathite. And the sons of Shimon *were* Amnon, Rinnah, Ben-Hanan, and Tilon. And the sons of Ishi *were* Zoheth and Ben-Zoheth. The sons of Shelah the son of Judah *were* Er the father of Lecah, Laadah the father of Mareshah, and the families of the house of the linen workers of the house of Ashbea; also Jokim, the men of Chozeba, and Joash; Saraph, who ruled in Moab, and Jashubi-Lehem. Now the records are ancient. These *were* the potters and those who dwell at Netaim and Gederah; there they dwelt with the king for his work.

a. **The sons of Judah were**: Since the focus of these genealogies is the dynastic line of David, it makes sense that the tribe of **Judah** is listed first.

i. "Ezra expected his readers to recognize (from 2:5, 18, 50) that the five *descendants* of Judah, from Perez to Shobal, were not brothers but successive generations. 'Carmi' must therefore be a scribal error for Caleb." (Payne)

b. **Now Jabez was more honorable than his brothers**: This man **Jabez** is one of the more interesting briefly-mentioned people of the Old Testament. We only know of him from this text, and from the town of scribes that may have been named after him or associated with him (1 Chronicles 2:55).

i. "While through these genealogies, and indeed through all the history, we are occupied with those connected with government and the procession of events leading to universal issues, it is refreshing to be halted by the story of one man who took his need directly to God and obtained the answer of God's grace." (Morgan)

ii. "On these accounts he was *more honourable than his brethren*. He was of the same stock and the same lineage; he had neither nobility of birth, nor was distinguished by earthly titles; in all these respects he was on a level with his brethren: but God tells us that he was *more honourable than them all*; and why? because he *prayed*, because he *served his Maker*, and because he *lived to do good among men*; therefore he received the honour that cometh from God." (Clarke)

c. **His mother called his name Jabez**: This name is associated with pain or sorrow. For some reason, probably surrounding the circumstances of his birth, his mother named him this. Because of the strong importance of the idea of a *name* in ancient Hebrew culture, this idea of *pain* was connected to Jabez – perhaps especially in his growing up.

d. **And Jabez called on the God of Israel**: Jabez was honored, and we know little more of him than that he was a man of prayer and that his prayer was answered. One way to gain honor in the kingdom of God is through prayer, instead of through ambition and achievement. Jabez had four basic requests in his prayer.

i. First, Jabez prayed to be blessed **indeed**. There are many who are blessed, but they are not **blessed indeed**. That is, they have something that is in one sense a blessing (such as family, salvation, wealth, fame, health, security), but yet because of fundamental dissatisfaction in their life, they are not **blessed indeed**.

- Even worse, sometimes blessings turn out to be a curse to us in that we make an idol of the blessing. In this, we see the great wisdom of Jabez's prayer.

- In the same way, many things that are outwardly curses end up being blessings **indeed** to us.

ii. Jabez prayed for enlarged **territory**. Virtually all older commentators agree with Matthew Poole that Jabez **called on the God of Israel** "when he was undertaking some great and dangerous service," in particular the conquest of the land of Canaan. Therefore, when he prayed "**enlarge my territory**," it was to "drive out these wicked and cursed Canaanties, whom thou hast commanded us to root out, and therefore I justly beg and expect thy blessing in the execution of thy command." (Poole)

- Adam Clarke quotes a Chaldean translation of this prayer, with the line: *and enlarge my borders with disciples*. This, together with the scribal city associated with his name, indicates (but does not prove) that Jabez's desire for more territory was not only to displace the wicked but also to advance the cause of godliness through the multiplication of disciples.

iii. Jabez asked that the **hand** of God would be **with** him. "The 'hand of the Lord' is a biblical term for God's power and presence in the lives of His people (see Joshua 4:24 and Isaiah 59:1)." (Wilkinson)

- The phrase *the hand of the LORD* is used many times in the Old Testament, and often in a negative sense – that is, in the sense of God's hand being *against* someone in judgment. Here Jabez prayed that the **hand** of the LORD would be **with** him.

- In Psalm 77:10, the Psalmist wrote: *I will remember the years of the right hand of the Most High.* Here Jabez prayed in advance for something to remember later – to see the **hand** of God **with** him now.

iv. Jabez asked to be kept from **evil** and that he would **not cause pain**. Some other translations render this with the idea that the **pain** Jabez did not want to cause was his own. "He used this expression in allusion to his name, which signifies *grief*; Lord, let me not have that grief which my name implies, and which my sin deserves." (Poole)

- In this Jabez recognized the evil in this world, no doubt because he had lived through much pain in his life.

- In this Jabez recognized that he needed God to keep him from evil.

- In this Jabez recognized that the hand of God could transform the evil and pain of his life.

e. **So God granted him what he requested**: This, of course, is the measure of effective prayer – that it is answered from heaven (allowing that "No" or "Wait" can also be an answer). Yet when we are close to the heart of God and pray for the things important to Him and His kingdom, we expect that our prayers will be **granted** (1 John 5:14).

i. "If we take up the character and conduct of Jabez in the view given by the *Chaldee*, we shall not only see him as a *pious* and *careful* man, deeply interested in behalf of *himself* and his *family*, but we shall see him as a *benevolent* man, labouring for the welfare of others, and especially for the religious instruction of *youth*. He founded *schools*, in which the young and rising generation were taught useful knowledge, and especially the knowledge of God. He had *disciples*, which were divided into *three classes*, who distinguished themselves by their *fervour* in the *worship of God*, by their *docility* in obediently hearing and treasuring up the advices and instructions of their teachers, and by their deep piety to God in bringing forth the fruits of the Spirit. The *spirit of prophecy*, that is, of *prayer* and *supplication, rested upon them*." (Clarke)

ii. "Reader, imitate the conduct of this worthy Israelite that thou mayest be a partaker of his blessings." (Clarke)

f. **And these were the sons of Bithiah the daughter of Pharaoh, whom Mered took**: "The wife of Mered here intended is Bithiah (v. 18). Her identification as a daughter of Pharaoh would locate this event during the early part of Israel's sojourn in Egypt (before 1800 B.C.), the union probably being made possible because of Joseph's prominence." (Payne)

g. **These were the potters and those who dwell at Netaim and Gederah; there they dwelt with the king for his work**: Since the broad focus of these chapters is to point to the tribe of Judah and especially to the family of David, these men receive special mention because they worked for the king and lived with the king. Charles Spurgeon preached a wonderful sermon on this verse, with four points under the title *With the King for His Work!*

i. *Our King has many kinds of servants.* He has soldiers, watchmen, heralds, scribes, musicians, house servants, gardeners, servants for the children. We should therefore value the different servants and understand and value our own place of service.

ii. *All who live with our King must work.* "They did not live on the king's bounty and dwell on the king's country estates to do nothing, but they dwelt there for his work. I do not know whether all that call my Master 'Lord' have caught this idea. I have thought that some of our church members imagine that the cause of Christ was a coach, and that they were to ride on it, and that they would prefer the box seat." (Spurgeon)

iii. *Those that work for the King ought to live with Him.* "Now, those that live with Jesus Christ have a sort of secret alphabet between themselves and him. Oftentimes when a Christian man does the right thing.... Do you know why he had that knack? He lived with his Master, so he knew what you knew not. He knew the meaning of his Master's eye, and it guided him." (Spurgeon)

iv. *We are working for the King.* "And after you have received Christ then you shall go forth and serve him. Put out an empty hand and receive Christ into it by a little faith, and then go and serve him, and the Lord bless you henceforth and for ever." (Spurgeon)

2. (4:24-43) The descendants of Simeon.

The sons of Simeon *were* Nemuel, Jamin, Jarib, Zerah, *and* Shaul, Shallum his son, Mibsam his son, and Mishma his son. And the sons of Mishma *were* Hamuel his son, Zacchur his son, and Shimei his son.

Shimei had sixteen sons and six daughters; but his brothers did not have many children, nor did any of their families multiply as much as the children of Judah. They dwelt at Beersheba, Moladah, Hazar Shual, Bilhah, Ezem, Tolad, Bethuel, Hormah, Ziklag, Beth Marcaboth, Hazar Susim, Beth Biri, and at Shaaraim. These *were* their cities until the reign of David. And their villages *were* Etam, Ain, Rimmon, Tochen, and Ashan; five cities; and all the villages that *were* around these cities as far as Baal. These *were* their dwelling places, and they maintained their genealogy: Meshobab, Jamlech, and Joshah the son of Amaziah; Joel, and Jehu the son of Joshibiah, the son of Seraiah, the son of Asiel; Elioenai, Jaakobah, Jeshohaiah, Asaiah, Adiel, Jesimiel, and Benaiah; Ziza the son of Shiphi, the son of Allon, the son of Jedaiah, the son of Shimri, the son of Shemaiah; these mentioned by name *were* leaders in their families, and their father's house increased greatly. So they went to the entrance of Gedor, as far as the east side of the valley, to seek pasture for their flocks. And they found rich, good pasture, and the land *was* broad, quiet, and peaceful; for some Hamites formerly lived there. These recorded by name came in the days of Hezekiah king of Judah; and they attacked their tents and the Meunites who were found there, and utterly destroyed them, as it is to this day. So they dwelt in their place, because *there was* pasture for their flocks there. Now *some* of them, five hundred men of the sons of Simeon, went to Mount Seir, having as their captains Pelatiah, Neariah, Rephaiah, and Uzziel, the sons of Ishi. And they defeated the rest of the Amalekites who had escaped. They have dwelt there to this day.

> a. **The sons of Simeon.... these were the dwelling places**: Simeon and Levi, two of the sons of Jacob, massacred the men of the city of Shechem (Genesis 34:24-30, 49:5-7) and were therefore cursed to be scattered. Therefore, the tribe of Simeon did not have a province to call their own, only these cities, villages, and **dwelling places**.
>
>> i. "Simeon was granted lands in Palestine only within the arid southwestern portions of Judah (Joshua 19:1-9; cf. 15:26, 28-32); and it campaigned cooperatively with Judah in their conquest (Judges 1:3)." (Payne)
>>
>> ii. "For after the division of Solomon's kingdom in 930 B.C., elements of Simeon either moved to the north or at least adopted its religious practices (cf. the inclusion of Beersheba along with the shrines of Ephraim that are condemned in Amos 5:5).... Other Simeonites carried on in a seminomadic life in isolated areas that they could occupy, such as those noted at the close of this chapter." (Payne)

iii. "This genealogy is very different from that given in Genesis 46:10, and Numbers 26:12. This may be occasioned by the same person having several names, one *list* taking one name, another list some other, and so on: to reconcile is impossible; to attempt it, useless." (Clarke)

b. **But his brothers did not have many children, nor did any of their families multiply as much as the children of Judah**: The census data both at the beginning and the end of the Book of Numbers indicates that the population of the tribe of Simeon decreased radically during the wilderness years of the exodus. They were among the largest tribes at the beginning and among the smallest tribes at the end.

i. "Of this tribe was that shameless fornicator, Zimri (Numbers 25), as also Judas Iscariot, as Jerome affirmeth." (Trapp)

B. The tribes of Israel settling east of the Jordan River.

1. (5:1-10) The descendants of Reuben.

Now the sons of Reuben the firstborn of Israel; he *was* indeed the firstborn, but because he defiled his father's bed, his birthright was given to the sons of Joseph, the son of Israel, so that the genealogy is not listed according to the birthright; yet Judah prevailed over his brothers, and from him *came* a ruler, although the birthright was Joseph's; the sons of Reuben the firstborn of Israel were Hanoch, Pallu, Hezron, and Carmi. The sons of Joel *were* Shemaiah his son, Gog his son, Shimei his son, Micah his son, Reaiah his son, Baal his son, and Beerah his son, whom Tiglath-Pileser king of Assyria carried into captivity. He *was* leader of the Reubenites. And his brethren by their families, when the genealogy of their generations was registered: the chief, Jeiel, and Zechariah, and Bela the son of Azaz, the son of Shema, the son of Joel, who dwelt in Aroer, as far as Nebo and Baal Meon. Eastward they settled as far as the entrance of the wilderness this side of the River Euphrates, because their cattle had multiplied in the land of Gilead. Now in the days of Saul they made war with the Hagrites, who fell by their hand; and they dwelt in their tents throughout the entire *area* east of Gilead.

a. **Reuben the firstborn of Israel; he was indeed the firstborn, but because he defiled his father's bed, his birthright was given**: This answers the question, "If Reuben was the first-born son, why is he not listed first?" It was because of the sin described in this verse, which disqualified Reuben from being first among the sons of Israel.

b. **Now in the days of Saul they made war with the Hagrites**: "The *Hagarites* were tribes of *Nomade*, or *Scenite*, Arabs; people who lived in *tents*, without any fixed dwellings, and whose property consisted in *cattle*.

The descendants of Reuben extirpated these Hagarites, seized on their property and their tents, and dwelt in their place." (Clarke)

2. (5:11-22) The descendants of Gad.

And the children of Gad dwelt next to them in the land of Bashan as far as Salcah: Joel *was* **the chief, Shapham the next, then Jaanai and Shaphat in Bashan, and their brethren of their father's house: Michael, Meshullam, Sheba, Jorai, Jachan, Zia, and Eber; seven** *in all.* **These** *were* **the children of Abihail the son of Huri, the son of Jaroah, the son of Gilead, the son of Michael, the son of Jeshishai, the son of Jahdo, the son of Buz; Ahi the son of Abdiel, the son of Guni,** *was* **chief of their father's house. And** *the Gadites* **dwelt in Gilead, in Bashan and in its villages, and in all the common-lands of Sharon within their borders. All these were registered by genealogies in the days of Jotham king of Judah, and in the days of Jeroboam king of Israel. The sons of Reuben, the Gadites, and half the tribe of Manasseh** *had* **forty-four thousand seven hundred and sixty valiant men, men able to bear shield and sword, to shoot with the bow, and skillful in war, who went to war. They made war with the Hagrites, Jetur, Naphish, and Nodab. And they were helped against them, and the Hagrites were delivered into their hand, and all who** *were* **with them, for they cried out to God in the battle. He heeded their prayer, because they put their trust in Him. Then they took away their livestock; fifty thousand of their camels, two hundred and fifty thousand of their sheep, and two thousand of their donkeys; also one hundred thousand of their men; for many fell dead, because the war** *was* **God's. And they dwelt in their place until the captivity.**

a. **For they cried out to God in the battle**: As these men of Gad did what God called them to do, they trusted in Him in the midst of the **battle**. Because **they put their trust in Him**, God delivered them in the battle.

i. Trapp on **for they cried to God in the battle**: "So did Jabez (chapter 4); Jehoshaphat (2 Chronicles 20); the thundering legion; the late king of Sweden, whose prayer before the great battle of Lutzen - where he fell, - was, 'Jesus vouchsafe this day to be my strong helper; and give me courage to fight for the honour of thy name.' In prayer alone he held the surest piece of his whole armour."

b. **Also one hundred thousand of their men; for many fell dead, because the war was God's**: This describes the unique wars of judgment God called Israel to bring against the Canaanites when they came into the Promised Land.

i. "This was a war of extermination as to the political state of the people, which nothing could justify but a special direction of God; and this he could never give against any, unless the cup of their iniquity had been full. The Hagrites were full of idolatry: see 1 Chronicles 5:25." (Clarke)

3. (5:23-26) The descendants of the eastern tribe of Manasseh.

So the children of the half-tribe of Manasseh dwelt in the land. Their *numbers* increased from Bashan to Baal Hermon, that is, to Senir, or Mount Hermon. These *were* the heads of their fathers' houses: Epher, Ishi, Eliel, Azriel, Jeremiah, Hodaviah, and Jahdiel. They were mighty men of valor, famous men, *and* heads of their fathers' houses. And they were unfaithful to the God of their fathers, and played the harlot after the gods of the peoples of the land, whom God had destroyed before them. So the God of Israel stirred up the spirit of Pul king of Assyria, that is, Tiglath-Pileser king of Assyria. He carried the Reubenites, the Gadites, and the half-tribe of Manasseh into captivity. He took them to Halah, Habor, Hara, and the river of Gozan to this day.

a. **They were mighty men of valor, famous men, and heads of their fathers' houses**: These original settlers of the eastern tribe of Manasseh were godly and bold men. Their desire to settle east of the Jordan River did not reflect an ungodly desire on *their* part.

b. **And they were unfaithful to the God of their fathers, and played the harlot after the gods of the peoples of the land**: Despite the good start for the eastern tribe of Manasseh, this is how they ended up. Their distance from the people of Israel in general and the spiritual life of the nation, in particular, seemed to weaken their devotion to God and strengthen their attraction to **the gods of the peoples of the land**.

i. "The remaining verses of chapter 5 describe an early, joint military campaign (vv. 18-22, elaborating v. 10) – in which God rewarded their faith and their prayers with a great victory over the Ishmaelites – and their later deportation to Assyria (vv. 25-26), as the result of collective apostasy." (Payne)

C. The tribe of Levi.

1. (6:1-30) The descendants of Levi.

The sons of Levi *were* Gershon, Kohath, and Merari. The sons of Kohath *were* Amram, Izhar, Hebron, and Uzziel. The children of Amram *were* Aaron, Moses, and Miriam. And the sons of Aaron *were* Nadab, Abihu, Eleazar, and Ithamar. Eleazar begot Phinehas, *and* Phinehas begot Abishua; Abishua begot Bukki, and Bukki begot Uzzi; Uzzi begot Zerahiah, and Zerahiah begot Meraioth; Meraioth begot Amariah, and

Amariah begot Ahitub; Ahitub begot Zadok, and Zadok begot Ahimaaz; Ahimaaz begot Azariah, and Azariah begot Johanan; Johanan begot Azariah (it was he who ministered as priest in the temple that Solomon built in Jerusalem); Azariah begot Amariah, and Amariah begot Ahitub; Ahitub begot Zadok, and Zadok begot Shallum; Shallum begot Hilkiah, and Hilkiah begot Azariah; Azariah begot Seraiah, and Seraiah begot Jehozadak. Jehozadak went *into captivity* when the LORD carried Judah and Jerusalem into captivity by the hand of Nebuchadnezzar. The sons of Levi *were* Gershon, Kohath, and Merari. These are the names of the sons of Gershon: Libni and Shimei. The sons of Kohath *were* Amram, Izhar, Hebron, and Uzziel. The sons of Merari *were* Mahli and Mushi. Now these *are* the families of the Levites according to their fathers: Of Gershon *were* Libni his son, Jahath his son, Zimmah his son, Joah his son, Iddo his son, Zerah his son, *and* Jeatherai his son. The sons of Kohath *were* Amminadab his son, Korah his son, Assir his son, Elkanah his son, Ebiasaph his son, Assir his son, Tahath his son, Uriel his son, Uzziah his son, and Shaul his son. The sons of Elkanah *were* Amasai and Ahimoth. *As for* Elkanah, the sons of Elkanah *were* Zophai his son, Nahath his son, Eliab his son, Jeroham his son, *and* Elkanah his son. The sons of Samuel *were Joel* the firstborn, and Abijah the second. The sons of Merari *were* Mahli, Libni his son, Shimei his son, Uzzah his son, Shimea his son, Haggiah his son, *and* Asaiah his son.

a. **The sons of Levi were**: This chapter describes the descendants of **Levi** and of **Aaron**. The entire tribe of Levi had a special place in Israel, given over to the service of God generally. Within the tribe of Levi was a special priestly family descended from **Aaron**. All priests were therefore Levites, but not all Levites were priests.

i. "It has been well remarked that the genealogy of *Levi* is given here more ample and correct than that of any of the others. And this is perhaps an additional proof that the author was a *priest*, felt much for the priesthood, and took care to give the genealogy of the Levitical and [priestly] families, from the most correct tables; for with such tables we may presume he was intimately acquainted." (Clarke)

ii. As previously seen, Simeon and Levi were both cursed to be scattered because of their massacre of the men of Shechem (Genesis 34:24-30, 49:5-7). God did in fact both divide the tribes of Simeon and Levi and scatter them among Israel. Yet the way it happened for each tribe was different. The tribe of Simeon, because of their lack of faithfulness, was effectively dissolved as a tribe, and was absorbed into the tribal area of Judah. The tribe of Levi was also scattered, but because of the faithfulness of this tribe during the rebellion of the golden calf (Exodus 32:26-28), the tribe was scattered as a blessing throughout the whole nation of Israel. Both were scattered, but one as a blessing and the other as a curse.

b. **In the temple that Solomon built in Jerusalem**: "So called to distinguish it from the second temple, which was built or in building when these books were written." (Poole)

c. **When the LORD carried Judah and Jerusalem into captivity by the hand of Nebuchadnezzar**: According to pattern, the inspired historian saw the hand of God even in the great tragedy that still afflicted Judah at the time of writing Chronicles. It was not the Babylonian Empire that **carried Judah and Jerusalem into captivity**, but it was the LORD.

2. (6:31-48) The musicians for the House of the LORD.

Now these are the men whom David appointed over the service of song in the house of the LORD, after the ark came to rest. They were ministering with music before the dwelling place of the tabernacle of meeting, until Solomon had built the house of the LORD in Jerusalem, and they served in their office according to their order. And these *are* the ones who ministered with their sons: Of the sons of the Kohathites *were* Heman the singer, the son of Joel, the son of Samuel, the son of Elkanah, the son of Jeroham, the son of Eliel, the son of Toah, the son of Zuph, the son of Elkanah, the son of Mahath, the son of Amasai, the son of Elkanah, the son of Joel, the son of Azariah, the son of Zephaniah, the son of Tahath, the son of Assir, the son of Ebiasaph, the son of Korah, the son of Izhar, the son of Kohath, the son of Levi, the son of Israel. And his brother Asaph, who stood at his right hand, *was* Asaph the son of Berachiah, the son of Shimea, the son of Michael, the son of Baaseiah, the son of Malchijah, the son of Ethni, the son of Zerah, the son of Adaiah, the son of Ethan, the son of Zimmah, the son of Shimei, the son of Jahath, the son of Gershon, the son of Levi. Their brethren, the sons of Merari, on the left hand, *were* Ethan the son of Kishi, the son of Abdi, the son of Malluch, the son of Hashabiah, the son of Amaziah, the son of Hilkiah, the son of Amzi, the son of Bani, the son of Shamer, the son of Mahli, the son of Mushi, the son of Merari, the son of Levi. And their brethren, the Levites, *were* appointed to every kind of service of the tabernacle of the house of God.

a. **Whom David appointed over the service of song in the house of the LORD, after the ark came to rest**: The dramatic entry of the ark of the covenant into Jerusalem is described in both 2 Samuel 6 and 1 Chronicles 15-16.

i. The fact that David **appointed** these men over the **service of song** shows that the musical worship of God is *important*, it is *worthy of attention*, and *should be organized*. In fact, it is specifically said **they served in their office according to their order**.

ii. It could perhaps be said that the artistic temperament resists organization, and it is certainly possible to be too ordered and too rigid, refusing to allow proper flexibility in the Holy Spirit. Nevertheless, organization and order remain part of a good music ministry.

iii. **They were ministering with music**: Their *ministry* was *music*. It was sacred service before the LORD, worthy of their dedication and hard work.

b. **Heman the singer**: This man is mentioned several times in connection with temple worship in the days of David and Solomon (1 Chronicles 15:17-19, 16:41-42, 25:1-7, 2 Chronicles 5:12-13). He was an important part of the ceremonies connected with bringing the ark of the covenant to Jerusalem and the dedication of the temple.

i. Psalm 88 is attributed to Heman: *A Song. A Psalm of the sons of Korah. To the Chief Musician. Set to "Mahalath Leannoth." A Contemplation [Maschil] of Heman the Ezrahite.*

ii. Psalm 88 shows us a man well acquainted with sorrow and trouble: *For my soul is full of troubles* (88:3).... *I am like a man who has no strength* (88:4).... *Your wrath lies heavy upon me* (88:7). Some of the sweetest songs come from the heaviest sorrow.

iii. Psalm 88 also shows us a man who could take his grief to the LORD: *But to You I have cried out, O LORD, and in the morning my prayer comes before You* (88:13). It is not a confident or triumphant psalm, but the undercurrent of trust and refuge in God runs through the song of sorrow.

c. **And his brother Asaph, who stood at his right hand**: Partnered with **Heman the singer** was **Asaph**, making for one of the great worship-leading combinations in history.

i. This is the first mention of Asaph in the Bible; the Asaph listed in 2 Kings 18:18 and 18:37 is a different man. Asaph was a man of wide and long-lasting influence among God's people.

- 1 Chronicles 15:17-19 mentions Asaph as a fellow singer with Heman and Ethan.
- 1 Chronicles 16:5 describes Asaph as *the chief* at the ceremony bringing the ark of the covenant into Jerusalem.

- 1 Chronicles 16:7 says that David delivered a psalm to Asaph and his brethren at that ceremony. Apparently, David wrote the psalm and Asaph and his brethren performed it.
- 1 Chronicles 16:37 says that Asaph was left with the responsibility to daily minister before the ark of the covenant when it was brought into Jerusalem in David's time.
- 1 Chronicles 25:6 says that Asaph, Jeduthun, and Heman served in music under the authority of King David.
- 2 Chronicles 20:14 and 29:13 indicate that the influence of Asaph lasted far beyond his death, in that future worship leaders and musicians were known as the *sons of Asaph*, even to the days of Ezra (Ezra 2:41, 3:10; Nehemiah 7:44, 11:17 and 22).

ii. 12 Psalms are attributed to Asaph (Psalm 50 and Psalms 73 through 83).

d. **Appointed to every kind of service of the tabernacle of the house of God**: The Levites served God in almost every conceivable way, both practical and spiritual. **Every kind of service** is important and precious to God.

3. (6:49-53) The family of Aaron.

But Aaron and his sons offered sacrifices on the altar of burnt offering and on the altar of incense, for all the work of the Most Holy *Place,* and to make atonement for Israel, according to all that Moses the servant of God had commanded. Now these *are* the sons of Aaron: Eleazar his son, Phinehas his son, Abishua his son, Bukki his son, Uzzi his son, Zerahiah his son, Meraioth his son, Amariah his son, Ahitub his son, Zadok his son, *and* Ahimaaz his son.

a. **But Aaron and his sons offered sacrifices on the altar**: The priesthood descended from Aaron and Aaron only. He, his sons, and their descendants were the only ones authorized to offer **sacrifices on the altar**.

b. **And to make atonement for Israel**: Only an authorized priest could make atonement. Though Jesus was not descended from Aaron, He was nevertheless an authorized priest according to the order of Melchizedek, not Aaron (Hebrews 7).

c. **Now these are the sons of Aaron**: *Not* listed are the two disobedient sons of Aaron (Nadab and Abihu) who were judged for bringing a strange fire of corrupt worship to the altar (Leviticus 10).

4. (6:54-81) The cities and common-lands of the Levites.

Now these *are* their dwelling places throughout their settlements in their territory, for they were *given* by lot to the sons of Aaron, of the family of the Kohathites: They gave them Hebron in the land of Judah, with its surrounding common-lands. But the fields of the city and its villages they gave to Caleb the son of Jephunneh. And to the sons of Aaron they gave *one of* the cities of refuge, Hebron; also Libnah with its common-lands, Jattir, Eshtemoa with its common-lands, Hilen with its common-lands, Debir with its common-lands, Ashan with its common-lands, and Beth Shemesh with its common-lands. And from the tribe of Benjamin: Geba with its common-lands, Alemeth with its common-lands, and Anathoth with its common-lands. All their cities among their families *were* thirteen. To the rest of the family of the tribe of the Kohathites *they gave* by lot ten cities from half the tribe of Manasseh. And to the sons of Gershon, throughout their families, *they gave* thirteen cities from the tribe of Issachar, from the tribe of Asher, from the tribe of Naphtali, and from the tribe of Manasseh in Bashan. To the sons of Merari, throughout their families, *they gave* twelve cities from the tribe of Reuben, from the tribe of Gad, and from the tribe of Zebulun. So the children of Israel gave *these* cities with their common-lands to the Levites. And they gave by lot from the tribe of the children of Judah, from the tribe of the children of Simeon, and from the tribe of the children of Benjamin these cities which are called by *their* names. Now some of the families of the sons of Kohath *were given* cities as their territory from the tribe of Ephraim. And they gave them *one of* the cities of refuge, Shechem with its common-lands, in the mountains of Ephraim, also Gezer with its common-lands, Jokmeam with its common-lands, Beth Horon with its common-lands, Aijalon with its common-lands, and Gath Rimmon with its common-lands. And from the half-tribe of Manasseh: Aner with its common-lands and Bileam with its common-lands, for the rest of the family of the sons of Kohath. From the family of the half-tribe of Manasseh the sons of Gershon *were given* Golan in Bashan with its common-lands and Ashtaroth with its common-lands. And from the tribe of Issachar: Kedesh with its common-lands, Daberath with its common-lands, Ramoth with its common-lands, and Anem with its common-lands. And from the tribe of Asher: Mashal with its common-lands, Abdon with its common-lands, Hukok with its common-lands, and Rehob with its common-lands. And from the tribe of Naphtali: Kedesh in Galilee with its common-lands, Hammon with its common-lands, and Kirjathaim with its common-lands. From the tribe of Zebulun the rest of the children of Merari *were given* Rimmon with its common-lands and Tabor with its common-lands. And on the other side of the Jordan, across from Jericho, on the east side of the Jordan, *they were given* from the tribe of Reuben: Bezer in the wilderness with its common-lands, Jahzah with its common-lands, Kedemoth with its common-lands, and Mephaath with its common-lands. And from the tribe of Gad: Ramoth in Gilead with its common-lands, Mahanaim with its common-lands, Heshbon with its common-lands, and Jazer with its common-lands.

a. **Now these are their dwelling places throughout their settlements**: According to Numbers 18:20-24, the tribe of Levi had no province of land as the other tribes did. Their inheritance was the Lord Himself and the tithes that the people of God brought to them.

b. **They gave them Hebron in the land of Judah, with its surrounding common-lands**: After this pattern, the Levites were "sprinkled" throughout the land of Israel by giving them cities in the different tribal provinces, cities together with surrounding **common-lands** (Numbers 35:1-8).

D. The other tribes of Israel.

1. (7:1-5) The descendants of Issachar.

The sons of Issachar *were* **Tola, Puah, Jashub, and Shimron; four** *in all*. **The sons of Tola** *were* **Uzzi, Rephaiah, Jeriel, Jahmai, Jibsam, and Shemuel, heads of their father's house.** *The sons* **of Tola** *were* **mighty men of valor in their generations; their number in the days of David** *was* **twenty-two thousand six hundred. The son of Uzzi** *was* **Izrahiah, and the sons of Izrahiah** *were* **Michael, Obadiah, Joel, and Ishiah. All five of them** *were* **chief men. And with them, by their generations, according to their fathers' houses,** *were* **thirty-six thousand troops ready for war; for they had many wives and sons. Now their brethren among all the families of Issachar** *were* **mighty men of valor, listed by their genealogies, eighty-seven thousand in all.**

a. **Thirty-six thousand troops ready for war**: "For Israhiah and his four sons, even with 'many wives,' to have '36,000' warriors seems unlikely, as does the total (vv. 2-5) of 145,600 for just one tribe of the Twelve. This appears to be the first of nine passages in Chronicles where *elep* ('thousand') might be better interpreted as *allup* ('chief')." (Payne)

2. (7:6-12) The descendants of Benjamin.

The sons of Benjamin *were* **Bela, Becher, and Jediael; three** *in all*. **The sons of Bela were Ezbon, Uzzi, Uzziel, Jerimoth, and Iri; five** *in all*. **They** *were* **heads of** *their* **fathers' houses, and they were listed by their genealogies, twenty-two thousand and thirty-four mighty men of valor. The sons of Becher** *were* **Zemirah, Joash, Eliezer, Elioenai, Omri, Jerimoth, Abijah, Anathoth, and Alemeth. All these** *are* **the sons of Becher. And they were**

recorded by genealogy according to their generations, heads of their fathers' houses, twenty thousand two hundred mighty men of valor. The son of Jediael *was* Bilhan, and the sons of Bilhan *were* Jeush, Benjamin, Ehud, Chenaanah, Zethan, Tharshish, and Ahishahar. All these sons of Jediael *were* heads of their fathers' houses; *there were* seventeen thousand two hundred mighty men of valor fit to go out for war *and* battle. Shuppim and Huppim *were* the sons of Ir, *and* Hushim *was* the son of Aher.

a. **Ehud**: This was the famous leader for Israel noted in Judges 3:12-30.

b. **The son of Aher**: Many believe that is better rendered *the sons of Aher* and is a veiled reference to the tribe of Dan, who is not otherwise mentioned in this genealogy.

i. "*The sons of Aher*, but divers take the Hebrew word *aher* for a common, not proper name, and render the words this, *another son*, or *the son of another* family or tribe, to wit, of Dan, as may be gathered." (Poole)

ii. There are at least four things that support the idea that this is a veiled reference to the tribe of Dan:

- In Genesis 46:23 **Hushim** is mentioned as the son of Dan.
- The next verse in 1 Chronicles (7:13) mentions **the sons of Bilhah**, who was mother to both Dan and **Naphtali**, also mentioned in that verse.
- Otherwise, the genealogy of Dan is left out.
- Hebrew writers sometimes used the word *another* (aher) to describe "an abominable thing which the writer disdained to mention; whence they call a swine, which to them was a very unclean and loathsome creature, *another thing*." (Poole)

iii. "And it must be remembered that the tribe of Dan had made themselves and their memory infamous and detestable by that gross idolatry, which began first and continued longest in that tribe, Judges 18." (Poole)

3. (7:13) The descendants of Naphtali.

The sons of Naphtali *were* Jahziel, Guni, Jezer, and Shallum, the sons of Bilhah.

4. (7:14-19) The descendants of the Western Tribe of Manasseh.

The descendants of Manasseh: his Syrian concubine bore him Machir the father of Gilead, the father of Asriel. Machir took as his wife *the*

sister of Huppim and Shuppim, whose name *was* **Maachah. The name of** *Gilead's* **grandson** *was* **Zelophehad, but Zelophehad begot only daughters. (Maachah the wife of Machir bore a son, and she called his name Peresh. The name of his brother** *was* **Sheresh, and his sons** *were* **Ulam and Rakem. The son of Ulam** *was* **Bedan.) These** *were* **the descendants of Gilead the son of Machir, the son of Manasseh. His sister Hammoleketh bore Ishhod, Abiezer, and Mahlah. And the sons of Shemida were Ahian, Shechem, Likhi, and Aniam.**

> a. **But Zelophehad begot only daughters**: Zelophehad is the one mentioned in Numbers 26:33, 27:1-11 and 36:1-12 when the question came to Moses about female inheritance rights.

5. (7:20-29) The descendants of Ephraim.

The sons of Ephraim *were* **Shuthelah, Bered his son, Tahath his son, Eladah his son, Tahath his son, Zabad his son, Shuthelah his son, and Ezer and Elead. The men of Gath who were born in** *that* **land killed** *them* **because they came down to take away their cattle. Then Ephraim their father mourned many days, and his brethren came to comfort him. And when he went in to his wife, she conceived and bore a son; and he called his name Beriah, because tragedy had come upon his house. Now his daughter** *was* **Sheerah, who built Lower and Upper Beth Horon and Uzzen Sheerah; and Rephah** *was* **his son,** *as well* **as Resheph, and Telah his son, Tahan his son, Laadan his son, Ammihud his son, Elishama his son, Nun his son, and Joshua his son. Now their possessions and dwelling places** *were* **Bethel and its towns: to the east Naaran, to the west Gezer and its towns, and Shechem and its towns, as far as Ayyah and its towns; and by the borders of the children of Manasseh** *were* **Beth Shean and its towns, Taanach and its towns, Megiddo and its towns, Dor and its towns. In these dwelt the children of Joseph, the son of Israel.**

> a. **The sons of Ephraim**: "The Ephraimites were famous for their wealth, power, and prowess; but withal they are noted for insolent, proud, and quarrelsome." (Trapp)

6. (7:30-40) The descendants of Asher.

The sons of Asher *were* **Imnah, Ishvah, Ishvi, Beriah, and their sister Serah. The sons of Beriah** *were* **Heber and Malchiel, who was the father of Birzaith. And Heber begot Japhlet, Shomer, Hotham, and their sister Shua. The sons of Japhlet** *were* **Pasach, Bimhal, and Ashvath. These** *were* **the children of Japhlet. The sons of Shemer** *were* **Ahi, Rohgah, Jehubbah, and Aram. And the sons of his brother Helem** *were* **Zophah, Imna, Shelesh, and Amal. The sons of Zophah** *were* **Suah, Harnepher, Shual, Beri, Imrah, Bezer, Hod, Shamma, Shilshah, Jithran, and Beera.**

The sons of Jether *were* Jephunneh, Pispah, and Ara. The sons of Ulla *were* Arah, Haniel, and Rizia. All these *were* the children of Asher, heads of *their* fathers' houses, choice men, mighty men of valor, chief leaders. And they were recorded by genealogies among the army fit for battle; their number *was* twenty-six thousand.

    a. **Their sister Serah.... their sister Shua**: "The rabbins say that the daughters of Asher were very beautiful, and were all matched with *kings* or *priests*." (Clarke)

7. (8:1-40) The descendants of Benjamin.

Now Benjamin begot Bela his firstborn, Ashbel the second, Aharah the third, Nohah the fourth, and Rapha the fifth. The sons of Bela *were* Addar, Gera, Abihud, Abishua, Naaman, Ahoah, Gera, Shephuphan, and Huram. These *are* the sons of Ehud, who were the heads of the fathers' *houses* of the inhabitants of Geba, and who forced them to move to Manahath: Naaman, Ahijah, and Gera who forced them to move. He begot Uzza and Ahihud. Also Shaharaim had children in the country of Moab, after he had sent away Hushim and Baara his wives. By Hodesh his wife he begot Jobab, Zibia, Mesha, Malcam, Jeuz, Sachiah, and Mirmah. These *were* his sons, heads of their fathers' *houses*. And by Hushim he begot Abitub and Elpaal. The sons of Elpaal *were* Eber, Misham, and Shemed, who built Ono and Lod with its towns; and Beriah and Shema, who *were* heads of their fathers' *houses* of the inhabitants of Aijalon, who drove out the inhabitants of Gath. Ahio, Shashak, Jeremoth, Zebadiah, Arad, Eder, Michael, Ispah, and Joha *were* the sons of Beriah. Zebadiah, Meshullam, Hizki, Heber, Ishmerai, Jizliah, and Jobab *were* the sons of Elpaal. Jakim, Zichri, Zabdi, Elienai, Zillethai, Eliel, Adaiah, Beraiah, and Shimrath *were* the sons of Shimei. Ishpan, Eber, Eliel, Abdon, Zichri, Hanan, Hananiah, Elam, Antothijah, Iphdeiah, and Penuel *were* the sons of Shashak. Shamsherai, Shehariah, Athaliah, Jaareshiah, Elijah, and Zichri *were* the sons of Jeroham. These *were* heads of the fathers' *houses* by their generations, chief men. These dwelt in Jerusalem. Now the father of Gibeon, whose wife's name *was* Maacah, dwelt at Gibeon. And his firstborn son *was* Abdon, then Zur, Kish, Baal, Nadab, Gedor, Ahio, Zecher, and Mikloth, *who* begot Shimeah. They also dwelt alongside their relatives in Jerusalem, with their brethren. Ner begot Kish, Kish begot Saul, and Saul begot Jonathan, Malchishua, Abinadab, and Esh-Baal. The son of Jonathan *was* Merib-Baal, and Merib-Baal begot Micah. The sons of Micah *were* Pithon, Melech, Tarea, and Ahaz. And Ahaz begot Jehoaddah; Jehoaddah begot Alemeth, Azmaveth, and Zimri;

and Zimri begot Moza. Moza begot Binea, Raphah his son, Eleasah his son, *and* Azel his son. Azel had six sons whose names *were* these: Azrikam, Bocheru, Ishmael, Sheariah, Obadiah, and Hanan. All these *were* the sons of Azel. And the sons of Eshek his brother *were* Ulam his firstborn, Jeush the second, and Eliphelet the third. The sons of Ulam were mighty men of valor; archers. *They* had many sons and grandsons, one hundred and fifty *in all.* These *were* all sons of Benjamin.

a. **Now Benjamin**: The tribe was already mentioned in 1 Chronicles 7:6-12, but is given more attention here. One reason for this is because most of these settlements were in the area of Jerusalem, which was the main area that the returning exiles came to in the days when Chronicles was written.

i. "Chronicles elaborates this material, not simply because of the significance of King Saul and his family, as it continued a dozen generations after him, but primarily because of the importance of Benjamin as a tribe, which ranked second only to Judah in postexilic society." (Payne)

b. **Ner begot Kish, Kish begot Saul**: "This Ner is also called Abiel (1 Samuel 9:1). The Hebrews tell us that his proper name was Abiel; and that he was called Ner – that is, a lamp or torch – because he outshone in holiness."

c. **The son of Jonathan *was* Merib-Baal**: "The same as *Mephi-bosheth*; for, as the Israelites detested *Baal*, which signifies *lord*, they changed it into *bosheth*, which signifies *shame* or *reproach*." (Clarke)

d. **Azel had six sons whose names were these**: "Of the six sons of Azel, mentioned 1 Chronicles 8:38, R.S. Jarchi says that their allegorical expositions were sufficient to load *thirteen thousand* camels! No doubt these were reputed to be *deeply learned* men. There was a time when the *allegorizers* and *metaphor-men* ranked very high among *theologians*, even in our own enlightened and critical country. At present they are almost totally out of fashion. May they never recover their footing! But what a shameful hyperbole is that of Jarchi! The writings of six men a load for *thirteen thousand camels!*" (Clarke)

e. **The sons of Ulam were mighty men of valor; archers**: Archers is in "Hebrew, *that tread the bow*; for the bows of steel, which these used, required great strength to bend them; which therefore they did by treading the bow with their feet, and pulling the string with both their hands." (Poole)

1 Chronicles 9 – Leaders in Jerusalem

A. Leaders in Jerusalem at the return from exile.

1. (1-2) Summary of the genealogies.

So all Israel was recorded by genealogies, and indeed, they *were* inscribed in the book of the kings of Israel. But Judah was carried away captive to Babylon because of their unfaithfulness. And the first inhabitants who *dwelt* in their possessions in their cities *were* Israelites, priests, Levites, and the Nethinim.

> a. **So all Israel was recorded**: The first eight chapters of 1 Chronicles list these genealogical records. These records were **inscribed in the book of the kings of Israel**, but these are not the same books we know today as 1 or 2 Kings.
>
>> i. "Not in that sacred and canonical book so called, but (as hath been oft observed before) in the public records, wherein there was an account of that kingdom, and of several families in it, according to their genealogies." (Poole)
>
> b. **But Judah was carried away captive to Babylon because of their unfaithfulness**: In one sentence, the Chronicler reminds us that it was not the clash of empires or the intrigues of the geopolitical scene that doomed the kingdom of Judah. It was their **unfaithfulness** to God. If they had remained faithful, God would have protected them amid the rise and fall of a hundred powerful empires.
>
> c. **And the first inhabitants who dwelt in their possessions in their cities were Israelites**: The Chronicler completely skips over the 70 years of captivity between verses 1 and 2. His interest is not only in the past (demonstrated by 8 previous chapters of genealogies) but also in the present and in the future. The **Israelites** were back in the land.

i. "All this means that Chronicles has taken the history of Israel a stage further than 1 and 2 Kings. Although 2 Kings ends on a note of genuine hope (2 Kings 25:27-30), it is restrained and Israel is still in exile. But now winter is over, and these lists are a definite sign that spring has begun to arrive." (Selman)

ii. No longer was there a kingdom of Judah and another kingdom of Israel; now they were *all* **Israelites**. "Called here by the general name of *Israelites*, which was given to them before that unhappy division of the two kingdoms, and now is restored to them when the Israelites are united with the Jews in one and the same commonwealth, so that all the names and signs of their former division might be blotted out." (Poole)

d. **Who dwelt in their possessions**: The idea is that the people of the tribes of Israel came back to their ancestral lands, promised to them by God and first possessed in the days of Moses and Joshua.

i. **In their possessions**: "'Their ancestral land' (NEB; *their own property*, NIV) is a term rarely found in Chronicles (only 1 Chronicles 7:28; 2 Chronicles 11:14; 31:1). Its occurrence here evokes its frequent use in of Moses (e.g. Leviticus 25:10ff, Numbers 27:4) and Joshua." (Selman)

ii. God kept the land empty for them during the exile. "A wonderful providence of God it was, that as the land kept her Sabbaths for those seventy years, so the country should be all that while kept empty, till the return of the natives." (Trapp)

d. **Priests, Levites, and the Nethinim**: These were three categories of workers at the temple, who had the work of restoring the temple and its worship in the days of Ezra.

- **Priests** were the descendants of Aaron who had the right to offer sacrifice and take care of the Holy Place in the temple.
- **Levites** were the much broader class of religious workers, who served in many ways: practical, artistic, and spiritual.
- **The Nethinim** were special servants given to the temple.

i. "The 'temple servants' were literally 'given ones.' They might consist of captives who had been spared but enslaved to temple service. Early Hebrew examples include the certain Midianite women (Numbers 31:35, 47) or the people of Gibeon (Joshua 9:22-23), but their organization as a class is credited to David (Ezra 8:20)." (Payne)

2. (3-9) Leading post-exilic citizens of Jerusalem.

Now in Jerusalem the children of Judah dwelt, and some of the children of Benjamin, and of the children of Ephraim and Manasseh: Uthai the son of Ammihud, the son of Omri, the son of Imri, the son of Bani, of the descendants of Perez, the son of Judah. Of the Shilonites: Asaiah the firstborn and his sons. Of the sons of Zerah: Jeuel, and their brethren; six hundred and ninety. Of the sons of Benjamin: Sallu the son of Meshullam, the son of Hodaviah, the son of Hassenuah; Ibneiah the son of Jeroham; Elah the son of Uzzi, the son of Michri; Meshullam the son of Shephatiah, the son of Reuel, the son of Ibnijah; and their brethren, according to their generations; nine hundred and fifty-six. All these men *were* heads of a father's *house* in their fathers' houses.

> a. **Now in Jerusalem the children of Judah dwelt**: This begins a list (1 Chronicles 9:2-17) that is in some ways similar to a list in Nehemiah 11 and in some ways different. Biblical researchers debate if the lists are more similar or more different, and the exact points of connection and difference can be difficult to assess.

B. Other post-exilic leaders in Jerusalem.

1. (10-13) Leaders among the priests.

Of the priests: Jedaiah, Jehoiarib, and Jachin; Azariah the son of Hilkiah, the son of Meshullam, the son of Zadok, the son of Meraioth, the son of Ahitub, the officer over the house of God; Adaiah the son of Jeroham, the son of Pashur, the son of Malchijah; Maasai the son of Adiel, the son of Jahzerah, the son of Meshullam, the son of Meshillemith, the son of Immer; and their brethren, heads of their fathers' *houses;* **one thousand seven hundred and sixty.** *They were* **very able men for the work of the service of the house of God.**

> a. **They were very able men**: This same phrase is translated *mighty men of valor* in many other Old Testament passages (Joshua 1:14, Judges 6:12, 1 Samuel 16:18, and many others). It shows that when it came to doing **the work of the service of the house of God**, it takes a man of strength and courage, the same qualities that are needed in a warrior.
>
>> i. "The phrase 'very able men' means 'mighty men of valour' and is so rendered in this historic connection in Nehemiah (11:14). The description is usually employed with reference to military men, and that makes its use here the more arresting." (Morgan)

2. (14-16) Leaders among the Levites.

Of the Levites: Shemaiah the son of Hasshub, the son of Azrikam, the son of Hashabiah, of the sons of Merari; Bakbakkar, Heresh, Galal, and Mattaniah the son of Micah, the son of Zichri, the son of Asaph;

Obadiah the son of Shemaiah, the son of Galal, the son of Jeduthun; and Berechiah the son of Asa, the son of Elkanah, who lived in the villages of the Netophathites.

3. (17-34) Levite gatekeepers and temple workers.

And the gatekeepers *were* Shallum, Akkub, Talmon, Ahiman, and their brethren. Shallum *was* the chief. Until then *they had been* gatekeepers for the camps of the children of Levi at the King's Gate on the east. Shallum the son of Kore, the son of Ebiasaph, the son of Korah, and his brethren, from his father's house, the Korahites, *were* in charge of the work of the service, gatekeepers of the tabernacle. Their fathers had been keepers of the entrance to the camp of the LORD. And Phinehas the son of Eleazar had been the officer over them in time past; the LORD *was* with him. Zechariah the son of Meshelemiah *was* keeper of the door of the tabernacle of meeting. All those chosen as gatekeepers *were* two hundred and twelve. They were recorded by their genealogy, in their villages. David and Samuel the seer had appointed them to their trusted office. So they and their children *were* in charge of the gates of the house of the LORD, the house of the tabernacle, by assignment. The gatekeepers were assigned to the four directions: the east, west, north, and south. And their brethren in their villages *had* to come with them from time to time for seven days. For in this trusted office *were* four chief gatekeepers; they were Levites. And they had charge over the chambers and treasuries of the house of God. And they lodged *all* around the house of God because they *had* the responsibility, and they *were* in charge of opening *it* every morning. Now *some* of them were in charge of the serving vessels, for they brought them in and took them out by count. *Some* of them *were* appointed over the furnishings and over all the implements of the sanctuary, and over the fine flour and the wine and the oil and the incense and the spices. And *some* of the sons of the priests made the ointment of the spices. Mattithiah of the Levites, the firstborn of Shallum the Korahite, had the trusted office over the things that were baked in the pans. And some of their brethren of the sons of the Kohathites *were* in charge of preparing the showbread for every Sabbath. These are the singers, heads of the fathers' *houses* of the Levites, *who lodged* in the chambers, *and were* free *from other duties;* for they were employed in *that* work day and night. These heads of the fathers' *houses* of the Levites *were* heads throughout their generations. They dwelt at Jerusalem.

> a. **And the gatekeepers were**: This describes the re-institution of the organization of the temple work and workers in the early days of the

second temple. They were anxious to organize things in the same manner as King David did originally.

>i. It also denotes that there was definite organization and division of labor among the Levites. "When the morning broke, it called to duty first the porters who opened the House of God; and then, after due ablution, each band of white-robed Levites began its special service. There was no running to and fro in disorder, no intrusion on one another's office, no clashing in duty, no jealousy of each other's ministry. It was enough to know that each had been appointed to his task, and was asked to be faithful to it. The right ordering of the whole depended on the punctuality, fidelity, and conscientiousness of each." (Meyer)

>ii. "Since both Meshelemiah and Zechariah served under David (1 Chronicles 26:8-11), this 'Tent of Meeting' would seem to refer to the curtained form of God's house erected prior to Solomon's permanent temple." (Payne)

b. **Phinehas the son of Eleazar had been the officer over them in time past; the LORD was with him**: The Chronicler remembered the faithful work of Phinehas in the days of Moses (Numbers 25:7-13), and linked his faithfulness to the work of the gatekeepers in the days of Ezra.

>i. "The fact that *the LORD was with him* [Phinehas] indicates that the Lord was also with those gatekeepers of the Chronicler's day who followed in the same living tradition of divine service." (Selman)

4. (35-44) The ancestors and descendants of King Saul.

Jeiel the father of Gibeon, whose wife's name *was* Maacah, dwelt at Gibeon. His firstborn son *was* Abdon, then Zur, Kish, Baal, Ner, Nadab, Gedor, Ahio, Zechariah, and Mikloth. And Mikloth begot Shimeam. They also dwelt alongside their relatives in Jerusalem, with their brethren. Ner begot Kish, Kish begot Saul, and Saul begot Jonathan, Malchishua, Abinadab, and Esh-Baal. The son of Jonathan *was* Merib-Baal, and Merib-Baal begot Micah. The sons of Micah *were* Pithon, Melech, Tahrea, *and Ahaz*. And Ahaz begot Jarah; Jarah begot Alemeth, Azmaveth, and Zimri; and Zimri begot Moza; Moza begot Binea, Rephaiah his son, Eleasah his son, and Azel his son. And Azel had six sons whose names *were* these: Azrikam, Bocheru, Ishmael, Sheariah, Obadiah, and Hanan; these *were* the sons of Azel.

>a. **Kish begot Saul, and Saul begot Jonathan**: For emphasis, some of the genealogy of the line of Saul (both before him and after him) is listed. This

was to emphasize the fact that God did not wipe out the line of Saul, and that his descendants lived to the days of Ezra and the return from exile.

i. "Since the genealogy continues for twelve generations after Saul, the fact that his dynasty crashed and his kingship was transferred to David did not remove his family's place in Israelite history. They too had lived in *Jerusalem* (1 Chronicles 9:38), and though we do not know whether this continued after the exile, even for them there were signs of hope." (Selman)

1 Chronicles 10 – The Death of Saul

"Having established Israel's historical setting and ethnic bounds in the preceding genealogies, the Chronicler now enters on his main subject, the history of the Hebrew kingdom, with its theological conclusions." (Payne)

A. The death of King Saul.

1. (1-2) The battle on Mount Gilboa.

Now the Philistines fought against Israel; and the men of Israel fled from before the Philistines, and fell slain on Mount Gilboa. Then the Philistines followed hard after Saul and his sons. And the Philistines killed Jonathan, Abinadab, and Malchishua, Saul's sons.

a. **Now the Philistines fought against Israel**: The Philistines were an immigrant people from the military aristocracy of the island of Crete (Amos 9:7). Small numbers of Philistines were in the land at the time of Abraham, but they only came in force soon after Israel came to Canaan from Egypt. They were organized into five city-states. Archaeologists tell us two other things about the Philistines: they were hard drinkers, and they were the first in the region to effectively use iron, and they made the most of it.

i. The Philistines were a sea-faring people and traded with distant lands. Therefore they imported newer and better military technology from the Greeks and became a powerful enemy of the people of Israel. At that time, Israel could compete on more equal terms with Moab and Ammon, but Greek military equipment (helmets, shields, coats of mail, swords and spears) made the Philistines much more formidable opponents.

b. **The men of Israel fled from before the Philistines**: The Philistines had attacked deep into Israeli territory (1 Samuel 28:4), and Saul's army assembled and prepared for battle at Mount Gilboa (1 Samuel 28:4).

Because of his deep rebellion against the LORD, Saul was not ready for battle: *When Saul saw the army of the Philistines, he was afraid, and his heart trembled greatly* (1 Samuel 28:5). It doesn't surprise us that with such a leader the soldiers of Israel could not stand **before the Philistines**.

> i. "Wonder not that Saul fell by the hands of the Philistines, who were armed against him by his own sin and by God's vengeance for it." (Poole)

c. **And the Philistines killed Jonathan, Abinadab, and Malchishua, Saul's sons**: Tragically, Saul's sons were affected by the judgment of God against their father Saul. The brave and worthy **Jonathan** died as he had lived – loyally fighting to the very end for his God, his country, and his father the king.

2. (3-6) Saul dies in battle.

The battle became fierce against Saul. The archers hit him, and he was wounded by the archers. Then Saul said to his armorbearer, "Draw your sword, and thrust me through with it, lest these uncircumcised men come and abuse me." But his armorbearer would not, for he was greatly afraid. Therefore Saul took a sword and fell on it. And when his armorbearer saw that Saul was dead, he also fell on his sword and died. So Saul and his three sons died, and all his house died together.

a. **The battle became fierce against Saul**: Saul, struck by many arrows and **wounded**, knew the battle was completely lost. He pled with his armorbearer to kill him, and when he would not, Saul killed himself (**Saul took a sword and fell on it**).

> i. "The flower of his army lay strewn around him; the chivalry of Israel was quenched in rivers of blood. Then, leaving all others, the Philistines concentrated their attack on that lordly figure which towered amid the fugitives, the royal crown on the helmet, the royal bracelet flashing on his arm." (Meyer)

> ii. In the way most people think of suicide, Saul's death was not suicide. Clarke explains well: "He was to all appearance mortally wounded, when he begged his armourbearer to extinguish the remaining spark of life...though this wound accelerated his death, yet it could not be properly the cause of it, as he was mortally wounded before, and did it on the conviction that he could not survive." (Clarke on 1 Samuel)

> iii. Taking the Bible's teaching on this point in its entirety, we can say that God does regard suicide as sin; it is the sin of self-murder. Yet, we are wrong if we regard it as the unforgivable sin. Anyone who does

commit suicide has given in to the lies and deceptions of Satan, whose purpose is to kill and destroy (John 10:10).

iv. "Suicide is always the ultimate action of cowardice. In the case of Saul, and in many similar cases, it is perfectly natural; but let it never be glorified as heroic. It is the last resort of the man who dare not stand up to life." (Morgan)

b. **So Saul and his three sons died, and all his house died together**: So was the tragic end of this first king of Israel, who started with great promise but ended his reign in disaster for himself, his sons, and his kingdom.

i. There were still some surviving members of Saul's family, yet "Every branch of his family that had followed him to the war was cut off; his *three sons* are mentioned as being the chief." (Clarke)

ii. "The Amalekite's story of Saul's death in 2 Samuel 1 is ignored, perhaps because its authenticity was doubted in ancient as well as in modern times." (Selman)

B. The aftermath of King Saul's death.

1. (7) Israel is defeated in battle.

And when all the men of Israel who *were* in the valley saw that they had fled and that Saul and his sons were dead, they forsook their cities and fled; then the Philistines came and dwelt in them.

a. **Saw that the men of Israel had fled and that Saul and his sons were dead**: When the leader (King Saul) was struck, it spread panic among God's people. Jesus knew this same principle would be used against His own disciples: *Then Jesus said to them, "All of you will be made to stumble because of Me this night, for it is written: 'I will strike the Shepherd, and the sheep will be scattered.'"* (Mark 14:27)

i. Saul's sin, hardened rebellion, and eventual ruin affected far more than himself and even his immediate family. It literally endangered the entire nation of Israel.

b. **They forsook the cities and fled; and the Philistines came and dwelt in them**: The victory of the Philistines was so complete that even those *on the other side of the Jordan* (1 Samuel 31:7) fled in terror before the Philistines. With the Philistine army occupying territory *on the other side of the Jordan* they had cut Israel in half, drawing a line from west to east. The rest of the nation was ripe for total conquest by the Philistines.

2. (8-10) Saul is further disgraced after his death.

So it happened the next day, when the Philistines came to strip the slain, that they found Saul and his sons fallen on Mount Gilboa. And they stripped him and took his head and his armor, and sent word *throughout* the land of the Philistines to proclaim the news *in the temple* of their idols and among the people. Then they put his armor in the temple of their gods, and fastened his head in the temple of Dagon.

    a. **To proclaim the news in the temple of their idols and among the people**: Saul's tragic death gave opportunity for the enemies of the LORD to disgrace His name. First, they gave the ultimate insult to Saul; in that culture, to have your dead body treated this way was considered a fate worse than death itself. Second, Saul's death was used to glorify pagan gods and to mock the living God.

3. (11-12) The courage and faithfulness of the men of Jabesh Gilead.

And when all Jabesh Gilead heard all that the Philistines had done to Saul, all the valiant men arose and took the body of Saul and the bodies of his sons; and they brought them to Jabesh, and buried their bones under the tamarisk tree at Jabesh, and fasted seven days.

    a. **And when all Jabesh Gilead**: These heroic men are recognized for their *gratitude*. Many years before, Saul delivered their city from the Ammonites (1 Samuel 11:1-11), and they repay the kindness God showed them from the hand of Saul. Upon taking the throne, David rightly thanked these **valiant men** for their kindness to the memory of Saul, Jonathan, and Saul's other sons (2 Samuel 2:4-7).

    b. **All the valiant men arose**: In a time of disgrace, loss, and tragedy like this, God still has His **valiant men** to do His work. The men of Jabesh Gilead took down the bodies of Saul and his sons from their place of humiliation and gave them a proper burial.

        i. God always has His **valiant men**. When one servant passes the scene, another arises to take his place. If Saul is gone, God raises up a David. If the army of Israel is utterly routed, God still has His **valiant men**. God's work is bigger than any man, or any group of people.

4. (13-14) The spiritual reason for the tragedy of King Saul.

So Saul died for his unfaithfulness which he had committed against the LORD, because he did not keep the word of the LORD, and also because he consulted a medium for guidance. But *he* did not inquire of the LORD; therefore He killed him, and turned the kingdom over to David the son of Jesse.

    a. **So Saul died for his unfaithfulness**: The story of King Saul is one of the great tragedies of the Bible. He was humble at his beginning, yet seeming to lack any genuine spiritual connection with God, he was easily and quickly corrupted by pride and fear. Saul becomes a tragic example of wasted potential.

> i. "Saul was a man than whom no other had greater opportunities, but his failure was disastrous. Of good standing in the nation, distinctly called and commissioned by God, honored with the friendship of Samuel, surrounded by a band of men whose hearts God had touched, everything was in his favor. From the beginning he failed; step by step he declined in conduct and character, until he went out." (Morgan)

b. **But he did not inquire of the Lord**: Saul did not have a genuine connection with God and did not seek God for the difficulties of his life. He **consulted a medium for guidance**, but not the Lord God.

> i. "When a human being is called of God to service, there is always given to that one the guidance of God, in direct spiritual communication. If there be disobedience, this guidance is necessarily withdrawn. Then, the forsaken man or woman, craving for supernatural aid, turns to sorcery, witchcraft, spiritism; and the issue is always destructive." (Morgan)

> ii. It does say in 1 Samuel 28:6 that Saul did inquire of the Lord. "Such an inconsiderable and trifling inquiry as Saul made, is justly accounted to be no inquiry at all; as they are said *not to eat the Lord's supper*, 1 Corinthians 11:20, who did eat it in a sinful and irregular manner." (Poole)

c. **And turned the kingdom over to David the son of Jesse**: In 1 Samuel 13:14, God promised to take the kingdom from Saul and give it to *a man after His own heart*. This took many years to become a fact, but at the death of Saul, David became king over Israel.

> i. "Upon the whole subject of responsible service, the story of Saul throws the light of the most solemn warning." (Morgan)

1 Chronicles 11 – David's Reign and Mighty Men

A. David becomes king over Israel.

1. (1-3) The elders declare David king at Hebron.

Then all Israel came together to David at Hebron, saying, "Indeed we *are* your bone and your flesh. Also, in time past, even when Saul was king, you *were* the one who led Israel out and brought them in; and the LORD your God said to you, 'You shall shepherd My people Israel, and be ruler over My people Israel.'" Therefore all the elders of Israel came to the king at Hebron, and David made a covenant with them at Hebron before the LORD. And they anointed David king over Israel, according to the word of the LORD by Samuel.

a. **Then all Israel came together to David**: Prior to this, only one of the tribes of Israel recognized David as king. The other tribes recognized the pretended king Ishbosheth, a son of Saul. Ishbosheth was murdered (2 Samuel 4) so now the tribes turned to David.

i. "It is significant that the chronicler makes no reference to the seven years in which David reigned over Judah. He begins with the crowning at Hebron, when all Israel acknowledged his kingship." (Morgan)

ii. This was actually David's third anointing. The first was before his family and Samuel when David was very young (1 Samuel 16:1-13). The second was an anointing and recognition by the tribe of Judah after the death of Saul (2 Samuel 2:4). This third anointing was after the defeat of Ishbosheth, a son of Saul who claimed the right to the throne.

iii. It is sad that the tribes only turned to David when their previous choice (Ishbosheth, a son of Saul) was taken away. On the same principle, it's sad when Christians only really recognize Jesus as king when other choices crumble. We should choose Jesus outright, not just when other options fail.

b. **We are your bone and your flesh**: The elders of Israel received David's leadership because he was an Israelite himself. This was significant because for a period of time David lived as a Philistine among the Philistines. The elders of Israel put that away and embrace David as one of their own.

c. **You were the one who led Israel out and brought them in**: The elders of Israel received David's leadership because he had already displayed his ability to lead.

d. **The LORD your God said to you, "You shall shepherd My people Israel, and be ruler over Israel"**: The elders of Israel received David's leadership because it was evident God called him to lead.

i. These three characteristics should mark anyone who leads God's people.

- A leader must belong to God's people in heritage and heart.
- A leader must demonstrate the capability to lead.
- A leader must have an evident call from God.

ii. The elders of Israel received David's leadership when they saw these things in David. When we see these same things in leaders we should also receive their leadership.

iii. "The image of the shepherd, who in ancient times was normally an employee or a dependent, also confirms that David as king was answerable to Yahweh for his flock." (Selman)

e. **According to the word of the LORD by Samuel**: This was prophesied by Samuel in passages like 1 Samuel 13:14 and 16:11-13.

2. (4-9) David takes control of Jerusalem, making it his capital city.

And David and all Israel went to Jerusalem, which is Jebus, where the Jebusites *were*, the inhabitants of the land. But the inhabitants of Jebus said to David, "You shall not come in here!" Nevertheless David took the stronghold of Zion (that is, the City of David). Now David said, "Whoever attacks the Jebusites first shall be chief and captain." And Joab the son of Zeruiah went up first, and became chief. Then David dwelt in the stronghold; therefore they called it the City of David. And he built the city around it, from the Millo to the surrounding area. Joab repaired the rest of the city. Then David went on and became great, and the LORD of hosts *was* with him.

a. **David and all Israel went to Jerusalem, which is Jebus**: To this point, Jerusalem was a small Canaanite city in the center of Israel. Some 400 years after God commanded Israel to take the whole land, this city was still in Canaanite hands.

b. **You shall not come in here**: Because of its location, Jerusalem was an easily defended city. This made the Jebusites overconfident and quick to mock David and his troops. **Nevertheless David took the stronghold of Zion**: Despite the difficulty, David and his men took the city.

i. At this time **Joab the son of Zeruiah** was captain of David's armies, yet David said that whoever led the charge into Jerusalem's walls **shall be chief and captain**. It may be that David hoped that someone would replace Joab, but the stubborn Joab successfully broke into Jerusalem first and retained his position.

c. **David dwelt in the stronghold**: Jerusalem became the capital city of David's kingdom. It was a good choice because:

- It had no prior tribal association and was therefore good for a unified Israel.
- The geography of the city made it easy to defend against a hostile army.

d. **Then David went on and became great**: David knew greatness, but he was by no means an "overnight success." David was long prepared for the greatness he later enjoyed, and he came to the place of greatness because **the LORD of hosts was with him**.

i. In God's plan, there is almost always a hidden price of greatness. Often those who become great among God's people experience much pain and difficulty in God's training process.

B. David's mighty men.

1. (10) David needed these faithful men for his success.

Now these *were* the heads of the mighty men whom David had, who strengthened themselves with him in his kingdom, with all Israel, to make him king, according to the word of the LORD concerning Israel.

a. **Now these were the heads of the mighty men whom David had**: It's important to understand that David was nothing without his mighty men, and they were nothing without him. He was their leader, but a leader is nothing without followers – and David had **the mighty men** to follow him. These men didn't necessarily *start* as mighty men; many were the distressed, indebted, and discontented people who followed David at Adullam Cave (1 Samuel 22:1-2).

2. (11-14) Two of David's mighty men.

And this *is* the number of the mighty men whom David had: Jashobeam the son of a Hachmonite, chief of the captains; he had lifted up his spear against three hundred, killed *by him* at one time. After him *was* Eleazar the son of Dodo, the Ahohite, who *was one* of the three mighty men. He was with David at Pasdammim. Now there the Philistines were gathered for battle, and there was a piece of ground full of barley. So the people fled from the Philistines. But they stationed themselves in the middle of *that* field, defended it, and killed the Philistines. So the LORD brought about a great victory.

a. **Jashobeam the son of a Hachmonite, chief of the captains**: This man is also mentioned in 2 Samuel 23:8 which records a slightly different name for him, and records that he killed 800 instead of **three hundred** here in 1 Chronicles. The difference is probably due to scribal error in copying.

i. The fact that **Jashobeam** was a **chief of the captains** shows that he was a leader among leaders. This means that even leaders need leaders. Also, his victory alone was counted, showing that numbers are important, but they are not the only measure.

b. **After him was Eleazar the son of Dodo, the Ahohite**: This man led a singular battle against a far more numerous foe, so much so that his hand was stuck to his sword (2 Samuel 23:10).

3. (15-19) David's mighty men and the mission of the water of Bethlehem.

Now three of the thirty chief men went down to the rock to David, into the cave of Adullam; and the army of the Philistines encamped in the Valley of Rephaim. David *was* then in the stronghold, and the garrison of the Philistines *was* then in Bethlehem. And David said with longing, "Oh, that someone would give me a drink of water from the well of Bethlehem, which is by the gate!" So the three broke through the camp of the Philistines, drew water from the well of Bethlehem that *was* by the gate, and took *it* and brought *it* to David. Nevertheless David would not drink it, but poured it out to the LORD. And he said, "Far be it from me, O my God, that I should do this! Shall I drink the blood of these men *who have put* their lives *in jeopardy?* For at the risk of their lives they brought it." Therefore he would not drink it. These things were done by the three mighty men.

a. **Into the cave of Adullam**: David spent time in this cave when those who would become his mighty men first came to him in 1 Samuel 22:1-2. This passage describes something that happened either during that time or a later time of battle against the Philistines when David went back to **the cave of Adullam**.

b. **The garrison of the Philistines was then in Bethlehem**: This shows how extensively the Philistines had invaded Israel in the days of Saul.

c. **And David said with longing**: Hiding in Adullam Cave, David nostalgically remembered the taste of the water from his boyhood village. He probably longed for it all the more because it seemed that he couldn't have it.

> i. We can be caught in the trap of these wistful longings. "Sometimes longings like his take possession of us. We desire to drink again the waters of comparative innocence, of childlike trust and joy; to drink again of the fountains of human love; to have the bright, fresh rapture in God, and nature, and home. But it is a mistake to look back. Here and now, within us, Jesus is waiting to open the well of living water which springs up to eternal life, of which if we drink we never thirst." (Meyer)

> ii. Instead, we should look to the Lord right now with confidence for the future instead of dreaming about the past. "Purity is better than innocence; the blessedness which comes through suffering is richer than the gladsomeness of childhood; the peace of the heart is more than peace of circumstances." (Meyer)

d. **So the three broke through the camp of the Philistines**: In response to David's longing – which wasn't a command or even a request, just a vocalized longing – three of David's mighty men decided to give him what he was **longing** for. They had to break through the **garrison of the Philistines** to do it, and to bring the water all the way back to Adullam Cave. It was a dangerous and difficult mission, but the courage and persistence of the mighty men made it happen.

e. **Nevertheless David would not drink it, but poured it out to the LORD**: David was so honored by the self-sacrifice of these three mighty men he felt that the water was too good for him – and worthy to be **poured** out in sacrifice to the LORD. He believed that the great sacrifice of these men could only be honored by giving the water to the LORD.

> i. "The point of David's pouring Bethlehem's precious *water* on the ground is threefold. It highlights a great act of Israelite bravery, it exalts David's ability to inspire extraordinary loyalty, and it was recognized as an act of worship." (Selman)

4. (20-25) Other accomplishments of David's mighty men.

Abishai the brother of Joab was chief of *another* three. He had lifted up his spear against three hundred *men,* killed *them,* and won a name among *these* three. Of the three he was more honored than the other two men. Therefore he became their captain. However he did not attain to the *first* three. Benaiah was the son of Jehoiada, the son of a valiant man from Kabzeel, who had done many deeds. He had killed two lion-like heroes of Moab. He also had gone down and killed a lion in the midst of a pit on a snowy day. And he killed an Egyptian, a man of *great* height, five cubits tall. In the Egyptian's hand *there was* a spear like a weaver's beam; and he went down to him with a staff, wrested the spear out of the Egyptian's hand, and killed him with his own spear. These *things* Benaiah the son of Jehoiada did, and won a name among three mighty men. Indeed he was more honored than the thirty, but he did not attain to the *first* three. And David appointed him over his guard.

    a. **Abishai the brother of Joab**: This leader among David's mighty men was famous for his battle against **three hundred men**. His leadership is also recorded in passages like 1 Samuel 26:6-9, 2 Samuel 3:30 and 2 Samuel 10:10-14.

    b. **Benaiah the son of Jehoiada**: This leader among David's mighty men was famous for his battles against both men (**two lion-like heroes of Moab…an Egyptian, a spectacular man**) and beasts (**a lion in the midst of a pit on a snowy day**).

5. (26-47) The honor roll of David's mighty men.

Also the mighty warriors *were* Asahel the brother of Joab, Elhanan the son of Dodo of Bethlehem, Shammoth the Harorite, Helez the Pelonite, Ira the son of Ikkesh the Tekoite, Abiezer the Anathothite, Sibbechai the Hushathite, Ilai the Ahohite, Maharai the Netophathite, Heled the son of Baanah the Netophathite, Ithai the son of Ribai of Gibeah, of the sons of Benjamin, Benaiah the Pirathonite, Hurai of the brooks of Gaash, Abiel the Arbathite, Azmaveth the Baharumite, Eliahba the Shaalbonite, the sons of Hashem the Gizonite, Jonathan the son of Shageh the Hararite, Ahiam the son of Sacar the Hararite, Eliphal the son of Ur, Hepher the Mecherathite, Ahijah the Pelonite, Hezro the Carmelite, Naarai the son of Ezbai, Joel the brother of Nathan, Mibhar the son of Hagri, Zelek the Ammonite, Naharai the Berothite (the armorbearer of Joab the son of Zeruiah), Ira the Ithrite, Gareb the Ithrite, Uriah the Hittite, Zabad the son of Ahlai, Adina the son of Shiza the Reubenite (a chief of the Reubenites) and thirty with him, Hanan the son of Maachah, Joshaphat the Mithnite, Uzzia the Ashterathite, Shama and Jeiel the sons of Hotham the Aroerite, Jediael the son of Shimri, and Joha his

brother, the Tizite, Eliel the Mahavite, Jeribai and Joshaviah the sons of Elnaam, Ithmah the Moabite, Eliel, Obed, and Jaasiel the Mezobaite.

a. **Also the mighty warriors were**: These remarkable men were the foundation of the greatness of David's reign. They did not come to David as great men. But God used David's leadership to transform them from the men who met David back at Adullam Cave; men who were *in distress, in debt* and *discontented* (1 Samuel 22:1-2).

> i. "More than all his victories against outside foes, the influence of his life and character on the men nearest to him testify to his essential greatness." (Morgan)

b. **Asahel the brother of Joab**: As recorded in 2 Samuel 2:18-23, Asahel was tragically killed in battle by Abner, who was the commander of Ishbosheth's armies (this was the son of Saul who tried to follow him on the throne of Israel).

c. **Uriah the Hittite**: He is notable among the mighty men because he was the husband of Bathsheba. When David heard of Bathsheba's relation to **Uriah** and **Eliam** and **Ahithophel** (2 Samuel 11:3) he should have put away every idea of adultery.

> i. The list of David's mighty men recorded in 2 Samuel 23 ends with the mention of **Uriah the Hittite**. This list adds a few more names. "But here some others are added to the number, because though they were not of the thirty, yet they were men of great valour and renown amongst David's commanders." (Poole)

1 Chronicles 12 – David's Army

"Every word of this chapter carries the mind on to great David's greater Son, and the men He gathers about Him." (G. Campbell Morgan)

A. The devotion of David's army.

1. (1-2) Even the Benjaminites, the tribal relatives of Saul, come to David.

Now these *were* the men who came to David at Ziklag while he was still a fugitive from Saul the son of Kish; and they *were* among the mighty men, helpers in the war, armed with bows, using both the right hand and the left in *hurling* stones and *shooting* arrows with the bow. They *were* of Benjamin, Saul's brethren.

> a. **Now these were the men who came to David at Ziklag**: David's time in Ziklag is described in 1 Samuel 27 and 30. This was a time when David lived in the territory of the Philistines to escape the murderous pursuit of King Saul.

> b. **They were among the mighty men, helpers in the war, armed with bows, using both the right hand and the left**: During David's time in Ziklag, certain mighty warriors came and expressed their allegiance to David and his cause. This was especially remarkable because they **were of Benjamin, Saul's brethren** and therefore had much to gain from Saul's continued reign. They chose David over Saul because they knew that God was with David.

>> i. Judges 3:15 and 20:16 make special reference to *left-handed* warriors; how much more if the soldiers can use **both the right hand and the left!**

2. (3-15) David's diverse army.

The chief *was* Ahiezer, then Joash, the sons of Shemaah the Gibeathite; Jeziel and Pelet the sons of Azmaveth; Berachah, and Jehu the

Anathothite; Ishmaiah the Gibeonite, a mighty man among the thirty, and over the thirty; Jeremiah, Jahaziel, Johanan, and Jozabad the Gederathite; Eluzai, Jerimoth, Bealiah, Shemariah, and Shephatiah the Haruphite; Elkanah, Jisshiah, Azarel, Joezer, and Jashobeam, the Korahites; and Joelah and Zebadiah the sons of Jeroham of Gedor. *Some* Gadites joined David at the stronghold in the wilderness, mighty men of valor, men trained for battle, who could handle shield and spear, whose faces *were like* the faces of lions, and *were* as swift as gazelles on the mountains: Ezer the first, Obadiah the second, Eliab the third, Mishmannah the fourth, Jeremiah the fifth, Attai the sixth, Eliel the seventh, Johanan the eighth, Elzabad the ninth, Jeremiah the tenth, and Machbanai the eleventh. These *were* from the sons of Gad, captains of the army; the least was over a hundred, and the greatest was over a thousand. These *are* the ones who crossed the Jordan in the first month, when it had overflowed all its banks; and they put to flight all *those* in the valleys, to the east and to the west.

> a. **A mighty man among the thirty, and over the thirty**: As mentioned in the previous chapter, David's army seemed to be organized in groups of **thirty** or the leaders of **thirty**. In the same way, a Roman centurion was supposedly a leader of one hundred soldiers.
>
>> i. "Certainly 'Thirty' is not to be understood in precise numerical terms, as the lists demonstrate, and either is a rather elastic number, or refers to a special kind of military leader. The word 'Thirty' may in fact mean an officer of some kind, either an 'officer of the third rank' or a member of a special three-man squad directly answerable to the king." (Selman)
>
> b. **Mighty men of valor, men trained for battle, who could handle shield and spear, whose faces were like the faces of lions, and were as swift as gazelles on the mountains**: These Gadites were impressive soldiers.
>
> - **Mighty men of valor**: They were men of courage and of a warrior spirit.
> - **Men trained for battle**: They were men who patiently received the training they needed to be mighty warriors.
> - **Who could handle shield and spear**: They were men who were skilled in the use of their essential weapons (both defensive and offensive), with skill gained from their training.
> - **Whose faces were like the faces of lions**: They had the calm demeanor of men who were confident in God; they had the countenance of fierce and calm warriors. "Undaunted, fierce, and

terrible to their enemies. They durst look death itself in the face upon great adventures in the field." (Trapp)

- **And were as swift as gazelles on the mountains**: They were mobile, active men, ready to fight wherever they were needed.
  - i. "The grace of God can make us like them. The grace of God can make us brave as lions, so that, wherever we are, we can hold our own, or rather can hold our Lord's truth, and never blush nor be ashamed to speak a good word for him at all times. He can make us quick and active too, so that we shall be like the roes upon the mountains." (Spurgeon)

c. **These are the ones who crossed the Jordan in the first month, when it had overflowed all its banks**: As an example of the might of these men, the Chronicler records an instance when these brave warriors crossed the Jordan at a dangerous time (Joshua 3:15 and 4:18).

> i. Adam Clarke on **the first month**: "Perhaps this was the month Nisan, which answers to a part of our *March* and *April*. This was probably before the snows on the mountains were melted, just as Jordan began to overflow its banks, it made their attempt more hazardous, and afforded additional proof of their heroism."

> ii. "These Gadites likewise furnish us with a noble example of strong devotion. When the eleven men determined to join David, they were living the other side of a deep river, which at that season of the year had overflowed its banks, so that it was extremely deep and broad. But they were not to be kept from joining David, when he wanted them, by the river. They swam through the river that they might come to David." (Spurgeon)

3. (16-22) David receives loyal soldiers at the stronghold.

Then some of the sons of Benjamin and Judah came to David at the stronghold. And David went out to meet them, and answered and said to them, "If you have come peaceably to me to help me, my heart will be united with you; but if to betray me to my enemies, since *there is* **no wrong in my hands, may the God of our fathers look and bring judgment." Then the Spirit came upon Amasai, chief of the captains,** *and he said:*

"*We are* **yours, O David;**
We *are* **on your side, O son of Jesse!**
Peace, peace to you,
And peace to your helpers!
For your God helps you."

So David received them, and made them captains of the troop. And *some from Manasseh defected to David when he was going with the Philistines to battle against Saul; but they did not help them, for the lords of the Philistines sent him away by agreement, saying, "He may defect to his master Saul *and endanger* our heads." When he went to Ziklag, those of Manasseh who defected to him were Adnah, Jozabad, Jediael, Michael, Jozabad, Elihu, and Zillethai, captains of the thousands who *were* from Manasseh. And they helped David against the bands *of raiders,* for they *were* all mighty men of valor, and they were captains in the army. For at *that* time they came to David day by day to help him, until *it was* a great army, like the army of God.

a. **And David went out to meet them**: This shows both David's large heart and his trust in God. He received these soldiers whom he had some reason to suspect. In his words to the **sons of Benjamin**, he appealed to God for wisdom and righteousness.

b. **Then the Spirit came upon Amasai**: Literally, this "The Spirit clothed Amasai." This Old Testament phrase is only used in Judges 6:34 and 2 Chronicles 24:20, but it may have been in the mind of Jesus when He promised that His followers would be *clothed with power from on high* (Luke 24:49).

i. "*Amasai* might be identified with Amasa, Absalom's army commander who was later reinstated by David (2 Samuel 19:13)." (Selman)

c. **For your God helps you**: Whatever the **sons of Benjamin** knew about David, they knew that God helped David. This made them want to follow him.

i. "We have observed God's singular and gracious care of thee, and kindness to thee, and if we should oppose thee, we should be fighters against God and his word and providence." (Poole)

d. **The lords of the Philistines sent him away by agreement**: During his time in Ziklag, David attempted to fight with the Philistines against Saul and the army of Israel. The Philistine lords, fearing that David planned to **defect to his master Saul**, refused to allow David and his mighty men to fight in the battle (1 Samuel 27).

e. **Until it was a great army, like the army of God**: Under the hand of God and His servant David, these mighty men – who began as disaffected people with nowhere else to go (1 Samuel 22:1-2) – developed into an amazing force. David and his mighty men needed each other and were each nothing without the other.

B. The royal army at Hebron.

1. (23-37) The army of the tribes of Israel.

Now these *were* the numbers of the divisions *that were* equipped for war, *and* came to David at Hebron to turn *over* the kingdom of Saul to him, according to the word of the LORD: of the sons of Judah bearing shield and spear, six thousand eight hundred armed for war; of the sons of Simeon, mighty men of valor fit for war, seven thousand one hundred; of the sons of Levi four thousand six hundred; Jehoiada, the leader of the Aaronites, and with him three thousand seven hundred; Zadok, a young man, a valiant warrior, and from his father's house twenty-two captains; of the sons of Benjamin, relatives of Saul, three thousand (until then the greatest part of them had remained loyal to the house of Saul); of the sons of Ephraim twenty thousand eight hundred, mighty men of valor, famous men throughout their father's house; of the half-tribe of Manasseh eighteen thousand, who were designated by name to come and make David king; of the sons of Issachar who had understanding of the times, to know what Israel ought to do, their chiefs were two hundred; and all their brethren were at their command; of Zebulun there were fifty thousand who went out to battle, expert in war with all weapons of war, stouthearted men who could keep ranks; of Naphtali one thousand captains, and with them thirty-seven thousand with shield and spear; of the Danites who could keep battle formation, twenty-eight thousand six hundred; of Asher, those who could go out to war, able to keep battle formation, forty thousand; of the Reubenites and the Gadites and the half-tribe of Manasseh, from the other side of the Jordan, one hundred and twenty thousand armed for battle with every *kind* of weapon of war.

> a. **Of the sons of Levi four thousand six hundred**: Some think that the Levites were prohibited from going to war, but this is not specifically stated. Numbers 1:47-53 says that in that census they were not to be *counted* among the other tribes when the men ready for war were numbered, but it does not say that they could never fight for Israel.
>
>> i. "The Levites were never prohibited from engaging in the military activity, despite their religious duties." (Selman)
>
> b. **The sons of Issachar who had understanding of the times, to know what Israel ought to do**: Some ancient traditions attribute this **understanding of the times** to skill in astrology, yet there is no foundation for this speculation. Instead, we should simply see that these **sons of Issachar** were men who supported King Saul *up until the right time* and *at the right time* gave their support to David.

i. "And particularly they showed this point of their wisdom at this time; for as they had adhered to Saul whilst he lived, as knowing the time was not yet come for David to take possession of the kingdom." (Poole)

ii. "Such as well knew what was to be done, and when to do it, by a singular sagacity, gotten by long experience, rather than by skill astrology." (Trapp)

c. **Stouthearted men who could keep ranks**: The idea behind the word **stouthearted** is that these were men of a single or whole heart in their devotion to King David. This is reflected in several other translations:

- *They were not of double heart* (KJV).
- *To help David with undivided loyalty* (NIV).
- *Helped David with an undivided heart* (NASB).
- *Completely loyal to David* (NLT).

i. "We read in verse 33 of Zebulon, whose warriors were not of a double heart; the margin says that they were 'without a heart and a heart.' The double-minded man is unstable in all his ways; he is not to be relied upon in his loyalty or service to his king." (Meyer)

ii. Because they were completely committed to their king, they could also **keep ranks** – that is, they stayed tight in their formations even in the heat of battle. Their single devotion to their king made them able to stay together as a single unit.

iii. "Too many like to break the ranks, and do God's work independently. Fifty men who act together will do greater execution than five hundred acting apart.... Unity is strength; and in their efforts to overthrow the kingdom of Satan it is most essential that the soldiers of Christ move in rank and keep step." (Meyer)

2. (38-40) Their great support of Israel's great king

All these men of war, who could keep ranks, came to Hebron with a loyal heart, to make David king over all Israel; and all the rest of Israel *were* of one mind to make David king. And they were there with David three days, eating and drinking, for their brethren had prepared for them. Moreover those who were near to them, from as far away as Issachar and Zebulun and Naphtali, were bringing food on donkeys and camels, on mules and oxen; provisions of flour and cakes of figs and cakes of raisins, wine and oil and oxen and sheep abundantly, for *there was* joy in Israel.

a. **To make David king over Israel**: This celebration came late (some seven years after the death of Saul), but it did come. The people of God together recognized David as their king. Significantly, David would not force his reign upon the people; he waited until they were willing **to make David king over Israel**.

> i. "From the whole it appears most evident that the great majority of the tribes of Israel wished to see the kingdom confirmed in the hands of David; nor was there ever in any country a man more worthy of the public choice." (Clarke)

b. **For there was joy in Israel**: Receiving their rightful and anointed king brought joy to Israel.

> i. "The paragraph as a whole, however, shows that the people of God are the real heroes of the chapter. Those Israelites exemplify the principle that when God's people become committed to one another in obedient service to God's chosen king, they find both unity and joy." (Selman)

> ii. "The enthroning of David was the uniting of the kingdom. Herein is the secret of the unity of the Church. We shall never secure it by endeavouring to bring about an unity in thought, or act, or organization. It is as each individual heart enthrones the Saviour that each will become one with all kindred souls in the everlasting kingdom." (Meyer)

1 Chronicles 13 – King David Brings the Ark of the Covenant to Jerusalem

A. The attempt to bring the ark of the covenant to Jerusalem.

1. (1-4) The plan to bring the ark of the covenant to Jerusalem.

Then David consulted with the captains of thousands and hundreds, *and* with every leader. And David said to all the assembly of Israel, "If *it seems* good to you, and if it is of the LORD** our God, let us send out to our brethren everywhere *who are* left in all the land of Israel, and with them to the priests and Levites *who are* in their cities *and* their common-lands, that they may gather together to us; and let us bring the ark of our God back to us, for we have not inquired at it since the days of Saul." Then all the assembly said that they would do so, for the thing was right in the eyes of all the people.**

> a. **David consulted with the captains of thousands and hundreds, and with every leader**: Notably, the text does not say that David consulted with the LORD. A group of godly men with good intentions would soon make a significant mistake because they took counsel with each other, but not with the LORD.
>
> > i. Payne on **to our brethren everywhere who are left**: "Literally 'our brothers that are left.' This may reflect something of the seriousness of the third major Philistine oppression against Israel, 1010-1003 B.C., which David had just broken (2 Samuel 5:20, 25)."
>
> b. **Let us bring the ark of our God back to us**: This was the *ark of the covenant*, which God commanded Moses to make more than 400 years before David's time. It was a wood box (the word **ark** means "box" or "chest") completely covered with gold and with an ornate gold lid or top known as the *mercy seat*.

i. The **ark of our God** was 3 feet 9 inches long, 2 feet 3 inches wide and 2 feet 3 inches high. In it were the tablets of the law that Moses brought down from Mount Sinai, a jar of manna, and Aaron's rod that miraculously budded as a confirmation of his leadership.

ii. The **ark of our God** had come back from the land of the Philistines some 70 years before this (1 Samuel 7:1). In those years it sat at the house of Abinadab, but now David and the people wanted to bring it back to the center of the national consciousness.

c. **For the thing was right in the eyes of all the people**: The idea of bringing the ark of the covenant back to the center of Israel's consciousness was good; their method of bringing it would soon be exposed as faulty.

i. It was good for both David and for the Israelites to have the ark in Jerusalem. "He knew that not he, but Jehovah, was their true King. His own rule must depend upon the will and counsel of God. Thus it was not only necessary for him to know, the fact must be recognized by the people." (Morgan)

2. (5-8) The procession of the ark from Kirjath Jearim.

So David gathered all Israel together, from Shihor in Egypt to as far as the entrance of Hamath, to bring the ark of God from Kirjath Jearim. And David and all Israel went up to Baalah, to Kirjath Jearim, which belonged to Judah, to bring up from there the ark of God the LORD, who dwells *between* the cherubim, where *His* name is proclaimed. So they carried the ark of God on a new cart from the house of Abinadab, and Uzza and Ahio drove the cart. Then David and all Israel played *music* before God with all *their* might, with singing, on harps, on stringed instruments, on tambourines, on cymbals, and with trumpets.

a. **To bring up from there the ark of God the LORD, who dwells between the cherubim, where His name is proclaimed**: The **ark of God** represented the immediate presence and glory of God in Israel. David considered it a high priority to bring the ark out of obscurity and back into prominence. David wanted Israel to be alive with a sense of the near presence and glory of God.

b. **So they carried the ark of God on a new cart**: Transporting the ark on a cart was against God's specific command. The ark was designed to be carried (Exodus 25:12-15) and was only to be carried by Levites of the family of Kohath (Numbers 4:15).

i. "There it was expressly ordained that the Ark should be carried on the shoulders of the priests, because the cause of God must proceed through the world by the means of consecrated men, rather than by mechanical instrumentality." (Meyer)

ii. We can imagine what these men thought. "Look – we have a **new cart** for the ark of God. God will be very pleased with our fancy **new cart**." They thought that a new technology or luxury could cover over their ignorant disobedience.

iii. "The long neglect of the Ark may have rendered these men unfamiliar with the very explicit commands concerning the method of its removal. Or they may have grown careless as to the importance of attending to such details." (Morgan)

iv. The Philistines transported the ark on a cart in 1 Samuel 6:10-11. They got away with it because they were Philistines, but God expected more from His people. Israel was to take their example from God's Word, not from the innovations of the Philistines. "Israel got into difficulties because they failed to recognize that worship of the true God meant they could no longer simply follow contemporary pagan practices." (Selman)

c. **Uzza and Ahio drove the new cart**: The meaning of the names of these sons of Abinadab paint a meaningful picture. **Uzza** means "strength" and **Ahio** means "friendly."

i. Much service for the LORD is like this – a new cart, a big production, with *strength* leading and *friendly* out front – yet all done without inquiring of God or looking to His will. Surely David prayed for God's blessing on this big production, but he didn't inquire of God regarding the production itself. This was a good thing done the wrong way.

d. **Then David and all Israel played music before God**: Judging from the importance of the occasion and all the instruments mentioned, this was quite a production. The atmosphere was joyful, exciting, and engaging. The problem was that none of it pleased God because it was all in disobedience to His word.

i. We are often tempted to judge a worship experience by how it makes *us* feel. But when we realize that worship is about *pleasing God*, we are driven to His word so we can know how He wants to be worshipped.

ii. "If you read the story through, you will see that it appears to be an affair of singing, and harps, and psalteries, and timbrels, and cymbals, and trumpets, and of a new cart and cattle; that is about all there is in it. There is not even a mention of humiliation of heart, or of solemn awe in the presence of that God of whom the ark was but the outward symbol. I am afraid that this first attempt was too much after the will of the Flesh, and the energy of nature." (Spurgeon)

B. The death of Uzza and its aftermath.

1. (9-11) Uzza touches the ark and is killed in judgment.

And when they came to Chidon's threshing floor, Uzza put out his hand to hold the ark, for the oxen stumbled. Then the anger of the LORD was aroused against Uzza, and He struck him because he put his hand to the ark; and he died there before God. And David became angry because of the Lord's outbreak against Uzza; therefore that place is called Perez Uzza to this day.

a. **When they came to Chidon's threshing floor**: At a **threshing floor** the whole stalks of wheat are gathered and the *chaff* is separated from the *wheat*. There was a lot of *chaff* in this production, and God would blow away the chaff at **Chidon's threshing floor**.

b. **Uzza put out his hand to hold the ark**: This was strictly forbidden. Regarding the transporting of the ark Numbers 4:15 says, *they shall not touch any holy thing lest they die*. He did it because **the oxen stumbled** (perhaps seeing the grain on the threshing floor) and he feared that perhaps the ark might fall off the new cart and crash to the ground. He believed that his hand on the ark was better than the ark on the ground.

i. Uzza decided in a moment to disregard God's command and do what seemed right to him. This shows us that even our decisions made in a moment matter before God.

c. **He struck him because he put his hand to the ark**: God fulfilled the ominous promise of Numbers 4:15 and **struck** Uzza. David wanted Israel to know the presence of the LORD and God showed up at **Chidon's threshing floor** – but not in the way anyone wanted.

i. The sin of Uzza was more than just a reflex action or instinct. God **struck** Uzza because his action was based upon critical errors in his thinking.

- Uzza erred in thinking it didn't matter who transported the ark.
- Uzza erred in thinking it didn't matter how the ark was transported.
- Uzza erred in thinking he knew all about the ark because it was in his father's house for so long (2 Samuel 6:3)
- Uzza erred in thinking that God couldn't take care of the ark Himself.

- Uzza erred in thinking that the ground of Chidon's threshing floor was less holy than his own hand.

ii. "He saw no difference between the ark and any other valuable article. His intention to help was right enough; but there was a profound insensibility to the awful sacredness of the ark, on which even its Levitical bearers were forbidden to lay hands." (Maclaren)

d. **David became angry because of the Lord's outbreak**: David's anger was rooted in confusion. He couldn't understand why his good intentions weren't enough. God is concerned with both our intentions and our actions.

3. (12-14) David's fear and God's blessing on Obed-Edom's house.

David was afraid of God that day, saying, "How can I bring the ark of God to me?" So David would not move the ark with him into the City of David, but took it aside into the house of Obed-Edom the Gittite. The ark of God remained with the family of Obed-Edom in his house three months. And the LORD blessed the house of Obed-Edom and all that he had.

a. **David was afraid of God that day**: He did not need to be afraid of God, but afraid of his own sin. There was no problem with God or with the ark itself (as the blessing on the house of **Obed-Edom** demonstrated). The problem was with the lack of knowledge and obedience on the part of David and those who helped him plan the entrance of the ark into Jerusalem.

i. "If Chronicles' readers wanted Israel's former glories restored, they too must reckon with a God whose dynamic holiness could not be contained within human limitations." (Selman)

b. **How can I bring the ark of God to me?** David knew it was important to bring the **ark of God** into the center of Israel's life. He wanted all Israel to be excited about the presence and glory of God. Because of what happened to Uzza, David felt he couldn't do what God wanted him to do.

i. David's response in the following chapter shows that he found the answer to his question. He answered the question with the thought later expressed in Isaiah 8:20: *To the law and to the testimony!* David found the answer in God's word.

ii. The whole account reinforces the principle that God is interested in the *process* as well as in the *outcome*. It would never do for David or Israel to have the attitude, "As long as we get the ark to Jerusalem, it doesn't matter how we do it." *How* they did it really did matter, and how we do things today (especially in serving God) also matters.

c. **Took it aside into the house of Obed-Edom**: David did this in fulfillment of God's word. **Obed-Edom** was a Levite of the clan of Kohath, of the family of Korah (1 Chronicles 26:4). This was the family within the tribe of Levi that God commanded to transport and take care of the ark (Numbers 4:15).

d. **And the LORD blessed the house of Obed-Edom and all that he had**: When God's word was obeyed and His holiness was respected blessing followed. God wanted the ark to be a blessing for Israel, not a curse. We might say that the curse didn't come from God's heart but from man's disobedience.

> i. Selman believes that the name **Obed-Edom the Gittite** means that he was from Gath, and the blessing on his house is therefore an example of the undeserved blessing of God, with the Lord displaying His grace to both Obed-Edom and to David. However, it seems better to take the observation of Adam Clarke: "That this man was only a sojourner at Gath, whence he was termed a Gittite, and that he was originally a *Levite*, is evident from 1 Chronicles 15:17-18."

1 Chronicles 14 – David's Throne Is Secured at Jerusalem

A. David's home in Jerusalem.

1. (1-2) The royal palace of David.

Now Hiram king of Tyre sent messengers to David, and cedar trees, with masons and carpenters, to build him a house. So David knew that the LORD had established him as king over Israel, for his kingdom was highly exalted for the sake of His people Israel.

> a. **To build him a house**: This shows David's influence and importance. Neighboring kings honor him with the finest craftsmen and wood to build him a palace. This relationship with **Hiram king of Tyre** also shows that David was more than a man of war. He knew how to build important political alliances.
>
> b. **So David knew**: David knew two things that made his reign great. Every godly leader should know these two things well.
>
> - **David knew that the LORD had established him as king over Israel**: David knew that God called him and established him over Israel.
>
> - **His kingdom was highly exalted for the sake of His people Israel**: David knew God wanted to use him as a channel to bless His people. It was not for David's sake that he was lifted up, but for the **sake of His people Israel**.

2. (3-7) The sons born to David in Jerusalem.

Then David took more wives in Jerusalem, and David begot more sons and daughters. And these are the names of his children whom he had in Jerusalem: Shammua, Shobab, Nathan, Solomon, Ibhar, Elishua, Elpelet, Nogah, Nepheg, Japhia, Elishama, Beeliada, and Eliphelet.

a. **David took more wives**: This was in direct disobedience to Deuteronomy 17:17: *Neither shall he multiply wives for himself, lest his heart turn away.* 2 Samuel 5:13 tells us that David also took more *concubines* when he lived in Jerusalem.

i. Chronicles makes no mention of David's sin with Bathsheba but after the murder of her husband she was one of the **more wives** that David added to his household in Jerusalem.

ii. "That David took 'more wives' was a historical fact but a moral failure, directly contrary to the law.... This sin led to a whole series of disasters later on." (Payne)

b. **David begot more sons and daughters**: Certainly, David (and everyone else) saw these many children as God's sign of blessing upon David and his many wives. Yet most of the trouble to come in David's life comes from his relationships with women and his children.

i. It is often true that the seeds of our future trouble are sown in times of great success and prosperity. In some ways, David handled trials better than success.

B. Victory over the Philistines.

1. (8-10) David seeks God in battle against the Philistines at the Valley of Rephaim.

Now when the Philistines heard that David had been anointed king over all Israel, all the Philistines went up to search for David. And David heard *of it* and went out against them. Then the Philistines went and made a raid on the Valley of Rephaim. And David inquired of God, saying, "Shall I go up against the Philistines? Will You deliver them into my hand?" And the LORD said to him, "Go up, for I will deliver them into your hand."

a. **All the Philistines went up to search for David**: David's success brought new challenges from the *outside*. As God worked mightily in David's life, the devil also got to work and brought opposition against David.

i. "The Valley of Rephaim lay southwest of Jerusalem and formed part of the boundary between Judah and Benjamin (Joshua 15:8). It may correspond to the 'Valley of Baca' (Psalm 84:6), due to the balsam trees that were there (1 Chronicles 14:14-15). These are named, literally, 'weepers' because of their drops of milky sap." (Payne)

b. **David inquired of God**: As David sought God and looked to Him for guidance he was blessed. God honored David's dependence on Him and gave him the promise of victory.

2. (11-12) David defeats the Philistines at Baal Perazim.

So they went up to Baal Perazim, and David defeated them there. Then David said, "God has broken through my enemies by my hand like a breakthrough of water." Therefore they called the name of that place Baal Perazim. And when they left their gods there, David gave a commandment, and they were burned with fire.

> a. **God has broken through my enemies**: At the battle of **Baal Perazim**, David defeated the Philistines with an overwhelming force, **like a breakthrough of water**.
>
>> i. "God's 'breakout' in judgment (1 Chronicles 13:9-12) now becomes a 'breakout' in blessing for Israel as well as for Obed-Edom's household." (Selman)
>
> b. **They left their gods there**: The Philistines brought their idols to the battle, thinking they would help defeat the Israelites. Because David inquired of God and obeyed God, they burned the Philistine idols.

3. (13-17) David defeats the Philistines again.

Then the Philistines once again made a raid on the valley. Therefore David inquired again of God, and God said to him, "You shall not go up after them; circle around them, and come upon them in front of the mulberry trees. And it shall be, when you hear a sound of marching in the tops of the mulberry trees, then you shall go out to battle, for God has gone out before you to strike the camp of the Philistines." So David did as God commanded him, and they drove back the army of the Philistines from Gibeon as far as Gezer. Then the fame of David went out into all lands, and the LORD brought the fear of him upon all nations.

> a. **David inquired again of God**: After the first victory over the Philistines, David was wise enough to wait on the LORD before the second battle. It is easy for many in the same situation to say, "I've fought this battle before. I know how to win. This will be easy." *David always triumphed when he sought and obeyed God.*
>
> b. **You shall not go up after them; circle around them**: God directed David differently in this battle. Even against the same enemy, not every battle is the same.
>
>> i. In his commentary on this account in 2 Samuel 5, Adam Clarke noted the remarkable guidance of God in David's life and asked a good question. "How is it that such supernatural directions and assistances are not communicated now? Because they are not asked for; and they are not asked for because they are not expected; and they

are not expected because men have not faith; and they have not faith because they are under a refined spirit of atheism, and have no spiritual intercourse with their Maker." (Clarke)

c. **God has gone out before you to strike the camp of the Philistines**: At this battle, David waited for the LORD to **strike the camp** of the enemy first. The sign of God's work was **a sound of marching in the tops of the mulberry trees**.

> i. "It was not merely a fitful breeze stealing through the leaves; it was not the going of the wind; but of angel squadrons who were proceeding against the enemies of Israel." (Meyer)

> ii. At the signal that the LORD was at work, David and his troops rushed forward to victory. This principle is true in our every-day walk with God. When we sense that the LORD is at work, we must **go out to battle** (*advance quickly*, 2 Samuel 5:24) and we will see a great victory won. "We must also, in the spiritual warfare, observe and obey the motions of the Spirit, when he setteth up his standard; for those are the sounds of God's goings, the footsteps of his anointed." (Trapp)

> iii. There is something wonderful about the King James Version translation of this account in 2 Samuel 5:24: *when thou hearest the sound of a going in the tops of the mulberry trees, that then thou shalt bestir thyself*. When you hear the work of God happening, *bestir thyself* – **go out to battle**. Spurgeon liked to point out that it said *bestir thyself* – often we think we must stir others up. That often just becomes hype and emotionalism. Instead, stir yourself.

> iv. When we see the work of God happening around us, it is like the sound in the mulberry trees - the rustling sound should awaken us to prayer and devotion. A time of crisis or tragedy is also like the sound in the mulberry trees - the rustling sound should awaken us to confession and repentance. "Now, what should I do? The first thing I will do is, I will bestir myself. But how shall I do it? Why, I will go home this day, and I will wrestle in prayer more earnestly than I have been wont to do that God will bless the minister, and multiply the church." (Spurgeon)

> v. "Oh, believe in the co-operation of the Holy Spirit. Lonely missionary in some distant station of the foreign field, listen for the moving of the tops of the mulberry trees! God is stirring for thy succor." (Meyer)

> vi. "The precise species of the *balsam* trees is uncertain. Other possibilities include the pear-tree (LXX), mulberry (AV), or aspen (REB, NEB)." (Selman)

d. **So David did as God commanded him**: He did this by waiting for evidence of God's work and then giving himself completely to the battle. The victory that sprang from this obedience made David and Israel respected and feared among neighboring nations.

i. "Because he looked to the Lord for his strength and for his strategy, he was able to beat back the Philistine offences, to secure the independence of God's people, and to terminate forever the threat of Philistine conquest and oppression." (Payne)

1 Chronicles 15 – The Ark Is Brought to Jerusalem

A. The assembly of the priests and the Levites

1. (1-2) David's directions for bringing in the Ark.

David **built houses for himself in the City of David; and he prepared a place for the ark of God, and pitched a tent for it. Then David said, "No one may carry the ark of God but the Levites, for the LORD has chosen them to carry the ark of God and to minister before Him forever."**

a. **David built houses for himself…he prepared a place for the ark of God, and pitched a tent for it**: At this moment of great triumph – bringing the ark into Jerusalem – the Chronicler reminds us that David lived in a house (or several **houses**) and the ark of the covenant was in **a tent**.

i. Significantly, this **tent** David **prepared** for the ark of God was not the tabernacle itself. The tabernacle of Moses was at Gibeon (1 Chronicles 16:39-40). There were several reasons to explain why David did not bring the tabernacle from Gibeon to Jerusalem:

- He may have believed if the tabernacle was there the people would be satisfied with that and they would lose the passion and vision for the temple God wanted to be built.
- It may be that the tabernacle was only moved when it was absolutely necessary – as when disaster came upon it at Shiloh or Nob.
- It may be that David simply focused on building the temple, not continuing the tabernacle.

b. **No one may carry the ark of God but the Levites**: This shows that David learned from his past mistake when Uzza was struck dead at the first attempt to bring the ark of the covenant into Jerusalem.

2. (3-10) A list of the priests and Levites who supervised the coming of the ark of the covenant into Jerusalem.

And David gathered all Israel together at Jerusalem, to bring up the ark of the LORD to its place, which he had prepared for it. Then David assembled the children of Aaron and the Levites: of the sons of Kohath, Uriel the chief, and one hundred and twenty of his brethren; of the sons of Merari, Asaiah the chief, and two hundred and twenty of his brethren; of the sons of Gershom, Joel the chief, and one hundred and thirty of his brethren; of the sons of Elizaphan, Shemaiah the chief, and two hundred of his brethren; of the sons of Hebron, Eliel the chief, and eighty of his brethren; of the sons of Uzziel, Amminadab the chief, and one hundred and twelve of his brethren.

> a. "A major problem for many readers is the way that the narrative is interrupted by repetitious lists. For example, just at the moment when the ark is raised on to the Levites' shoulders, apparently unrelated lists of musicians and gatekeepers occur…the lists actually have an important function in anticipating the next section of narrative. The Levites who sanctified themselves are shown to have had a valid ancestry; this was a live issue in post-exilic Israel." (Selman)

3. (11-15) The ark is brought to Jerusalem in the right way.

And David called for Zadok and Abiathar the priests, and for the Levites: for Uriel, Asaiah, Joel, Shemaiah, Eliel, and Amminadab. He said to them, "You *are* the heads of the fathers' *houses* **of the Levites; sanctify yourselves, you and your brethren, that you may bring up the ark of the LORD God of Israel to** *the place* **I have prepared for it. For because you** *did* **not** *do it* **the first** *time,* **the LORD our God broke out against us, because we did not consult Him about the proper order." So the priests and the Levites sanctified themselves to bring up the ark of the LORD God of Israel. And the children of the Levites bore the ark of God on their shoulders, by its poles, as Moses had commanded according to the word of the LORD.**

> a. **Sanctify yourselves, you and your brethren, that you may bring up the ark of the LORD God of Israel to the place I have prepared for it**: This demonstrates David's commitment to bringing the ark of the covenant into Jerusalem in the *right* way. He had learned the lesson that the process also matters to God, not only the result.
>
>> i. It also demonstrates that David understood that it was not only a matter of doing the right things in the process but in having **sanctified** men to carry the ark. Ministry that pleases God is done the *right way*, by *sanctified men*, for the *right end result*.

ii. "Sanctification required separation from every form of 'uncleanness' (Leviticus 16:19; 2 Samuel 11:4), and in the Old Testament might include temporary abstinence from sexual intercourse (Exodus 19:15), dirty clothing (Exodus 19:14), or contact with corpses (Leviticus 21:1-4), or more permanently for the priests, not marrying a divorcee, prostitute, or even a widow (Leviticus 21:13-15)." (Selman)

b. **For because you did not do it the first time, the L**ORD **our God broke out against us, because we did not consult Him about the proper order**: 1 Chronicles 13:1-4 makes it clear that David consulted with his leaders and with the people in a highly democratic way. What he did not do was **consult Him** [God] **about the proper order**.

B. The celebration at bringing the ark of the covenant into Jerusalem.

1. (16-24) Names of the musicians at the ceremony.

Then David spoke to the leaders of the Levites to appoint their brethren *to be* **the singers accompanied by instruments of music, stringed instruments, harps, and cymbals, by raising the voice with resounding joy. So the Levites appointed Heman the son of Joel; and of his brethren, Asaph the son of Berechiah; and of their brethren, the sons of Merari, Ethan the son of Kushaiah; and with them their brethren of the second** *rank:* **Zechariah, Ben, Jaaziel, Shemiramoth, Jehiel, Unni, Eliab, Benaiah, Maaseiah, Mattithiah, Elipheleh, Mikneiah, Obed-Edom, and Jeiel, the gatekeepers; the singers, Heman, Asaph, and Ethan,** *were* **to sound the cymbals of bronze; Zechariah, Aziel, Shemiramoth, Jehiel, Unni, Eliab, Maaseiah, and Benaiah, with strings according to Alamoth; Mattithiah, Elipheleh, Mikneiah, Obed-Edom, Jeiel, and Azaziah, to direct with harps on the Sheminith; Chenaniah, leader of the Levites, was instructor** *in charge of* **the music, because he** *was* **skillful; Berechiah and Elkanah** *were* **doorkeepers for the ark; Shebaniah, Joshaphat, Nethanel, Amasai, Zechariah, Benaiah, and Eliezer, the priests, were to blow the trumpets before the ark of God; and Obed-Edom and Jehiah, doorkeepers for the ark.**

a. **David spoke to the leaders of the Levites to appoint their brethren to be the singers**: King David knew a lot about music and singing, but he did not over-manage this ceremony. He delegated responsibility and allowed **the leaders of the Levites to appoint their brethren to be the singers**.

i. **Chenaniah**: "This appears to have been the master singer; he gave the *key* and the *time*, for he presided in the *elevation*, probably meaning what is called *pitching the tune*, for *he was skilful* in music, and powerful in his voice, and well qualified to lead the band: he might have been *precentor*." (Clarke)

b. **By raising the voice with resounding joy**: The several musical instruments mentioned were important, but not more important than these joyful voices. The singing was loud and joyful.

i. "The phrase 'according to *alamoth*' occurs also in the title to Psalm 46. Since the noun means 'maidens, virgins,' such as are mentioned as beating tambourines in ceremonial processions of singers and other musicians (Psalm 68:25), it may indicate music produced in a soprano register." (Payne)

ii. "The phrase 'according to *sheminith*' occurs also in the titles to Psalms 6 and 12. The word is derived from the root for 'eight' and is usually thought to indicate music in a lower octave, in contrast to the preceding verse, though it might indicate an instrument that had eight strings." (Payne)

iii. **Berechia and Elkanah were doorkeepers for the ark**: "They were appointed to keep the door of the tent, in which the ark was to be put and kept, that no unallowed person might press in and touch it; and in like manner they were to attend upon the ark in the way, and to guard it from the press and touch of profane hands." (Poole)

2. (25-28) The ark comes into Jerusalem.

So David, the elders of Israel, and the captains over thousands went to bring up the ark of the covenant of the LORD from the house of Obed-Edom with joy. And so it was, when God helped the Levites who bore the ark of the covenant of the LORD, that they offered seven bulls and seven rams. David was clothed with a robe of fine linen, as were all the Levites who bore the ark, the singers, and Chenaniah the music master *with* the singers. David also wore a linen ephod. Thus all Israel brought up the ark of the covenant of the LORD with shouting and with the sound of the horn, with trumpets and with cymbals, making music with stringed instruments and harps.

a. **To bring up the ark of the covenant of the LORD from the house of Obed-Edom to the City of David with joy**: David was glad to know that the presence and glory of God could bring a blessing instead of a curse. He was also glad to see that when they obeyed God they were blessed.

i. When the worship was in *the proper order* it was filled **with joy** and gladness. It is a mistake to feel that "real" worship must be subdued or solemn or only in a minor key.

b. **God helped the Levites who bore the ark**: It wasn't so much that the ark of the covenant was so heavy that they needed God's help to carry it. Rather, there was considerable pressure and stress in bearing a burden that had recently resulted in a sudden death. They needed God's help to deal with the spiritual pressure of this ministry.

c. **They offered seven bulls and seven rams**: David was careful *not* to neglect the institution of sacrifice in this second attempt to bring the ark of the covenant into Jerusalem.

> i. 2 Samuel 6:13 says that they sacrificed every six steps in the procession, "Because Uzzah perished when he had gone but six paces, say some. Every man that seeth another stricken, and himself spared, is to offer sacrifices, yea, to keep a passover for himself." (Trapp)

d. **David also wore a linen ephod**: It is a mistake to think that David was immodest. **As were all the Levites** indicates that David was dressed just like all the other priests and Levites in this procession.

e. **Thus all Israel brought up the ark of the covenant of the LORD with shouting**: This shows that David brought the ark to Jerusalem with a big production – bigger than the first attempt. David was wise enough to know that the problem with the first attempt wasn't that it was a big production, but that it was a big production that came from man and not from God.

> i. This is essentially the same account recorded in 2 Samuel 6, except in 2 Samuel the leadership of David is emphasized, and in 1 Chronicles 15 the participation and support of **all Israel** is emphasized. Both accounts are correct; David was the leader, but it wasn't a one-man show; **all Israel brought up the ark**.
>
> ii. "The primary change is that the homecoming of the ark…has become a corporate act of *all Israel* rather than an expression of David's personal faith." (Selman)

3. (29) David's wife Michal despises David.

And it happened, *as* the ark of the covenant of the LORD came to the City of David, that Michal, Saul's daughter, looked through a window and saw King David whirling and playing music; and she despised him in her heart.

> a. **Michal, Saul's daughter, looked through a window and saw King David whirling and playing music**: David didn't hold back anything in his own expression of worship. He didn't dance out of obligation but out of heartfelt worship. He was glad to bring the **ark of the covenant of the LORD** into Jerusalem according to God's word.

i. This expression of David's heart showed that he had a genuine *emotional link* to God. There are two great errors in this area – the error of making emotions the center of our Christian life and the error of an emotionally detached Christian life. In the Christian life, emotions must not be manipulated and they must not be repressed.

ii. From our knowledge of ancient and modern culture, we can surmise that David's dance wasn't a solo performance. The context clearly puts him together with the priests and Levites, and he probably danced with simple rhythmic steps together with other men in the way one might see Orthodox Jewish men dance today. In this context, David's **linen ephod** means he set aside his royal robes and dressed just like everyone else in the procession.

iii. It should also be observed that David's dancing was appropriate in the context. This was a parade with a marching band, a grand procession. David's dancing fit right in. If David did this as the nation gathered on the Day of Atonement it would be out of context and wrong.

b. **And she despised him in her heart**: 2 Samuel 6:20-23 tell us more of Michal's complaint and of David's response to her. She sarcastically said to him, *How glorious was the king of Israel today, uncovering himself today*. Michal seemed to indicate that she didn't object to David's dancing, but to what David wore when he set aside his royal robes and danced as a man just like the other men celebrating in the procession. David acted as if he were just another worshipper in Israel, and this offended Michal.

i. In response, David told Michal that his actions were *before the* LORD. In simple terms, David told Michal: "I did it for God, not for you." He went on to explain, *and will be humble in my own sight*. What David did was *humbling* to him. He didn't dance to show others how spiritual he was.

ii. "The incident illustrates the perpetual inability of the earthly minded to appreciate the gladness of the spiritual." (Morgan)

1 Chronicles 16 – David's Psalm of Thanks

A. The ark is brought into the prepared tent.

1. (1-3) David gives the assembly a feast.

So they brought the ark of God, and set it in the midst of the tabernacle that David had erected for it. Then they offered burnt offerings and peace offerings before God. And when David had finished offering the burnt offerings and the peace offerings, he blessed the people in the name of the LORD. Then he distributed to everyone of Israel, both man and woman, to everyone a loaf of bread, a piece *of meat*, **and a cake of raisins.**

> a. **They brought the ark of God, and set it in the midst of the tabernacle**: After many years – since the ark was lost in battle – the ark is returned to the center of Israel's national consciousness. The emblem of God's presence and glory was set in its proper place in Israel.
>
> b. **When David had finished offering the burnt offerings and peace offerings**: The **burnt offerings** spoke of *consecration*. The **peace offerings** spoke of *fellowship*. This was a day of great consecration and fellowship with God. It was also a great barbeque and meal for all the people.
>
> > i. These sacrifices were an important part of the ceremony, neglected in the first attempt to bring the ark of the covenant to Jerusalem. "These pointed them to Christ, freeing them from their sins, both from the crime and from the curse; these taught them thankfulness for Christ, and all benefits in and by him." (Trapp)
> >
> > ii. "The second item of food (known only here and in 2 Samuel 6:19) was either a *cake of dates* or a 'portion of meat' (REB, NEB, NSRV; *cf.* GNB, AV) – if the latter is correct, it was an especially generous act since meat rarely appeared on domestic menus in ancient Israel." (Selman)

iii. "Most flesh from the peace offerings was eaten by the people themselves, sitting down, as it were, as guests of God's table, in a meal celebrating the restoration of their peace with him." (Payne)

2. (4-6) Worship leaders are appointed to lead the congregation.

And he appointed some of the Levites to minister before the ark of the LORD, to commemorate, to thank, and to praise the LORD God of Israel: Asaph the chief, and next to him Zechariah, *then* Jeiel, Shemiramoth, Jehiel, Mattithiah, Eliab, Benaiah, and Obed-Edom: Jeiel with stringed instruments and harps, but Asaph made music with cymbals; Benaiah and Jahaziel the priests regularly *blew* the trumpets before the ark of the covenant of God.

a. **And he appointed some of the Levites to minister before the ark**: At the end of this spectacular day of celebration, David established an *enduring* institution of worship and commemoration at the ark of the covenant. It wasn't to be a one-day high, but an ongoing ministry to God.

i. "David's appointment then of Levites to minister in music and praise to God marks a significant advance in the history of Israel's worship. His previous arrangements for music had been devised for just one occasion; but now a continuing service is envisioned." (Payne)

b. **He appointed some of the Levites…to commemorate**: In the Levitical appointments for that day and beyond, David selected some Levites to focus on *commemorating* what great things God had done. Simply *remembering* God's great works is an important and often neglected part of the Christian life. Spurgeon (in his sermon *The Recorders*) noted several ways that we can help ourselves remember the great things of God:

- Make an actual record of what God has done, keeping a written journal.
- Be sure to praise God thoroughly at the time you receive His goodness.
- Set apart time for meditation on the good things God has done.
- Talk about His mercy often to other people.
- Use everything around you as reminders of the goodness of God.

c. **Asaph the chief**: Previously, the Levites had appointed Heman as the leader of worship (1 Chronicles 15:17). At this time David elevated **Asaph** to this position.

i. "No reason is given, though Asaph did represent the senior Levitical clan of Gershon (1 Chronicles 6:39-43). Personal ability may also have been a contributing factor, for Asaph and his descendants are listed as composers for twelve of the inspired Old Testament psalms." (Payne)

B. David's song of thanksgiving.

1. (7) The psalm written for the special occasion.

On that day David first delivered *this psalm* into the hand of Asaph and his brethren, to thank the LORD:

> a. **David first delivered this psalm**: David was known as *the sweet psalmist of Israel* (2 Samuel 23:1), and he especially wrote the following psalm **to thank the LORD** on the day the ark of the covenant was brought to Jerusalem.
>
>> i. "The Psalm is found in the Book of Psalms; its first movement (8-22) in Psalm 105:1-15; its second movement (23-33) in Psalm 96:1b-13a; its third movement (34-36) consisting of a quotation of the opening and closing sentences of Psalm 106:1-47 and 48." (Morgan)
>>
>> ii. "All three of the canonical psalms that he quoted are anonymous, 'orphan psalms' (without title) in the Old Testament Psalter; but on the basis of the king's use of them here, they should indeed be classed as his." (Payne)

2. (8-13) The call to praise.

Oh, give thanks to the LORD!
Call upon His name;
Make known His deeds among the peoples!
Sing to Him, sing psalms to Him;
Talk of all His wondrous works!
Glory in His holy name;
Let the hearts of those rejoice who seek the LORD!
Seek the LORD and His strength;
Seek His face evermore!
Remember His marvelous works which He has done,
His wonders, and the judgments of His mouth,
O seed of Israel His servant,
You children of Jacob, His chosen ones!

> a. **Oh, give thanks to the LORD!** Like many psalms, this one begins with a call to praise, virtually in the form of a commandment. Yet the psalm breathes with too much excitement for this to be a true command; it is an exhortation to the community of God's people to join in praise to their God.

i. "All the good that we enjoy comes from God. Recollect that! Alas, most men forget it. Rowland Hill used to say that worldlings were like the hogs under the oak, which eat the acorns, but never think of the oak from which they fell, nor lift up their heads to grunt out a thanksgiving. Yes, so it is. They munch the gift and murmur at the giver." (Spurgeon)

b. **Give thanks.... Call upon...Make known.... Sing...Talk.... Glory.... Seek.... Remember**: In a few verses, David lists a remarkable number of ways (at least eight) one can praise and glorify God. Some of them speak directly to God (such as **sing psalms to Him**), some speak to others about God's greatness (**make known His deeds among the peoples**), and some are a conversation with one's self (**remember His marvelous works**).

i. Meyer on **talk of all His wondrous works**: "We do not talk sufficiently about God. Why it is so may not be easy to explain; but there seems to be too great reticence among Christian people about the best things.... We talk about sermons, details of worship and church organization, or the latest phase of Scripture criticism; we discuss men, methods, and churches; but our talk in the home, and in the gatherings of Christians for social purposes, is too seldom about the wonderful works of God. Better to speak less, and to talk more of Him."

ii. "If we talked more of God's wondrous works, *we should be free from talking of other people's works*. It is easy to criticise those we could not rival, and carp at those we could not emulate. He who could not carve a statue, or make a single stroke of the chisel correctly, affects to point out where the handicraft of the greatest sculptor might have been improved. It is a poor, pitiful occupation, that of picking holes in other people's coats, and yet some people seem so pleased when they can perceive a fault, that they roll it under their tongue as a sweet morsel." (Spurgeon)

iii. "There is no gifted tongue requisite, there are no powers of eloquence invoked; neither laws of rhetoric nor rules of grammar are pronounced indispensable in the simple talk that my text inculcates, '*Talk* ye of all his wondrous works.' I beg your pardon when you say you cannot do this. You cannot because you will not." (Spurgeon)

c. **O seed of Israel...His chosen ones**: This call to praise is directed to the people of God. As will be noted later in the psalm, *all* creation has a responsibility to praise its Creator; but this is the *special* responsibility of God's people.

3. (14-19) Remembering God's covenant with His people.

He *is* the LORD our God;
His judgments *are* in all the earth.
Remember His covenant forever,
The word which He commanded, for a thousand generations,
***The covenant which* He made with Abraham,**
And His oath to Isaac,
And confirmed it to Jacob for a statute,
To Israel *for* an everlasting covenant,
Saying, "To you I will give the land of Canaan
As the allotment of your inheritance,"
When you were few in number,
Indeed very few, and strangers in it.

a. **His judgments are in all the earth**: David will soon begin to sing about the special relationship between the LORD and His covenant people. Yet he prefaced those ideas with the thought that God is the Lord of **all the earth**. His authority is not limited to His covenant people.

b. **Remember His covenant forever**: God wanted His people to never forget the **covenant** He made with them. God's dealing with man through history has been based on the idea of **covenant**.

- God made a covenant with Abraham regarding a land, a nation, and a particular messianic blessing (Genesis 12:1-3).
- God made a covenant with Israel as a nation, regarding a law, sacrifice, and choice of blessing or cursing (Exodus 19:5-8).
- God made a covenant with David regarding the specific lineage of the Messiah (2 Samuel 7).
- God made a covenant with all who would believe on His Son, the New Covenant through Jesus Christ (Luke 22:20).

i. It was entirely appropriate that this psalm focuses on the idea of **His covenant** because it was written for the arrival of the *ark of the covenant* into the place David prepared for it in Jerusalem.

ii. "In the restoration of the Ark after a period of neglect, the people found a sure token of that mercy." (Morgan)

c. **To you I will give the land of Canaan**: David here highlighted the promise of **land** that God made to Abraham as part of His covenant with the patriarch (Genesis 12:1 and 13:14-17). The land belonged to the descendants of Abraham, Isaac, and Jacob through this covenant.

i. In this, we see that this portion of the psalm is largely meant for *teaching*. This stanza was not primarily intended as a declaration of praise to God, but as informing the worship of God's people.

4. (20-22) God's protection upon His people.

When they went from one nation to another,
And from *one* kingdom to another people,
He permitted no man to do them wrong;
Yes, He rebuked kings for their sakes,
***Saying,* "Do not touch My anointed ones,**
And do My prophets no harm."

a. **When they went from one nation to another**: In the story of the arrival of the ark of the covenant recorded in 2 Samuel, this psalm of David is not included. Here we see why the Chronicler – writing shortly *after* the Babylonian exile – was anxious to include it. This line of David's psalm praises God for His providential protection of His people when they were *out of* the Promised Land.

b. **He permitted no man to do them wrong**: One might say that this was inaccurate – after all, the oppressive Pharaohs seemed to do much **wrong** to Israel. Yet, in the longer view of seeing God's good work even through such painful times, David can truthfully say "**He permitted no man to do them wrong.**"

c. **Do not touch My anointed ones, and do My prophets no harm**: This seems to refer to God's people as a whole instead of particular **anointed** individuals or individual **prophets**.

5. (23-30) The command to praise the LORD.

Sing to the LORD, all the earth;
Proclaim the good news of His salvation from day to day.
Declare His glory among the nations,
His wonders among all peoples.
For the LORD *is* great and greatly to be praised;
He *is* also to be feared above all gods.
For all the gods of the peoples *are* idols,
But the LORD made the heavens.
Honor and majesty *are* before Him;
Strength and gladness are in His place.
Give to the LORD, O families of the peoples,
Give to the LORD glory and strength.
Give to the LORD the glory *due* His name;
Bring an offering, and come before Him.

Oh, worship the LORD in the beauty of holiness!
Tremble before Him, all the earth.
The world also is firmly established,
It shall not be moved.

> a. **Sing to the LORD, all the earth**: God's covenant people have a special responsibility to praise Him, but **all the earth** should also **proclaim the good news of His salvation day to day**.
>
>> i. It is only **good news** when it is **His salvation**. *My* salvation isn't enough to save me. I need **His salvation** to save me. This is something worth proclaiming.
>>
>> ii. "There is not one of us but has cause for song, and certainly not one saint but ought specially to praise the name of the Lord." (Spurgeon)
>
> b. **Declare His glory among the nations**: David is back to a particular address to the people of God, imploring them to tell everyone of the greatness of God, and His superiority **above all gods**.
>
>> i. The reason for His superiority is simple: **all the gods of the peoples are idols, but the LORD made the heavens**. The covenant God of Israel is real and is the Creator of all things, in contrast to the mere statues of the nations.
>
> c. **Give to the LORD glory and strength**: This is *not* in the sense of giving something to God that He does not already have. It is in the sense of *crediting* to God what He actually does possess, but what man is often blind to.
>
> d. **Worship the LORD in the beauty of holiness!** God's holiness – His "set-apart-ness" – has a wonderful and distinct **beauty** about it. It is *beautiful* that God is God and not man; that He is more than the greatest man or a super-man. His holy love, grace, justice, and majesty are *beautiful*.

6. (31-33) Creation praises God.

Let the heavens rejoice, and let the earth be glad;
And let them say among the nations, "The LORD reigns."
Let the sea roar, and all its fullness;
Let the field rejoice, and all that *is* in it.
Then the trees of the woods shall rejoice before the LORD,
For He is coming to judge the earth.

> a. **Let the heavens rejoice, and let the earth be glad**: David knew that creation itself praised God. He knew that the beauty and power and skill and majesty of creation was itself a testimony of praise to its Creator.

b. **Let them say among the nations**: Israel had the word of God to tell them of God's reign and His coming judgment. The **nations** have the testimony of creation to tell them what they should know about God (Romans 1:19-23).

c. **The LORD reigns**: The creation itself tells us of a God of infinite wisdom, power, and order; it logically deduces that this God **reigns** and will **judge the earth**, understanding that His order and power and wisdom are expressed *morally* as well as *materially*.

> i. Payne on **for He is coming to judge the earth**: "While earlier messianic prophecies had foretold our Lord's universal, millennial reign (Genesis 49:10; Numbers 24:17; 1 Samuel 2:10), these words – 'he comes' – may be the first in all of written Scripture (Job 19:25 may well have been *spoken* earlier) to set forth the doctrine of the glorious second coming of Jesus Christ."

7. (34-36) Conclusion: Celebrating God's faithfulness to His people.

Oh, give thanks to the LORD, for *He is* good!
For His mercy *endures* forever.
And say, "Save us, O God of our salvation;
Gather us together, and deliver us from the Gentiles,
To give thanks to Your holy name,
To triumph in Your praise."
Blessed *be* the LORD God of Israel
From everlasting to everlasting!
And all the people said, "Amen!" and praised the LORD.

a. **Gather us together, and deliver us from the Gentiles**: This is yet another demonstration of why the Chronicler chose to include this psalm of David in the account of the ark's coming into Jerusalem. These ancient words of David would have special relevance to the returned exiles. They would not only have confidence in God's ability to **gather** and **deliver**, but they would also be motivated to **give thanks** and **to triumph in Your praise**.

> i. "The words…do not presuppose that the people had been previously led away into the Chaldean exile, but only the dispersion of prisoners of war, led away captive into an enemy's land after a defeat.... It was just such cases Solomon had in view in his prayer, 1 Kings 8:46-50." (Payne citing Keil)

b. **And all the people said, "Amen!" and praised the LORD**: This reminds us that David's psalm was not sung as a solo. The hearts – and perhaps the voices – of the people were in complete agreement with him through the psalm.

8. (37-43) Postscript: Maintaining the worship of God.

So he left Asaph and his brothers there before the ark of the covenant of the LORD to minister before the ark regularly, as every day's work required; and Obed-Edom with his sixty-eight brethren, including Obed-Edom the son of Jeduthun, and Hosah, *to be* **gatekeepers; and Zadok the priest and his brethren the priests, before the tabernacle of the LORD at the high place that** *was* **at Gibeon, to offer burnt offerings to the LORD on the altar of burnt offering regularly morning and evening, and** *to do* **according to all that is written in the Law of the LORD which He commanded Israel; and with them Heman and Jeduthun and the rest who were chosen, who were designated by name, to give thanks to the LORD, because His mercy** *endures* **forever; and with them Heman and Jeduthun, to sound aloud with trumpets and cymbals and the musical instruments of God. Now the sons of Jeduthun** *were* **gatekeepers. Then all the people departed, every man to his house; and David returned to bless his house.**

a. **So he left Asaph and his brothers there before the ark of the covenant**: This emphasizes the point made previously in 1 Chronicles 16:4-6, that David deliberately planned for this to be more than a one day spectacular. He instituted ongoing service and worship before the ark of the covenant at its new resting place in Jerusalem.

b. **Before the tabernacle of the LORD at the high place that was at Gibeon, to offer burnt offerings to the LORD**: This reminds us that the center of *sacrifice* was still at the tabernacle's altar at Gibeon.

i. "For the time being, Israel's worship activities and personnel were to be divided between the ark at Jerusalem and the tended altar at Gibeon." (Selman)

ii. "How long the service at Gibeon was continued we cannot tell; the principle functions were no doubt performed at Jerusalem." (Clarke)

1 Chronicles 17 – A House for God and a House for David

"This chapter lies at the heart of the Chronicler's presentation of history." (Martin J. Selman)

A. God's promise to David.

1. (1-2) Nathan's premature advice to David.

Now it came to pass, when David was dwelling in his house, that David said to Nathan the prophet, "See now, I dwell in a house of cedar, but the ark of the covenant of the LORD *is* under tent curtains." Then Nathan said to David, "Do all that *is* in your heart, for God *is* with you."

> a. **Now it came to pass**: "Chronologically chapter 17 came after the termination of the wars chronicled in chapter 18 and it should be dated about 995 B.C." (Payne)
>
> b. **I dwell in a house of cedar**: **Cedar** wood was especially valued. This means that David lived in an expensive, beautiful home. When he remembered that **the ark of the covenant of the LORD is under tent curtains**, the contrast bothered him. David was troubled by the thought that he lived in a nicer house than the ark of the covenant.
>
>> i. Without saying the specific words, David told Nathan that he wanted to build a *temple* to replace the *tabernacle*. More than 400 years before this, when Israel was in the wilderness, God commanded Moses to build a tent of meeting according to a specific pattern (Exodus 25:8-9). God never asked for a permanent building to replace the tent, but now David wanted to do this for God.
>>
>> ii. The tent of meeting – also known as the tabernacle – was perfectly suited to Israel in the wilderness, because they constantly moved. Now that Israel was securely in the land, and the tabernacle was in

Jerusalem (2 Samuel 6:17), David thought it would be better and more appropriate to build a temple to replace the tabernacle.

c. **Do all that is in your heart, for God is with you**: Nathan said this to David because it seemed good and reasonable. What could be wrong with David building a temple?

i. **All that is in your heart** shows that David's heart was filled with this question: "What can I do for God?" He was so filled with gratitude and concern for God's glory that he wanted to do something special for God.

2. (3-6) God corrects Nathan's hasty approval of David's plan to build a temple.

But it happened that night that the word of God came to Nathan, saying, "Go and tell My servant David, 'Thus says the Lord: "You shall not build Me a house to dwell in. For I have not dwelt in a house since the time that I brought up Israel, even to this day, but have gone from tent to tent, and from *one* **tabernacle** *to another*. **Wherever I have moved about with all Israel, have I ever spoken a word to any of the judges of Israel, whom I commanded to shepherd My people, saying, 'Why have you not built Me a house of cedar?'"'"**

a. **That night that the word of God came to Nathan**: Nathan's response to David was presumptuous. He answered according to human judgment and common sense, but before the **word of God** came to him.

i. "It is of the utmost importance that we should ever test our desires, even the highest and holiest of them, by His will. Work, excellent in itself, should never be undertaken, save at the express command of God. The passing of time will always vindicate the wisdom of the Divine will." (Morgan)

b. **For I have not dwelt in a house since the time that I brought up Israel, even to this day**: God seemed honored and "surprised" that David offered to build Him a house. "You want to build Me a house? No one has ever offered to do that before, and I never commanded anyone to do it."

i. "The Hebrew text says literally, 'build me *the* house.' The idea of there being such a house *was* legitimate, just that David was not the one to build it." (Payne)

ii. David wanted to do more than God commanded. This is a wonderful place to be in our relationship with God. Most of us are so stuck in the thinking, "How little can I do and still please the Lord?" that we never really want to do *more* than God commands.

iii. "Though the Lord refused to David the realization of his wish, he did it in a most gracious manner. He did not put the idea away from him in anger or disdain, as though David had cherished an unworthy desire; but he honored his servant even in the non-acceptance of his offer." (Spurgeon)

iii. David now knew that God didn't want him to build the temple, but David didn't respond by doing *nothing*. Instead of building the temple, David gathered all the materials for its construction so Solomon could build a glorious temple to God (1 Chronicles 29:2-9).

iv. "If you cannot have what you hoped, do not sit down in despair and allow the energies of your life to run to waste; but arise, and gird yourself to help others to achieve. If you may not build, you may gather materials for him that shall. If you may not go down the mine, you can hold the ropes." (Meyer)

3. (7-10) God promises to build David a house.

Now therefore, thus shall you say to My servant David, "Thus says the Lord of hosts: 'I took you from the sheepfold, from following the sheep, to be ruler over My people Israel. And I have been with you wherever you have gone, and have cut off all your enemies from before you, and have made you a name like the name of the great men who *are* on the earth. Moreover I will appoint a place for My people Israel, and will plant them, that they may dwell in a place of their own and move no more; nor shall the sons of wickedness oppress them anymore, as previously, since the time that I commanded judges *to be* over My people Israel. Also I will subdue all your enemies. Furthermore I tell you that the Lord will build you a house.'"

a. **I took you from the sheepfold, from following the sheep, to be ruler over My people**: God was about to make David an amazing promise – one that might be hard for David to believe. Therefore, He first reminded David of His *past* work in His life. The same God who was with David wherever he had gone would also fulfill this promise.

b. **I will appoint a place for My people Israel**: God promised David that under his reign, God would establish a permanent, secure, Israel. God promised this first because He knew that David, being a godly shepherd, was first concerned about the welfare of his people.

c. **Furthermore I tell you that the Lord will build you a house**: God promised David that He would build *him* a house in the sense of establishing a dynasty for the house of David. This was an enduring legacy for David long after his death.

i. David wanted to build God a temple. God said, "Thank you David, but no thanks. Let me **build you a house** instead." This was a greater promise than David's offer to God because David's house would last longer and be more glorious than the temple David wanted to build.

ii. "The oracle's significance depends on the various meanings of the Hebrew *bayit*, 'house', which can mean 'dynasty', 'temple', and even 'household' (1 Chronicles 16:43)." (Selman)

iii. Why did God say, "No" to David's offer? Because David was a man of war, and God wanted a man of peace to build His temple. 1 Chronicles 22:8-10 explains this: *But the word of the LORD came to me, saying, 'You have shed much blood and have made great wars; you shall not build a house for My name, because you have shed much blood on the earth in My sight…a son shall be born to you, who shall be a man of rest… He shall build a house for My name.*

iv. The explanation to David recorded in 1 Chronicles 22:8 came years afterwards. "It would have wounded David needlessly to have been told this at the time…. Meanwhile David possessed his soul in patience, and said to himself, 'God has a reason; I cannot understand it, but it is well.' " (Meyer)

v. "Our relationship with God is always based upon what He does for us, never upon what we do for Him. If He wills that we build a Temple, it is ours to do it, but the doing of it creates no merit by which we may claim anything from Him." (Morgan)

4. (11-15) God promises to build David a house instead.

"And it shall be, when your days are fulfilled, when you must go *to be* with your fathers, that I will set up your seed after you, who will be of your sons; and I will establish his kingdom. He shall build Me a house, and I will establish his throne forever. I will be his Father, and he shall be My son; and I will not take My mercy away from him, as I took *it* from *him* who was before you. And I will establish him in My house and in My kingdom forever; and his throne shall be established forever." According to all these words and according to all this vision, so Nathan spoke to David.

a. **I will set up your seed after you**: In this, God specifically promised a hereditary monarchy for the house of David. It was important for God to repeat this promise specifically because there had never yet been a king succeeded by his son in Israel.

i. "The ambiguity inherent in the Hebrew word *zera*, like its English equivalents 'seed' (AV) or *offspring* (NIV, NRSV, RSV), means it can apply both to the dynasty as a whole and to individual members of it (*cf.* the use of the same word in Genesis 3:15; 12:7; 17:7; 17:16)." (Selman)

ii. "While God did not here employ the term covenant, what he revealed was one; and it is so designated subsequently (2 Samuel 23:5; Psalm 89:3, 34; Psalm 132:11-12)." (Payne)

b. **He shall build Me a house**: Though David would not build a temple for God, David's descendant would.

i. "Like circumcision in the case of the Abrahamic covenant (Genesis 17), building the temple is the act of human obedience by which God's covenant promise is accepted and confirmed." (Selman)

c. **I will establish his throne forever**: The family of David did rule over Israel for more than four centuries but was eventually removed because of evil added upon evil. Yet out of the "stump" of Jesse, God raised up a new branch that would reign forever and ever (Isaiah 11:1-2).

d. **I will be his Father, and he shall be My son**: This descendant of David would enjoy a special relationship with God.

e. **His throne shall be established forever**: God promised David that the reign of his dynasty would last forever.

i. Each of these great promises was *partially* fulfilled in Solomon, David's son and the successor to his throne.

- Solomon ruled on David's throne.
- God's mercies never departed from Solomon, though he sinned.
- Solomon built God a magnificent house.

ii. Yet God's promise to David was all the more important because of when the Chronicler wrote about it – *after* the exile when there was no independent kingdom of Israel and the throne of David seemed vacant. The Chronicler had the faith to see that this promise was not broken even when it plainly seemed to be. He knew that Messiah would indeed come from the seemingly dead line of David and reign forever. He had faith in what the prophets foretold as a greater fulfillment of these promises:

- *Behold, the days are coming, says the* LORD, *that I will raise to David a Branch of righteousness; a King shall reign and prosper, and execute judgment and righteousness in the earth.... Now this is His name by which He will be called: THE* LORD *OUR RIGHTEOUSNESS.* (Jeremiah 23:5-6)

- *For unto us a Child is born, unto us a Son is given; and the government will be upon His shoulder.... Upon the throne of David and over His kingdom, to order it and establish it...from that time forward, even forever.* (Isaiah 9:6-7)

- *And behold, you will conceive in your womb and bring forth a Son, and shall call His name JESUS. He will be great, and will be called the Son of the Highest; and the Lord God will give Him the throne of His father David. And He will reign over the house of Jacob forever, and of His kingdom there will be no end.* (Luke 1:31-33)

iii. God did not want the earthly house built until the spiritual house was promised and established. The more important house had to be in place first, and that house was the dynasty that would result in the throne of God's Messiah.

iv. As for David, God's blessing was upon him in a unique way. The New Testament identifies Jesus with David more than with any other human ancestor.

- *Hosanna to the Son of David!* (Matthew 21:9)

- *The Lord God will give Him the throne of His father David.* (Luke 1:32)

- *I am the Root and Offspring of David, the Bright and Morning Star.* (Revelation 22:16)

v. It also seems that David will be God's chosen prince over a restored Israel in the millennial earth. Hosea 3:5 says, *Afterward the children of Israel shall return and seek the LORD their God and David their king. They shall fear the LORD and His goodness in the latter days.* Other passages which set forth this idea are Ezekiel 37:24-25, Ezekiel 34:23-24, and Jeremiah 30:9.

B. David's thankful response.

1. (16-22) David's humble thanksgiving and praise to God.

Then King David went in and sat before the LORD; and he said: "Who *am* I, O LORD God? And what is my house, that You have brought me this far? And *yet* this was a small thing in Your sight, O God; and You have *also* spoken of Your servant's house for a great while to come, and have regarded me according to the rank of a man of high degree, O LORD God. What more can David *say* to You for the honor of Your servant? For You know Your servant. O LORD, for Your servant's sake, and according to Your own heart, You have done all this greatness, in making known all these great things. O LORD, *there is* none like You,

nor *is there any* God besides You, according to all that we have heard with our ears. And who *is* like Your people Israel, the one nation on the earth whom God went to redeem for Himself *as* a people—to make for Yourself a name by great and awesome deeds, by driving out nations from before Your people whom You redeemed from Egypt? For You have made Your people Israel Your very own people forever; and You, Lord, have become their God."

> a. **Who am I, O Lord God?.... O Lord, there is none like You**: When David received this spectacular gift, he didn't think it made *him* any greater. In David's eyes it made *God* greater.
>
> > i. "Thou hast treated me as if I had been born the son of a great monarch, and not a poor shepherd, as indeed I was, O Lord God." (Poole)
> >
> > ii. David's attitude wasn't "I am so great that even God's gives me gifts." His attitude was, "God is so great that He gives even me gifts." We should receive salvation and every blessing with the same attitude. God's giving reflects the greatness of the Giver, not the receiver.
>
> b. **Your servant**: David's humble reception of this gift is shown by the repetition of the phrase **Your servant** – ten times in this prayer.
>
> > i. It shows that David humbly accepted God's "no" when he wanted to build the temple. "There are some professors who would do a great thing if they might, but if they are not permitted to act a shining part they are in the sulks and angry with their God. David when his proposal was set aside found it in his heart not to murmur, but to pray." (Spurgeon)
> >
> > ii. "The king's sitting 'before the Lord' suggests that he went to the tent that was enshrining the ark." (Payne)

2. (23-27) David boldly asks that the promise be fulfilled as spoken.

"And now, O Lord, the word which You have spoken concerning Your servant and concerning his house, *let it* be established forever, and do as You have said. So let it be established, that Your name may be magnified forever, saying, 'The Lord of hosts, the God of Israel, *is* Israel's God.' And let the house of Your servant David be established before You. For You, O my God, have revealed to Your servant that You will build him a house. Therefore Your servant has found it *in his heart* to pray before You. And now, Lord, You are God, and have promised this goodness to Your servant. Now You have been pleased to bless the house of Your servant, that it may continue before You forever; for You have blessed it, O Lord, and *it shall be* blessed forever."

a. **Let it be established forever, and do as You have said**: David's prayer boldly asked God to *do* what He *promised*. This wasn't *passive* prayer that said, "Well God, do whatever You want to do – I don't really care one way or another." This wasn't *arrogant* prayer that said, "Well God, let me tell You what to do." This was *bold* prayer that said, "God, here is Your promise – now I trust You to fulfill it grandly and to be faithful to Your word."

i. The phrase "**therefore Your servant has found it in his heart to pray before You**" emphasizes this. David was saying, "I'm only praying because You promised. You told me that this is what You want to do."

ii. "There is hardly any position more utterly beautiful, strong, or safe than to put the finger upon some promise of the Divine Word, and claim it.... It is far better to claim a few things specifically than a score vaguely." (Meyer)

iii. This kind of prayer *appropriates* God's promise. Just because God promises does not mean that we possess. Through believing prayer like this, God promises and we appropriate. If we don't appropriate in faith, God's promise is left unclaimed.

- We may appropriate His promise for forgiveness: *If we confess our sins, He is faithful and just to forgive us our sins and to cleanse us from all unrighteousness* (1 John 1:9).
- We may appropriate His promise for peace: *Peace I leave with you, My peace I give to you: not as the world gives do I give to you. Let not your heart be troubled, neither let it be afraid* (John 14:27).
- We may appropriate His promise for guidance: *I will instruct you and teach you in the way you should go: I will guide you with My eye* (Psalm 32:8).
- We may appropriate His promise for growth: *He who has begun a good work in you will complete it until the day of Jesus Christ* (Philippians 1:6).
- We may appropriate His promise for help: *Let us therefore come boldly to the throne of grace, that we may obtain mercy and find grace to help in time of need* (Hebrews 4:16).

b. **Therefore Your servant has found it in his heart to pray before You**: Notice that David prayed from the **heart**. Some people pray from a book; others pray from their mind. The right place to pray from is the **heart**.

c. **Lord, You are God, and have promised this goodness to Your servant**: This was David's foundation of faith. He knew that God was **God** and that His promise was true. God *can* be trusted.

i. "The great sin of not believing in the Lord Jesus Christ is often spoken of very lightly and in a very trifling spirit, as though it were scarcely any sin at all; yet, according to my text, and, indeed, according to the whole tenor of the Scriptures, unbelief is the giving of God the lie, and what can be worse?" (Spurgeon)

1 Chronicles 18 – The Security of David's Kingdom

A. David conquers neighboring nations.

1. (1) David subdues the Philistines.

After this it came to pass that David attacked the Philistines, subdued them, and took Gath and its towns from the hand of the Philistines.

a. **David attacked the Philistines, subdued them**: The Philistines had troubled Israel for centuries, and often dominated Israel. Under the reign of David, he both **attacked** and **subdued** these troublesome enemies.

i. David didn't avoid fighting the Philistines because Israel had lost to them so many times before. "The thing that fascinates me about this complete victory is the utter contempt with which David treated the great power of his adversaries." (Redpath)

b. **And took Gath**: When David became king, the Philistines were *taking* territory from God's people. Under his leadership, God's people began to *take* territory from the enemy.

i. "Evidence for David's conquest of *Gath and its surrounding villages* is found in the presence of 600 Gittites in David's entourage (2 Samuel 15:18)." (Selman)

2. (2) The Moabites put under tribute.

Then he defeated Moab, and the Moabites became David's servants, *and* brought tribute.

a. **He defeated Moab**: David's war against Moab and his harsh treatment of their army seems out of place considering that David's great-grandmother was a Moabite (Ruth) and that he entrusted his mother and father into the care of the Moabites (1 Samuel 22:3-4). It may be that the Moabites killed or mistreated David's parents.

b. **Brought tribute**: God did not want Israel to *destroy* every neighbor nation. Generally, God wanted Israel to be so blessed and strong that other nations were "taxed" by Israel, in recognition of their strength and dominance.

3. (3-8) David conquers a Syrian alliance.

And David defeated Hadadezer king of Zobah *as far as* Hamath, as he went to establish his power by the River Euphrates. David took from him one thousand chariots, seven thousand horsemen, and twenty thousand foot soldiers. Also David hamstrung all the chariot *horses*, except that he spared enough of them for one hundred chariots. When the Syrians of Damascus came to help Hadadezer king of Zobah, David killed twenty-two thousand of the Syrians. Then David put *garrisons* in Syria of Damascus; and the Syrians became David's servants, *and* brought tribute. So the LORD preserved David wherever he went. And David took the shields of gold that were on the servants of Hadadezer, and brought them to Jerusalem. Also from Tibhath and from Chun, cities of Hadadezer, David brought a large amount of bronze, with which Solomon made the bronze Sea, the pillars, and the articles of bronze.

a. **As he went to establish his power by the River Euphrates**: The king of **Zobah** (a Syrian kingdom) ran into David on his way to capture territory to the Euphrates. David's dominance extended all the way to the Euphrates River.

i. "The border of Israel was carried to the line of the Euphrates, so that promise made by God to Abraham was fulfilled: 'Unto thy seed I have given this land, from the river of Egypt unto the great river, the river Euphrates.' " (Meyer)

ii. "Then there was Syria, the great heathen nation to the north, divided into two groups with capitals at Zobah and Damascus. They united together for protection but found themselves helpless against the might of David." (Redpath)

b. **David also hamstrung all the chariot horses**: This was military necessity instead of mere animal cruelty. David could not care for so many horses while on military campaign and he could not give them back to the enemy.

c. **He spared enough of them for one hundred chariots**: That David kept such a small number shows remarkable self-control and trust in God. David obeyed the principle of Deuteronomy 17:15-16 and absolutely refused to trust in horses as military weapons. His trust was in God instead (Psalm 20:7 and 33:16-17).

d. **David took the shields of gold that were on the servants of Hadadezer**: David took what was the glory of the enemy and transformed it into trophies of the power and goodness of God. David displayed those **shields of gold**, testifying to God's work in and through David.

e. **David brought a large amount of bronze, with which Solomon made the bronze Sea, the pillars, and the articles of bronze**: The gathering of this treasure to Jerusalem, later used in the building of the temple, shows the reason why the Chronicler chose particular events from the records of 2 Samuel to emphasize.

> i. "At first glance, this is a somewhat artificial record of David's military successes, which has been produced by leaving out the more interesting narratives and those less favourable to David. This view is rather inaccurate, however, since positive elements such as the birth of Solomon, David's magnanimity to Saul's family, and David's psalms are omitted…. The reason is that Chronicles has chosen to focus on the relationship of David's wars with the Davidic covenant and the temple preparations." (Selman)
>
> ii. One needed two things to build the temple: security and money. These chapters show how David, though he could not build the temple himself, obtained the security and money necessary for his son to build the temple.
>
> iii. "In view of the desire of the king to build the Temple of God, the chapter is of special interest; it shows how in these wars he was amassing treasure with that purpose in view, not for himself, but for his son." (Meyer)
>
> iv. Even when God shuts the door for us to do a work, we may still be vitally involved in it – often by amassing treasure for that work, as David did for the temple his son would build. "To be willing to do the work of preparation, when not permitted to undertake the principal service, is proof of real devotion." (Morgan)

4. (9-13) The glory and security of David's kingdom.

Now when Tou king of Hamath heard that David had defeated all the army of Hadadezer king of Zobah, he sent Hadoram his son to King David, to greet him and bless him, because he had fought against Hadadezer and defeated him (for Hadadezer had been at war with Tou); and *Hadoram brought with him* **all kinds of articles of gold, silver, and bronze. King David also dedicated these to the LORD, along with the silver and gold that he had brought from all** *these* **nations; from Edom, from Moab, from the people of Ammon, from the Philistines, and from**

Amalek. Moreover Abishai the son of Zeruiah killed eighteen thousand Edomites in the Valley of Salt. He also put garrisons in Edom, and all the Edomites became David's servants. And the LORD preserved David wherever he went.

> a. **Tou…sent Hadoram his son to King David, to greet him and bless him**: Neighboring nations saw the hand of God on David and brought him honor and gifts. They knew that a strong, godly leader of Israel was good for the whole community of nations, not just good for Israel itself.
>
>> i. Not every pagan nation surrounding Israel was hostile to Israel or their God, and David did not treat them as if they were hostile. We make a mistake if we treat every unbeliever as an openly hostile enemy of the Lord.
>>
>> ii. "Tou's son was probably called *Hadoram* rather than 'Joram' (2 Samuel 8:10), since the latter's Yahwistic form is unlikely in a non-Israelite state." (Selman)
>
> b. **King David also dedicated these to the LORD**: When David received this acclaim from the nations he **dedicated** it all to the LORD. He knew that the praise and glory belonged to God, not himself. David could handle success as well as apparent failure.
>
> c. **From Edom, from Moab, from the people of Ammon, from the Philistines, and from Amalek**: By citing these subdued nations we learn that David's victories were complete. God used David to lead Israel to victory over enemies in every direction.
>
>> i. Israel possessed more of the land God promised to Abraham (Genesis 15:18-21) under David's reign than at any other time.
>>
>> ii. David was able to accomplish so much against God's enemies because he, unlike Saul, was not consumed with fighting against the people of God.
>
> d. **The LORD preserved David wherever he went**: This is the summary of this whole chapter. Every victory and every enemy subdued was a testimony to the Lord's preserving power in the life and reign of David.

B. David's administration.

1. (14) A general description of David's government.

So David reigned over all Israel, and administered judgment and justice to all his people.

> a. **So David reigned**: This chapter of victory, blessing, and prosperity describes the national life of Israel during the reign of David. This is one

reason why he is generally regarded as the greatest king or ruler Israel ever had.

> i. This is how God wanted to reign in the life of Saul, but Saul resisted the Lord and rejected His Spirit. Because David allowed God to subdue Him, the nations were subdued before David.

b. **Administered judgment and justice to all his people**: This shows that David was a great king to his own people, not only against neighboring nations. He fulfilled what is the fundamental duty of government – to administer **judgment and justice** (Romans 13:1-7).

2. (15-17) Key people in David's government.

Joab the son of Zeruiah *was* **over the army; Jehoshaphat the son of Ahilud** *was* **recorder; Zadok the son of Ahitub and Abimelech the son of Abiathar** *were* **the priests; Shavsha** *was* **the scribe; Benaiah the son of Jehoiada** *was* **over the Cherethites and the Pelethites; and David's sons** *were* **chief ministers at the king's side.**

> a. **Joab…Jehoshaphat…Zadok…Abimelech…Shavsha…Benaiah**: No great ruler succeeds by himself. Only the smallest organizations can be governed well without a gifted and committed team. Part of David's success as a ruler was in his ability to assemble, train, empower, and maintain such a team.
>
> i. We never find such a list regarding the organization of King Saul's government. This is because David's government had much more form and structure than Saul's.
>
> ii. There is a limit to what we can be and what we can do for the Lord without order and organization. It isn't that order and organization are requirements for progress in the Christian life; they *are* progress in the Christian life; in becoming more like the Lord.
>
> iii. *Nothing* is accomplished in God's kingdom without order and organization. While it may *seem* so to us, it is only an illusion – behind the scenes God is moving with utmost order and organization though sometimes we cannot see it.

b. **Zadok the son of Ahitub and Abimelech the son of Abiathar were the priests**: There were two priestly centers at this time, thus two priests. One was at Gibeon, with the tabernacle of Moses and the altar of burnt offering. The other was at Jerusalem, with the special tent David made for the ark of the covenant. Thus there were two priests, **Zadok** and **Abiathar**.

c. **The Cherethites and Pelethites**: These were hired soldiers from Crete. "By employing foreign guards to ensure the safety of the king, David would minimize the possibility of becoming the victim of inter-tribal rivalries; these men from Crete could give whole-hearted allegiance to him." (Baldwin, commentary on 2 Samuel 8)

1 Chronicles 19 – War with Ammon and Syria

A. The offense of the Ammonites.

1. (1-2) David sends ambassadors to the Ammonites at the death of their king.

It happened after this that Nahash the king of the people of Ammon died, and his son reigned in his place. Then David said, "I will show kindness to Hanun the son of Nahash, because his father showed kindness to me." So David sent messengers to comfort him concerning his father. And David's servants came to Hanun in the land of the people of Ammon to comfort him.

> a. **I will show kindness**: David was the dominant ruler of his region, but he was not a cruel tyrant. Here he showed kindness towards a pagan king in sympathy with the loss of his father.
>
> b. **So David sent messengers to comfort him**: David wasn't content to *feel* kindness towards Hanun. He *did* something to bring the grieving man comfort.

2. (3-5) Hanun, the new king of the Ammonites, treats Israel's ambassadors shamefully.

And the princes of the people of Ammon said to Hanun, "Do you think that David really honors your father because he has sent comforters to you? Did his servants not come to you to search and to overthrow and to spy out the land?" Therefore Hanun took David's servants, shaved them, and cut off their garments in the middle, at their buttocks, and sent them away. Then *some* went and told David about the men; and he sent to meet them, because the men were greatly ashamed. And the king said, "Wait at Jericho until your beards have grown, and *then* return."

> a. **Do you think that David really honors your father because he has sent comforters to you?** It's hard to explain why these advisers to Hanun said this to the king of Ammon. It is possible that they genuinely suspected

David, or they may have just used this as a way to appear wise and cunning to King Hanun. It is common for liars to always suspect others of lying.

b. Hanun took David's servants, shaved them, and cut off their garments in the middle…and sent them away: This was a disgraceful insult to these ambassadors from Israel. One suggested reason for this is the idea that to be clean-shaven was the mark of a slave. Free men wore beards. Therefore in that culture, many men would rather die than to have their beard removed.

i. "With the value universally set upon the beard by the Hebrews and other Oriental nations, as being man's greatest ornament, the cutting off of one-half of it was the greatest insult that could have been offered to the ambassadors, and through them to David their king." (Keil and Delitzsch in their commentary on 2 Samuel 10)

ii. "The *beard* is held in high respect in the East: the possessor considers it his greatest ornament; often swears by it; and, in matters of great importance, *pledges* it. Nothing can be more secure than a pledge of this kind; its owner will redeem it at the hazard of his life." (Clarke on 2 Samuel 10)

iii. To **cut off their garments in the middle** was also an obvious insult and humiliation. "That the shame of their nakedness might appear, and especially that of their circumcision, so derided by the heathen." (Trapp on 2 Samuel 10)

iv. "This is check to the fashion-mongers of our time, saith Piscator; who wear their clothes so close, and cloaks so short, that they cover not their buttocks." (Trapp) One must only wonder what the Puritan preacher John Trapp would say about those who today wear their garments so low that they do not cover their buttocks.

v. To insult the ambassador is to insult the king. It was just as if they had done this to David himself. The same principle is true with King Jesus and His ambassadors. Jesus reminded His disciples: *If the world hates you, you know that it hated Me before it hated you.* (John 15:18)

vi. "The attitude of Ammon does not detract from the nobleness of the action of David. In that action he proved that he had not forgotten the kindness which had been shown to him by Nahash." (Morgan)

c. Wait at Jericho until your beards have grown, and then return: David didn't use these men as political tools to whip up anger against the Ammonites. He cared more for their own dignity and honor and allowed them to wait before returning to Jerusalem.

3. (6-8) The Ammonites and Israelites prepare for war.

When the people of Ammon saw that they had made themselves repulsive to David, Hanun and the people of Ammon sent a thousand talents of silver to hire for themselves chariots and horsemen from Mesopotamia, from Syrian Maachah, and from Zobah. So they hired for themselves thirty-two thousand chariots, with the king of Maachah and his people, who came and encamped before Medeba. Also the people of Ammon gathered together from their cities, and came to battle. Now when David heard *of it*, he sent Joab and all the army of the mighty men.

a. **When the people of Ammon saw that they had made themselves repulsive**: They knew that *they* did this. David didn't reject the Ammonites, they **made themselves repulsive** to Israel.

b. **The people of Ammon sent a thousand talents of silver to hire for themselves chariots and horsemen**: This was a common practice in the ancient world. The Ammonites had no hope of protecting themselves, so they hired mercenary armies.

c. **When David heard of it, he sent Joab and all the army of the mighty men**: It's important to understand that David was nothing without his mighty men, and they were nothing without him. He was their leader, but a leader is nothing without followers – and David had **an army of the mighty men** to follow him. These men didn't necessarily *start* as mighty men; many were the distressed, indebted, and discontented people who followed David at Adullam Cave (1 Samuel 22:1-2).

i. One of these mighty men was Adino the Eznite – famous for killing 800 men at one time (2 Samuel 23:8). Another was Jashobeam who killed 300 men at one time (1 Chronicles 11:11). Another was Benaiah who killed a lion in a pit on a snowy day and took on a huge Egyptian warrior and killed the Egyptian with his own spear (1 Chronicles 11:22-23).

B. Victory for Israel.

1. (9-13) Joab divides the army into two groups.

Then the people of Ammon came out and put themselves in battle array before the gate of the city, and the kings who had come *were* by themselves in the field. When Joab saw that the battle line was against him before and behind, he chose some of Israel's best and put *them* in battle array against the Syrians. And the rest of the people he put under the command of Abishai his brother, and they set *themselves* in battle array against the people of Ammon. Then he said, "If the Syrians are

too strong for me, then you shall help me; but if the people of Ammon are too strong for you, then I will help you. Be of good courage, and let us be strong for our people and for the cities of our God. And may the LORD do *what is* good in His sight."

> a. **Joab saw that the battle line was against him before and behind**: As the army of the mighty men approached the Ammonite city they found themselves surrounded. In front of them were the Ammonites **in battle array before the gate of the city**. Behind them were the mercenary kings **in the field**. It looked bad for the army of Israel.
>
> b. **If the Syrians are too strong for me, then you shall help me**: Joab had only one strategy in battle – *attack*. Many generals would consider surrender when surrounded on both sides by the enemy, but not Joab. He called the army to courage and faith and told them to press on.
>
>> i. "It is interesting to observe that in his arrangements he made no allowance for the possibility of ultimate defeat in his conflict with Ammon…it does not seem to have occurred to him that the combination might have been too much for both of them." (Morgan)
>
> c. **Be of good courage, and let us be strong for our people and for the cities of our God. And may the LORD do what is good in His sight**: This was a great speech by Joab before the battle. He made at least three persuasive points.
>
>> i. **Be of good courage, and let us be strong**: Courage and strength are not matters of feeling and circumstance. They are matters of choice, especially when God makes His strength available to us. We can *be strong in the Lord and in the power of His might* (Ephesians 6:10).
>>
>> ii. **Let us be strong for our people and for the cities of our God**: Joab called them to remember all they had to lose. If they lost this battle they would lose both their **people** and their **cities**. This was a battle bigger than themselves, and the army of the mighty men had to remember that.
>>
>> iii. **And may the LORD do what is good in His sight**: Joab wisely prepared for the battle to the best of his ability and worked hard for the victory. At the same time, he knew that the outcome was ultimately in God's hands.
>>
>> iv. Joab trusted God to work, *and* he did all that he could do. "To believe that God will do all, and therefore to do nothing, is as bad as to believe that God leaves us to our unaided endeavours." (Meyer)

2. (14-15) Joab defeats the Syrians, and the Ammonites retreat to the city of Rabbah.

So Joab and the people who *were* with him drew near for the battle against the Syrians, and they fled before him. When the people of Ammon saw that the Syrians were fleeing, they also fled before Abishai his brother, and entered the city. So Joab went to Jerusalem.

> a. **They fled before him**: It doesn't even say that Joab engaged the Syrians in battle. This mercenary army **fled before** the army of the mighty men because God was with them. God promised this kind of blessing upon an obedient Israel (Deuteronomy 28:7).
>
> b. **They also fled before Abishai his brother, and entered the city**: When the Ammonites saw the mercenaries retreating, they also retreated. They could no more stand before the army of the mighty men than the Syrians could.
>
>> i. "Joab did not at this time follow up the victory by laying siege to Rabbah; it may have been too late in the year." (Payne)

3. (16-19) David wipes out the Syrian reinforcements.

Now when the Syrians saw that they had been defeated by Israel, they sent messengers and brought the Syrians who were beyond the River, and Shophach the commander of Hadadezer's army *went* before them. When it was told David, he gathered all Israel, crossed over the Jordan and came upon them, and set up in battle array against them. So when David had set up in *battle* array against the Syrians, they fought with him. Then the Syrians fled before Israel; and David killed seven thousand charioteers and forty thousand foot soldiers of the Syrians, and killed Shophach the commander of the army. And when the servants of Hadadezer saw that they were defeated by Israel, they made peace with David and became his servants. So the Syrians were not willing to help the people of Ammon anymore.

> a. **When the Syrians saw that they had been defeated by Israel, they sent messengers and brought the Syrians who were beyond the River**: The enemies of Israel wouldn't quit after one defeat. They were a persistent enemy and came back to fight again.
>
> b. **When it was told David, he gathered all Israel**: David gathered the rest of the army of Israel to prevent this army of Syrian reinforcements from crushing the army of the mighty men. The result was glorious: **the Syrians fled before Israel**.

i. The emphasis on **all Israel** is important. "The whole incident therefore shows 'all Israel' cooperating under David and establishing the required 'rest' for building the temple." (Selman)

ii. The chapter ends with unfinished business at Rabbah. The offending Ammonites are still in their city and Joab has returned to Jerusalem. In the Spring King David will send Joab and the army out again to deal with Rabbah as he waits in Jerusalem. While he waited comfortably in Jerusalem he fell into sin with Bathsheba.

iii. Most of us know about David's sin with Bathsheba, and how it happened when David waited in Jerusalem when he should have led the battle at Rabbah. We see in 2 Samuel 10 that God gave David a warning by showing it necessary for him to come out against the Syrians. David *tried* to leave the battle to Joab in 1 Chronicles 19 (and 2 Samuel 10), but his army *needed* him and God tried to show him that by blessing it when David did go out to battle. These events were God's gracious warning that David sadly wasted.

iv. When it comes to sin such as David fell into, "Constant watchfulness is the only guarantee of safety. Not even true desire and great blessing are sufficient if the heart be not personally watchful." (Morgan)

1 Chronicles 20 – Ammon is Defeated at Rabbah

A. The defeat of Ammon.

1. (1) Joab goes back out the next year to get Rabbah of Ammon.

It happened in the spring of the year, at the time kings go out *to battle*, that Joab led out the armed forces and ravaged the country of the people of Ammon, and came and besieged Rabbah. But David stayed at Jerusalem. And Joab defeated Rabbah and overthrew it.

> a. **In the spring of the year, at the time kings go out to battle**: In that part of the world, wars were not normally fought during the winter months because rains and cold weather made travel and campaigning difficult. Fighting resumed in the spring.
>
> b. **Joab led out the armed forces.... But David remained at Jerusalem**: David should have been out at the battle but he remained behind. In 1 Chronicles 19 Joab and the army of the mighty men were preserved against the Syrians and the Ammonites but they did not win a decisive victory. The decisive victory came when David led the battle at the end of 1 Chronicles 19. Both through custom and experience God told David, "You need to be at the battle." **But David remained at Jerusalem**.
>
>> i. What happened when **David remained at Jerusalem** was so well known that the Chronicler did not need to record it. In his leisure he saw a woman bathing, acting upon his feelings of lust he committed adultery with her making her pregnant, and conspired with Joab to murder her husband (Uriah, one of David's mighty men) to cover up his crime. A lot happened between **David stayed at Jerusalem** and **Joab defeated Rabbah**.
>>
>> ii. "Beware of moments and hours of ease. It is in these that we most easily fall into the power of Satan. The sultriest summer days are most laden with blight.... If we cannot fill our days with our own matters,

there is always plenty to be done for others.... Watch and pray in days of vacation and ease, even more than at other times." (Meyer)

iii. "There is nothing more full of subtle danger in the life of any servant of God than that he should remain inactive when the enterprises of God demand that he be out on the fields of conflict." (Morgan)

c. **Joab defeated Rabbah**: The account in 2 Samuel 12:26-31 tells us that Joab essentially conquered Rabbah, but called David to help with the final conquest of the city *after* David's sin and subsequent repentance. Then, 2 Samuel 12:29 tells us, *David gathered all the people together and went to Rabbah*. This was the final phase of David's restoration. He went back to doing what he should have done all along – leading Israel out to battle, instead of remaining in Jerusalem. This means that David was in victory once again. His sin did not condemn him to a life of failure and defeat. There was chastisement for David's sin, but it did not mean that his life was ruined.

i. "David's fall should put those who have not fallen on their guard, and save from despair those who have." (Augustine)

2. (2-3) David wears the crown of Ammon.

Then David took their king's crown from his head, and found it to weigh a talent of gold, and *there were* precious stones in it. And it was set on David's head. Also he brought out the spoil of the city in great abundance. And he brought out the people who *were* in it, and put *them* to work with saws, with iron picks, and with axes. So David did to all the cities of the people of Ammon. Then David and all the people returned *to* Jerusalem.

a. **David took their king's crown.... it was set on David's head**: David's sin didn't take away his crown. Had David refused the voice of Nathan the prophet it might have. Because David responded with confession and repentance, there was still a crown for **David's head**.

i. "David's rule over Ammon seems to be part of a complex four-stage system of administration of the empire outside the land of Israel.... Ammon was most restricted of all, apparently demoted to provincial status." (Selman)

b. **He brought out the spoil of the city in great abundance.... David and all the people returned to Jerusalem**: David again increases in might and in wealth, bringing the riches back to Jerusalem for the sake of later building the temple.

i. This example of extending Israel's security with its neighbors fits in with the Chronicler's broader purpose of showing how David prepared the way for his son to build the temple.

B. Other Israeli victories over Philistine giants.

1. (4-7) Three victories over three giants.

Now it happened afterward that war broke out at Gezer with the Philistines, at which time Sibbechai the Hushathite killed Sippai, *who was one* **of the sons of the giant. And they were subdued. Again there was war with the Philistines, and Elhanan the son of Jair killed Lahmi the brother of Goliath the Gittite, the shaft of whose spear** *was* **like a weaver's beam. Yet again there was war at Gath, where there was a man of** *great* **stature, with twenty-four fingers and toes, six** *on each hand* **and six** *on each foot;* **and he also was born to the giant. So when he defied Israel, Jonathan the son of Shimea, David's brother, killed him.**

a. **Now it happened afterward**: This description of victory over Philistine giants shows that Israel could slay giants without David. **Sibbechai.... Elhanan.... Jonathan**: These men accomplished heroic deeds when David was finished fighting giants. God will continue to raise up leaders when the leaders of the previous generation pass from the scene.

i. David's legacy lay not only in what he accomplished but in what he left behind – a people prepared for victory. David's triumphs were meaningful not only for himself but for others who learned victory through his teaching and example.

ii. "The compiler of these books passes by also the incest of Amnon with his sister Tamar, and the rebellion of Absalom, and the awful consequences of all these. These should have preceded the fourth verse. These facts could not be unknown to him, for they were notorious to all; but he saw that they were already amply detailed in books which were accredited among the people, and the relations were such as no friend to piety and humanity could delight to repeat. On these grounds the reader will give him credit for the *omission*." (Clarke)

b. **With twenty-four fingers and toes, six on each hand and six on each foot**: This described an unnamed **man of great stature** from Gath. Commentators like Adam Clarke can't resist reminding us that this is a known phenomenon. "This is not a solitary instance: *Tavernier* informs us that the eldest son of the emperor of Java, who reigned in 1649, had *six fingers* on each hand, and *six toes* on each foot.... I once saw a young girl, in the county of Londonderry, in Ireland, who had six fingers on each hand, and six toes on each foot, but her stature had nothing gigantic in it."

i. **The shaft of whose spear was like a weaver's beam**: This was true of Lahmi, a brother of Goliath. "Also has known parallels and is not the unhistorical creation which some have alleged. It was actually a javelin with a loop and cord round the shaft for greater distance and stability, and was known in the Aegean area from the twelfth century B.C. Even the Old Testament reports one in the possession of another non-Israelite (1 Chronicles 11:23)." (Selman)

2. (8) Summary of the victories over the Philistine giants.

These were born to the giant in Gath, and they fell by the hand of David and by the hand of his servants.

a. **These were born to the giant in Gath**: Since Goliath was from **Gath** (1 Samuel 17:4) these were Goliath's sons or brothers.

i. "The Philistine warriors are also all called 'Rephaites' (RSV) or *descendants of Rapha* ('giants', NRSV), who were one of the pre-Israelite groups in Canaan (*e.g.* Genesis 15:20) and famous for their size." (Selman)

b. **Fell by the hand of David and by the hand of his servants**: Part of the idea is that David is conquering enemies now so it will be better for Solomon in the future. Our present victory is not only good for us now but it passes something important on to the next generation.

i. The defeat of these four giants is rightly credited to **the hand of David** *and* **the hand of his servants**. David had a role in this through his example, guidance, and influence.

ii. "Let those who after long service find themselves waning in strength, be content to abide with the people of God, still shining for them as a lamp, and thus enabling them to carry on the same Divine enterprises. Such action in the last days of life is also great and high service." (Morgan)

1 Chronicles 21 – Where to Build the Temple

A. David commands a census to be taken.

1. (1-2) David is moved to take a census.

Now Satan stood up against Israel, and moved David to number Israel. So David said to Joab and to the leaders of the people, "Go, number Israel from Beersheba to Dan, and bring the number of them to me that I may know *it*."

> a. **Now Satan stood up against Israel, and moved David to number Israel**: In 2 Samuel 24:1, it tells us that this was initially prompted because *the anger of the Lord was aroused against Israel*. So we see that Satan **moved David** yet the LORD expressly allowed it as a chastisement against David.
>
>> i. There is quite a gap in the historical record that the Chronicler passes over, including many family problems and a civil war. "His reasons for a gap of this length are not difficult to surmise: little of what transpired during those two decades would encourage a postexilic Judah, before whom Ezra was seeking to portray a piety that characterized David at his best." (Payne)
>>
>> ii. "For the first time in Scripture, the word 'Satan' appears without the definite article as a proper noun." (Payne)
>>
>> iii. "When Satan incites, he is interested merely in his own ends. He neither cares for righteous punishment nor looks for possible repentance, since they are as foreign to his nature as temptation to sin is to God's." (Selman)
>
> b. **Go, number Israel**: This was dangerous because of a principle stated in Exodus 30:12: *When you take the census of the children of Israel for their number, then every man shall give a ransom for himself to the LORD, when you number them, that there may be no plague among them when you number them.*

i. The principle of Exodus 30:12 speaks to *God's ownership of His people*. In the thinking of these ancient cultures, a man only had the right to count or number what belonged to him. Israel didn't belong to David; Israel belonged to God. It was up to the LORD to command a counting, and if David counted he should only do it at God's command and should receive ransom money to "atone" for the counting.

ii. "Numbering the hosts of Jehovah is not essentially or necessarily wrong; everything depends on the motive.... When it is born of pride, it is the subtlest of perils, inclining us to trust in the multitude of a host, and thus to cease to depend upon God." (Morgan)

iii. "When we are moved to number the people, we may rest assured that the impulse is Divine or Satanic, and we may determine which by the motive. If the motive is service, it is God. If the motive is pride, it is Satanic." (Morgan)

2. (3-4) Joab objects to the census.

And Joab answered, "May the LORD make His people a hundred times more than they are. But, my lord the king, *are* they not all my lord's servants? Why then does my lord require this thing? Why should he be a cause of guilt in Israel?" Nevertheless the king's word prevailed against Joab. Therefore Joab departed and went throughout all Israel and came to Jerusalem.

a. **Why then does my lord require this thing?** Joab wasn't afraid to speak to David when he thought the king was wrong. With the best interest of both David and Israel in mind, Joab tactfully asked David to reconsider this foolish desire to count the nation.

i. Joab also hints at the *motive* behind the counting - pride in David. The **this thing** that David desired was the increase of the nation, and he perhaps wanted to measure the size of his army to know if he had enough force to conquer a neighboring nation. "He did it out of curiosity and creature-confidence." (Trapp)

ii. We gather from 2 Samuel 24 that this took place late in his reign. So late in his reign, David was tempted to take some of the glory for himself. He looked at how Israel had grown and prospered during his reign – it was remarkable indeed. The count was a way to take credit for himself. "The spirit of vainglory in numbers had taken possession of the people and the king, and there was a tendency to trust in numbers and forget God." (Morgan)

b. **Nevertheless the king's word prevailed against Joab**: 2 Samuel 24:4 tells us that it wasn't only Joab who tried to tell David not to do this – the *captains of the army* also warned David not to count the soldiers in Israel. But David did so anyway.

3. (5-8) The census is made, and David is immediately sorry.

Then Joab gave the sum of the number of the people to David. All Israel *had* **one million one hundred thousand men who drew the sword, and Judah** *had* **four hundred and seventy thousand men who drew the sword. But he did not count Levi and Benjamin among them, for the king's word was abominable to Joab. And God was displeased with this thing; therefore He struck Israel. So David said to God, "I have sinned greatly, because I have done this thing; but now, I pray, take away the iniquity of Your servant, for I have done very foolishly."**

a. **Joab gave the sum of the number of the people to the king**: The results showed that there were 1,300,000 fighting men among the twelve tribes, reflecting an estimated total population of 6 million in Israel.

i. 2 Samuel 24:5-9 indicates that it took almost 10 months to complete the census. David should have called off this foolish census during the ten months, but he didn't.

ii. The number given in 2 Samuel 24:5-9 is different than the sum arrived at here. "To attempt to reconcile them in every part is lost labour; better at once acknowledge what cannot be successfully denied, that although the original writers of the Old Testament wrote under the influence of the Divine Spirit, yet we are not told that the same influence descended on all *copiers* of their words, so as absolutely to prevent them from making mistakes." (Clarke)

iii. **But he did not count Levi and Benjamin**: "The rabbis give the following reason for this: Joab, seeing that this would bring down destruction upon the people, purposed to save two tribes. Should David ask, Why have you not numbered the Levites? Joab purposed to say, Because the Levites are not reckoned among the children of Israel. Should he ask, Why have you not numbered Benjamin? he would answer, Benjamin has been already sufficiently punished, on account of the treatment of the woman at Gibeah: if, therefore, this tribe were to be again punished, who would remain?" (Clarke)

b. **Therefore He struck Israel**: God would strike Israel with a choice of judgments offered to David. Yet God had already struck Israel by deeply convicting the king of Israel with an acute sense of his sin.

c. **I have sinned greatly**: The man after God's heart was not sinless, but he had a heart sensitive to sin when he did commit it. David kept a short account with God.

i. "The chief interest of this chapter for us lies in the revelation of the true character of David. His sins were the lapses and accidents of his life. This is not to condone them. It is, however, to emphasize that the habitual set of his life was far otherwise than these sins suggest, and the deepest truth concerning him is revealed, not by the failures, but by his action afterwards." (Morgan)

d. **Take away the iniquity of Your servant, for I have done very foolishly**: David now saw the pride and vainglory that prompted him to do such a foolish thing.

4. (9-12) David is allowed to choose the judgment.

Then the LORD spoke to Gad, David's seer, saying, "Go and tell David, saying, 'Thus says the LORD: "I offer you three *things;* choose one of them for yourself, that I may do *it* to you."'" So Gad came to David and said to him, "Thus says the LORD: 'Choose for yourself, either three years of famine, or three months to be defeated by your foes with the sword of your enemies overtaking *you,* or else for three days the sword of the LORD; the plague in the land, with the angel of the LORD destroying throughout all the territory of Israel.' Now consider what answer I should take back to Him who sent me."

a. **I offer you three things**: God used David's sin and the resulting chastisement to reveal David's heart and wisdom. His choice of the following three options would test David:

- **Three years of famine**: This would surely be the death of some in Israel, but the wealthy and resourceful would survive. Israel would have to depend on neighboring nations for food.

- **Three months to be defeated by your foes**: This would be the death of some in Israel, but mostly only of soldiers. Israel would have to contend with **enemies** among neighboring nations.

- **For three days…the plague in the land**: This would be the death of some in Israel, but *anyone* could be struck by this plague – rich or poor, influential or anonymous, royal or common.

    i. "This was a great mercy: David must be whipped; but he may choose his own rod." (Trapp)

b. **Now consider what answer I should take back to Him who sent me**: God wanted David to use the prophet as a mediator, and to answer to the prophet instead of directly to God.

5. (13) David chooses the three days of plague.

And David said to Gad, "I am in great distress. Please let me fall into the hand of the LORD, for His mercies *are* very great; but do not let me fall into the hand of man."

> a. **Please let me fall into the hand of the LORD**: This meant that David chose the three days of plague. In the other two options, the king and his family could be insulated against the danger, but David knew that he had to expose *himself* to the chastisement of God.
>
>> i. "Had he chosen *war*, his own *personal safety* was in no danger, because there was already an ordinance preventing him from going to battle. Had he chosen *famine*, his own wealth would have secured his and his own family's support. But he showed the greatness of his mind in choosing the *pestilence*, to the ravages of which himself and his household were exposed equally with the meanest of his subjects." (Clarke)
>
> b. **Do not let me fall into the hand of man**: This meant that David chose the three days of plague. In the other two options, Israel would either be at the mercy of neighbors (as in the famine) or attacked by enemies. David knew that God is far more merciful and gracious than man is.

B. The course of the plague

1. (14-15) The plague of destruction hits Israel severely.

So the LORD sent a plague upon Israel, and seventy thousand men of Israel fell. And God sent an angel to Jerusalem to destroy it. As he was destroying, the LORD looked and relented of the disaster, and said to the angel who was destroying, "It is enough; now restrain your hand." And the angel of the LORD stood by the threshing floor of Ornan the Jebusite.

> a. **Seventy thousand men of Israel fell**: This was a great calamity upon Israel - a devastating plague striking this many in such a short period of time.
>
> b. **The LORD looked and relented of the disaster**: This justified David's wisdom in leaving himself in God's hands. He could not trust man to relent from destruction.

2. (16-19) David's intercession; and God's instruction.

Then David lifted his eyes and saw the angel of the LORD standing between earth and heaven, having in his hand a drawn sword stretched out over Jerusalem. So David and the elders, clothed in sackcloth, fell on their faces. And David said to God, "Was it not I who commanded the people to be numbered? I am the one who has sinned and done evil indeed; but these sheep, what have they done? Let Your hand, I pray,

O LORD my God, be against me and my father's house, but not against Your people that they should be plagued." Therefore, the angel of the LORD commanded Gad to say to David that David should go and erect an altar to the LORD on the threshing floor of Ornan the Jebusite. So David went up at the word of Gad, which he had spoken in the name of the LORD.

a. **Having in his hand a drawn sword stretched out over Jerusalem**: At this point, God had relented from the severity of judgment, yet the threat was still imminent. So **David and the elders** humbled themselves before God and David repented.

b. **Let Your hand, I pray, O LORD my God, be against me and my father's house**: Like a true shepherd, David asked that the punishment be upon him and his own household. Having another purpose to accomplish, God did not accept David's offer.

c. **Erect an altar to the LORD on the threshing floor of Ornan the Jebusite**: This is where David met the Angel of the LORD, and where God relented from the plague before it came upon Jerusalem. Now God wanted David to meet Him there in worship.

> i. "Threshing floors were usually on a height, in order to catch every breeze; some area to the north of David's city is indicated" (Baldwin)
>
> ii. The **threshing floor of Ornan** had both a rich history and a rich future. 2 Chronicles 3:1 tells us that the threshing floor of Ornan was on Mount Moriah; the same hill where Abraham offered Isaac (Genesis 22:2), and the same set of hills where Jesus died on the cross (Genesis 22:14).
>
> iii. "In fact, David's altar was the only one in pre-exilic times which God explicitly commanded to be built." (Selman)
>
> iv. "The decision of God to establish his altar and temple at Moriah in Jerusalem has affected all history (cf. Revelation 11:1); for this mountain became the focus of the Holy City, where His Son was crucified. And it will continue to affect history; for from this 'city he loves', he will some day rule the nations of the earth (Isaiah 2:2-4)." (Payne)

3. (20-25) David buys the threshing floor of Ornan.

Now Ornan turned and saw the angel; and his four sons *who were* with him hid themselves, but Ornan continued threshing wheat. So David came to Ornan, and Ornan looked and saw David. And he went out from the threshing floor, and bowed before David with *his* face to the ground. Then David said to Ornan, "Grant me the place of *this*

threshing floor, that I may build an altar on it to the LORD. You shall grant it to me at the full price, that the plague may be withdrawn from the people." But Ornan said to David, "Take *it* to yourself, and let my lord the king do *what is* good in his eyes. Look, I *also* give *you* the oxen for burnt offerings, the threshing implements for wood, and the wheat for the grain offering; I give *it* all." Then King David said to Ornan, "No, but I will surely buy *it* for the full price, for I will not take what is yours for the LORD, nor offer burnt offerings with *that which* costs *me* nothing." So David gave Ornan six hundred shekels of gold by weight for the place.

a. **Now Ornan turned and saw the angel; and his four sons who were with him hid themselves**: "Partly because of the glory and majesty in which the angel appeared, which men's weak and sinful natures are not able to bear; and partly for the fear of God's vengeance, which was at this time riding circuit in the land, and now seemed to be coming to their family." (Poole)

b. **Grant me the place of this threshing floor…at full price**: David wanted to transform this place where chaff was separated from wheat into a place of sacrifice and worship. It would remain a place of sacrifice and worship because this land purchased by David became the site of Solomon's temple (1 Chronicles 21:28-22:5).

i. "So David bought 'the site' – *hammaqom*, which may have included the whole area of Mount Moriah – for 240 ounces of gold. This was worth about one hundred thousand dollars. Second Samuel 24:24 notes a much smaller amount, 20 ounces of silver, for the threshing floor itself." (Payne)

c. **Take it to yourself, and let my lord the king do what is good in his eyes**: Ornan had a good, generous heart and wanted to *give* David anything he wanted.

i. "Had Araunah's [Ornan's] noble offer been accepted, it would have been *Araunah's sacrifice*, not *David's*; nor would it have answered the end of turning away the displeasure of the Most High." (Clarke)

d. **No, but I will surely buy it for the full price, for I will not take what is yours for the LORD, nor offer burnt offerings with that which costs me nothing**: David knew that it would not be a *gift* nor a *sacrifice* to the LORD if it did not cost him something. He didn't look for the cheapest way possible to please God.

i. "He who has a religion that *costs him nothing*, has a religion that is *worth nothing*: nor will any man esteem the ordinances of God, if those ordinances cost him nothing." (Clarke)

ii. "Where there is true, strong love to Jesus, it will cost us something. Love is the costliest of all undertakings…. But what shall we mind if we gain Christ? You cannot give up for Him without regaining everything you have renounced, but purified and transfigured." (Meyer)

4. (26-27) God is satisfied and relents of the judgment.

And David built there an altar to the Lord, and offered burnt offerings and peace offerings, and called on the Lord; and He answered him from heaven by fire on the altar of burnt offering. So the Lord commanded the angel, and he returned his sword to its sheath.

a. **And offered burnt offerings and peace offerings**: This shows that David understood that the death of the 70,000 in Israel in the plague did not *atone* for his and Israel's sin. Atonement could only be made through the blood of an approved substitute.

i. **Burnt offerings** were to atone for sin; **peace offerings** were to enjoy fellowship with God. This shows us from beginning to end, David's life was marked by fellowship with God.

ii. "We finally see the man after God's own heart turning the occasion of his sin and its punishment into an occasion of worship." (Morgan)

iii. "Abraham taught the fact of the sacrifice, while to David the reason of that sacrifice of Christ was explained. He was sacrificed to stay the plague – the plague of sin, the punishment of our iniquities." (Spurgeon)

b. **He answered him from heaven by fire on the altar**: God showed His acceptance of David's sacrifice by consuming it with fire from **heaven**. The Lord honored David's desire to be right with God and to fellowship with Him, by answering with Divine blessing from heaven. So it always is when God's children draw near to their God and Father for cleansing and fellowship.

i. The sending of fire from heaven answered a question that had burned in the heart of David for a long time. For many years, he had wondered where God wanted the temple to be built, and he sought for that place, as shown in Psalm 132:1-5:

*Lord, remember David
And all his afflictions;
How he swore to the Lord,*

And vowed to the Mighty One of Jacob:
"Surely I will not go into the chamber of my house,
Or go up to the comfort of my bed;
I will not give sleep to my eyes
Or slumber to my eyelids,
Until I find a place for the LORD,
A dwelling place for the Mighty One of Jacob."

ii. The **fire on the altar** from heaven confirmed the previous word of the prophet Gad that *this* was the place to build the altar and the temple. We see that God simply used Satan's provocation at the opening of this chapter to lead to the answer of this important question for David and for the nation of Israel. There were certainly other purposes of God at work, but this was one of them.

5. (28-22:1) David decides to build the temple at the place where God showed mercy to Israel.

At that time, when David saw that the LORD had answered him on the threshing floor of Ornan the Jebusite, he sacrificed there. For the tabernacle of the LORD and the altar of the burnt offering, which Moses had made in the wilderness, *were* **at that time at the high place in Gibeon. But David could not go before it to inquire of God, for he was afraid of the sword of the angel of the LORD. Then David said, "This** *is* **the house of the LORD God, and this** *is* **the altar of burnt offering for Israel."**

a. **When David saw that the LORD had answered him on the threshing floor of Ornan the Jebusite, he sacrificed there**: David knew that there was something special about this threshing floor; he understood that God had sanctified the place Himself with fire from heaven.

i. "Having seen his prayers answered and his sacrifices accepted, the site had already become a 'house of prayer' and a 'temple for sacrifices' *cf.* 2 Chronicles 7:12; Isaiah 56:7)." (Selman)

ii. **He sacrificed there**: "Do not believe for a moment that visible grandeur is necessary to the place where God will meet with you. Go to your threshing floor and pray; aye, while the unmuzzled oxen take their rest, bow your knee and cry to the Lord of the harvest, and you shall meet with God there amongst the straw and the grain. Fear not to draw nigh to God in these streets, but consecrate all space to the Lord your God." (Spurgeon)

b. **This is the house of the LORD God, and this is the altar of burnt offering for Israel**: David understood that the future temple should be built on this spot in Jerusalem. God had sanctified this humble threshing floor to Himself.

i. **This is the house**: "This is that very place foretold by Moses (Deuteronomy 12:11)." (Trapp)

ii. The character of Ornan's threshing floor shows us something about where and how God wants to meet with men. Ornan's threshing floor was:

- A simple, unadorned place – not like a fancy church at all.
- A place of ordinary work.
- A place bought with money.
- A place from where bread came from.
- A place where the justice of God was evident.
- A place where sin was confessed.
- A place where sacrifice was offered and accepted.

1 Chronicles 22 – David's Charge to Solomon

A. David gathers men, material, and a vision.

1. (2-4) David gathers men and material for building the temple.

So David commanded to gather the aliens who *were* in the land of Israel; and he appointed masons to cut hewn stones to build the house of God. And David prepared iron in abundance for the nails of the doors of the gates and for the joints, and bronze in abundance beyond measure, and cedar trees in abundance; for the Sidonians and those from Tyre brought much cedar wood to David.

> a. **David commanded to gather the aliens who were in the land of Israel**: 1 Kings 5:15-18 describes how these people were actually put to work in the building of the temple in Solomon's day. There were some 70,000 slaves.
>
> b. **Cedar trees in abundance**: The cedar trees of Lebanon were legendary for their excellent timber. This means David (and Solomon after him) wanted to build the temple out of the best materials possible.
>
>> i. It also means that they were willing to build this great temple to God with "Gentile" wood and using "Gentile" labor. This was a temple to the God of Israel, but it was not only for Israel. Only Jews built the tabernacle, "But the temple is not built without the aid of the Gentile Tyrians. They, together with us, make up the Church of God." (Trapp)
>>
>> ii. Payne on **iron in abundance**: "The king's provision of 'a large amount of iron' reflects how conditions had changed during his time – known archaeologically as Iron I – due, no doubt, to the incorporation of iron-producing Philistines within the sphere of Hebrew control."

2. (5) David's vision for the preparation of the temple.

Now David said, "Solomon my son *is* young and inexperienced, and the house to be built for the LORD** *must be* exceedingly magnificent, famous and glorious throughout all countries. I will now make preparation for it." So David made abundant preparations before his death.**

a. **Solomon my son is young and inexperienced**: Even after David's death, Solomon knew that he was **young and inexperienced** (1 Kings 3:7), so when offered a choice of anything he asked for wisdom to lead God's people.

b. **The house to be built for the L**ORD **must be exceeding magnificent**: Solomon had the same vision for the glory of the temple, and he indeed built it according to David's vision of a **magnificent, famous, and glorious** building. Solomon had this vision breathed into him through his father's influence.

i. We can almost picture the old David and the young Solomon pouring over the plans and ideas for the temple together with excitement. David knew that it was not his place to build it, but had the right vision for what the temple should be in general terms, and he passed that vision on to his son.

ii. **So David made abundant preparations before his death**: This indicates that David was at peace with the idea that he himself could not build the temple and was content to prepare the way for his son to build it successfully. "This is a picture of a man who through stress and storm had found his way into the quiet calm assurance of his place in the divine economy.... It is a condition of peace and power." (Morgan)

iii. "The Chronicler was vitally concerned to ensure support for the Jerusalem temple in his day. No more fitting stimulus for dedication in this regard could then be found than in the example set by David when he made preparations for the construction of that temple in his day." (Payne)

B. David's exhortation to his son Solomon.

1. (6-10) David's testimony of the call to build the temple.

Then he called for his son Solomon, and charged him to build a house for the LORD **God of Israel. And David said to Solomon: "My son, as for me, it was in my mind to build a house to the name of the L**ORD **my God; but the word of the L**ORD **came to me, saying, 'You have shed much blood and have made great wars; you shall not build a house for My name, because you have shed much blood on the earth in My sight. Behold, a son shall be born to you, who shall be a man of rest; and I will give him rest from all his enemies all around. His name shall be**

Solomon, for I will give peace and quietness to Israel in his days. He shall build a house for My name, and he shall be My son, and I *will be his Father*; and I will establish the throne of his kingdom over Israel forever.'"

> a. **And charged him to build a house for the Lord God of Israel**: This was not a suggestion or an idea offered to Solomon. It was a sacred *charge* for him to fulfill. David knew that he could not fulfill this last great work himself; he could only do it *through* Solomon after David went to his reward. There was a sense in which if Solomon failed, David failed also.
>
>> i. Specifically, David wanted to **build a house to the name of the Lord my God**. "That the temple was to be built 'for the Name of the Lord' means more than his reputation or honor but ultimately for his Person." (Payne)
>
> b. **You have shed much blood and have made great wars; you shall not build a house for My name**: This explanation was not previously recorded, either in 2 Samuel or in 1 Chronicles. Here we find one of the reasons why God did not want David to build the temple, and why He chose Solomon instead. God wanted **a man of rest** and **peace** to build a **house** to Him.
>
>> i. It wasn't that David's wars were wrong or ungodly, or that he often acted unrighteously when he shed blood. It was that God wanted His house built from the context of peace and rest and victory; the Lord wanted it to be built *after* and *from* the victory, not from the midst of struggle.
>
>> ii. "Principally for mystical signification, to teach us that the church (whereof the temple was a manifest and illustrious type) should be built by Christ, *the Prince of peace*, Isaiah 9:6; and that it should be gathered and built up, *not by might or power*, or by force of arms, but *by God's Spirit*, Zechariah 4:6, and by the preaching of the gospel of peace." (Poole)

2. (11-13) David warns Solomon to stay faithful to God and His word.

"Now, my son, may the Lord be with you; and may you prosper, and build the house of the Lord your God, as He has said to you. Only may the Lord give you wisdom and understanding, and give you charge concerning Israel, that you may keep the law of the Lord your God. Then you will prosper, if you take care to fulfill the statutes and judgments with which the Lord charged Moses concerning Israel. Be strong and of good courage; do not fear nor be dismayed."

> a. **May the Lord be with you; and may you prosper, and build the house of the Lord your God**: The Chronicler emphasized David's legacy

and Solomon's mission to build the temple. This would become by far Solomon's greatest accomplishment.

b. **That you may keep the law of the LORD your God**: David knew that Solomon could not be strong or courageous without obedient fellowship with God. In this place of obedient fellowship, Solomon would **prosper** in all that he did.

c. **Be strong and of good courage; do not fear nor be dismayed**: Solomon could take courage and reject fear because God promised David that as long as his sons walked in obedience, they would keep the throne of Israel (1 Kings 2:1-4).

i. This is an amazing promise. No matter what the Assyrians or the Egyptians or the Babylonians did, as long as David's sons were *obedient* and followed God with all their heart and with all their soul, God would establish their kingdom. He would take care of the rest.

3. (14-16) What David did to prepare for the building of the temple.

"Indeed I have taken much trouble to prepare for the house of the LORD one hundred thousand talents of gold and one million talents of silver, and bronze and iron beyond measure, for it is so abundant. I have prepared timber and stone also, and you may add to them. Moreover *there are* workmen with you in abundance: woodsmen and stonecutters, and all types of skillful men for every kind of work. Of gold and silver and bronze and iron *there is* no limit. Arise and begin working, and the LORD be with you."

a. **I have taken much trouble to prepare for the house of the LORD**: David took seriously his mission to **prepare** the way by bringing both *security* and *treasure* to Israel and his successor Solomon. With these two advantages he could build **the house of the LORD**.

i. The Bible tells us that Jesus – the greater Son of David – is also building a temple (Ephesians 2:19-22). He could only do this after security and treasure were won, but the greater Son of David made this peace and plundered the enemy *Himself* at the cross. Jesus could also say that He took **much trouble to prepare for the house of the LORD** and that He has prepared the building materials (His people, according to Ephesians 2:19-22).

b. **One hundred thousand talents of gold**: This is an enormous amount of gold. Some Bible commentators believe this large number is accurate and some feel it is a scribal error. Even allowing for possible scribal error, David clearly amassed significant resources for a temple he would never build.

i. Even so, David also told Solomon to receive these enormous resources and **add to them**. "Save as I have saved, out of the revenues of the state, and thou mayest also add something for the erection and splendour of this house. This was a gentle though pointed hint, which was not lost on Solomon." (Clarke)

ii. "Cannot I put my hand on some young man's shoulder, and say to him, 'Thou mayest add thereto; thou hast a good voice; thou hast an active brain; begin to speak for God; there are numbers of godly men in the gospel ministry; if thou art called of God, thou mayest add thereto'?" (Spurgeon)

c. **Arise and begin working, and the Lord be with you**: David made all the preparation, but it was in vain if Solomon did not **begin working**. He had to actually do the work, and do it with the confidence that the Lord was with him.

i. David is an example of someone who works in the background, who receives none or little credit for his work, but the job cannot be done without him.

- David gathered the materials for the temple.
- David prepared some of those materials.
- David won the peace with surrounding nations that Israel needed to build the temple.
- David found and purchased the site to build the temple.
- David established the plans for the temple.
- David organized and commanded the administration and servants of the temple.

ii. Yet no one calls it "David's temple." It seems that all the credit, all the name, all the glory goes to Solomon. It doesn't seem to have bothered David, because he was a man after God's heart.

iii. "So, if you go to a country town or village, and you preach the gospel to a few poor folk, you may never have seemed very successful; but you have been preparing the way for somebody else who is coming after you." (Spurgeon)

iv. "But *this is a terrible blow at self*. Self says, 'I like to begin something of my own, and I like to carry it out; I do not want any interference from other people.' A friend proposed, the other day, to give you a little help in your service. You looked at him as if he had been a thief. You do not want any help; you are quite up to the mark; you are like a wagon and four horses, and a dog under the wagon as well! There is everything about you that is wanted; you need no help from anybody; you can do all things almost without the help of God! I am very sorry for you if that is your opinion." (Spurgeon)

4. (17-19) David's command to the leaders of Israel.

David also commanded all the leaders of Israel to help Solomon his son, saying, "Is not the LORD your God with you? And has He *not* given you rest on every side? For He has given the inhabitants of the land into my hand, and the land is subdued before the LORD and before His people. Now set your heart and your soul to seek the LORD your God. Therefore arise and build the sanctuary of the LORD God, to bring the ark of the covenant of the LORD and the holy articles of God into the house that is to be built for the name of the LORD."

a. **David also commanded all the leaders of Israel to help Solomon his son**: David knew that one leader – even a great leader – was not enough to get a great work done. When God calls a leader He also calls other **leaders…to help**.

b. **Now set your heart and your soul to seek the LORD your God**: This command of David's is interesting in its context. David gave this command in the context of *work*, not the context of leisurely repose before God. David knew that it was possible to keep one's heart set on seeking God even in the midst of doing a great work before the LORD.

i. "They must *seek the LORD* (v. 19) as David had sought him (*cf.* 1 Chronicles 13:3; 14:10, 14). David explains how to seek ('devote your heart and soul'; *cf.* REB, NEB, JB) and what it meant in practice (*Build the sanctuary*). As elsewhere, 'seeking' is an act of obedience rather than a search for guidance, and David will yet again underline its importance (1 Chronicles 28:8-9)." (Selman)

ii. "Thus Solomon came to the Jewish throne with every possible advantage. Had he made a proper use of his state and of his talents, he would have been the greatest as well as the wisest of sovereigns. But alas! How soon did this pure gold become dim! He began with an unlawful matrimonial connection; this led him to a commerce that was positively forbidden by the law of God: he then multiplied his matrimonial connections with pagan women; they turned his heart away from God, and the once wise and holy Solomon died a fool and an idolater." (Clarke)

iii. "Did David live in vain? Can it be truly said that he failed in the grandest project of his life? Assuredly not; he did all that he was permitted to do, and by making those elaborate preparations, he was really the means of the building of the temple." (Spurgeon)

iv. "God buries the workman, but the devil himself cannot bury the work. The work is everlasting, though the workmen die. We pass away, as star by star grows dim; but the eternal light is never-fading. God shall have the victory." (Spurgeon)

1 Chronicles 23 – New Duties for the Levites

A. The groupings of the Levites.

1. (1-2) David passes the kingdom to Solomon.

So when David was old and full of days, he made his son Solomon king over Israel. And he gathered together all the leaders of Israel, with the priests and the Levites.

> a. **When David was old and full of days, he made his son Solomon king over Israel**: David had other sons who might also claim the throne of Israel after his death (especially Adonijah). 1 Kings 1:31-40 describes in greater detail how David made sure that Solomon, and not Adonijah, took the throne after his death.
>
>> i. "Not that he did resign the kingdom to him, but that he declared his mind concerning his succession into the throne after his death." (Poole)
>
> b. **He gathered together all the leaders of Israel**: David gathered these for the purpose of organizing them to help Solomon with the work of building the temple and administering the affairs of the kingdom.

2. (3-6) The number and the main groupings of the Levites.

Now the Levites were numbered from the age of thirty years and above; and the number of individual males was thirty-eight thousand. Of these, twenty-four thousand *were* **to look after the work of the house of the LORD, six thousand** *were* **officers and judges, four thousand** *were* **gatekeepers, and four thousand praised the LORD with** *musical instruments,* **"which I made,"** *said David,* **"for giving praise." Also David separated them into divisions among the sons of Levi: Gershon, Kohath, and Merari.**

a. **The Levites were numbered from the age of thirty years and above**: This was based on the ancient command found in Numbers 4:1-3, indicating that a Levite's service began at 30 years of age.

b. **The number of individual males was thirty-eight thousand**: These 38,000 qualified Levites were divided into different duties.

   i. **To look after the work of the house of the LORD**: The temple was a busy place constantly flowing with worshippers, sacrifice, and service to God. It took many skilled people to take care of all the practical matters behind this activity.

   ii. **Officers and judges**: The Levites were also the civil servants for the kingdom of Israel. Governmental records, decisions, and administration were all in the hands of the Levites.

   iii. **Gatekeepers**: These had the responsibility for security, both in a practical and spiritual sense. They made sure that only those who were ready to serve and worship God could come to the temple and its associated building.

   iv. **Four thousand praised the LORD**: These Levites had the job of worshipping God both with their voices and musical instruments. They did this both to honor God directly and also to encourage *others* to worship God.

c. **David separated them into divisions among the sons of Levi: Gershon, Kohath, and Merari**: These family groupings within the tribe of Levi were described hundreds of years before in Numbers 3 and 4.

   i. **Gershon**: The Gershonites were to take care of the skins that covered the tabernacle itself.

   ii. **Kohath**: The Kohathites were to take care of the furniture of the tabernacle including the ark of the covenant, the table of showbread, and so forth, under the direction of Eleazar the priest, son of Aaron.

   iii. **Merari**: The family of Merari was to take care of the structural aspects of the tabernacle including the pillars, the boards, and so forth

3. (7-11) The Gershonites.

Of the Gershonites: Laadan and Shimei. The sons of Laadan: the first Jehiel, then Zetham and Joel; three *in all*. The sons of Shimei: Shelomith, Haziel, and Haran; three *in all*. These were the heads of the fathers' *houses* **of Laadan. And the sons of Shimei: Jahath, Zina, Jeush, and Beriah. These *were* the four sons of Shimei. Jahath was the first and Zizah the second. But Jeush and Beriah did not have many sons; therefore they were assigned as one father's house.**

4. (12-13) The Kohathites.

The sons of Kohath: Amram, Izhar, Hebron, and Uzziel; four *in all*. The sons of Amram: Aaron and Moses; and Aaron was set apart, he and his sons forever, that he should sanctify the most holy things, to burn incense before the LORD**, to minister to Him, and to give the blessing in His name forever.**

a. **And Aaron was set apart, he and his sons forever**: Among the Levites, the descendants of Aaron were chosen for the priestly duties described in these verses. Being a member of the tribe of Levi was not enough to be a priest; one had to be a descendant of this particular family of Aaron.

b. **That he should sanctify the most holy things, to burn incense before the L**ORD**, to minister to Him, and to give the blessing in His name forever**: This is a brief but powerful description of the duties of the priests of Israel.

- **That he should sanctify the most holy things**: The priest was to have an active concern for holiness, and to be able to discern between what was holy and what was not. This means that holiness had to touch the life of the priest; he had to represent God before the people.

- **To burn incense before the L**ORD: Incense is a picture of intercessory prayer. The priest had to represent the people before the Lord. "The fragrant incense stealing heavenward is a beautiful emblem of intercessory prayer. Let us pray more, not for ourselves so much as for others. This is the sign of growth in grace, when our prayers are fragrant with the names of friend and foe, and mingled with the coals of the golden altar." (Meyer)

- **To minister to Him**: The priest was busy with people and the work of ministry, but he must never forget his ministry to God Himself. He was to spend time in personal devotion, worship, and attention given to God in the secret place.

- **To give the blessing in His name forever**: The priest was blessed so that he could bless others. "It is not enough to linger in soft prayer within the vail, we must come forward to bless mankind. He who is nearest to God is closest to man." (Meyer)

5. (14-20) The sons of Moses, of the family of Kohath.

Now the sons of Moses the man of God were reckoned to the tribe of Levi. The sons of Moses *were* Gershon and Eliezer. Of the sons of Gershon, Shebuel *was* the first. Of the descendants of Eliezer, Rehabiah was the first. And Eliezer had no other sons, but the sons of Rehabiah

were very many. Of the sons of Izhar, Shelomith *was* the first. Of the sons of Hebron, Jeriah *was* the first, Amariah the second, Jahaziel the third, and Jekameam the fourth. Of the sons of Uzziel, Michah *was* the first and Jesshiah the second.

6. (21-23) The family of Merari.

The sons of Merari *were* **Mahli and Mushi. The sons of Mahli** *were* **Eleazar and Kish. And Eleazar died, and had no sons, but only daughters; and their brethren, the sons of Kish, took them** *as wives.* **The sons of Mushi** *were* **Mahli, Eder, and Jeremoth; three** *in all.*

B. David changes the duties of the Levites.

1. (24-26) The reason for the change of duty.

These *were* **the sons of Levi by their fathers' houses; the heads of the fathers'** *houses* **as they were counted individually by the number of their names, who did the work for the service of the house of the LORD, from the age of twenty years and above. For David said, "The LORD God of Israel has given rest to His people, that they may dwell in Jerusalem forever"; and also to the Levites, "They shall no longer carry the tabernacle, or any of the articles for its service."**

> a. **From the age of twenty years and above**: David first changed the year when service began for the Levites from 30 to 20.
>
>> i. One reason he did this was because the new temple would require more workers, and he wanted to keep the Levites busy. "Temple service will certainly have brought increased work, even though the occasional duty of transporting the ark was now to be abolished. In fact, the Levites and their duties had suffered from long-standing neglect." (Selman)
>
> b. **The LORD God of Israel has given rest to His people**: Now that the tabernacle and its furnishings would **rest** permanently at the temple David planned and Solomon would build, there could and should be a change in the duties of the Levites.

2. (27-32) The new duties of the Levites.

For by the last words of David the Levites *were* **numbered from twenty years old and above; because their duty** *was* **to help the sons of Aaron in the service of the house of the LORD, in the courts and in the chambers, in the purifying of all holy things and the work of the service of the house of God, both with the showbread and the fine flour for the grain offering, with the unleavened cakes and** *what is baked in* **the pan, with what is mixed and with all kinds of measures and sizes; to stand every**

morning to thank and praise the LORD, and likewise at evening; and at every presentation of a burnt offering to the LORD on the Sabbaths and on the New Moons and on the set feasts, by number according to the ordinance governing them, regularly before the LORD; and that they should attend to the needs of the tabernacle of meeting, the needs of the holy *place*, and the needs of the sons of Aaron their brethren in the work of the house of the LORD.

> a. **For by the last word of David the Levites were numbered**: "Never was the true kingliness of David more manifest, than when he sought to make these arrangements for the consolidation around the Throne of God of that kingdom which he was so soon to leave." (Morgan)
>
>> i. 2 Chronicles 29:25 tells us that David commanded these arrangements as he worked together with *Gad the king's seer* and *Nathan the prophet*. It also tells us that these arrangements were *the commandment of the LORD by his prophets*. This was Holy Spirit guided organization and administration.
>>
>> ii. "Guided by the prophets (2 Chronicles 29:25), the king exercised his administrative genius to establish a system of procedures that helped maintain legitimate worship under his successors." (Payne)
>
> b. **Because their duty was to help the sons of Aaron in the service of the house of the LORD**: Since the tabernacle and its service was now to come to a place of permanent rest, the Levites who once had the responsibility to manage and move the mobile structure could now become the helpers of the priests, the **sons of Aaron**.
>
> c. **To stand every morning to thank and praise the LORD**: The Chronicler mentioned many specific duties of the Levites (**purifying all holy things…with the showbread…what is baked in the pan**). Yet he included among them this most important duty: **to stand every morning to thank and praise the LORD**. This was essential among the duties of the Levites and the priests, and could never be neglected.
>
>> i. "The specific work of the Levites is beautifully described by the chronicler in the closing verses of the chapter. They were the servants of the priest and of the house. They were also to stand at morning and evening to praise the Lord. High and holy calling, this." (Morgan)
>>
>> ii. "It was the priests' business to kill, flay, and dress, as well as to *offer*, the victims; but being *few*, they were obliged to employ the Levites to flay those animals. The Levites were, properly speaking, servants to the priests, and were employed about the more servile part of divine worship." (Clarke)

iii. "As assistants, they were active in side-rooms and courtyards rather than the main building, preparing food and offerings rather than actually offering sacrifices." (Selman)

1 Chronicles 24 – The Sections of the Priesthood

A. The twenty-four divisions of the priesthood.

1. (1-6) The sons of Aaron and what became of them.

Now these are the divisions of the sons of Aaron. The sons of Aaron were Nadab, Abihu, Eleazar, and Ithamar. And Nadab and Abihu died before their father, and had no children; therefore Eleazar and Ithamar ministered as priests. Then David with Zadok of the sons of Eleazar, and Ahimelech of the sons of Ithamar, divided them according to the schedule of their service. There were more leaders found of the sons of Eleazar than of the sons of Ithamar, and thus they were divided. Among the sons of Eleazar were sixteen heads of their fathers' houses, and eight heads of their fathers' houses among the sons of Ithamar. Thus they were divided by lot, one group as another, for there were officials of the sanctuary and officials of the house of God, from the sons of Eleazar and from the sons of Ithamar. And the scribe, Shemaiah the son of Nethanel, one of the Levites, wrote them down before the king, the leaders, Zadok the priest, Ahimelech the son of Abiathar, and the heads of the fathers' houses of the priests and Levites, one father's house taken for Eleazar and one for Ithamar.

    a. **Nadab and Abihu died before their father**: God judged Nadab and Abihu because they dared to bring *strange fire* before the LORD, blaspheming God's commandments for sacrifice (Leviticus 10:1-2).

    b. **Divided them according to the schedule of their service**: David took the descendants of Aaron – the priestly family of Israel – and together with **Zadok** he divided them into 24 sections, to serve **according to the schedule of their service**.

        i. "Two aspects of this service are emphasized – that it is to be regulated in an orderly system of twenty-four courses (vv. 1-19), and that it provides a pattern to be followed by the priests' Levitical assistants (vv. 20-31)." (Selman)

2. (7-19) The priesthood is divided by lot into 24 sections.

Now the first lot fell to Jehoiarib, the second to Jedaiah, the third to Harim, the fourth to Seorim, the fifth to Malchijah, the sixth to Mijamin, the seventh to Hakkoz, the eighth to Abijah, the ninth to Jeshua, the tenth to Shecaniah, the eleventh to Eliashib, the twelfth to Jakim, the thirteenth to Huppah, the fourteenth to Jeshebeab, the fifteenth to Bilgah, the sixteenth to Immer, the seventeenth to Hezir, the eighteenth to Happizzez, the nineteenth to Pethahiah, the twentieth to Jehezekel, the twenty-first to Jachin, the twenty-second to Gamul, the twenty-third to Delaiah, the twenty-fourth to Maaziah. This *was* the schedule of their service for coming into the house of the LORD according to their ordinance by the hand of Aaron their father, as the LORD God of Israel had commanded him.

> a. **This was the schedule of their service for coming into the house of the LORD:** David knew that because there were so many descendants of Aaron by this time, the priests should be divided so they could be fairly assigned the privileged service of the temple.
>
>> i. "In later Jewish practice, the number of twenty-four courses was based on a lunar calendar of forty-eight weeks, with each course serving for a week at a time and thus twice in a year." (Selman)
>>
>> ii. "With the passage of time, some of the Davidic courses died out or had to be consolidated with others, and new ones were formed to take their places. At the first return from exile in 527 B.C., only four courses were registered.... By 520 twenty-two were again operative, (Nehemiah 12:1-7), but only half of them were the courses as originally organized by David." (Payne)

B. The rest of the sons of Levi.

1. (20-30) A list of the remaining sons of Levi.

And the rest of the sons of Levi: of the sons of Amram, Shubael; of the sons of Shubael, Jehdeiah. Concerning Rehabiah, of the sons of Rehabiah, the first *was* Isshiah. Of the Izharites, Shelomoth; of the sons of Shelomoth, Jahath. Of the sons *of Hebron,* Jeriah *was the first,* Amariah the second, Jahaziel the third, *and* Jekameam the fourth. *Of* the sons of Uzziel, Michah; of the sons of Michah, Shamir. The brother of Michah, Isshiah; of the sons of Isshiah, Zechariah. The sons of Merari *were* Mahli and Mushi; the son of Jaaziah, Beno. The sons of

Merari by Jaaziah *were* **Beno, Shoham, Zaccur, and Ibri. Of Mahli: Eleazar, who had no sons. Of Kish: the son of Kish, Jerahmeel. Also the sons of Mushi** *were* **Mahli, Eder, and Jerimoth. These** *were* **the sons of the Levites according to their fathers' houses.**

> a. **And the rest of the sons of Levi**: These were the descendants of Kohath's son Amram who were *not* of the family of Moses and Aaron (Exodus 6:18-27).

2. (31) How their lots were chosen.

These also cast lots just as their brothers the sons of Aaron did, in the presence of King David, Zadok, Ahimelech, and the heads of the fathers' *houses* **of the priests and Levites. The chief fathers** *did* **just as their younger brethren.**

> a. **These also cast lots just as their brothers the sons of Aaron did**: These other descendants of the family of Kohath were divided according to the schedule for their service, along the same pattern as the priests.
>
> b. **The chief fathers did just as their younger brethren**: "The lots of the elder and younger brethren were promiscuously put together, and the order was settled as the lots came forth, without any regard to the age, or dignity, or number of the persons or families, the youngest family having the first course if they had the first lot." (Poole)
>
>> i. "There was a tactful mingling in the arrangement of the older and the younger men, so that in this highest and holiest national service the experience of age and the enthusiasm of youth were naturally inspiring." (Morgan)

1 Chronicles 25 – Musicians for the Temple

A. The musicians for the temple.

1. (1) Musicians separated for service.

Moreover David and the captains of the army separated for the service *some* of the sons of Asaph, of Heman, and of Jeduthun, who *should* prophesy with harps, stringed instruments, and cymbals. And the number of the skilled men performing their service was:

a. **David and the captains of the army separated for the service**: Interestingly, the **captains of the army** took part in the selection and organization of the musicians or "worship leaders" for Israel. David sensed a connection between the security of the kingdom and the worship and honoring of God.

i. "Chapter 25 concerns David's organization of the four thousand Levitical musicians (23:5) into courses of service that correspond to those of the priests and temple Levites (chapter 24)." (Payne)

ii. "David did give high regard to the counsel of his military commanders (1 Chronicles 11:10; 12:32; 28:1), even in liturgical affairs (cf. 1 Chronicles 13:1; 15:25)." (Payne)

b. **Who should prophesy with harps, stringed instruments, and cymbals**: Their service was connected with the dynamic of prophecy in the sense that it was inspired by God. Their ministry in music was not merely the product of good musicianship; it was a gift of the Holy Spirit being exercised through them.

i. "This work of praise is thrice described by a somewhat singular, and, in this connection, arresting word, 'prophecy.' The use of this word here is a revelation of the true value of the service of music in the sanctuary of God." (Morgan)

ii. "Either they supplied messages direct from God in the manner of the classical prophets, for which the Levite Jahaziel (2 Chronicles 20:14-17) provides an obvious analogy, or their praise was itself seen as 'prophecy' in that it proclaimed God's word with God's authority." (Selman)

2. (2-6) The sons of Asaph, Jeduthun, and Heman.

Of the sons of Asaph: Zaccur, Joseph, Nethaniah, and Asharelah; the sons of Asaph *were* **under the direction of Asaph, who prophesied according to the order of the king. Of Jeduthun, the sons of Jeduthun: Gedaliah, Zeri, Jeshaiah, Shimei, Hashabiah, and Mattithiah, six, under the direction of their father Jeduthun, who prophesied with a harp to give thanks and to praise the LORD. Of Heman, the sons of Heman: Bukkiah, Mattaniah, Uzziel, Shebuel, Jerimoth, Hananiah, Hanani, Eliathah, Giddalti, Romamti-Ezer, Joshbekashah, Mallothi, Hothir,** *and* **Mahazioth. All these** *were* **the sons of Heman the king's seer in the words of God, to exalt his horn. For God gave Heman fourteen sons and three daughters. All these** *were* **under the direction of their father for the music** *in* **the house of the LORD, with cymbals, stringed instruments, and harps, for the service of the house of God. Asaph, Jeduthun, and Heman** *were* **under the authority of the king.**

a. **Asaph, who prophesied according to the order of the king**: 12 Psalms are attributed to Asaph (Psalm 50 and Psalms 73 through 83).

b. **Jeduthun, who prophesied with a harp to give thanks and to praise the LORD**: Jeduthun's music ministry was so inspired by the Spirit of God that it could be said that he **prophesied with a harp**.

c. **Heman the king's seer**: "He is called *the king's seer*, either because the king took special delight in him, or because he frequently attended upon the king in his palace, executing his sacred office there, while the rest were constantly employed in the tabernacle." (Poole)

d. **Asaph, Jeduthun, and Heman were under the authority of the king**: These enormously talented and Spirit-anointed men knew how to submit themselves under the leadership of David, **under the authority of the king**.

i. We note the prominent place of the **sons of Heman**, and that **all these were under the direction of their father for the music in the house of the LORD**. "How one would like to have seen Heman coming into the Temple with his children! It was largely owing to him and their mother that they were what they were." (Meyer)

ii. **Under the direction of their father**: "Heman's children were 'under the hands of their father.' Young people must not get the upper hand." (Meyer)

iii. Yet we also see that **Heman** was among those **under the authority of the king**. "But if you would rule well, you must obey. Asaph, Heman, and Jeduthun, were under the king. The man who is himself under authority, can say, Go, come, do this or that, with the calm assurance of being obeyed." (Meyer)

B. The result of the casting of lots for their duty.

1. (7-8) The number of skillful musicians.

So the number of them, with their brethren who were instructed in the songs of the LORD, all who were skillful, *was* two hundred and eighty-eight. And they cast lots for their duty, the small as well as the great, the teacher with the student.

a. **They cast lots for their duty, the small as well as the great, the teacher with the student**: David didn't give the choice worship assignments only to the most talented and greatest. He let God do the choosing and it was both a prevention of pride for the **great** and the **teacher**, and a learning opportunity for the **small** and the **student**.

2. (9-31) The divisions of the musicians.

Now the first lot for Asaph came out for Joseph; the second for Gedaliah, him with his brethren and sons, twelve; the third for Zaccur, his sons and his brethren, twelve; the fourth for Jizri, his sons and his brethren, twelve; the fifth for Nethaniah, his sons and his brethren, twelve; the sixth for Bukkiah, his sons and his brethren, twelve; the seventh for Jesharelah, his sons and his brethren, twelve; the eighth for Jeshaiah, his sons and his brethren, twelve; the ninth for Mattaniah, his sons and his brethren, twelve; the tenth for Shimei, his sons and his brethren, twelve; the eleventh for Azarel, his sons and his brethren, twelve; the twelfth for Hashabiah, his sons and his brethren, twelve; the thirteenth for Shubael, his sons and his brethren, twelve; the fourteenth for Mattithiah, his sons and his brethren, twelve; the fifteenth for Jeremoth, his sons and his brethren, twelve; the sixteenth for Hananiah, his sons and his brethren, twelve; the seventeenth for Joshbekashah, his sons and his brethren, twelve; the eighteenth for Hanani, his sons and his brethren, twelve; the nineteenth for Mallothi, his sons and his brethren, twelve; the twentieth for Eliathah, his sons and his brethren, twelve; the twenty-first for Hothir, his sons and his brethren, twelve; the twenty-second for Giddalti, his sons and his brethren, twelve; the twenty-third

for Mahazioth, his sons and his brethren, twelve; the twenty-fourth for Romamti-Ezer, his sons and his brethren, twelve.

1 Chronicles 26 – The Gatekeepers for the Temple

A. The divisions of the gatekeepers.

1. (1-5) The divisions of the gatekeepers.

Concerning the divisions of the gatekeepers: of the Korahites, Meshelemiah the son of Kore, of the sons of Asaph. And the sons of Meshelemiah *were* Zechariah the firstborn, Jediael the second, Zebadiah the third, Jathniel the fourth, Elam the fifth, Jehohanan the sixth, Eliehoenai the seventh. Moreover the sons of Obed-Edom *were* Shemaiah the firstborn, Jehozabad the second, Joah the third, Sacar the fourth, Nethanel the fifth, Ammiel the sixth, Issachar the seventh, Peulthai the eighth; for God blessed him.

a. **Divisions of the gatekeepers**: These had the responsibility for security, both in a practical and spiritual sense. They made sure that only those who were ready to serve and worship God could come to the temple and its associated building. Their work had to be organized and arranged just as much as the work of the priests who officiated at the sacrifices.

i. "Though less prominent than some of their Levitical colleagues, from time to time the gatekeepers made a vital contribution to national life, notably under the high priest Jehoiada (2 Chronicles 23:4-6, 19), and in the reigns of Hezekiah (2 Chronicles 31:14-19) and Josiah (2 Chronicles 34:9-13)." (Selman)

ii. "Essentially their duty was to make ordinary people aware of the practical limits of holiness, for anyone entering the sanctuary unlawfully did so on penalty of death." (Selman)

iii. Though some might see their work as humble, it was actually of great privilege. Remember the envy of the Psalmist: *I would rather be a doorkeeper in the house of my God than dwell in the tents of wickedness.* (Psalm 84:10)

b. **Of the sons of Asaph**: "Not that famous *Asaph* the singer, but another *Asaph*, called also *Ebiasaph*, 1 Chronicles 6:37." (Trapp)

2. (6-8) Shemaiah and his sons, and the other sons of Obed-Edom.

Also to Shemaiah his son were sons born who governed their fathers' houses, because they *were* men of great ability. The sons of Shemaiah *were* Othni, Rephael, Obed, and Elzabad, whose brothers Elihu and Semachiah *were* able men. All these *were* of the sons of Obed-Edom, they and their sons and their brethren, able men with strength for the work: sixty-two of Obed-Edom.

a. **Who governed their fathers' houses, because they were men of great ability**: Shemaiah was of the family of gatekeepers, yet his sons rose to positions of high responsibility because they were **men of great ability**. They are also described as **able men with strength for the work**.

i. "*Able men* might be better translated, 'strong men'. The job might entail removal of unwelcome people or objects (*cf.* 2 Chronicles 26:16-20)." (Selman)

3. (9-12) Other gatekeepers.

And Meshelemiah had sons and brethren, eighteen able men. Also Hosah, of the children of Merari, had sons: Shimri the first (for *though he was not the firstborn, his father made him the first*), Hilkiah the second, Tebaliah the third, Zechariah the fourth; all the sons and brethren of Hosah *were* thirteen. Among these *were* the divisions of the gatekeepers, among the chief men, *having* duties just like their brethren, to serve in the house of the LORD.

a. **Having duties just like their brethren, to serve in the house of the LORD**: Some would make a distinction between the *spiritual* work of the temple and the *practical* work of the temple and regard the spiritual work as more important. The Chronicler is careful to remind us that the work of these **gatekeepers**, whose service was more practical in nature, was esteemed by God as just as valuable.

i. "A very important point is made by the inclusion of these groups, even though they might seem to represent a diversion from Chronicles' main theme. As God's people pay proper attention to their status as a worshipping community, the distinction between the sacred and the secular disappears. All tasks, whether mundane or specialized, 'religious' or 'lay', have value in the eyes of God." (Selman)

4. (13-19) The lot for each family of the gatekeepers.

And they cast lots for each gate, the small as well as the great, according to their father's house. The lot for the East *Gate* fell to Shelemiah. Then they cast lots *for* his son Zechariah, a wise counselor, and his lot came out for the North Gate; to Obed-Edom the South Gate, and to his sons the storehouse. To Shuppim and Hosah *the lot came out* for the West Gate, with the Shallecheth Gate on the ascending highway; watchman opposite watchman. On the east were *six* Levites, on the north four each day, on the south four each day, and for the storehouse two by two. As for the Parbar on the west, *there were* four on the highway *and* two at the Parbar. These were the divisions of the gatekeepers among the sons of Korah and among the sons of Merari.

a. **They cast lots for each gate**: They determined the order and arrangement of the service for the gatekeepers the same way that they determined the order and arrangement for the priests in their service.

b. **The small as well as the great**: This means that David let the LORD decide when it came to organizing and ordering these offices, and he did not let prestige or position determine their appointments.

i. "Our method is not that of casting lots, but of seeking the direct guidance of the Spirit. But we need to remember that in our choice of men for office in the work of the Church of God, the things of privilege, which too often count in human affairs, must have no weight with us." (Morgan)

ii. "But chiefly we are concerned with the temple of the heart. We surely need the doorkeeper there, for in the history of the inner life there is so much going and coming; such troops of thoughts pour into the shrine of the soul, and pour out. And often, in the crowd, disloyal and evil thoughts intrude, which, before we know it, introduce a sense of distance and alienation from God." (Meyer)

B. Other Levitical servants to the temple.

1. (20-25) Overseers for the treasuries of the house of God.

Of the Levites, Ahijah *was* over the treasuries of the house of God and over the treasuries of the dedicated things. The sons of Laadan, the descendants of the Gershonites of Laadan, heads of their fathers' *houses***, of Laadan the Gershonite: Jehieli. The sons of Jehieli, Zetham and Joel his brother,** *were* **over the treasuries of the house of the LORD. Of the Amramites, the Izharites, the Hebronites, and the Uzzielites: Shebuel the son of Gershom, the son of Moses,** *was* **overseer of the treasuries. And his brethren by Eliezer** *were* **Rehabiah his son, Jeshaiah his son, Joram his son, Zichri his son, and Shelomith his son.**

a. **Over the treasuries of the house of God and over the treasuries of the dedicated things**: David set in order the financial organization necessary to administrate the building of the temple, including oversight of all the riches brought in by David's conquest of neighboring peoples (**the dedicated things**).

2. (26-28) Shelomith, a notable overseer of the treasuries of the house of God.

This Shelomith and his brethren *were* over all the treasuries of the dedicated things which King David and the heads of fathers' *houses*, the captains over thousands and hundreds, and the captains of the army, had dedicated. Some of the spoils won in battles they dedicated to maintain the house of the LORD. And all that Samuel the seer, Saul the son of Kish, Abner the son of Ner, and Joab the son of Zeruiah had dedicated, every dedicated *thing*, was under the hand of Shelomith and his brethren.

3. (29-32) Other servants for the kingdom of Israel.

Of the Izharites, Chenaniah and his sons *performed* duties as officials and judges over Israel outside Jerusalem. Of the Hebronites, Hashabiah and his brethren, one thousand seven hundred able men, had the oversight of Israel on the west side of the Jordan for all the business of the LORD, and in the service of the king. Among the Hebronites, Jerijah *was* head of the Hebronites according to his genealogy of the fathers. In the fortieth year of the reign of David they were sought, and there were found among them capable men at Jazer of Gilead. And his brethren *were* two thousand seven hundred able men, heads of fathers' *houses*, whom King David made officials over the Reubenites, the Gadites, and the half-tribe of Manasseh, for every matter pertaining to God and the affairs of the king.

> a. **For every matter pertaining to God and the affairs of the king**: "Expounding also of the law, and therehence answering cases, solving doubts; superintendents, some say they were, throughout the whole kingdom." (Trapp)
>
>> i. "The statistic that 2,700 Levites maintained the laws of 'God and… the king' among the tribes west of the Jordan (v.30) seems strange… but contains a hint of the importance of the district of Gilead." (Payne)

1 Chronicles 27 – Tribal Leaders and Officials of State

A. Captains over the army of Israel.

1. (1) The military divisions of Israel.

And the children of Israel, according to their number, the heads of fathers' *houses,* **the captains of thousands and hundreds and their officers, served the king in every matter of the** *military* **divisions.** ***These divisions*** **came in and went out month by month throughout all the months of the year, each division** *having* **twenty-four thousand.**

a. **And the children of Israel…served the king in every matter of the military divisions**: Under David and most every other king of Israel or Judah, Israel never relied on mercenary soldiers. Israelites themselves **served the king in every matter of the military.**

b. **These divisions came in and went out month by month**: David's army was also divided into units of twelve, with one group of the twelve on alert each month of the year. This was an effective way to keep troops always ready and the inactive troops regularly trained.

i. "All these men were prepared, disciplined, and ready at a call, without the smallest expense to the state or the king. These were, properly speaking, the *militia* of the Israelitish kingdom." (Clarke)

2. (2-15) Captains over David's army.

Over the first division for the first month *was* **Jashobeam the son of Zabdiel, and in his division** *were* **twenty-four thousand;** *he was* **of the children of Perez, and the chief of all the captains of the army for the first month. Over the division of the second month** *was* **Dodai an Ahohite, and of his division Mikloth also** *was* **the leader; in his division** *were* **twenty-four thousand. The third captain of the army for the third**

month *was* Benaiah, the son of Jehoiada the priest, who was chief; in his division *were* twenty-four thousand. This was the Benaiah *who was* mighty *among* the thirty, and was over the thirty; in his division *was* Ammizabad his son. The fourth *captain* for the fourth month *was* Asahel the brother of Joab, and Zebadiah his son after him; in his division *were* twenty-four thousand. The fifth *captain* for the fifth month *was* Shamhuth the Izrahite; in his division were twenty-four thousand. The sixth *captain* for the sixth month *was* Ira the son of Ikkesh the Tekoite; in his division *were* twenty-four thousand. The seventh *captain* for the seventh month *was* Helez the Pelonite, of the children of Ephraim; in his division *were* twenty-four thousand. The eighth *captain* for the eighth month *was* Sibbechai the Hushathite, of the Zarhites; in his division *were* twenty-four thousand. The ninth *captain* for the ninth month *was* Abiezer the Anathothite, of the Benjamites; in his division *were* twenty-four thousand. The tenth *captain* for the tenth month *was* Maharai the Netophathite, of the Zarhites; in his division *were* twenty-four thousand. The eleventh *captain* for the eleventh month *was* Benaiah the Pirathonite, of the children of Ephraim; in his division *were* twenty-four thousand. The twelfth *captain* for the twelfth month *was* Heldai the Netophathite, of Othniel; in his division *were* twenty-four thousand.

a. **Of the first division**: This section explains the twelve divisions mentioned in the previous verses.

b. **Benaiah, the son of Jehoiada**: 2 Samuel 23:20-21 describes this same Benaiah as a great hero in Israel, someone who killed two mighty Moabites, a lion in a pit on a snowy day, and a formidable Egyptian.

c. **Asahel the brother of Joab**: As recorded in 2 Samuel 2:18-23, Asahel was tragically killed in battle by Abner, who was the commander of Ishbosheth's armies (this was the son of Saul who tried to follow him on the throne of Israel).

B. Tribal leaders over Israel and officials in King David's government.

1. (16-22) Tribal leaders.

Furthermore, over the tribes of Israel: the officer over the Reubenites *was* Eliezer the son of Zichri; over the Simeonites, Shephatiah the son of Maachah; *over* **the Levites, Hashabiah the son of Kemuel; over the Aaronites, Zadok;** *over* **Judah, Elihu,** *one* **of David's brothers;** *over* **Issachar, Omri the son of Michael;** *over* **Zebulun, Ishmaiah the son of Obadiah;** *over* **Naphtali, Jerimoth the son of Azriel;** *over* **the children of Ephraim, Hoshea the son of Azaziah;** *over* **the half-tribe of Manasseh, Joel the son of Pedaiah;** *over* **the** *half-***tribe of Manasseh in Gilead, Iddo**

the son of Zechariah; *over* **Benjamin, Jaasiel the son of Abner;** *over* **Dan, Azarel the son of Jeroham. These** *were* **the leaders of the tribes of Israel.**

a. The officer over the Reubenites was Eliezer the son of Zichri: This list describes tribal leaders who were not priests or military leaders, but administrators in the civil service of the kingdom of Israel.

i. "We have the account of the order of the *civil* service, that which related simply to the *political state* of the king and the kingdom." (Clarke)

b. These were the leaders of the tribes of Israel: For some reason, the tribes of Asher and Gad are excluded from this list. "In this enumeration there is no mention of the tribes of Asher and Gad. Probably the account of these has been lost from this register. These rulers appear to have been all honorary men, like the lords lieutenants of our counties." (Clarke)

2. (23-34) Officials in King David's government.

But David did not take the number of those twenty years old and under, because the Lord **had said He would multiply Israel like the stars of the heavens. Joab the son of Zeruiah began a census, but he did not finish, for wrath came upon Israel because of this census; nor was the number recorded in the account of the chronicles of King David. And Azmaveth the son of Adiel** *was* **over the king's treasuries; and Jehonathan the son of Uzziah was over the storehouses in the field, in the cities, in the villages, and in the fortresses. Ezri the son of Chelub was over those who did the work of the field for tilling the ground. And Shimei the Ramathite** *was* **over the vineyards, and Zabdi the Shiphmite was over the produce of the vineyards for the supply of wine. Baal-Hanan the Gederite was over the olive trees and the sycamore trees that** *were* **in the lowlands, and Joash** *was* **over the store of oil. And Shitrai the Sharonite** *was* **over the herds that fed in Sharon, and Shaphat the son of Adlai was over the herds** *that were* **in the valleys. Obil the Ishmaelite** *was* **over the camels, Jehdeiah the Meronothite** *was* **over the donkeys, and Jaziz the Hagrite** *was* **over the flocks. All these** *were* **the officials over King David's property. Also Jehonathan, David's uncle,** *was* **a counselor, a wise man, and a scribe; and Jehiel the son of Hachmoni** *was* **with the king's sons. Ahithophel** *was* **the king's counselor, and Hushai the Archite** *was* **the king's companion. After Ahithophel** *was* **Jehoiada the son of Benaiah, then Abiathar. And the general of the king's army** *was* **Joab.**

a. David did not take the number of those twenty years old and under, because the L**ord** had said He would multiply Israel like the stars of

the heavens: David wisely refrained from completing an unwise census, trusting that God would increase the kingdom and make them great.

b. **Treasuries…storehouses…. work of the field for tilling the ground … vineyards…. olive trees…. herds…. camels…donkeys…flocks**: David had trusted men to oversee these areas, and they were just as important to the kingdom as the more obvious spiritual leaders.

> i. "The greatness of David as a king was manifested in the acts of peaceful administration, as surely as in his victories on the fields of battle. The tilling of the ground, and its careful cultivation; the rearing of cattle; and all the things pertaining to the welfare of his people were arranged for, under duly qualified and appointed oversight." (Morgan)

> ii. "Each of these different men had his distinct sphere for which he was doubtless specially qualified; and it was his duty – not to be jealous of others, nor eager to imitate them, but – to be faithful in his own province." (Meyer)

> iii. The key was that **all these were the officials over King David's property**. "How great an error it would have been had any of these begun to account the produce of cattle or ground as his own! He had nothing that he had not received, and whatever he controlled had been entrusted to his care for the emolument and advantage of his sovereign." (Meyer)

> iv. "It is worthy of remark, that Obil, an Ishmaelite or Arab, was put over the camels which is a creature of Arabia; and that Jaziz, a Hagarene, (the Hagarenes were shepherds by profession,) was put over the flocks: nothing went by favour; each was appointed to the office for which he was best qualified; and thus men of worth were encouraged, and the public service effectually promoted." (Clarke)

c. **Hushai the Archite was the king's companion**: "Hushai's post of 'king's friend' (cf. 2 Samuel 15:37) may have begun on an informal and personal basis; but it became an official advisory position (cf. 1 Kings 4:5)." (Payne)

d. **The general of the king's army was Joab**: Joab is one of the more complex characters of the Old Testament. He was fiercely loyal to David, yet not strongly obedient. He disobeyed David when he thought it was in David's best interest, and he was cunning and ruthless in furthering his own position.

1 Chronicles 28 – David's Public Charge to Solomon

A. David's public words to the assembly of Israel and to Solomon.

1. (1) The assembly of Israel gathers to hear King David.

Now David assembled at Jerusalem all the leaders of Israel: the officers of the tribes and the captains of the divisions who served the king, the captains over thousands and captains over hundreds, and the stewards over all the substance and possessions of the king and of his sons, with the officials, the valiant men, and all the mighty men of valor.

a. **Now David assembled at Jerusalem all the leaders of Israel**: This was David's public "passing of the torch" ceremony to Solomon, with an emphasis on the responsibility to build the temple. Despite this, another son of David (Adonijah, in 1 Kings 1-2) tried to take the throne when David died.

b. **All the leaders of Israel**: It may be that this was the group of people collectively mentioned in the previous chapters.

i. "The occasion for the final chapters of 1 Chronicles is a continuation of what was introduced in chapter 23: the assembling by the king of the leaders of Israel (23:2 = 28:1 and 29:1)." (Payne)

2. (2-8) David speaks to the assembly of Israel.

Then King David rose to his feet and said, "Hear me, my brethren and my people: I *had* it in my heart to build a house of rest for the ark of the covenant of the LORD, and for the footstool of our God, and had made preparations to build it. But God said to me, 'You shall not build a house for My name, because you *have been* a man of war and have shed blood.' However the LORD God of Israel chose me above all the house of my father to be king over Israel forever, for He has chosen Judah *to be*

the ruler; and of the house of Judah, the house of my father, and among the sons of my father, He was pleased with me to make *me* king over all Israel. And of all my sons (for the LORD has given me many sons) He has chosen my son Solomon to sit on the throne of the kingdom of the LORD over Israel. Now He said to me, 'It is your son Solomon *who* shall build My house and My courts; for I have chosen him *to be* My son, and I will be his Father. Moreover I will establish his kingdom forever, if he is steadfast to observe My commandments and My judgments, as it is this day.' Now therefore, in the sight of all Israel, the assembly of the LORD, and in the hearing of our God, be careful to seek out all the commandments of the LORD your God, that you may possess this good land, and leave *it* as an inheritance for your children after you forever."

> a. **Then King David rose to his feet**: Since this happened towards the end of David's life, he was in declining health (1 Kings 1:1-4). The Chronicler noted David's standing posture because considering his age and the setting, it was a dramatic scene.
>
> b. **You shall not build a house for My name**: Though David wanted to build God a house, God politely refused David's offer and proposed to build him a house instead, in the sense of a lasting royal dynasty (2 Samuel 7).
>
>> i. Significantly, David calls the temple **a house of rest**. "As in the case of God's sabbath rest at creation (Genesis 2:1-3), God's rest represents the completion of his work. The idea of rest was so significant for the temple that even though David's role as a 'man of war' was a vital part of the temple preparations in creating the necessary conditions for the work, it disqualified him from building the temple himself. Only Solomon, the 'man of rest' (22:9), was sufficiently fitted for the task." (Selman)
>
> c. **He has chosen my son Solomon to sit on the throne**: This was a significant event because there had never been a hereditary monarchy in Israel before. Saul, the previous king of Israel, was not succeeded by any son of his.
>
> d. **Moreover I will establish his kingdom forever**: God promised that if the royal descendants of David remained obedient, the LORD would protect their throne and the kingdom of Israel, and there would always be a descendant of David reigning over Israel.
>
> e. **Be careful to seek out all the commandments of the LORD**: This was an important and well-chosen exhortation to the people of Israel.

- They were exhorted to **be careful**, in the sense that they had to regard this responsibility as important and worthy of attention.
- They were exhorted to **seek out** the commandments of God, searching the Scriptures diligently.
- They were exhorted to seek out **all the commandments**, and not compromise by focusing on a few favored commandments.

3. (9-10) David speaks to Solomon.

"As for you, my son Solomon, know the God of your father, and serve Him with a loyal heart and with a willing mind; for the LORD searches all hearts and understands all the intent of the thoughts. If you seek Him, He will be found by you; but if you forsake Him, He will cast you off forever. Consider now, for the LORD has chosen you to build a house for the sanctuary; be strong, and do it."

a. **Know the God of your father**: David's exhortation to Solomon begins with the most important aspect – emphasizing a genuine commitment to a real relationship with the living God. David essentially told Solomon, "The secret of my success has been my relationship with God. You need to pursue the same relationship."

b. **Serve Him with a loyal heart and with a willing mind**: David also exhorted Solomon to serve God with *both* his **heart** and **mind**. Some people are all heart and no mind in their service to God; others are all mind and no heart. Both of these are important to truly **serve Him**.

  i. We notice that the command to **know** came before the command to **serve**. "To know God is to serve Him. All failure in service is the result of loss of vision of God, misapprehension of Him, due to some distance from Him." (Morgan)

  ii. David gave Solomon a *reason* to commit his **heart** and **mind** to God: **for the LORD searches all hearts and understands all the intent of the thoughts**. When we properly understand God and His omniscience we will much more naturally serve Him as we should.

c. **If you seek Him, He will be found by you; but if you forsake Him, He will cast you off forever**: Both of these proved true in the life of Solomon. When Solomon sought the LORD at Gibeon, he definitely **found** Him (1 Kings 3:1-15). When Solomon forsook God, he was in some sense **cast... off** (1 Kings 11:1-13).

  i. "Solomon's response, typical of humanity, was inconsistent. Though he did seek God (2 Chronicles 1:5), it was not with a 'whole heart' and his divided devotion led ultimately to a divided kingdom." (Selman)

d. **The LORD has chosen you to build a house for the sanctuary; be strong, and do it**: David concluded his exhortation to Solomon with the single most *urgent* command – to build the temple. All of David's exhaustive preparations would be for nothing if Solomon did not complete the job that David started.

B. The plans for the temple.

1. (11-13) David gives Solomon the plans for the temple.

Then David gave his son Solomon the plans for the vestibule, its houses, its treasuries, its upper chambers, its inner chambers, and the place of the mercy seat; and the plans for all that he had by the Spirit, of the courts of the house of the LORD, of all the chambers all around, of the treasuries of the house of God, and of the treasuries for the dedicated things; also for the division of the priests and the Levites, for all the work of the service of the house of the LORD, and for all the articles of service in the house of the LORD.

a. **Then David gave his son Solomon the plans**: Considered together, David did almost everything for the building of the temple except actually build it. He gave Solomon security, a location, the land, money, materials, supervisory staff, workers, and an organized team to run the temple. Here we also see that David also **gave his son Solomon the plans**.

b. **The plans for all that he had by the Spirit**: Even as with the organization of the temple servants (2 Chronicles 29:25), these practical details were inspired by the Holy Spirit, not by human ingenuity.

i. "Moreover, the temple was for God's own dwelling. Should not the Most High have a house after his own mind? If he was to be the Tenant, should it not be built to suit him? And who knows what God requires in a habitation but God himself?" (Spurgeon)

2. (14-19) The ornate furnishings for the temple.

***He gave* gold by weight for *things* of gold, for all articles used in every kind of service; also *silver* for all articles of silver by weight, for all articles used in every kind of service; the weight for the lampstands of gold, and their lamps of gold, by weight for each lampstand and its lamps; for the lampstands of silver by weight, for the lampstand and its lamps, according to the use of each lampstand. And by weight *he gave* gold for the tables of the showbread, for each table, and silver for the tables of silver; also pure gold for the forks, the basins, the pitchers of pure gold, and the golden bowls; *he gave gold* by weight for every bowl; and for the silver bowls, *silver* by weight for every bowl; and**

refined gold by weight for the altar of incense, and for the construction of the chariot, that is, the gold cherubim that spread *their wings* and overshadowed the ark of the covenant of the LORD. "All *this,*" said *David,* "the LORD made me understand in writing, by *His* hand upon me, all the works of these plans."

a. **He gave gold**: These six verses mention **gold** 11 times. David amassed an amazing amount of gold for the furnishings of the temple.

b. **For the construction of the chariot, that is, the gold cherubim**: "So called, because God sat between them (Psalm 99:1), rode upon them (Psalm 18:10); the angels – represented by those cherubims – are called the chariots of God (Psalm 68:17); and the Hebrews have a saying, that such as saw God of old saw only *Merchavah velo harocheb*, the chariot in which God rode, but not the rider in it." (Trapp)

i. "It is a good note also that is given here by some expositors – viz., that by this chariot of the cherubims God gave his people to understand that his presence in the ark was not so fixed among them, but that would leave them, and ride clean away from them, if they should thereunto provoke him by their sins." (Trapp)

c. **The LORD made me understand in writing, by His hand upon me, all the works of these plans**: As with the organization of the servants and builders of the temple and the plans for the temple, God also spoke to David about these furnishings of the temple.

3. (20-21) David's final charge to Solomon.

And David said to his son Solomon, "Be strong and of good courage, and do *it;* **do not fear nor be dismayed, for the LORD God; my God;** *will be* **with you. He will not leave you nor forsake you, until you have finished all the work for the service of the house of the LORD.** *"Here are* **the divisions of the priests and the Levites for all the service of the house of God; and every willing craftsman** *will be* **with you for all manner of workmanship, for every kind of service; also the leaders and all the people** *will be* **completely at your command."**

a. **Be strong and of good courage, and do it; do not fear nor be dismayed**: David here echoes God's exhortation to Joshua before he led the people of God into the Promised Land (Joshua 1:5-7). This was appropriate because Moses was a great leader who could only lead the people of Israel to a certain point – the rest was up to Joshua. The same pattern applied to David and his successor Solomon.

i. "In describing David's plans for building the temple, Chronicles has paid special attention to portray David as a second Moses and Solomon as a second Joshua." (Payne)

b. **And do it**: It is easy to see how important this was for David. He had spent enormous effort to prepare the temple, but all David's work would have been usless unless Solomon did in fact **do it**.

i. "Do not talk about it; do not sit down, and dream over the plans, and think how admirable they are, and then roll them up; but, 'Be strong and of good courage, and do it.'" (Spurgeon)

c. **Here are the divisions of the priests and the Levites**: We can picture David handing Solomon the scrolls with the plans for building the temple and organizing its service. The job was now in the hands of David's son Solomon.

1 Chronicles 29 – The End of David's Reign

A. David's offering for the temple.

1. (1-5) David's gifts to build the temple.

Furthermore King David said to all the assembly: "My son Solomon, whom alone God has chosen, *is* young and inexperienced; and the work *is* great, because the temple *is* not for man but for the LORD God. Now for the house of my God I have prepared with all my might: gold for *things to be made of* gold, silver for *things of* silver, bronze for *things of* bronze, iron for *things of* iron, wood for *things of* wood, onyx stones, *stones* to be set, glistening stones of various colors, all kinds of precious stones, and marble slabs in abundance. Moreover, because I have set my affection on the house of my God, I have given to the house of my God, over and above all that I have prepared for the holy house, my own special treasure of gold and silver: three thousand talents of gold, of the gold of Ophir, and seven thousand talents of refined silver, to overlay the walls of the houses; the gold for *things of* gold and the silver for *things of* silver, and for all kinds of work *to be done* by the hands of craftsmen. Who *then* is willing to consecrate himself this day to the LORD?"

   a. **The work is great, because the temple is not for man but for the LORD God**: One reason David did so much to prepare for the building of the temple was because he knew that the **work** was **great** and required great resources – more than a **young and inexperienced** king like Solomon could be expected to gather on his own.

      i. The **work** was **great** because it was for God. Before a great God there are no small works; everything should be done for the glory of God (Colossians 3:22).

b. **Now for the house of my God I have prepared with all my might**: This was certainly true. When we consider all that David did to provide security, a location, the land, money, materials, supervisory staff, workers, plans, and an organized team to run the temple, it is evident that David gave this work of preparation **all** of his **might**.

c. **Moreover, because I have set my affection on the house of my God, I have given to the house of my God**: David gave all he gave because he loved the house of God. We naturally give to and support that which we love. *For where your treasure is, there your heart will be also* (Matthew 6:21).

i. David specifically used the phrase **house of my God** to emphasize the personal connection; this was more personal than saying merely *the house of God*. Because God was David's God in a personal sense, David loved the **house of** God.

ii. **Over and above all that I have prepared for the holy house**: David loved the house of his God so much that he gave **over and above** what he gave before. David did an enormous amount of preparation and resource gathering to build the temple; but now he gave more, even giving **over and above**.

d. **Who then is willing to consecrate himself this day to the LORD?** David brought up *his* giving – especially the **over and above** giving – he used it as an occasion to challenge his fellow Israelites to also **consecrate** themselves to the LORD.

i. Given the massive amount that David gathered for the building of the temple, it might be argued that the gifts of the people were unnecessary. Yet David knew that it was important to give the people an opportunity to give, for *their sake* more than for the sake of the building project itself. Their giving was a legitimate and important way to **consecrate** themselves to God.

ii. "The king's appeal for each giver to 'consecrate himself' reads literally 'to fill his hand.' This was a technical phrase used to describe ordination to the priesthood; and Scripture, significantly, places the act of giving on this same level of devotion." (Payne)

2. (6-9) The giving of other Israelites.

Then the leaders of the fathers' *houses,* **leaders of the tribes of Israel, the captains of thousands and of hundreds, with the officers over the king's work, offered willingly. They gave for the work of the house of God five thousand talents and ten thousand darics of gold, ten thousand talents of silver, eighteen thousand talents of bronze, and one hundred thousand talents of iron. And whoever had** *precious* **stones gave** *them* to the treasury of the house of the LORD, into the hand of Jehiel the Gershonite. Then the people rejoiced, for they had offered willingly, because with a loyal heart they had offered willingly to the LORD; and King David also rejoiced greatly.

> a. **Then the leaders…offered willingly**: The people found it easy to give when they saw the greatness and the value of the project and when they had good examples of *over and above* giving like King David.

> b. **Then the people rejoiced, for they had offered willingly, because with a loyal heart they had offered willingly to the LORD**: The people found that it was a joyful thing to give so generously to God. They fulfilled the later New Testament idea of the cheerful giver (2 Corinthians 9:7).

B. David's Psalm blesses God before the people.

1. (10-12) David exalts the LORD.

Therefore David blessed the LORD before all the assembly; and David said:

"Blessed are You, LORD God of Israel, our Father, forever and ever.
Yours, O LORD, *is* the greatness,
The power and the glory,
The victory and the majesty;
For all *that is* in heaven and in earth *is Yours;*
Yours *is* the kingdom, O LORD,
And You are exalted as head over all.
Both riches and honor *come* from You,
And You reign over all.
In Your hand *is* power and might;
In Your hand *it is* to make great
And to give strength to all.

> a. **Therefore David blessed the LORD before all the assembly**: The generous giving made David rejoice and praise God. It wasn't for the sake of the wealth itself, but because it demonstrated that the hearts of the people were really interested in God and in His house.

> b. **Blessed are You, LORD God of Israel, our Father, forever and ever**: This is the first time in the Bible that God is addressed directly as a **Father** over His people.

>> i. Jesus taught His disciples to pray beginning with this phrase, **our Father** (Matthew 6:9-13). Jesus may have had this passage in mind when teaching His disciples about prayer because there are other similarities between the two passages.

ii. "This verse supplies the conclusion to the Lord's Prayer: 'For thine is the kingdom' (Matthew 6:13, KJV)." (Payne)

c. **Both riches and honor come from You**: David could say this as a man who had a life full of both **riches and honor**. David knew that those things came from God and not from himself.

2. (13-15) David expresses thanks for the privilege of giving

"**Now therefore, our God,**
We thank You
And praise Your glorious name.
But who *am* I, and who *are* my people,
That we should be able to offer so willingly as this?
For all things *come* from You,
And of Your own we have given You.
For we *are* aliens and pilgrims before You,
As *were* all our fathers;
Our days on earth *are* as a shadow,
And without hope.

a. **Who am I, and who are my people, that we should be able to offer so willingly as this?** David knew that both the *ability* and the *heart* to give were themselves gifts from God. He was actually humbled by having such a heart to give, both in himself and in the people of Israel as a group.

i. David knew this was true because he knew that **all things come from** God, and whatever they gave to God was His **own** to begin with.

ii. "That thou shouldst give us both such riches out of which we should be able to make such an offering, and such a willing and free heart to offer them; both of which are thy gifts, and the fruits of thy good grace and mercy to us." (Poole)

b. **Our days on earth are as a shadow, and without hope**: By emphasizing the weakness of man, David recognizes the greatness of God. He can take hopeless, alien pilgrims and shadows and use them to build a great house to a great God.

i. "A shadow seemeth to be something, when indeed it is nothing; so is man's life: and the longer this shadow seemeth to be, the nearer the sun is to setting." (Trapp)

3. (16-19) David commits the offering received from the people to God.

"**O Lord our God, all this abundance that we have prepared to build You a house for Your holy name is from Your hand, and *is* all Your own. I know also, my God, that You test the heart and have pleasure in** uprightness. As for me, in the uprightness of my heart I have willingly offered all these *things;* and now with joy I have seen Your people, who are present here to offer willingly to You. O LORD God of Abraham, Isaac, and Israel, our fathers, keep this forever in the intent of the thoughts of the heart of Your people, and fix their heart toward You. And give my son Solomon a loyal heart to keep Your commandments and Your testimonies and Your statutes, to do all *these things,* and to build the temple for which I have made provision."

> a. **In the uprightness of my heart I have willingly offered all these things**: David knew that it was important to emphasize that his offering had been made **willingly**. He gave because he wanted to, not merely as a demonstration to induce the people to give. David therefore also knew that the **people** made their offering **willingly** to God.
>
> b. **Keep this forever in the intent of the thoughts of the heart of Your people, and fix their heart toward You**: David knew that the people of Israel were in a godly, wonderful place on this day of offering to the temple.
>
>> i. "Praise then merged into prayer that the state of mind in which they had given might be maintained; and for Solomon, that he might be kept with a perfect heart to complete the work of Temple building. It was a fitting and glorious ending to a great reign." (Morgan)
>
> c. **And give my son Solomon a loyal heart to keep Your commandments**: David knew that this was the key to the lasting health of the kingdom of Israel and the security of his dynasty.

4. (20) David leads the congregation in praise to God.

Then David said to all the assembly, "Now bless the LORD your God." So all the assembly blessed the LORD God of their fathers, and bowed their heads and prostrated themselves before the LORD and the king.

> a. **Now bless the LORD your God**: When it came time to **bless the LORD**, it wasn't enough for the people to have a feeling in their heart. They had to *do* something to demonstrate their heart towards God, and they **bowed their heads and prostrated themselves before the LORD**.

C. The end of David's reign.

1. (21-25) The nation rejoices as Solomon is enthroned.

And they made sacrifices to the LORD and offered burnt offerings to the LORD on the next day: a thousand bulls, a thousand rams, a thousand lambs, with their drink offerings, and sacrifices in abundance for all Israel. So they ate and drank before the LORD with great gladness on that day. And they made Solomon the son of David king the second time, and

anointed *him* before the LORD *to be* the leader, and Zadok *to be* priest. Then Solomon sat on the throne of the LORD as king instead of David his father, and prospered; and all Israel obeyed him. All the leaders and the mighty men, and also all the sons of King David, submitted themselves to King Solomon. So the LORD exalted Solomon exceedingly in the sight of all Israel, and bestowed on him *such* royal majesty as had not been on any king before him in Israel.

> a. **A thousand bulls, a thousand rams, a thousand lambs, with their drink offerings, and sacrifices in abundance**: This was a special day, probably celebrated *after* the death of David when Solomon formally took the throne. These sacrifices were used to feed the people of Israel, and **they ate and drank before the LORD** in a great feast of communion with God and one another.
>
> b. **They made Solomon the son of David king the second time**: This was undoubtedly the enthronement after the rebellion of Adonijah had been defeated (1 Kings 1-2).
>
>> i. "For the first time (1 Kings 1:38-39) it was done hastily, suddenly, and in [an irregular manner], by reason of Adonijah's sedition; but this here was done with good respite and great solemnity, but whether before or after David's death is questionable." (Trapp)
>>
>> ii. **Submitted themselves to King Solomon**: "After Adonijah's death they all submitted themselves to Solomon the king. Hebrew, Gave the hand under Solomon the king; haply they laid their hand under his thigh – that ancient ceremony (Genesis 24:2, and 47:29), and sware to be faithful to him." (Trapp)
>
> c. **Then Solomon sat on the throne of the LORD as king**: "*On the throne of the Lord*, i.e. on the throne of Israel, which is called *the throne of the Lord*, either more generally, as all thrones are the Lord's, *by whom kings reign*, Proverbs 8:15, and magistrates are ordained, Romans 13:1-2…signifies *which the Lord gave him.*" (Poole)
>
> d. **And bestowed on him such royal majesty as had not been on any king before him in Israel**: This was true, but the wise reader understands that this was only because David had made this possible. The majesty of Solomon was really inherited from the work and wisdom and godliness and prayers of his father.

2. (26-30) The end of King David's reign.

Thus David the son of Jesse reigned over all Israel. And the period that he reigned over Israel *was* forty years; seven years he reigned in Hebron, and thirty-three *years* he reigned in Jerusalem. So he died in

a good old age, full of days and riches and honor; and Solomon his son reigned in his place. Now the acts of King David, first and last, indeed they *are* written in the book of Samuel the seer, in the book of Nathan the prophet, and in the book of Gad the seer, with all his reign and his might, and the events that happened to him, to Israel, and to all the kingdoms of the lands.

a. **The period that he reigned over Israel was forty years**: Other kings over Israel or Judah had reigns longer, more secure, or more prosperous than David's reign – but none were more glorious or godly. David remains Israel's model king, pointing us to Jesus the Messiah, Israel's greatest king.

b. **So he died in a good old age, full of days and riches and honor**: David was a great king and his greatness is especially seen in his connection with the Messiah. One of the great titles of Jesus is, *Son of David*.

i. "Albeit he swam to the throne through a sea of sorrows; and so must all saints to the kingdom of heaven." (Trapp)

ii. "By birth, a *peasant*; by merit, a *prince*; in youth, a *hero*; in manhood, a *monarch*; and in age, a *saint*. The matter of Uriah and Bath-sheba is his great but only *blot!* There he sinned deeply; and no man ever suffered more in his body, soul, and domestic affairs, than he did in consequence. His penitence was as deep and as extraordinary as his crime; and nothing could surpass both but that eternal mercy that took away the guilt, assuaged the sorrow, and restored this most humbled transgressor to character, holiness, and happiness. Let the God of David be exalted forever!" (Clarke)

2 Chronicles 1 – Solomon Seeks God

A. Solomon meets God at Gibeon.

1. (1-4) Solomon brings the leaders of Israel to the tabernacle at Gibeon.

Now Solomon the son of David was strengthened in his kingdom, and the LORD his God *was* with him and exalted him exceedingly. And Solomon spoke to all Israel, to the captains of thousands and of hundreds, to the judges, and to every leader in all Israel, the heads of the fathers' *houses*. **Then Solomon, and all the assembly with him, went to the high place that** *was* **at Gibeon; for the tabernacle of meeting with God was there, which Moses the servant of the LORD had made in the wilderness. But David had brought up the ark of God from Kirjath Jearim to** *the place* **David had prepared for it, for he had pitched a tent for it at Jerusalem.**

a. **Now Solomon the son of David was strengthened in his kingdom, and the LORD his God was with him**: Solomon made a great start to his reign as king, and God blessed it. His father David left him with almost every possible advantage and his kingdom was strong.

b. **Then Solomon…went to the high place that was at Gibeon**: Solomon made these special sacrifices at **Gibeon** because **the tabernacle of meeting with God was there**. Though the ark of the covenant had been brought to Jerusalem (**the place David had prepared for it**), the tabernacle itself stayed at Gibeon.

i. Morgan on the phrase, **tabernacle of meeting**: "That is, it was the place where the people met with God. That is always the idea; not the meeting of the people with each other, but their meeting with God."

ii. We can track the progress of the tabernacle and the ark of the covenant in the Promised Land:

- Joshua brought both the ark and the tabernacle to Shiloh (Joshua 18).

- In the days of Eli the ark was captured and the tabernacle wrecked (1 Samuel 4, Psalm 78:60-64, Jeremiah 7:12 and 26:9).
- The ark came back to Kirjath Jearim (1 Samuel 7:1-2).
- Saul restored the tabernacle at Nob (1 Samuel 21).
- Saul moved the tabernacle to Gibeon (1 Chronicles 16:39-40).
- David brought the ark to Jerusalem and built a temporary tent for it (2 Samuel 6:17, 2 Chronicles 1:4).

iii. There are several reasons that could explain why David did not bring the tabernacle from Gibeon to Jerusalem.

- He may have believed if the tabernacle was there the people would be satisfied with that, and they would lose the passion and vision for the temple God wanted built.
- It may be that the tabernacle was only moved when it was absolutely necessary – as when disaster came upon it at Shiloh or Nob.
- It may be that David was simply focused on building the temple, not continuing the tabernacle.

2. (5-6) Solomon and the assembly seek God together.

Now the bronze altar that Bezalel the son of Uri, the son of Hur, had made, he put before the tabernacle of the LORD; Solomon and the assembly sought Him *there*. And Solomon went up there to the bronze altar before the LORD, which *was* at the tabernacle of meeting, and offered a thousand burnt offerings on it.

a. **Now the bronze altar that Bezalel the son of Uri, the son of Hur, had made, he put before the tabernacle of the LORD**: This was the same altar made in the wilderness between Egypt and the Promised Land (Exodus 38:1-2). This altar was at least 500 years old and had received many sacrifices over Israel's long history since the Exodus.

b. **Solomon and the assembly sought Him there**: Solomon and the people of God **sought** the LORD *at the place of atoning sacrifice*. This was the Old Testament equivalent to "coming to the cross" in seeking God.

i. This was an important event marking the "ceremonial" beginning of Solomon's reign. Solomon wanted to demonstrate from the beginning that he would seek God and lead the kingdom to do so.

c. **And offered a thousand burnt offerings**: This almost grotesque amount of sacrifice demonstrated both Solomon's great wealth and his heart to use it to glorify God.

3. (7-10) Solomon's request.

On that night God appeared to Solomon, and said to him, "Ask! What shall I give you?" And Solomon said to God: "You have shown great mercy to David my father, and have made me king in his place. Now, O LORD God, let Your promise to David my father be established, for You have made me king over a people like the dust of the earth in multitude. Now give me wisdom and knowledge, that I may go out and come in before this people; for who can judge this great people of Yours?"

a. **God appeared to Solomon**: 1 Kings 3:5 tells us that this remarkable visitation from God happened *in a dream*. This is one of the more significant dreams in the Bible.

i. "It is interesting to note that notwithstanding the fact that the ark was not there, God met with Solomon and communed with him." (Morgan) Here God made it clear that His presence was not to be superstitiously restricted to an association with the ark of the covenant.

b. **Ask! What shall I give you?** This was an amazing promise. God seemed to offer Solomon whatever he wanted. This wasn't only because Solomon sacrificed 1,000 animals. It was because his heart was surrendered to God, and God wanted to work something in Solomon through this offer and his response.

i. The natural reaction to reading this promise of God to Solomon is to wish we had such promises. We do have them.

- *Ask, and it will be given to you; seek, and you will find; knock, and it will be opened to you* (Matthew 7:7).
- *If you abide in Me, and My words abide in you, you will ask what you desire, and it shall be done for you* (John 15:7).
- *Now this is the confidence that we have in Him, that if we ask anything according to His will, He hears us* (1 John 5:14).

ii. "The problem for many Christians, then, is not whether they will receive anything when they ask, but whether they will ask at all." (Selman)

c. **You have shown great mercy**: Before responding to God's offer and asking for something, Solomon remembered God's faithfulness to both David and now to himself.

d. **Now give me wisdom and knowledge**: Solomon asked for more than great **knowledge**; he wanted **wisdom**, and according to 1 Kings 3, he wanted it in his **heart**, not merely in his *head*.

e. **That I may go out and come in before this people**: This was a Hebrew expression that meant, "That I may fulfill my duties before this people." Solomon asked for the **knowledge** and **wisdom** necessary to be a good king.

> i. "Such words referred originally to military leadership (1 Chronicles 11:2; cf. 1 Samuel 18:13) but are here broadened into representing good governmental administratorship in general." (Payne)

B. God answers Solomon's request.

1. (11-12) Solomon receives wisdom and blessings from God.

Then God said to Solomon: "Because this was in your heart, and you have not asked riches or wealth or honor or the life of your enemies, nor have you asked long life; but have asked wisdom and knowledge for yourself, that you may judge My people over whom I have made you king; wisdom and knowledge *are* granted to you; and I will give you riches and wealth and honor, such as none of the kings have had who *were* before you, nor shall any after you have the like."

> a. **Because this was in your heart**: God was pleased by what Solomon *asked for*, in that he knew his great need for **knowledge** and **wisdom**. God was also pleased by what Solomon *did not ask for*, in that he did not ask for riches or fame or power for himself.
>
> i. Solomon's request was *not* bad. We are specifically told in 1 Kings 3:10 that *the speech pleased the LORD*. Yet we can also ask if this was *the best* Solomon could ask for. "Was this the highest gift that he could have asked or received? Surely the deep longings of his father for communion with God were yet better." (Maclaren)
>
> ii. Solomon did his job well – as well or better than anyone. Yet as his falling away in the end showed (1 Kings 11:1-11) there was something lacking in his spiritual life. "There is no sign in his biography that he ever had the deep inward devotion of his father. After the poet-psalmist came the prosaic and keen-sighted shrewd man of affairs." (Maclaren)
>
> b. **Wisdom and knowledge are granted to you; and I will give you riches and wealth and honor**: God not only answered Solomon's prayer, He answered it beyond all expectation. Solomon did not ask for **riches and wealth and honor**, but God gave him those also.
>
> i. "God's answer was a beautiful instance of the overflowing love and grace of the divine heart. All the things Solomon set aside for the sake of wisdom were also given to him." (Morgan)

ii. Appearing in his dream, God answered Solomon's prayer and made him wise, powerful, rich, and influential. His reign was glorious for Israel. At the same time, his end was tragic. We can fairly say that Solomon *wasted* these gifts God gave him. Though he accomplished much, he could have done much more – and his heart was led away from God in the end (1 Kings 11:4-11).

iii. "Instead of being the *wisest* of men, did he not become more *brutish* than any man? Did he not even lose the *knowledge of his Creator*, and worship the abominations of the Moabites, Zidonians, and [so forth]? And was not such idolatry a proof of the *grossest stupidity*? How few proofs does his life give that the gracious purpose of God was fulfilled in him! He received *much*; but he would have received *much more*, had he been faithful to the grace given. No character in the sacred writings disappoints us more than the character of Solomon." (Clarke, commenting in 1 Kings)

2. (13-17) The great wealth of King Solomon.

So Solomon came to Jerusalem from the high place that *was* at Gibeon, from before the tabernacle of meeting, and reigned over Israel. And Solomon gathered chariots and horsemen; he had one thousand four hundred chariots and twelve thousand horsemen, whom he stationed in the chariot cities and with the king in Jerusalem. Also the king made silver and gold as common in Jerusalem as stones, and he made cedars as abundant as the sycamores which *are* in the lowland. And Solomon had horses imported from Egypt and Keveh; the king's merchants bought them in Keveh at the *current* price. They also acquired and imported from Egypt a chariot for six hundred *shekels* of silver, and a horse for one hundred and fifty; thus, through their agents, they exported them to all the kings of the Hittites and the kings of Syria.

a. **So Solomon came to Jerusalem…and reigned over Israel**: Solomon actually reigned – or began his reign – in the great wisdom God gave him at Gibeon. A famous example of this wisdom is found in 1 Kings 3:16-28, where he wisely judged between two mothers who each claimed the same baby as their own.

b. **And Solomon gathered chariots and horsemen**: The famous stables of Solomon show what a vast cavalry he assembled for Israel. Unfortunately, it also shows that Solomon did not take God's word as seriously as he should. In Deuteronomy 17:16, God spoke specifically to the future kings of Israel: *But he shall not multiply horses for himself.*

c. **The king made silver and gold as common in Jerusalem as stones**: When we think of Solomon's great wealth, we also consider that he originally did not set his heart upon riches. He deliberately asked for wisdom to lead the people of God *instead* of riches or fame. God promised to *also* give Solomon riches and fame, and God fulfilled His promise.

i. We also consider that Solomon gave an eloquent testimony to the vanity of riches as the preacher in the Book of Ecclesiastes. He powerfully showed that there was no ultimate satisfaction through materialism. We don't have to be as rich as Solomon to learn the same lesson.

ii. Certainly, Solomon presided over a prosperous and wealthy kingdom. Yet the Chronicler is also warning us here. He assumes that we know of the instructions for future kings of Israel in Deuteronomy 17:14-20. He assumes we know verse 17 of that passage, which says: *nor shall he greatly multiply silver and gold for himself.* God blessed Solomon with great riches, but Solomon allowed that blessing to turn into a danger because he disobediently multiplied silver and gold for himself.

iii. "There was nothing wrong in all this, but it created a very subtle peril. Prosperity is always a more insidious danger to men of faith than adversity." (Morgan)

d. **Solomon had horses imported from Egypt and Keveh**: At the end of this great description of Solomon's wealth and splendor, we have the sound of this dark note. This was in direct disobedience to Deuteronomy 17:16, which said to the kings of Israel: *But he shall not multiply horses for himself, nor cause the people to return to Egypt to multiply horses, for the LORD has said to you, "You shall not return that way again."*

i. **Keveh** (also known as Cilicia) was "in what is now southern Turkey, at the east end of the Mediterranean…a prime ancient supplier of horses." (Payne)

e. **Thus, through their agents, they exported them to all the kings of the Hittites and the kings of Syria**: This may explain why Solomon broke such an obvious commandment. Perhaps the importation of horses from Egypt began as trading as an agent on behalf of other kings. From this, perhaps Solomon could say, "I'm importing horses from Egypt but I am not doing it for myself. I'm not breaking God's command." Many examples of gross disobedience begin as clever rationalizations.

i. It is hard to know in what order Solomon's compromise was expressed. Yet it is possible to say that this disobedience to this seemingly small command began the downfall of Solomon.

- *First*, in disobedience he multiplied horses for the service of his kingdom and he obtained them from the Egyptians (1 Kings 4:26, 10:28-29).
- *Then*, because of these connections with Egypt he married Pharaoh's daughter (1 Kings 3:1).
- *Then*, because he started by marrying an Egyptian he married many other foreign women (1 Kings 11:1-4).
- *Then*, because of the presence of the foreign wives he built temples to their gods for their use (1 Kings 11:7-8).
- *Then*, because of the presence of these temples he began to worship these other gods himself (1 Kings 11:4-5).

2 Chronicles 2 – Supplies and Workers for the Temple

A. An overview of the work of building the temple.

1. (1) Solomon's determination to build the temple.

Then Solomon determined to build a temple for the name of the LORD, and a royal house for himself.

> a. **Then Solomon determined to build a temple**: His determination was fitting because of all that his father David did to prepare for the building and because of the charge David gave him to do the work.
>
>> i. We might think that the greatest thing about Solomon was his wisdom, his riches, his proverbs or his writings. Clearly, for the Chronicler the most important thing about Solomon was the temple he built. This was most important because it was most relevant to a community of returning exiles who struggled to build a new temple and to make a place for Israel among the nations again.
>>
>> ii. "Chronicles' record of Solomon's achievements moves straight away to the construction of the temple. Several important items in the account of his reign in Kings are left out as a result, such as his wisdom in action, administration, educational reforms, and some building activities (*e.g.* 1 Kings 3:16-4:34; 7:1-12). These were not unimportant, but, for Chronicles, they were all subsidiary to the temple." (Selman)
>
> b. **And a royal house for himself**: Solomon's great building works did not end with the temple. He also built a spectacular palace (1 Kings 7:1-12) and more.

2. (2) The magnitude of the work

Solomon selected seventy thousand men to bear burdens, eighty thousand to quarry *stone* in the mountains, and three thousand six hundred to oversee them.

> a. **Seventy thousand men to bear burdens, eighty thousand to quarry stone**: This seems to describe the number of Canaanite slave laborers that Solomon used.
>
>> i. Ginzberg relates some of the legends surrounding the building of the temple. "During the seven years it took to build the Temple, not a single workman died who was employed about it, nor even did a single one fall sick. And as the workmen were sound and robust from first to last, so the perfection of their tools remained unimpaired until the building stood complete. Thus the work suffered no sort of interruption." (Ginzberg)
>
> b. **And three thousand six hundred to oversee them**: This was the middle management team administrating the work of building the temple.
>
>> i. "The number of *thirty-six hundred* foremen differs from 1 Kings 5:16 (3,300), but the LXX of Kings is quite insecure here, and Chronicles may preserve the better reading." (Selman)

B. Solomon's correspondence with Hiram king of Tyre.

1. (3-6) Solomon describes the work to Hiram.

Then Solomon sent to Hiram king of Tyre, saying: As you have dealt with David my father, and sent him cedars to build himself a house to dwell in, *so deal with me*. Behold, I am building a temple for the name of the LORD my God, to dedicate *it* to Him, to burn before Him sweet incense, for the continual showbread, for the burnt offerings morning and evening, on the Sabbaths, on the New Moons, and on the set feasts of the LORD our God. This *is an ordinance* forever to Israel. And the temple which I build *will be* great, for our God is greater than all gods. But who is able to build Him a temple, since heaven and the heaven of heavens cannot contain Him? Who *am* I then, that I should build Him a temple, except to burn sacrifice before Him?

> a. **Solomon sent to Hiram king of Tyre, saying: As you have dealt with David my father**: Solomon appealed to Hiram based on his prior good relationship with his father David. This shows us that David did not regard every neighboring nation as an enemy. David wisely built alliances and friendships with neighboring nations, and the benefit of this also came to Solomon.

i. "Hiram is an abbreviation of Ahiram which means 'Brother of Ram,' or 'My brother is exalted,' or 'Brother of the lofty one'.... Archaeologists have discovered a royal sarcophagus in Byblos of Tyre dated about 1200 B.C. inscribed with the king's name, 'Ahiram.' Apparently it belonged to the man in this passage." (Dilday, commentary on 1 Kings)

b. **Then Solomon sent to Hiram**: "According to Josephus, copies of such a letter along with Hiram's reply were preserved in both Hebrew and Tyrian archives and were extant in his day (*Antiquities*, 8.2.8)." (Dilday)

c. **I am building a temple for the name of the LORD my God**: Of course, Solomon did not build a temple for a **name** but for a living God. This is a good example of avoiding the direct mention of the name of God in Hebrew writing and speaking. They did this out of reverence to God.

i. Solomon also used this phrase because he wanted to explain that he didn't think the temple would be the house of God in the way pagans thought. This is especially shown in his words, **who is able to build Him a temple, since heaven and the heaven of heavens cannot contain Him?** By the standards of the paganism of his day, Solomon's conception of God was both Biblical and high.

ii. "He never conceived it as a place to which God would be confined. He did expect, and he received, manifestations of the Presence of God in that house. Its chief value was that it afforded man a place in which he should offer incense; that is, the symbol of adoration, praise, worship, to God." (Morgan)

iii. God is, "good without quality, great without quantity, everlasting without time, present everywhere without place, containing all without extent...he is within all things, and contained of nothing: without all things, and sustained of nothing." (Trapp)

2. (7-10) Solomon's request to Hiram.

Therefore send me at once a man skillful to work in gold and silver, in bronze and iron, in purple and crimson and blue, who has skill to engrave with the skillful men who are with me in Judah and Jerusalem, whom David my father provided. Also send me cedar and cypress and algum logs from Lebanon, for I know that your servants have skill to cut timber in Lebanon; and indeed my servants *will be* with your servants, to prepare timber for me in abundance, for the temple which I am about to build *shall be* great and wonderful. And indeed I will give to your servants, the woodsmen who cut timber, twenty thousand kors of ground wheat, twenty thousand kors of barley, twenty thousand baths of wine, and twenty thousand baths of oil.

a. **Therefore send me at once a man skillful to work in gold and silver**: Solomon wanted the temple to be the best it could be, so he used Gentile labor when it was better. This means that Solomon was willing to build this great temple to God with "Gentile" wood and using "Gentile" labor. This was a temple to the God of Israel, but it was not only for Israel.

   i. "The leading craftsmen for the Tent, Bezalel and his assistant Oholiab, were both similarly skilled in a range of abilities (*cf.* Exodus 31:1-6; 35:30-36:2)." (Selman)

   ii. "Despite a growing number of 'skilled craftsmen' in Israel, their techniques remained inferior to those of their northern neighbors, as is demonstrated archaeologically by less finely cut building stones and by the lower level of Israelite culture in general." (Payne)

b. **To prepare timber for me in abundance**: The cedar trees of Lebanon were legendary for their excellent timber. This means Solomon wanted to build the temple out of the best materials possible.

   i. "The Sidonians were noted as timber craftsmen in the ancient world, a fact substantiated on the famous Palmero Stone. Its inscription from 2200 B.C. tells us about timber-carrying ships that sailed from Byblos to Egypt about four hundred years previously. The skill of the Sidonians was expressed in their ability to pick the most suitable trees, know the right time to cut them, fell them with care, and then properly treat the logs." (Dilday)

3. (11-16) Hiram's response to Solomon.

Then Hiram king of Tyre answered in writing, which he sent to Solomon: Because the LORD loves His people, He has made you king over them. Hiram also said: Blessed *be* the LORD God of Israel, who made heaven and earth, for He has given King David a wise son, endowed with prudence and understanding, who will build a temple for the LORD and a royal house for himself! And now I have sent a skillful man, endowed with understanding, Huram my master *craftsman* (the son of a woman of the daughters of Dan, and his father was a man of Tyre), skilled to work in gold and silver, bronze and iron, stone and wood, purple and blue, fine linen and crimson, and to make any engraving and to accomplish any plan which may be given to him, with your skillful men and with the skillful men of my lord David your father. Now therefore, the wheat, the barley, the oil, and the wine which my lord has spoken of, let him send to his servants. And we will cut wood from Lebanon, as much as you need; we will bring it to you in rafts by sea to Joppa, and you will carry it up to Jerusalem.

a. **Then Hiram king of Tyre answered in writing**: "We find…that kings could *write* and *read* in what were called by the proud and insolent *Greeks* and *Romans* barbarous nations. Nearly *two thousand* years after this we find a king on the British throne who could not sign his own name." (Clarke)

b. **Blessed be the Lord God of Israel**: We can't say if Hiram was a saved man, but he certainly respected the God of Israel. This was no doubt due to David's godly influence on Hiram.

c. **I have sent a skillful man, endowed with understanding, Huram my master craftsman**: King Hiram answered Solomon's request for a **skillful man** (2 Chronicles 2:7). **Huram** had a Jewish mother and a Gentile father.

d. **The wheat, the barley, the oil, and the wine which my lord has spoken of, let him send to his servants**: Hiram agreed to work for the arrangement suggested by Solomon, though he could have asked for more (1 Kings 5:6).

> i. This shows us that Hiram did expect to be paid. His service and the service of his people were not a gift or a sacrifice. "There are a good many people who get mixed up with religious work, and talk as if it were very near their hearts, who have as sharp an eye to their own advantage as he had. The man who serves God because he gets paid for it, does not serve Him." (Maclaren)

4. (17-18) The laborers who built the temple.

Then Solomon numbered all the aliens who *were* in the land of Israel, after the census in which David his father had numbered them; and there were found to be one hundred and fifty-three thousand six hundred. And he made seventy thousand of them bearers of burdens, eighty thousand stonecutters in the mountain, and three thousand six hundred overseers to make the people work.

a. **All the aliens who were in the land of Israel**: This specifically tells us where the **seventy thousand** man labor force described here and in 2 Chronicles 2:2 came from.

> i. "The temple, then, did not become a house of prayer for all nations by accident. The nations even played a part in its construction!" (Selman)

2 Chronicles 3 – The Building of the Temple

A. Where and when the temple construction began.

1. (1) The location of the temple.

Now Solomon began to build the house of the LORD at Jerusalem on Mount Moriah, where *the Lord* had appeared to his father David, at the place that David had prepared on the threshing floor of Ornan the Jebusite.

> a. **Now Solomon began to build the house of the LORD at Jerusalem on Mount Moriah**: This place had been previously identified as the **threshing floor of Ornan the Jebusite**. Here it is specifically located as **Mount Moriah**. This was the same hill where Abraham offered Isaac (Genesis 22:2), and the same set of hills where Jesus would later die on the cross (Genesis 22:14).
>
>> i. "Where Isaac, as a type of Christ, bore the wood, obeyed his father, and should have been sacrificed. Calvary, where our Saviour suffered, was either a part of this mount, or very near unto it." (Trapp)
>
> b. **Began to build the house of the LORD**: This was when the actual construction began. All David's prior plans and preparations anticipated the actual beginning of the work. One can plan and prepare endlessly and never begin to build, but Solomon **began to build the house of the LORD**.

2. (2) When the construction began.

And he began to build on the second *day* of the second month in the fourth year of his reign.

> a. **On the second day of the second month in the fourth year of his reign**: This was probably in the year 967 B.C. Connecting this with 1 Kings 6:1, this marking point shows just how long Israel lived in the Promised Land without a temple. The tabernacle served the nation well for more than

400 years. The prompting to build the temple was more at the direction and will of God than out of absolute necessity.

b. **In the fourth year of his reign**: This doesn't mean that Solomon delayed his obedience for four years. He probably started to organize the work right away. There is some evidence that it took three years to prepare timber from Lebanon for use in building. If Solomon began the construction of the temple in the **fourth year** of his reign, he probably started organizing the construction in the very first year of his reign.

B. A Description of the temple.

1. (3-7) The building in general.

This is the foundation which Solomon laid for building the house of God: The length *was* **sixty cubits (by cubits according to the former measure) and the width twenty cubits. And the vestibule that** *was* **in front** *of the sanctuary* **was twenty cubits long across the width of the house, and the height** *was* **one hundred and twenty. He overlaid the inside with pure gold. The larger room he paneled with cypress which he overlaid with fine gold, and he carved palm trees and chainwork on it. And he decorated the house with precious stones for beauty, and the gold** *was* **gold from Parvaim. He also overlaid the house; the beams and doorposts, its walls and doors; with gold; and he carved cherubim on the walls.**

a. **For building the house of God**: This chapter will describe the building of the temple and its associated areas. There are four main structures described.

- The temple proper (**the foundation which Solomon laid**), divided into two rooms (the holy place and the Most Holy Place).

- The vestibule or entrance hall on the east side of the temple proper (**the vestibule that was in front of the sanctuary**). It was thirty feet (10 meters) wide and fifteen feet (5 meters) deep, and the same height as the temple proper. "Its height measurement should read *twenty cubits high* (NIV, REB, NEB), as against a literal translation of MT, 'and its height 120'." (Selman)

- The three-storied side chambers (described in 1 Kings 6:5) which surrounded the temple proper on the north, south, and west sides.

- A large courtyard surrounding the whole structure (the *inner court* mentioned in 1 Kings 6:36).

b. **He decorated the house with precious stones for beauty**: This is one description among many that give us an idea of how beautiful the temple was and how Solomon spared no expense in making it beautiful.

> i. "The reference to 'precious stones' may suggest mosaics, inlaid in the floor." (Payne)

c. **He carved cherubim on the walls**: This was after the pattern of the tabernacle, which had woven designs of cherubim on the inner covering. Therefore when one entered the temple they saw **cherubim** all around – as one would see in heaven (Psalm 80:1, Isaiah 37:16, and Ezekiel 10:3). These angelic beings worship God perpetually in heaven.

> i. One might say that we don't worship angels but we do worship *with* them.

2. (8-14) The **Most Holy Place**.

And he made the Most Holy Place. Its length was according to the width of the house, twenty cubits, and its width twenty cubits. He overlaid it with six hundred talents of fine gold. The weight of the nails *was* fifty shekels of gold; and he overlaid the upper area with gold. In the Most Holy Place he made two cherubim, fashioned by carving, and overlaid them with gold. The wings of the cherubim *were* twenty cubits in *overall* length: one wing *of the one cherub was* five cubits, touching the wall of the room, and the other wing *was* five cubits, touching the wing of the other cherub; *one* wing of the other cherub *was* five cubits, touching the wall of the room, and the other wing *also was* five cubits, touching the wing of the other cherub. The wings of these cherubim spanned twenty cubits overall. They stood on their feet, and they faced inward. And he made the veil of blue, purple, crimson, and fine linen, and wove cherubim into it.

> a. **And he made the Most Holy Place**: Special attention was given to the Holy of Holies or **Most Holy Place**. It was a 30-foot (10 meter) cube, completely overlaid with gold. It also had two large sculptures of cherubim (15-foot or 5 meters in height), which were overlaid with gold.
>
> b. **He overlaid it with six hundred talents of fine gold**: There was gold everywhere in the temple, but especially in the **Most Holy Place**. The walls were covered with gold (1 Kings 6:20-22), the floor was covered with gold (1 Kings 6:30) and gold was hammered into the carvings on the doors (1 Kings 6:32).
>
> > i. There was gold everywhere on the inside of the temple. "Such was Christ's inside (Colossians 2:9); in his outside was no such desirable

beauty (Isaiah 53:2); so the Church's glory is inward (Psalm 45:13), in the hidden man of the heart (1 Peter 3:4)." (Trapp)

c. **Two cherubim, fashioned by carving, and overlaid them with gold**: These two large sculptures inside the Most Holy Place faced the entrance to this inner room, so as soon as the High Priest entered he saw these giant guardians of the presence of God facing him.

i. "If it were image work – cherubims were made like boys – yet this is no plea for Popish images; since they are flatly forbidden; and God made the law for us, not for himself." (Trapp)

d. **And he made the veil**: This was the important barrier separating the holy place from the **Most Holy Place**. Only one man, once a year, could go behind the veil and enter the **Most Holy Place**.

i. "To most Israelites, therefore, the temple was an unseen world. God had drawn near to them, but the way to him was hedged around with many restrictions." (Selman)

ii. Spiritually speaking, in dying for our sins Jesus *with His own blood…entered the Most Holy Place once for all, having obtained eternal redemption* (Hebrews 9:12).

iii. In the temple, this veil was torn from top to bottom at the death of Jesus (Matthew 27:51), showing that through His death, there is no longer a barrier to the Most Holy place.

iv. Now the Most Holy Place is open to us: *brethren, having boldness to enter the Holiest by the blood of Jesus, by a new and living way which He consecrated for us, through the veil, that is, His flesh* (Hebrews 10:19-20). The torn veil of Matthew 27:51 also symbolizes the broken body of Jesus, through which we have access to the Most Holy Place.

3. (15-17) The pillars of the temple.

Also he made in front of the temple two pillars thirty-five cubits high, and the capital that *was* on the top of each of *them* was five cubits. He made wreaths of chainwork, as in the inner sanctuary, and put *them* on top of the pillars; and he made one hundred pomegranates, and put *them* on the wreaths of chainwork. Then he set up the pillars before the temple, one on the right hand and the other on the left; he called the name of the one on the right hand Jachin, and the name of the one on the left Boaz.

a. **In front of the temple two pillars thirty-five cubits high**: 1 Kings 7:15 tells us that these pillars were actually made of bronze. They were two very impressive adornments to the **front of the temple**.

b. **He called the name of the one on the right hand Jachin, and the name of the one on the left Boaz**: These two pillars were so impressive that they were actually given names. **Jachin** means *He shall establish* and **Boaz** means *in strength*.

> i. Every time someone came to the house of the LORD in the days of Solomon they said, "Look! There is 'He Shall Establish.' And there is 'In Him Is Strength.'" It set them in the right frame of mind to worship the LORD. When the crowds gathered at the morning and evening sacrifice to worship the LORD, the Levites led the people standing in front of the temple with these two great, bronze pillars behind them. It was always before them: *He Shall Establish* and *In Him Is Strength*.
>
> ii. One could say that the house of God itself was **Jachin** and **Boaz**. That temple was *established* by God, and built by the *strength* of God. Every time they looked at that temple, they knew that God liked to establish and strengthen things.
>
> iii. The house of God was a place where people experienced what the pillars were all about. At that house, people were *established* in their relationship with God. At that house, people were given *strength* from the LORD. From this building, it should go out to the whole community: "Come here and get *established*. Come here and receive the *strength* of God."

2 Chronicles 4 – Furnishings for the Temple and Its Court

A. The furnishings of the temple.

1. (1) The bronze altar.

Moreover he made a bronze altar: twenty cubits was its length, twenty cubits its width, and ten cubits its height.

> a. **He made a bronze altar**: The idea behind the Hebrew word for **altar** is essentially, "killing-place." This was the place of sacrifice, the center for worship and service for the priests and the people.
>
>> i. "Just as in the tabernacle, the altar was the first main object to be met as one entered the sanctuary court. It demonstrates that God may be approached only through sacrifices." (Payne)
>>
>> ii. We also have an altar: *We have an altar from which those who serve the tabernacle have no right to eat* (Hebrews 13:10). Our altar – our "killing-place" – is the cross, where Jesus died for our sins and we follow by dying to self and living for Jesus.
>
> b. **Twenty cubits**: Essentially, this altar was large (about 30 feet or 10 meters square) and about twice as large as the altar originally built for the tabernacle (Exodus 27:1-2).
>
> c. **Ten cubits its height**: The altar was raised significantly. The altar was set up high, "That all the people might see the burnt-offerings, and be reminded of their sins and of their Saviour; for the ceremonial law was their gospel." (Trapp)

2. (2-6) The washing basins for the temple.

Then he made the Sea of cast *bronze,* ten cubits from one brim to the other; *it was* completely round. Its height *was* five cubits, and a line of thirty cubits measured its circumference. And under it *was* the likeness

of oxen encircling it all around, ten to a cubit, all the way around the Sea. The oxen *were* cast in two rows, when it was cast. It stood on twelve oxen: three looking toward the north, three looking toward the west, three looking toward the south, and three looking toward the east; the Sea *was set* upon them, and all their back parts *pointed* inward. It *was* a handbreadth thick; and its brim was shaped like the brim of a cup, *like* a lily blossom. It contained three thousand baths. He also made ten lavers, and put five on the right side and five on the left, to wash in them; such things as they offered for the burnt offering they would wash in them, but the Sea *was* for the priests to wash in.

> a. **Then he made the Sea of cast bronze, ten cubits from one brim to the other**: The huge laver was more than 15 feet (5 meters) across, and was used for the ceremonial washings connected with the priests themselves.
>
>> i. "Priests who did not wash to make themselves clean would die (Exodus 30:20)." (Selman)
>>
>> ii. Wiseman explains in his commentary on 1 Kings: "It was used by priests for cleansing their hands and feet and perhaps also to supply water to the standing basins for the rinsing of offerings (2 Chronicles 4:10)." Poole believes that perhaps water came out of the bulls that formed the foundation of the Sea.
>
> b. **It stood on twelve oxen**: This large pool of water was set upon sculptured **oxen**. "Prefiguring, say some, the twelve apostles, who carried the water of life all the world over." (Trapp)
>
>> i. **It contained three thousand baths**: "In 1 Kings 7:26, it is said to hold only *two thousand baths*. Since this book was written *after* the Babylonian captivity, it is very possible that reference is here made to the Babylonian *bath*, which might have been *less* than the Jewish." (Clarke)
>
> c. **He also made ten lavers**: These additional basins were used for washing and cleaning the animal parts in the rituals of sacrifice.

3. (7-8) The lampstands, tables, and bowls.

And he made ten lampstands of gold according to their design, and set *them* in the temple, five on the right side and five on the left. He also made ten tables, and placed *them* in the temple, five on the right side and five on the left. And he made one hundred bowls of gold.

> a. **And he made ten lampstands…. He also made ten tables**: The work of the temple required **lampstands** for light and **tables** to hold the *showbread*, the bread that represented the continual fellowship of Israel with God.

Notably, the old tabernacle had *one* lampstand and *one* table. The temple fittingly displayed a greater light and a greater dynamic of fellowship.

b. And he made one hundred bowls of gold: "The 'sprinkling bowls' were not particularly associated with the tables but seem rather to have been used for collecting the blood of sacrifices, which was then sprinkled about the altar in the temple services of atonement." (Payne)

4. (9-10) The court of the temple.

Furthermore he made the court of the priests, and the great court and doors for the court; and he overlaid these doors with bronze. He set the Sea on the right side, toward the southeast.

a. **He made the court of the priests**: This was also known as the *inner* court, the court of the temple open only to the priests.

b. **And the great court**: This was the *outer* court, the place in the temple precincts open to the assembly of Israel as a whole.

i. "Yet this very division into two courts (2 Kings 23:12) gave concrete expression to the fact that under the older testament there had not yet been achieved that universal priesthood of the believers that would come about through Jesus Christ. In him all the people of God have direct access to the Father." (Payne)

B. The work of Huram from Tyre.

1. (11-17) Huram's furnishings for the temple.

Then Huram made the pots and the shovels and the bowls. So Huram finished doing the work that he was to do for King Solomon for the house of God: the two pillars and the bowl-shaped capitals *that were* on top of the two pillars; the two networks covering the two bowl-shaped capitals which *were* on top of the pillars; four hundred pomegranates for the two networks (two rows of pomegranates for each network, to cover the two bowl-shaped capitals that *were* on the pillars); he also made carts and the lavers on the carts; one Sea and twelve oxen under it; also the pots, the shovels, the forks; and all their articles Huram his master *craftsman* made of burnished bronze for King Solomon for the house of the LORD. In the plain of Jordan the king had them cast in clay molds, between Succoth and Zeredah.

a. **Then Huram made**: Huram was half Israeli and half Gentile, and he was the best craftsman around. Solomon hired him to do all his work – that is, the fine artistic work of the temple.

b. **The pots and the shovels and the bowls**: These articles were of special note for the Chronicler, because these were some of the only articles that were recovered and used from the first temple period into the days of the Chronicler.

> i. "The emphasis on the temple vessels, as well as the association between Tent and temple, underlines the continuity represented by the temple. The return of the temple vessels to the second temple was one of the chief signs that post-exilic Israel remained a worshipping community of covenant people (*cf.* Ezra 1:7-11; 6:5; 8:24-34)." (Selman)

2. (18-22) Summary of the furnishings for the temple.

And Solomon had all these articles made in such great abundance that the weight of the bronze was not determined. Thus Solomon had all the furnishings made for the house of God: the altar of gold and the tables on which *was* the showbread; the lampstands with their lamps of pure gold, to burn in the prescribed manner in front of the inner sanctuary, with the flowers and the lamps and the wick-trimmers of gold, of purest gold; the trimmers, the bowls, the ladles, and the censers of pure gold. As for the entry of the sanctuary, its inner doors to the Most Holy *Place*, and the doors of the main hall of the temple, *were* gold.

> a. **Such great abundance that the weight of the bronze was not determined**: "*The weight could not be found out.* This was as it should be. There was no attempt to keep an accurate account of what was given to the service of God. Even Solomon's left hand did not know what his right hand did. There is a tendency in all of us to keep a strict account of what we give to God…but the loftiest form of devotion overleaps such calculation." (Meyer)

> b. **With the flowers and the lamps**: "The symbolism of flora and fauna in the temple may either indicate God's sovereignty over the created order or be another allusion to the harmony of all created things in God's presence as in the Garden of Eden." (Selman)

2 Chronicles 5 – The Ark is brought to the Temple

A. The finished temple.

1. (1) Completion of the work.

So all the work that Solomon had done for the house of the LORD was finished; and Solomon brought in the things which his father David had dedicated: the silver and the gold and all the furnishings. And he put *them* in the treasuries of the house of God.

> a. **All the work that Solomon had done for the house of the LORD was finished**: This was the great achievement of Solomon's life. He began this ambitious project shortly after he came to the throne, and now it was finished, certainly much to his satisfaction.
>
> b. **Solomon brought in the things which his father David had dedicated**: This reminds us of just how much *David* did for the temple. He even designed, made, and **dedicated** some of the furnishings of the temple.

2. (2-5) The furniture of the temple is brought in before the assembled nation.

Now Solomon assembled the elders of Israel and all the heads of the tribes, the chief fathers of the children of Israel, in Jerusalem, that they might bring the ark of the covenant of the LORD up from the City of David, which *is* Zion. Therefore all the men of Israel assembled with the king at the feast, which *was* in the seventh month. So all the elders of Israel came, and the Levites took up the ark. Then they brought up the ark, the tabernacle of meeting, and all the holy furnishings that *were* in the tabernacle. The priests and the Levites brought them up.

> a. **Solomon assembled the elders of Israel and all the heads of the tribes**: The official installation of the ark of the covenant into the temple was an extremely important occasion. Solomon wanted representatives of the entire kingdom to have a part in this memorable event.

b. **The priests and the Levites brought them up**: This properly respected the pattern designated by the Mosaic Law. Solomon wanted representatives of the entire kingdom to witness the event, but not at the expense of obedience to God's command.

3. (6-10) The ark comes into the Most Holy Place of the temple.

Also King Solomon, and all the congregation of Israel who were assembled with him before the ark, were sacrificing sheep and oxen that could not be counted or numbered for multitude. Then the priests brought in the ark of the covenant of the LORD to its place, into the inner sanctuary of the temple, to the Most Holy *Place*, under the wings of the cherubim. For the cherubim spread *their* wings over the place of the ark, and the cherubim overshadowed the ark and its poles. And the poles extended so that the ends of the poles of the ark could be seen from *the holy place*, in front of the inner sanctuary; but they could not be seen from outside. And they are there to this day. Nothing was in the ark except the two tablets which Moses put *there* at Horeb, when the LORD made *a covenant* with the children of Israel, when they had come out of Egypt.

a. **Sacrificing sheep and oxen that could not be counted or numbered for multitude**: Solomon went "over-the-top" in his effort to honor and praise God on this great day.

b. **Then the priests brought in the ark of the covenant of the LORD**: The temple wasn't "open" until the ark of the covenant was set in the Most Holy Place. The ark was the most important item in the temple.

c. **Under the wings of the cherubim**: The interior of the temple was richly decorated with the designs of cherubim, which surround the throne of God in heaven. This design of the temple was after the pattern of the tabernacle, which had woven designs of cherubim on the inner covering.

> i. "The statement that 'they are still there today' must have been quoted by Ezra from his sources (2 Chronicles 9:29), particularly from 1 Kings (8:8), out of those portions that were written before the destruction of Jerusalem in 586 B.C. The ark had been gone for over a century by Ezra's day." (Payne)

d. **Nothing was in the ark except the two tablets which Moses put there at Horeb**: At an earlier point in Israel's history there were three items in the ark of the covenant. Earlier, inside the ark were the golden pot that had the manna (Exodus 16:33), Aaron's rod that budded (Numbers 17:6-11), and the tablets of the covenant (Exodus 25:16). We don't know what happened to the golden pot of manna and Aaron's rod, but they were not in the ark when Solomon set it in the Most Holy Place.

e. **When the LORD made a covenant with the children of Israel, when they had come out of Egypt**: The reminder of the deliverance from Egypt is significant because there is a sense in which this – some 500 years after the Exodus – is the culmination of the deliverance from Egypt. Israel came out of Egypt and into the wilderness, and out of necessity, lived in tents – and the dwelling of God was also a tent. Now since Solomon built the temple, the dwelling of God among Israel was a *building*, a place of permanence and security.

B. The glory of God fills the temple.

1. (11-12) The praise of the Levites at the installation of the ark of the covenant.

And it came to pass when the priests came out of the *Most* Holy *Place* (for all the priests who *were* present had sanctified themselves, without keeping to their divisions), and the Levites *who were* the singers, all those of Asaph and Heman and Jeduthun, with their sons and their brethren, stood at the east end of the altar, clothed in white linen, having cymbals, stringed instruments and harps, and with them one hundred and twenty priests sounding with trumpets;

a. **For all the priests who were present had sanctified themselves, without keeping to their divisions**: Normally the priests and Levites worked at the temple according to a strict schedule. Yet on this day, *all* the priests and Levites were on duty before the LORD.

b. **And the Levites who were the singers**: It was right that on this day praise should be focused on *the LORD*, and not on Solomon or David. In reality, this was the LORD's house, not David's or Solomon's.

2. (13-14) The cloud of God's glory fills the temple.

Indeed it came to pass, when the trumpeters and singers *were* as one, to make one sound to be heard in praising and thanking the LORD, and when they lifted up their voice with the trumpets and cymbals and instruments of music, and praised the LORD, *saying:*

***"For He is* good,**
For His mercy *endures* forever,"

that the house, the house of the LORD, was filled with a cloud, so that the priests could not continue ministering because of the cloud; for the glory of the LORD filled the house of God.

a. **That the house, the house of the LORD, was filled with a cloud**: This was the cloud of glory, seen often in the Old and New Testaments, sometimes called the cloud of Shekinah glory. It is hard to *define* the glory of God; we could call it the radiant outshining of His character and presence. Here it is manifested in a cloud.

- This is the cloud that stood by Israel in the wilderness (Exodus 13:21-22).
- This is the cloud of glory that God spoke to Israel from (Exodus 16:10).
- This is the cloud from which God met with Moses and others (Exodus 19:9, 24:15-18, Numbers 11:25, 12:5, 16:42).
- This is the cloud that stood by the door of the Tabernacle (Exodus 33:9-10).
- This is the cloud from which God appeared to the High Priest in the Holy Place inside the veil (Leviticus 16:2).
- This is the cloud of Ezekiel's vision, filling the temple of God with the brightness of His glory (Ezekiel 10:4).
- This is the cloud of glory that overshadowed Mary when she conceived Jesus by the power of the Holy Spirit (Luke 1:35).
- This is the cloud present at the transfiguration of Jesus (Luke 9:34-35).
- This is the cloud of glory that received Jesus into heaven at His ascension (Acts 1:9).
- This is the cloud that will display the glory of Jesus Christ when He returns in triumph to this earth (Luke 21:27, Revelation 1:7).

i. It is worthy of note that this great outpouring of the glory of God came in the context of intense and dedicated praise. God pours out His glory when His people praise Him. "We can never expect to have God in this house, or in our own houses, or in our own hearts, until we begin to praise him. Unless as a people we unanimously, with one heart, though with many tongues, extol the King of kings, farewell to the hope that he will give us his presence in the future." (Spurgeon)

ii. "There is an order in this work which we do well to consider. Work performed according to the divine order, offered in sacrifice and praise, is acceptable to God. Such work He receives by possessing it with His own presence and glory." (Morgan)

b. **So that the priests could not continue ministering because of the cloud**: The extreme presence of the glory of God made *normal* service impossible. The sense of the presence of God was so intense that the priests felt it was impossible to continue in the building.

i. "As soon as the temple is opened for business, all the carefully planned ceremonies and services have to be suspended because God takes over the entire building for himself. The temple is to be for God's glory, not for that of human beings." (Selman)

ii. Jesus Himself was greater than the cloud that filled the temple and when *He* came it was fitting for the priests' temple service to stop. "This showed that the Levitical ministry should cease when the Lord Christ came." (Trapp)

iii. "The glory of God had filled the house, and *the priests were set aside*. Where God is, man is forgotten. You will think little of the minister save for his work's sake – you will talk the less of the man when you shall see the Master." (Spurgeon)

2 Chronicles 6 – Solomon's Prayer of Dedication

A. Solomon blesses God.

1. (1-2) Acknowledgement of God's presence in the cloud.

Then Solomon spoke:

**"The LORD said He would dwell in the dark cloud.
I have surely built You an exalted house,
And a place for You to dwell in forever."**

> a. **The LORD said He would dwell in the dark cloud**: The cloud of God's glory has a long association with His presence.

> b. **I have surely built You an exalted house, and a place for You to dwell in forever**: Solomon rightly sensed that the presence of the cloud meant that God dwelt in the temple in a special way. As long as this did not slip into a superstitious misunderstanding, it was good to recognize a special place to come and meet with God.

>> i. "Though only Jesus is God incarnate, the temple was a clear sign that God in all his being was committed to living among his people." (Selman)

2. (3-9) Solomon blesses the people and blesses God.

Then the king turned around and blessed the whole assembly of Israel, while all the assembly of Israel was standing. And he said: "Blessed *be* the LORD God of Israel, who has fulfilled with His hands *what* He spoke with His mouth to my father David, saying, 'Since the day that I brought My people out of the land of Egypt, I have chosen no city from any tribe of Israel *in which* to build a house, that My name might be there, nor did I choose any man to be a ruler over My people Israel. Yet I have chosen Jerusalem, that My name may be there; and I have chosen David to be over My people Israel.' Now it was in the heart of my

father David to build a temple for the name of the LORD God of Israel. But the LORD said to my father David, 'Whereas it was in your heart to build a temple for My name, you did well in that it was in your heart. Nevertheless you shall not build the temple, but your son who will come from your body, he shall build the temple for My name.'"

> a. **Who has fulfilled with His hands what He spoke with His mouth to my father David**: Solomon recognized that the temple was the fulfillment of *God's* plan, not David's or Solomon's. David and Solomon were human instruments, but the work was God's.
>
>> i. "The mention of God's hands (lit. 'fulfilled with his hands') really means that God's actions have confirmed his words – it is as if God's unseen hands were active in all the human hands who contributed to the construction work (*cf.* 1 Chronicles 29:16)." (Selman)
>
> b. **Out of the land of Egypt**: Solomon presses the remembrance of the Exodus. Though it happened 500 years before, it was just as important and real for Israel as the day it happened.
>
> c. **Nevertheless you shall not build the temple**: Though Solomon built the temple and not David, we are reminded of the extensive preparations David made for the temple. David prepared for the temple in every way he could short of actually building it, and he was happy for the credit and honor for building it to go to his son Solomon.
>
>> i. "It confirms that David's disqualification was not due to sin, but because the concept of God's rest must be regarded as the unique and final stage in building the temple." (Selman)

3. (10-11) Solomon presents the finished temple to God.

"So the LORD has fulfilled His word which He spoke, and I have filled the position of my father David, and sit on the throne of Israel, as the LORD promised; and I have built the temple for the name of the LORD God of Israel. And there I have put the ark, in which *is* the covenant of the LORD which He made with the children of Israel."

> a. **I have filled the position of my father David, and sit on the throne of Israel, as the LORD promised**: Solomon recognized that his succession of David on the throne of Israel was a significant thing. He was the first king to follow his father as a hereditary monarch.
>
> b. **There I have put the ark, in which is the covenant of the LORD**: The chief glory of the temple was that it was the resting place for the **ark** of the **covenant**, a representation of God's covenantal presence with His people.

B. Solomon's prayer.

1. (12-14) Humility before, and praise to, God.

Then *Solomon* stood before the altar of the Lord in the presence of all the assembly of Israel, and spread out his hands (for Solomon had made a bronze platform five cubits long, five cubits wide, and three cubits high, and had set it in the midst of the court; and he stood on it, knelt down on his knees before all the assembly of Israel, and spread out his hands toward heaven); and he said: "Lord God of Israel, *there is* no God in heaven or on earth like You, who keep *Your* covenant and mercy with Your servants who walk before You with all their hearts.

a. **Stood before the altar of the Lord**: Solomon did not dedicate the temple from *within* the temple. It would be inappropriate for him to do so because he was a king and not a priest. The holy place and Most Holy Place were only for chosen descendants of the High Priest.

b. **And spread out his hands**: This was the most common posture of prayer in the Old Testament. Many modern people close their eyes, bow their heads, and fold their hands as they pray, but the Old Testament tradition was to spread out the hands toward heaven in a gesture of surrender, openness, and ready reception.

i. "It is worthy of remark concerning this prayer that it is as full and comprehensive as if it were meant to be the summary of all future prayers offered in the temple." (Spurgeon)

ii. "One is struck, moreover, with the fact that the language is far from new, and is full of quotations from the Pentateuch, some of which are almost word for word, while the sense of the whole may be found in those memorable passages in Leviticus and Deuteronomy." (Spurgeon)

c. **There is no God in heaven or on earth like You**: Solomon recognized that God was completely unique. The pretended gods of the nations could not compare to Him in any way.

2. (15-17) Solomon recognizes God as the maker and keeper of promises.

"You have kept what You promised Your servant David my father; You have both spoken with Your mouth and fulfilled *it* with Your hand, as *it is* this day. Therefore, Lord God of Israel, now keep what You promised Your servant David my father, saying, 'You shall not fail to have a man sit before Me on the throne of Israel, only if your sons take heed to their way, that they walk in My law as you have walked before Me.' And now, O Lord God of Israel, let Your word come true, which You have spoken to Your servant David."

a. **You have kept what You promised**: Solomon first thanked and praised God for His *past* fulfillment of promises.

b. **Now keep what You promised Your servant David.... let Your word come true**: Solomon called upon God to keep the promises that He made. This is the great secret to power in prayer – to take God's promises to heart in faith, and then boldly and reverently call upon Him to fulfill the promises.

> i. "God sent the promise on purpose to be used. If I see a Bank of England note, it is a promise for a certain amount of money, and I take it and use it. But oh my friend, do try and use God's promises; nothing pleases God better than to see his promises put in circulation; he loves to see his children bring them up to him, and say, 'Lord, do as thou hast said.' And let me tell you that it glorifies God to use his promises." (Spurgeon)

> ii. This kind of prayer *lays hold of* God's promise. Just because God promises does not mean that we possess. Through believing prayer like this, God promises and we appropriate. If we don't appropriate in faith, God's promise is left unclaimed.

3. (18-21) Solomon asks God to dwell in this place and honor those who seek Him here.

"But will God indeed dwell with men on the earth? Behold, heaven and the heaven of heavens cannot contain You. How much less this temple which I have built! Yet regard the prayer of Your servant and his supplication, O Lord my God, and listen to the cry and the prayer which Your servant is praying before You: that Your eyes may be open toward this temple day and night, toward the place where *You* said *You would* put Your name, that You may hear the prayer which Your servant makes toward this place. And may You hear the supplications of Your servant and of Your people Israel, when they pray toward this place. Hear from heaven Your dwelling place, and when You hear, forgive."

a. **How much less this temple which I have built!** We are glad that Solomon said this. From prior statements, such as his statement in 2 Chronicles 6:1-2, we might have thought that Solomon drifted towards a superstitious idea that God actually lived in the temple to the exclusion of other places. It was important to recognize that though God had a *special* presence in the temple, He was far too great to be restricted to the temple.

b. **May You hear the supplications of Your servant and of Your people Israel, when they pray toward this place**: Solomon asked God to incline His ear towards the king and the people when they prayed from the temple. For this reason, many observant Jews still pray facing the direction of the site of the temple in Jerusalem.

c. **When You hear, forgive**: Solomon knew that the most important thing Israel needed was *forgiveness*. This was the greatest answer to prayer Israel could expect from God.

4. (22-23) Hear when Your people take an oath at the temple.

"If anyone sins against his neighbor, and is forced to take an oath, and comes *and* takes an oath before Your altar in this temple, then hear from heaven, and act, and judge Your servants, bringing retribution on the wicked by bringing his way on his own head, and justifying the righteous by giving him according to his righteousness."

a. **And comes and takes an oath before Your altar in this temple**: The temple grounds were used as a place to verify and authorize oaths. When a dispute came down to one word against another, Solomon asked that the temple would be a place to properly swear by.

b. **Hear from heaven, and act, and judge Your servants**: Solomon asked the God who can see what man can't – who knows the hidden heart of man – to enforce from heaven the oaths made at the temple.

i. The old Puritan commentator John Trapp could not resist mentioning a fulfillment of this principle in his own day: "Anne Averies, who, forswearing herself, A.D. 1575, February 11, at a shop of Wood Street in London, praying God she might sink where she stood if she had not paid for the wares she took, fell down presently speechless, and with horrible stink died."

5. (24-25) Hear when Your people are defeated.

"Or if Your people Israel are defeated before an enemy because they have sinned against You, and return and confess Your name, and pray and make supplication before You in this temple, then hear from heaven and forgive the sin of Your people Israel, and bring them back to the land which You gave to them and their fathers."

a. **If Your people Israel are defeated before an enemy**: Many times in their history, Israel suffered defeat and could only cry out to God. It was even worse when the defeat was because they had **sinned against** the LORD Himself.

b. **Return and confess Your name, and pray and make supplication before You in this temple, then hear from heaven**: Solomon asked God to hear the prayers of a defeated, yet humble and penitent Israel. God answered this prayer of Solomon, and He forgave and restored His defeated people when they came in humble repentance.

6. (26-31) Hear in times of plague and famine.

"When the heavens are shut up and there is no rain because they have sinned against You, when they pray toward this place and confess Your name, and turn from their sin because You afflict them, then hear *in* heaven, and forgive the sin of Your servants, Your people Israel, that You may teach them the good way in which they should walk; and send rain on Your land which You have given to Your people as an inheritance. When there is famine in the land, pestilence or blight or mildew, locusts or grasshoppers; when their enemies besiege them in the land of their cities; whatever plague or whatever sickness *there is*; whatever prayer, whatever supplication is *made* by anyone, or by all Your people Israel, when each one knows his own burden and his own grief, and spreads out his hands to this temple: then hear from heaven Your dwelling place, and forgive, and give to everyone according to all his ways, whose heart You know (for You alone know the hearts of the sons of men), that they may fear You, to walk in Your ways as long as they live in the land which You gave to our fathers."

> a. **When the heavens are shut up and there is no rain**: Drought was a constant threat for the agriculturally based economy of Israel. If there was no rain, there was no food.
>
> b. **When they pray toward this place and confess Your name, and turn from their sin because You afflict them, then hear in heaven**: Solomon doesn't take it for granted that God would forgive and hear His repentant people. God's good response to our repentance comes from His *grace*, not from *justice*.
>
>> i. "It is not therefore to be wondered at that, when Solomon dedicated to the Lord the temple which he had built, his great petition was that God would hear every prayer that should be uttered in that place or toward that place. He wished the temple always to be to Israel the token that God's memorial is that he hears prayer." (Spurgeon)

7. (32-33) Hear when a foreigner prays.

"Moreover, concerning a foreigner, who is not of Your people Israel, but has come from a far country for the sake of Your great name and Your mighty hand and Your outstretched arm, when they come and pray in this temple; then hear from heaven Your dwelling place, and do according to all for which the foreigner calls to You, that all peoples of the earth may know Your name and fear You, as *do* Your people Israel, and that they may know that this temple which I have built is called by Your name."

> a. **Moreover, concerning a foreigner**: The temple was in Israel but it was always intended to be a house of prayer for *all* nations (Isaiah 56:7). God

wanted the court of the Gentiles to be a place where the nations could come and pray.

> i. The violation of this principle made Jesus angry. When He came to the temple and found the outer courts – the only place where the Gentile nations could come and pray – more like a swap meet than a house of prayer, He drove out the moneychangers and the merchants (Matthew 21:13).

b. **Hear from heaven Your dwelling place, and do according to all for which the foreigner calls to You, that all peoples of the earth may know Your name and fear You**: Solomon asked God to hear the prayer of the foreigner out of a *missionary* impulse. He knew that when God mercifully answered the prayers of foreigners, it drew those from other nations to the God of all nations.

> i. "What is especially notable is that foreigners could know and fear God 'like your people Israel.' This hope of equality in worship was rarely expressed in the Old Testament (*e.g.* Genesis 12:3; Isaiah 19:24-25; Zechariah 8:20-22), and even Jesus' closest disciples found its fulfillment hard to take (Acts 10:1-11:18)." (Selman)

8. (34-39) Hear when Israel goes out to battle and prays from captivity.

"When Your people go out to battle against their enemies, wherever You send them, and when they pray to You toward this city which You have chosen and the temple which I have built for Your name, then hear from heaven their prayer and their supplication, and maintain their cause. When they sin against You (for *there is* no one who does not sin), and You become angry with them and deliver them to the enemy, and they take them captive to a land far or near; *yet* when they come to themselves in the land where they were carried captive, and repent, and make supplication to You in the land of their captivity, saying, 'We have sinned, we have done wrong, and have committed wickedness'; and *when* they return to You with all their heart and with all their soul in the land of their captivity, where they have been carried captive, and pray toward their land which You gave to their fathers, the city which You have chosen, and toward the temple which I have built for Your name: then hear from heaven Your dwelling place their prayer and their supplications, and maintain their cause, and forgive Your people who have sinned against You."

a. **When Your people go out to battle against their enemies, wherever You send them**: Solomon prayed with the idea that God should answer the prayers for victory made in foreign lands towards the temple, but only when they battle as God *sent* them. This was not a blanket request for blessing on every military adventure.

b. **When they sin against You (for there is no one who does not sin)**: This is a succinct Old Testament statement of the principle most clearly stated in Romans 3:23: *for all have sinned and fall short of the glory of God*.

i. "The sense that sin is all-pervading dominates, epitomised in one of the clearest biblical statements about sin's universality (*there is no-one who does not sin*, v. 36). No greater indication of the need for a place of atonement and forgiveness could be given." (Selman)

c. **When they come to themselves in the land where they were carried captive**: Solomon also asked God to hear Israel's prayer from captivity in a foreign land. This recognized that the God of the temple could answer prayers made away from the temple.

9. (40-42) Conclusion to the prayer.

"**Now, my God, I pray, let Your eyes be open and *let* Your ears *be* attentive to the prayer *made* in this place.**

Now therefore,
Arise, O Lord God, to Your resting place,
You and the ark of Your strength.
Let Your priests, O Lord God, be clothed with salvation,
And let Your saints rejoice in goodness.
O Lord God, do not turn away the face of Your Anointed;
Remember the mercies of Your servant David."

a. **Arise, O Lord God, to Your resting place, You and the ark of Your strength**: This conclusion of prayer has Numbers 10:35-36 in mind, when Israel moved the ark of the covenant, the tabernacle, and the whole camp of Israel from place to place through the wilderness during the exodus. Solomon used the phrasing of that passage to emphasize that the ark of the covenant and the symbol of God's presence would wander no more and had finally come to its final **resting place**.

b. **Do not turn away the face of Your Anointed**: Solomon probably meant this in reference to himself because he was the anointed king of Israel. Nevertheless, it also reminds us of the principle in prayer of praying in the name of Jesus, the ultimate **Anointed** One.

i. "In his prayer 'do not reject your anointed one,' the king now meant himself, though in subsequent usage it would express Israel's hope in the coming Messiah." (Payne)

2 Chronicles 7 – The Temple Dedicated

A. Dedication by God and man.

1. (1-3) The temple is dedicated by God with fire from heaven.

When Solomon had finished praying, fire came down from heaven and consumed the burnt offering and the sacrifices; and the glory of the LORD filled the temple. And the priests could not enter the house of the LORD, because the glory of the LORD had filled the Lord's house. When all the children of Israel saw how the fire came down, and the glory of the LORD on the temple, they bowed their faces to the ground on the pavement, and worshiped and praised the LORD, *saying:*

"For *He is* **good,
For His mercy** *endures* **forever."**

> a. **Fire came down from heaven and consumed the burnt offering and the sacrifices**: This is one of the remarkable instances in the Old Testament of God sending fire from heaven to consume a sacrifice. It was a dramatic and visible proof of God's approval, **and the glory of the LORD filled the temple**.
>
>> i. "This fire was kept alive till the captivity of Babylon: and after that, it was said to have been miraculously renewed [in the days of the Maccabees]." (Trapp)
>
> b. **The priests could not enter the house of the LORD**: This repeats the occasion first described in 2 Chronicles 5:14.
>
> c. **They bowed their faces to the ground on the pavement, and worshiped and praised the LORD**: The people responded with a combination of reverence and worship. Their awe-filled praise glorified the goodness and mercy of God.

> i. One might think that consuming fire from heaven might make them more aware of the power and judgment of God. Yet the whole situation seems to have made them more aware of the goodness and mercy of God.
>
> d. **For He is good, for His mercy endures forever**: This familiar refrain is connected with Psalms 136 and 118, and with 2 Chronicles 5:13. Seeing all they could of God's great works, they could not help having this strong emphasis on the goodness and mercy of God.

2. (4-5) The temple is dedicated by man with a multitude of sacrifices.

Then the king and all the people offered sacrifices before the LORD. King Solomon offered a sacrifice of twenty-two thousand bulls and one hundred and twenty thousand sheep. So the king and all the people dedicated the house of God.

> a. **The king and all the people offered sacrifices before the LORD**: As wonderful as the program and the praise were, they could not replace the **sacrifices**. God still had to be honored through blood sacrifice, both for atonement and as a demonstration of fellowship with God.
>
> b. **King Solomon offered a sacrifice of twenty-two thousand bulls and one hundred and twenty thousand sheep**: This is a staggering – almost grotesque – amount of sacrifice. Each animal was ritually sacrificed and a portion was dedicated to the LORD, and a portion given to the priests and the people. It was enough to feed a vast multitude for two weeks.

3. (6-10) The days of praise and feasting for the dedication of the temple.

And the priests attended to their services; the Levites also with instruments of the music of the LORD, which King David had made to praise the LORD, saying, "For His mercy *endures* forever," whenever David offered praise by their ministry. The priests sounded trumpets opposite them, while all Israel stood. Furthermore Solomon consecrated the middle of the court that *was* in front of the house of the LORD; for there he offered burnt offerings and the fat of the peace offerings, because the bronze altar which Solomon had made was not able to receive the burnt offerings, the grain offerings, and the fat. At that time Solomon kept the feast seven days, and all Israel with him, a very great assembly from the entrance of Hamath to the Brook of Egypt. And on the eighth day they held a sacred assembly, for they observed the dedication of the altar seven days, and the feast seven days. On the twenty-third day of the seventh month he sent the people away to their tents, joyful and glad of heart for the good that the LORD had done for David, for Solomon, and for His people Israel.

a. **The priests attended to their services; the Levites also with instruments of the music of the LORD**: On such a great occasion everyone must be about their work. The priests had so many sacrifices to administer that they specially consecrated the area in front of the temple to receive sacrifices because **the bronze altar which Solomon had made was not able to receive the burnt offerings**.

b. **At that time Solomon kept the feast seven days, and all Israel with him**: From the time of year and the length of this **feast**, we understand that this was the Feast of Tabernacles, extended beyond its normal seven days on this special occasion.

> i. "Their unity is expressed in geographical terms as well as by a unity of spirit – *Lebo Hamath to the Wadi of Egypt* indicates the widest possible extent of Israel's occupation of the Promised Land." (Selman)

c. **For the good that the LORD had done for David, for Solomon, and for His people Israel**: This account of the dedication of the temple ends where the story of the temple began – with David, not Solomon. The writer remembers that it was David's heart and vision that started the work of the temple.

4. (11) Conclusion: the work successfully accomplished.

Thus Solomon finished the house of the LORD and the king's house; and Solomon successfully accomplished all that came into his heart to make in the house of the LORD and in his own house.

a. **Thus Solomon finished the house of the LORD and the king's house**: 1 Kings 7 goes into more detail about Solomon's palace. It seems that his palace was even more spectacular than the temple, based on the number of years it took him to build it.

b. **Solomon successfully accomplished all that came into his heart**: It was the end of a well-done job, a job that began with Solomon's father David.

B. God appears to Solomon again.

1. (12-16) The assurance of answered prayer from the temple.

Then the LORD appeared to Solomon by night, and said to him: "I have heard your prayer, and have chosen this place for Myself as a house of sacrifice. When I shut up heaven and there is no rain, or command the locusts to devour the land, or send pestilence among My people, if My people who are called by My name will humble themselves, and pray and seek My face, and turn from their wicked ways, then I will hear from heaven, and will forgive their sin and heal their land. Now My eyes

will be open and My ears attentive to prayer *made* in this place. **For now I have chosen and sanctified this house, that My name may be there forever; and My eyes and My heart will be there perpetually."**

a. **The LORD appeared to Solomon by night**: This was actually the *second* great appearance of God to Solomon (1 Kings 9:1-2). The first is described in 1 Kings 3:5-9. It was good of God to appear to Solomon the first time; it was even better of God to grant a unique appearance to Solomon the second time.

i. "Brethren, we want renewed appearances, fresh manifestations, new visitations from on high; and I commend to those of you who are getting on in life, that while you thank God for the past, and look back with joy to his visits to you in your early days, you now seek and ask for a second visitation of the Most High." (Spurgeon)

ii. After Solomon built the temple and his palace he came to the most dangerous period of his life – a season *after* great blessing and accomplishment. God graciously gave Solomon a fresh revelation of Himself before this dangerous period.

iii. "The words speak to us also. No height attained, no work done, no blessing received, is in itself sufficient to ensure our continuance in favour. Nothing but continued fidelity can do that." (Morgan)

b. **I have heard your prayer**: The great prayer of Solomon in 1 Kings 8 meant nothing unless God **heard** the prayer. The true measure of our prayer is if God in heaven *answers* the prayer.

i. This answer seems to have come many years after the actual dedication of the temple. Yet God also gave Solomon an immediate answer of approval at the time of dedication, when the sacrifices were consumed with fire from heaven (2 Chronicles 7:1-7).

c. **Have chosen this place for Myself as a house of sacrifice**: The building was Solomon's work, done in the power and inspiration of the LORD. The *consecration* of the building was God's work. Solomon could build a building, but only God could hallow it with His presence.

i. "It is to be a house of prayer and a (literal) 'house of sacrifice'…. This combination of the temple's functions is striking, and is one of the several indications in 2 Chronicles 5-7 that prayer and sacrifice are to be understood as 'two sides of the same coin.'" (Selman)

ii. "By presenting the temple as a place where right sacrifice and prayer could be accepted, an opening was being provided to exchange Israel's present bleak circumstances for a more positive future. It offered an opportunity to change the course of Israel's history." (Selman)

d. **If My people who are called by My name will humble themselves, and pray and seek My face**: This wonderful promise is in the context of God's promise to answer prayer from the temple which He chose to hallow with His presence. God promised something special to Israel when they did **humble themselves** and did **pray** and **seek** God's **face**.

> i. There is something naturally **humble** in true prayer because it recognizes that the answers are not in self and they are in God. God promises something special to **humble**, praying people.
>
> ii. The phrase **My people who are called by My name** had its first application to the people of Israel as they lived in the land God promised them. Nevertheless, the same God who made this promise to Israel still reigns in the heavens and will still respond to His humble praying people today.
>
> iii. "Although God's invitation is initially given to *my people* (2 Chronicles 7:14), 2 Chronicles 6:32-33 has made clear that anyone who acknowledges God's name and authority may pray with the same confidence of a hearing. This passage is therefore consistent with others where the invitation is explicitly extended to 'all who call upon the name of the LORD.'" (Selman)

e. **And turn from their wicked ways**: This great promise of answered prayer in 2 Chronicles 7:14 also includes the condition of repentance. As the people of God **humble** themselves, **pray and seek** the **face** of God, they must also **turn from their wicked ways**. It wasn't enough to merely turn their *hearts* to God; they must also turn their *lives* to God.

f. **Then I will hear from heaven, and will forgive their sin and heal their land**: God simply promises to hear the prayer of His humble, prayerful, seeking, repentant people. He will bring forgiveness to His people and healing to their land.

> i. "These expressions are best understood as four facets of one attitude, that sinners should seek God himself in humble repentance, rather than four separate steps on a long road to forgiveness." (Selman)
>
> - We can see what it means to **humble** one's self by looking at Rehoboam (2 Chronicles 12:6, 7, and 12), Hezekiah (2 Chronicles 32:26), and Manasseh (2 Chronicles 33:12, 19, and 23).
> - We can see what it means to **pray** by looking at Hezekiah (2 Chronicles 30:18 and 32:20) and Manasseh (2 Chronicles 33:13).

- We can see what it means to **seek** by looking at the returning priests and the faithful (2 Chronicles 11:13-16) and Jehoshaphat (2 Chronicles 20:3-4).
- We can see what it means to **turn** by looking at Hezekiah (2 Chronicles 30:6 and 30:9)

ii. "Healing throughout the Old Testament has a mixture of spiritual and physical applications. Sometimes healing is specifically equated with forgiveness (*e.g.* Hosea 14:4; Isaiah 53:5, 57:18-19; Psalm 41:4); at other times it relates to physical healing (*e.g.* Genesis 20:17; Numbers 12:13; 2 Kings 20:5, 8). When it is applied to the land, as here, it can refer to bringing the exiles back to the Promised Land (Jeremiah 30:17; 33:6-7) or restoring the land and its people to peace and security (Jeremiah 33:6; Isaiah 57:19)." (Selman)

g. **Now My eyes will be open and My ears attentive to prayer made in this place**: God promised to pay special attention to the prayers offered from the temple which Solomon, the son of David built. We can be much more confident of His attention to our prayers when we offer them in the name of Jesus, the Son of David. He is better access to God than even the temple was.

h. **My eyes and My heart will be there perpetually**: "The idea of God having a heart is extremely rare in the Bible, and the only other explicit reference speaks of God suffering heart pains because of the evil of humanity (Genesis 6:6; *cf.* also Genesis 8:21; 1 Samuel 13:14; Acts 13:22).... It is hard to think of a more intimate way to indicate God's nearness, or a greater encouragement to prayer." (Selman)

2. (17-22) God's warning to Solomon.

"As for you, if you walk before Me as your father David walked, and do according to all that I have commanded you, and if you keep My statutes and My judgments, then I will establish the throne of your kingdom, as I covenanted with David your father, saying, 'You shall not fail *to have* a man as ruler in Israel.' But if you turn away and forsake My statutes and My commandments which I have set before you, and go and serve other gods, and worship them, then I will uproot them from My land which I have given them; and this house which I have sanctified for My name I will cast out of My sight, and will make it a proverb and a byword among all peoples. And *as for* this house, which is exalted, everyone who passes by it will be astonished and say, 'Why has the LORD done thus to this land and this house?' Then they will answer, 'Because they forsook the LORD God of their fathers, who brought them

out of the land of Egypt, and embraced other gods, and worshiped them and served them; therefore He has brought all this calamity on them.'"

a. **If you walk before Me as your father David walked…then I will establish the throne of your kingdom**: God's answer to Solomon's previous prayer had a great *condition*. If Solomon walked before God in obedience and faithfulness, he could expect blessing on his reign and the reign of his descendants, and the dynasty of David would endure forever.

i. God did not demand perfect obedience from Solomon. David certainly did not walk perfectly before the Lord, and God told Solomon to **walk before Me as your father David walked**. This was not out of reach for Solomon.

b. **But if you turn away and forsake My statutes and My commandments… then I will uproot them**: The positive promise is followed by a negative promise. If Solomon or his descendants **turn away and forsake** God and His word, then God promised to correct a disobedient Israel.

c. **And this house which I have sanctified for My name I will cast out of My sight**: God's answer to Solomon's prayer was not an unqualified promise to bless the temple in any circumstance. God blessed the temple and filled it with the glory of His presence, but He would cast it out of His sight if the kings of Israel forsook the Lord.

i. With such a glorious temple, Israel would be tempted to forsake the God of the temple and make an idol of the temple of God. Here the Lord made them know that He could never bless this error.

d. **Will make it a proverb and a byword among all peoples.… everyone who passes by it will be astonished**: Under the Old Covenant, God promised to use Israel to exalt Himself among the nations one way or another. If Israel obeyed, He would bless them so much that others had to recognize the hand of God upon Israel. If Israel disobeyed, He would chastise them so severely that the nations would **be astonished** at the judgment of God among His disobedient people, and they would know that the Lord **has brought all this calamity on them**.

i. "The *manner* in which these disobedient people have been destroyed is truly *astonishing*: no nation was every so highly favoured, and none ever so severely and signally punished." (Clarke)

2 Chronicles 8 – Achievements of Solomon

A. Solomon and the surrounding nations.

1. (1-6) The dominion of Solomon.

It came to pass at the end of twenty years, when Solomon had built the house of the LORD and his own house, that the cities which Hiram had given to Solomon, Solomon built them; and he settled the children of Israel there. And Solomon went to Hamath Zobah and seized it. He also built Tadmor in the wilderness, and all the storage cities which he built in Hamath. He built Upper Beth Horon and Lower Beth Horon, fortified cities *with* walls, gates, and bars, also Baalath and all the storage cities that Solomon had, and all the chariot cities and the cities of the cavalry, and all that Solomon desired to build in Jerusalem, in Lebanon, and in all the land of his dominion.

> a. **At the end of twenty years**: It took Solomon seven years to build the temple and 13 years to build his palace. At the end of these **twenty years** his kingdom was secure, stable, and blessed.

> b. **He also built…. He built…. and all that Solomon desired to build in Jerusalem**: This passage reflects Solomon's great heart and ambition as a *builder*. He energetically **settled** new cities and built **storage cities**, fortifications, **chariot cities**, and **cities of the cavalry**.

>> i. A problem comes in reconciling the mention of the cities that Hiram gave to Solomon, because 1 Kings 9:11-14 indicates that they were given *by* Solomon to Hiram. "While textual disturbance is possible, it seems more probable that they had been returned to Solomon, either because they were unacceptable (1 Kings 9:12-13) or because they had been collateral for a loan (1 Kings 9:14)." (Selman)

>> ii. Sadly, this new emphasis on chariots and cavalry shows that Solomon did not take God's word as seriously as he should have. In

Deuteronomy 17:16, God spoke specifically to the future kings of Israel: *But he shall not multiply horses for himself.* It would have been much better if Solomon had possessed the heart reflected in Psalm 20:7: *Some trust in chariots, and some in horses; but we will remember the name of the LORD our God.*

2. (7-10) Solomon and the conquered peoples of his dominion.

All the people *who were* left of the Hittites, Amorites, Perizzites, Hivites, and Jebusites, who *were* not of Israel; that is, their descendants who were left in the land after them, whom the children of Israel did not destroy; from these Solomon raised forced labor, as it is to this day. But Solomon did not make the children of Israel servants for his work. Some *were* men of war, captains of his officers, captains of his chariots, and his cavalry. And others *were* chiefs of the officials of King Solomon: two hundred and fifty, who ruled over the people.

a. **From these Solomon raised forced labor**: Solomon's practice of using the people of neighboring conquered nations as **forced labor** is also described in 1 Kings 5:15-18.

b. **Solomon did not make the children of Israel servants for his work**: Israelites were used for the work of building the temple and Solomon's palace, but they were not forced labor (1 Kings 5:13-14). They were often used in the management of the forced labor (**who ruled over the people**).

B. Solomon and the daughter of Pharaoh.

1. (11) Solomon marries an Egyptian princess.

Now Solomon brought the daughter of Pharaoh up from the City of David to the house he had built for her, for he said, "My wife shall not dwell in the house of David king of Israel, because *the places* to which the ark of the LORD has come are holy."

a. **Solomon brought the daughter of Pharaoh up from the City of David to the house he had built for her**: This marriage to a princess of Egypt was the first of Solomon's many unwise marriages (1 Kings 11:1-3). These unwise marriages launched the spiritual downfall of Solomon.

b. **My wife shall not dwell in the house of David king of Israel, because the places to which the ark of the LORD has come are holy**: With this, Solomon *admitted* that his wife was an unbeliever and unholy – yet he married her just the same. This led Solomon along a remarkably wicked path (1 Kings 11:4-8).

i. "Is not this a *proof* that he considered his wife to be a *heathen*, and not proper to dwell in a place which had been sanctified? Solomon had not yet departed from the true God." (Clarke)

ii. "Solomon had, against the law of God, married this and other strange wives, for politic ends no doubt, and as hoping that by his wisdom he could reclaim them, or at least rule them.... Howbeit afterwards, overcome by the importunities of his strange wives, he yielded to them shamefully. Watch, therefore, and beware." (Trapp)

iii. "To build a house for Pharaoh's daughter outside the Holy City is to open its gates sooner or later to Pharaoh's gods." (Morgan)

iv. "The blessedness of the marriage tie depends on whether the twain are one in spirit, in a common love for Christ, and endeavour for his glory. Nothing is more terrible than when either admits in the secrecy of the heart, concerning the other, My husband or my wife cannot accompany me into the holy places where I was reared, and in which my best life finds its home." (Meyer)

2. (12-16) The order of Solomon's administration.

Then Solomon offered burnt offerings to the Lord on the altar of the Lord which he had built before the vestibule, according to the daily rate, offering according to the commandment of Moses, for the Sabbaths, the New Moons, and the three appointed yearly feasts; the Feast of Unleavened Bread, the Feast of Weeks, and the Feast of Tabernacles. And, according to the order of David his father, he appointed the divisions of the priests for their service, the Levites for their duties (to praise and serve before the priests) as the duty of each day required, and the gatekeepers by their divisions at each gate; for so David the man of God had commanded. They did not depart from the command of the king to the priests and Levites concerning any matter or concerning the treasuries. Now all the work of Solomon was well-ordered from the day of the foundation of the house of the Lord until it was finished. So the house of the Lord was completed.

a. **Solomon offered burnt offerings**: In accordance with the commanded morning and evening sacrifices (**according to the daily rate** as mentioned in Numbers 28:1-8) Solomon administrated the burnt offering for Israel. He also observed the other sacrifices commanded by the Law of Moses.

b. **According to the order of David his father, he appointed the divisions of the priests for their service**: Solomon carried out the administration for the temple service as it was originally organized by King David (1 Chronicles 24).

c. **Now all the work of Solomon was well-ordered**: This was a reflection of his great wisdom and an answer to his prayer for help in leading the kingdom of Israel (1 Kings 3).

3. (17-18) Solomon's sea trading.

Then Solomon went to Ezion Geber and Elath on the seacoast, in the land of Edom. And Hiram sent him ships by the hand of his servants, and servants who knew the sea. They went with the servants of Solomon to Ophir, and acquired four hundred and fifty talents of gold from there, and brought it to King Solomon.

a. **Then Solomon went to Ezion Geber and Elath on the seacoast**: This was unusual for an Israelite king because the people of Israel were not known for their accomplishments at sea. Solomon boldly led the people of Israel into new ventures.

i. "'Ezion Geber and Elath' were ports at the north end of the Gulf of Aqaba that provided a strategic commercial access southward into the Red Sea and beyond." (Payne)

ii. "Solomon probably bore the expenses, and his friend, the Tyrian king, furnished him with expert sailors; for the Jews, at no period of their history, had any skill in maritime affairs, their navigation being confined to the lakes of their own country, from which they could never acquire any nautical skill." (Clarke)

b. **They went with the servants of Solomon to Ophir, and acquired four hundred and fifty talents of gold from there**: It is hard to say with certainty where the land of **Ophir** was. Some suggest it was in southern Arabia or the eastern coast of Africa. This shows the great enterprise and industriousness of Solomon's administration.

i. "No man knows certainly, to this day, where this *Ophir* was situated. There were two places of this name; one somewhere in India, beyond the Ganges, and another in Arabia, near the country of the Sabaeans, mentioned by Job 22:24." (Clarke)

2 Chronicles 9 – More Achievements of Solomon

A. Solomon hosts the queen of Sheba.

1. (1-4) The queen of Sheba comes to Jerusalem.

Now when the queen of Sheba heard of the fame of Solomon, she came to Jerusalem to test Solomon with hard questions, *having* a very great retinue, camels that bore spices, gold in abundance, and precious stones; and when she came to Solomon, she spoke with him about all that was in her heart. So Solomon answered all her questions; there was nothing so difficult for Solomon that he could not explain it to her. And when the queen of Sheba had seen the wisdom of Solomon, the house that he had built, the food on his table, the seating of his servants, the service of his waiters and their apparel, his cupbearers and their apparel, and his entryway by which he went up to the house of the LORD, there was no more spirit in her.

> a. **The queen of Sheba**: Sheba (also known as *Sabea*) was where modern-day Yemen is today (Southern Arabia). We know from geography this was a wealthy kingdom, with much gold, spices, and precious woods. History also tells us that they were known to have queens as well as kings.
>
>> i. This was a long trip – up to about 1,500 miles (2,400 kilometers). She probably came as part of a trade delegation (1 Kings 10:2-5), but there is no doubt that she was highly motivated to see Solomon and his kingdom.
>
> b. **To test Solomon with hard questions**: Because Solomon was internationally famous for his wisdom, the queen of Sheba came to **test** this great wisdom.
>
> c. **Having a very great retinue**: This queen traveled in the manner of queens – with a large royal procession, heavily laden with gifts and goods for trade.

d. **When she came to Solomon, she spoke with him about all that was in her heart**: Solomon's kingdom was famous not only for its material prosperity but also for his great wisdom. The queen of Sheba had great, and seemingly difficult, questions and **Solomon answered all her questions**.

> i. "The hard questions were not just riddles, but included difficult diplomatic and ethical questions.... The test was not an academic exercise but to see if he would be a trustworthy business party and a reliable ally capable of giving help." (Wiseman)

> ii. "Bring your hard questions to Christ; He is greater than Solomon." (Meyer)

d. **When the queen of Sheba had seen the wisdom of Solomon, the house that he had built, the food on his table…there was no more spirit in her**: This queen was obviously familiar with the world of royal splendor and luxury. Yet she was completely overwhelmed by the wisdom of Solomon and the glory of his kingdom.

> i. "What happened to the queen of Sheba is a natural and not an uncommon effect which will be produced in a delicate sensible mind at the sight of rare and extraordinary productions of art." (Clarke)

2. (5-8) The reaction of the queen of Sheba.

Then she said to the king: *"It was* **a true report which I heard in my own land about your words and your wisdom. However I did not believe their words until I came and saw with my own eyes; and indeed the half of the greatness of your wisdom was not told me. You exceed the fame of which I heard. Happy** *are* **your men and happy** *are* **these your servants, who stand continually before you and hear your wisdom! Blessed be the LORD your God, who delighted in you, setting you on His throne** *to be* **king for the LORD your God! Because your God has loved Israel, to establish them forever, therefore He made you king over them, to do justice and righteousness."**

> a. **Indeed the half of the greatness of your wisdom was not told me**: The queen of Sheba heard wonderful things about Solomon and his kingdom, but upon seeing it with her own eyes she realized it was far greater than she had heard.

> b. **Happy are your men and happy are these your servants**: It is a joyful thing to serve a great, wise, and rich king. If it was a happy thing to serve Solomon, it is a much happier thing to serve Jesus.

> c. **Blessed be the LORD your God, who delighted in you**: This is an example of what God wanted to do for Israel under the promises of the Old Covenant. God promised Israel that if they obeyed under the Old

Covenant, He would bless them so tremendously that the world would notice and give glory to the Lord GOD of Israel.

> i. *Now it shall come to pass, if you diligently obey the voice of the LORD your God, to observe carefully all His commandments which I command you today, that the LORD your God will set you high above all nations of the earth.... Then all peoples of the earth shall see that you are called by the name of the LORD, and they shall be afraid of you.* (Deuteronomy 28:1, 10)
>
> ii. God wanted to reach the nations through an obedient and blessed Israel. If Israel did not obey, then God would speak to the nations through a thoroughly disciplined Israel.

d. **Blessed be the LORD your God**: It is fair to ask if this was a true confession of faith, expressing allegiance to the God of Israel. Taken in their context, these words may not be more than the queen's response to the astonishing blessing evident in Solomon's Jerusalem.

> i. "Her statement about the blessings of the Lord on Israel and Solomon in verse 9 were no more than a polite reference to Solomon's God.... There is no record that she accepted Solomon's God, who was so majestically edified by the temple." (Dilday)
>
> ii. "*Praise to the* LORD implies recognition of Israel's national God and need not necessarily be an expression of personal faith." (Wiseman)
>
> iii. If we take the queen of Sheba as an example of a *seeker*, we see that Solomon impressed her with his wealth and splendor, and also impressed her personally. But she returned home without an evident expression of faith in the God of Israel. This shows that impressing seekers with facilities and programs and organization and professionalism isn't enough.
>
> iv. Regardless of the result of her search, we can admire her seeking.
> - She came from a great distance.
> - She came with gifts to offer.
> - She came to question and to learn.
> - She came and saw the riches of the king.
> - She came for an extended period.
> - She came telling all that was on her heart.
>
> v. Jesus used the queen of Sheba as an example of a seeker: *The queen of the South will rise up in the judgment with this generation and condemn it, for she came from the ends of the earth to hear the wisdom of Solomon;*

and indeed a greater than Solomon is here. (Matthew 12:42) If the queen of Sheba sought Solomon and the splendor of his kingdom so diligently, *how much more* should people today seek Jesus and the glory of His Kingdom. She will certainly also rise up in judgment with this generation.

e. **Because your God has loved Israel forever…therefore He made you king over them**: This statement is especially meaningful because Solomon was not necessarily the most logical successor of his father David. There were several sons of David born before Solomon. "It was God's special act to make him king rather than his elder brother." (Poole)

3. (9-12) An exchange of gifts.

And she gave the king one hundred and twenty talents of gold, spices in great abundance, and precious stones; there never were any spices such as those the queen of Sheba gave to King Solomon. Also, the servants of Hiram and the servants of Solomon, who brought gold from Ophir, brought algum wood and precious stones. And the king made walkways *of* the algum wood for the house of the LORD and for the king's house, also harps and stringed instruments for singers; and there were none such *as these* seen before in the land of Judah. Now King Solomon gave to the queen of Sheba all she desired, whatever she asked, *much more* than she had brought to the king. So she turned and went to her own country, she and her servants.

a. **There never were any spices such as those the queen of Sheba gave to King Solomon**: She came from a region rich in spices and skilled in the processing of spices.

b. **Solomon gave to the queen of Sheba all she desired**: Solomon would not allow the queen of Sheba to give him more than he gave back to her. This description of Solomon's measure of generosity to the queen of Sheba also describes the measure of God's generosity towards us.

i. According to tradition – fanciful stories, perhaps – the queen of Sheba wanted a son by Solomon, and he obliged her. Her child was named Menilek, and he became the ancestor of all subsequent Ethiopian monarchs.

B. Solomon's great wealth.

1. (13-14) Solomon's yearly income.

The weight of gold that came to Solomon yearly was six hundred and sixty-six talents of gold, besides *what* the traveling merchants and

traders brought. And all the kings of Arabia and governors of the country brought gold and silver to Solomon.

a. **Six hundred and sixty-six talents of gold**: This is a vast amount of gold, which came to Solomon **yearly**. One commentator sets the value of the 666 talents of gold at $281,318,400. According to the 2016 price of gold ($1269 an ounce) the value would be $1,019,565,360. This speaks not only to the great wealth of Solomon, but it also makes him one of the only two people in the Bible associated with the number 666.

> i. The other Biblical connection to 666 is the end-times world dictator and opponent of God and His people often known as the Antichrist (Revelation 13:18). In fact, the Revelation passage specifically says that the number 666 is *the number of a man*, and the *man* may be Solomon.
>
> ii. This isn't to say that Solomon was the Antichrist or that the coming Antichrist will be some weird reincarnation of Solomon. But it may indicate that the Antichrist may not be someone purely evil from the very beginning. Instead, he may be like Solomon – a good man corrupted.

b. **Besides what the traveling merchants and traders brought**: Solomon received *more* than 666 talents of gold a year. The amount of 666 talents was just his beginning or base salary.

> i. The writer of Chronicles gave a subtle warning signal here. He assumed his readers knew the instructions for future kings of Israel in Deuteronomy 17:14-20. He assumed we know verse 17 of that passage, which says: *nor shall he greatly multiply silver and gold for himself*. God blessed Solomon with great riches, but Solomon allowed that blessing to turn into a danger because he disobediently multiplied silver and gold for himself.

2. (15-28) Examples of Solomon's wealth and prosperity.

And King Solomon made two hundred large shields of hammered gold; six hundred *shekels* of hammered gold went into each shield. *He* also made three hundred shields of hammered gold; three hundred *shekels* of gold went into each shield. The king put them in the House of the Forest of Lebanon. Moreover the king made a great throne of ivory, and overlaid it with pure gold. The throne *had* six steps, with a footstool of gold, *which were* fastened to the throne; there were armrests on either side of the place of the seat, and two lions stood beside the armrests. Twelve lions stood there, one on each side of the six steps; nothing like *this* had been made for any *other* kingdom. All King Solomon's drinking vessels *were* gold, and all the vessels of the House of the Forest

of Lebanon *were* pure gold. Not *one was* silver, for this was accounted as nothing in the days of Solomon. For the king's ships went to Tarshish with the servants of Hiram. Once every three years the merchant ships came, bringing gold, silver, ivory, apes, and monkeys. So King Solomon surpassed all the kings of the earth in riches and wisdom. And all the kings of the earth sought the presence of Solomon to hear his wisdom, which God had put in his heart. Each man brought his present: articles of silver and gold, garments, armor, spices, horses, and mules, at a set rate year by year. Solomon had four thousand stalls for horses and chariots, and twelve thousand horsemen whom he stationed in the chariot cities and with the king at Jerusalem. So he reigned over all the kings from the River to the land of the Philistines, as far as the border of Egypt. The king made silver *as common* in Jerusalem as stones, and he made cedar trees as abundant as the sycamores which *are* in the lowland. And they brought horses to Solomon from Egypt and from all lands.

a. **Two hundred large shields of hammered gold.... three hundred shields of hammered gold**: These shields made beautiful displays in the House of the Forest of Lebanon (1 Kings 10:17), but they were of no use in battle. Gold was too heavy and too soft to be used as a metal for effective shields. This shows Solomon had the *image* of a warrior king, but without the *substance*.

i. According to Dilday, each large shield was worth about $120,000. The smaller shields were worth $30,000. $33 million was invested in gold ceremonial shields. According to 2016 prices ($1269 an ounce) and assuming a 75-pound talent, the larger shields were worth $152,280, the smaller shields worth $76,140, and the total invested in ceremonial shields was more than $53 million.

b. **Not one was silver, for this was accounted as nothing in the days of Solomon**: This was a statement of wealth. If taken seriously, it shows the tremendous abundance of Solomon's kingdom. Truly, **King Solomon surpassed all the kings of the earth in riches and wisdom**, and the promises of Deuteronomy 28:1-14 were fulfilled in his reign: *The LORD will open to you His good treasure, the heavens, to give the rain to your land in its season, and to bless all the work of your hand. You shall lend to many nations, but you shall not borrow.* (Deuteronomy 28:12)

c. **All the kings of the earth sought the presence of Solomon to hear his wisdom, which God had put in his heart**: This was another fulfillment of the promises of Deuteronomy 28: *And the LORD will make you the head* *and not the tail; you shall be above only, and not be beneath, if you heed the commandments of the LORD your God.* (Deuteronomy 28:13)

d. **The king made silver as common in Jerusalem as stones**: When we think of Solomon's great wealth, we also consider that he originally did not set his heart upon riches. He deliberately asked for wisdom to lead the people of God *instead* of riches or fame. God promised to *also* give Solomon riches and fame, and God fulfilled His promise.

> i. We also consider that Solomon gave an eloquent testimony to the vanity of riches as the preacher in the Book of Ecclesiastes. He powerfully showed that there was no ultimate satisfaction through materialism. We don't have to be as rich as Solomon to learn the same lesson.

e. **They brought horses to Solomon from Egypt and from all lands**: At the end of this great description of Solomon's wealth and splendor, we have the sound of this dark note. This was in direct disobedience to Deuteronomy 17:16, which said to the kings of Israel: *But he shall not multiply horses for himself, nor cause the people to return to Egypt to multiply horses, for the LORD has said to you, "You shall not return that way again."*

4. (29-31) The end of Solomon's reign.

Now the rest of the acts of Solomon, first and last, *are* they not written in the book of Nathan the prophet, in the prophecy of Ahijah the Shilonite, and in the visions of Iddo the seer concerning Jeroboam the son of Nebat? Solomon reigned in Jerusalem over all Israel forty years. Then Solomon rested with his fathers, and was buried in the City of David his father. And Rehoboam his son reigned in his place.

a. **Solomon reigned in Jerusalem over all Israel forty years**: Many commentators believe that Solomon began his reign when he was about 20 years old. This means that Solomon did not live a particularly long life and the promise made in 1 Kings 3:14 was not fulfilled for Solomon, because of his disobedience.

> i. *So if you walk in My ways, to keep My statutes and My commandments, as your father David walked, then I will lengthen your days.* (1 Kings 3:14)
>
> ii. "When we consider the excess in which he lived, and the criminal passions which he must have indulged among his thousand wives, and their idolatrous and impure worship, this life was as long as could be reasonably expected." (Clarke)

b. **Then Solomon rested with his fathers**: This does not necessarily mean that Solomon died a saved man. It is a familiar phrase used in 1 and 2

Kings (used 25 times) and was used of such wicked kings as Ahab (1 Kings 22:40). It simply means that Solomon passed to the world beyond. We cannot say with certainty that he is in heaven.

i. "Yielding to certain lower things of his nature, he became a slave to them, and dragged down his nation with him. So long as he remained on the throne, the people were solaced and drugged by the material magnificence; but underneath, the spirit of rebellion and revolt was at work, ready to break out into open manifestation directly he was removed." (Morgan)

ii. "The story is perhaps one of the most striking illustrations of the fact that opportunity and privilege, even God bestowed, are not enough in themselves to assure full realisation." (Morgan)

2 Chronicles 10 – The Reign of Rehoboam

A. Rehoboam and the nation at Shechem.

1. (1-5) The elders of Israel offer Rehoboam the throne of Israel.

And Rehoboam went to Shechem, for all Israel had gone to Shechem to make him king. So it happened, when Jeroboam the son of Nebat heard *it* (he was in Egypt, where he had fled from the presence of King Solomon), that Jeroboam returned from Egypt. Then they sent for him and called him. And Jeroboam and all Israel came and spoke to Rehoboam, saying, "Your father made our yoke heavy; now therefore, lighten the burdensome service of your father and his heavy yoke which he put on us, and we will serve you." So he said to them, "Come back to me after three days." And the people departed.

> a. **Rehoboam went to Shechem, for all Israel had gone to Shechem to make him king**: This was a logical continuation of the Davidic dynasty. David was succeeded by his son Solomon, and now **Rehoboam**, the son of Solomon, was assumed to be the next king.
>
>> i. Rehoboam was the only son of Solomon that we know by name. Solomon had 1000 wives and concubines, yet we read of one son he had to bear up his name, and he was a fool. This demonstrates that sin is a bad way of building up a family.
>>
>> ii. "It is difficult to believe that he had no other sons; yet it is a fact that Rehoboam is the only one mentioned (1 Chronicles 3:10)." (Knapp)
>>
>> iii. **Shechem** was a city with a rich history. Abraham worshipped there (Genesis 12:6). Jacob built an altar and purchased land there (Genesis 33:18-20). Joseph was buried there (Joshua 24:32). It was also the geographical center of the northern tribes. All in all, it showed that Rehoboam was in a position of weakness, having to meet the ten northern tribes on *their* territory, instead of demanding that representatives come to Jerusalem.

b. **When Jeroboam the son of Nebat heard it**: Jeroboam was mentioned previously in 1 Kings 11:26-40. God told him through a prophet that he would rule over a portion of a divided Israel. Naturally, Jeroboam was interested in Solomon's successor. He was specifically part of the group of elders that addressed Rehoboam.

c. **Your father made our yoke heavy; now therefore, lighten the burdensome service of your father**: Solomon was a great king, but he *took* a lot from the people. The people of Israel wanted relief from the heavy taxation and forced service of Solomon's reign, and they offered allegiance to Rehoboam if he agreed to this.

i. God warned Israel about this in 1 Samuel 8:10-19, when through Samuel, the LORD spoke of what a king would *take* from Israel. After the warning, the people still wanted a king, and now they knew what it was like to be ruled by a *taking* king.

ii. Sadly, the elders of Israel made no *spiritual* demand or request on Rehoboam. Seemingly, the gross idolatry and apostasy of Solomon didn't bother them at all.

2. (6-7) The counsel from Rehoboam's older advisors.

Then King Rehoboam consulted the elders who stood before his father Solomon while he still lived, saying, "How do you advise *me* to answer these people?" And they spoke to him, saying, "If you are kind to these people, and please them, and speak good words to them, they will be your servants forever."

a. **Rehoboam consulted the elders who stood before his father Solomon while he still lived**: Wisely, Rehoboam asked for the counsel of these older, experienced men. They seemed to advise Solomon well, so it was fitting that Rehoboam asked for their advice.

b. **If you are kind to these people…they will be your servants forever**: The elders knew that Rehoboam was not Solomon, and could not expect the same from the people that Solomon did. Rehoboam had to relate to the people based on who *he* was, not on who his father was. If he showed kindness and a servant's heart to the people, they would love and serve him forever. This was good advice.

3. (8-11) The counsel from Rehoboam's younger advisors.

But he rejected the advice which the elders had given him, and consulted the young men who had grown up with him, who stood before him. And he said to them, "What advice do you give? How should we answer this people who have spoken to me, saying, 'Lighten the yoke which your father put on us'?" Then the young men who had grown up with

him spoke to him, saying, "Thus you should speak to the people who have spoken to you, saying, 'Your father made our yoke heavy, but you make *it* lighter on us'; thus you shall say to them: 'My little *finger* shall be thicker than my father's waist! And now, whereas my father put a heavy yoke on you, I will add to your yoke; my father chastised you with whips, but I *will chastise you* with scourges!'"

a. **But he rejected the advice which the elders had given him, and consulted the young men**: *Before* Rehoboam ever consulted with the younger men **he rejected the advice** of the elders.

> i. This is a common phenomenon today – what some call "advice shopping." The idea is that you keep asking different people for advice until you find someone who will tell you what you want to hear. This is an unwise and ungodly way to get counsel. It is better to have a few trusted counselors you will listen to – even when they tell you what you don't want to hear.

b. **And consulted the young men who had grown up with him**: These men were much more likely to tell Rehoboam what he already thought. By turning to those likely to think just as he did, it shows that Rehoboam only asked for advice for the sake of appearances.

> i. Their unwise advice shows the wisdom of seeking counsel from those *outside* our immediate situation and context. Sometimes an outsider can see things more clearly than those who share our same experiences.

> ii. "The 'young men' to who Rehoboam preferred to turn were probably some of Solomon's many sons, rendered callous by upbringing in the luxurious harem and court at Jerusalem." (Payne)

c. **And now, whereas my father put a heavy yoke on you, I will add to your yoke**: The younger men offered the opposite advice to the elders. They suggested an adversarial approach, one that would make Rehoboam more feared than Solomon was.

> i. Solomon asked a lot of Israel, in both taxes and service. Yet we don't have the impression that Israel followed Solomon out of fear, but out of a sense of shared vision and purpose. They believed in what Solomon wanted to do, and were willing to sacrifice to accomplish it. Rehoboam did not appeal to any sense of shared vision and purpose – he simply wanted the people to follow his orders out of the fear of a tyrant.

> ii. "He attempted to continue the despotism of his father, though he lacked his father's refinement and ability to fascinate." (Morgan)

iii. "With a dozen rash words, Rehoboam, the bungling dictator, opened the door for four hundred years of strife, weakness, and, eventually, the destruction of the entire nation." (Dilday)

iv. **My little finger shall be thicker than my father's waist!** A targum translates this, "My weakness shall be stronger than the might of my father." (Clarke)

4. (12-15) Rehoboam answers Jeroboam and the elders of Israel harshly.

So Jeroboam and all the people came to Rehoboam on the third day, as the king had directed, saying, "Come back to me the third day." Then the king answered them roughly. King Rehoboam rejected the advice of the elders, and he spoke to them according to the advice of the young men, saying, "My father made your yoke heavy, but I will add to it; my father chastised you with whips, but I *will chastise you* with scourges!" So the king did not listen to the people; for the turn *of events* was from God, that the LORD might fulfill His word, which He had spoken by the hand of Ahijah the Shilonite to Jeroboam the son of Nebat.

a. **So the king did not listen to the people**: In this case, Rehoboam clearly should have listened to the people. This is not to say that a leader should always lead by popular vote, but a leader needs the wisdom to know when what the people want is best for them.

i. Rehoboam was a fool. Ironically, his father Solomon worried about losing all he worked for under a foolish successor: *Then I hated all my labor in which I had toiled under the sun, because I must leave it to the man who will come after me. And who knows whether he will be wise or a fool? Yet he will rule over all my labor in which I toiled and in which I have shown myself wise under the sun. This also is vanity.* (Ecclesiastes 2:18-19)

ii. "Rehoboam was a fool; and through his folly he lost his kingdom. He is not the only example on record: the *Stuarts* lost the realm of England much in the same way." (Clarke)

iii. "Livy saith, when a state is ripe for ruin, all wholesome counsels are fatally but foolishly slighted." (Trapp)

b. **For the turn of events was from God**: God managed this whole series of events, but He did not *make* Rehoboam take this unwise and sinful action. God simply left Rehoboam alone and allowed him to make the critical errors his sinful heart *wanted* to make.

i. "It seemed to be altogether a piece of human folly and passion; but now we are suddenly brought into the presence of God, and told that beneath the plottings and plannings of man He was carrying out His eternal purpose.... He makes the wrath of man to praise Him, and weaves the malignant work of Satan into his plans." (Meyer)

ii. "Notice also, dear friends, that God is in events which are produced by the sin and the stupidity of men. This breaking up of the kingdom of Solomon into two parts was the result of Solomon's sin and Rehoboam's folly; yet God was in it: 'This thing is from me, saith the Lord.' God had nothing to do with the sin or the folly, but in some way which we can never explain, in a mysterious way in which we are to believe without hesitation, God was in it all." (Spurgeon)

B. The revolt against Rehoboam.

1. (16-17) Jeroboam leads those leaving Rehoboam's rule.

Now when all Israel *saw* that the king did not listen to them, the people answered the king, saying:

"What share have we in David?
***We have* no inheritance in the son of Jesse.**
Every man to your tents, O Israel!
Now see to your own house, O David!"

So all Israel departed to their tents. But Rehoboam reigned over the children of Israel who dwelt in the cities of Judah.

a. **What share have we in David?** Rehoboam's foolishness made Israel reject not only Rehoboam, but also the entire dynasty of David. They rejected the descendants of Israel's greatest king.

b. **Rehoboam reigned over the children of Israel who dwelt in the cities of Judah**: This signals the division of the twelve tribes into two kingdoms; a northern kingdom made up of ten tribes and a southern kingdom made up of **Judah** and Benjamin.

2. (18-19) Israel rebels against the house of David.

Then King Rehoboam sent Hadoram, who *was* in charge of revenue; but the children of Israel stoned him with stones, and he died. Therefore King Rehoboam mounted *his* chariot in haste to flee to Jerusalem. So Israel has been in rebellion against the house of David to this day.

a. **King Rehoboam sent Hadoram, who was in charge of the revenue; but the children of Israel stoned him with stones**: Apparently, Rehoboam did not take the rebellions seriously until this happened. When his chief tax collector was murdered, he knew that the ten tribes were serious about their rebellion.

i. Hadoram was the wrong man for Rehoboam to send. He was famous for his harsh policy of forced labor (1 Kings 4:6 and 5:14). "He was probably one of the most hated figures in the land, an embodiment of oppression." (Payne). Rehoboam probably sent Hadoram because he wanted to make good on his promise to punish those who opposed him. His tough-guy policy didn't work.

ii. "Rehoboam makes one pathetic effort to restore unity, perfectly illustrating the poverty of his policy." (Selman)

b. **So Israel has been in rebellion against the house of David to this day**: From this point on in the history of Israel, the name "Israel" referred to the ten northern tribes and the name "Judah" referred to the southern tribes of Benjamin and Judah.

i. There was a long-standing tension between the ten northern tribes and the combined group of Judah and Benjamin. There were two earlier rebellions along this line of potential division, in the days after Absalom's rebellion (2 Samuel 19:40-43), which developed into the rebellion of Sheba (2 Samuel 20:1-2).

ii. "Rehoboam ought to have been thankful that God's love to David had left him even two tribes." (Knapp)

2 Chronicles 11 – The Defection of the Levites

A. The reign of Rehoboam, the son of Solomon.

1. (1-4) A prophet prevents a civil war, allowing the northern tribes to secede.

Now when Rehoboam came to Jerusalem, he assembled from the house of Judah and Benjamin one hundred and eighty thousand chosen *men* who were warriors, to fight against Israel, that he might restore the kingdom to Rehoboam. But the word of the LORD came to Shemaiah the man of God, saying, "Speak to Rehoboam the son of Solomon, king of Judah, and to all Israel in Judah and Benjamin, saying, 'Thus says the LORD: "You shall not go up or fight against your brethren! Let every man return to his house, for this thing is from Me."'" Therefore they obeyed the words of the LORD, and turned back from attacking Jeroboam.

> a. **When Rehoboam came to Jerusalem, he assembled from the house of Judah and Benjamin one hundred and eighty thousand chosen men who were warriors**: This was the time of Jeroboam's rebellion against the house of David. Rehoboam intended to keep the kingdom united by force.
>
> b. **To fight against Israel, that he might restore the kingdom to Rehoboam**: Rehoboam intended to make war against the seceding tribes of Israel, but God spoke through a prophet and stopped him. To his credit – or perhaps due to a lack of courage – Rehoboam listened to God's word through **Shemaiah the man of God**.
>
>> i. "Here is one Shemaiah, - some of you never heard of him before, perhaps you will never hear of him again; he appears once in this history, and then he vanishes; he comes, and he goes, - only fancy this one man constraining to peace a hundred and eighty thousand chosen men, warriors ready to fight against the house of Israel, by giving to them in very plain, unpolished words, the simple command

of God.... Why have we not such power? Peradventure, brethren, we do not always speak in the name of the Lord, or speak God's Word as God's Word. If we are simply tellers out of our own thoughts, why should men mind us?" (Spurgeon)

2. (5-12) Rehoboam turns his attention to defense.

So Rehoboam dwelt in Jerusalem, and built cities for defense in Judah. And he built Bethlehem, Etam, Tekoa, Beth Zur, Sochoh, Adullam, Gath, Mareshah, Ziph, Adoraim, Lachish, Azekah, Zorah, Aijalon, and Hebron, which are in Judah and Benjamin, fortified cities. And he fortified the strongholds, and put captains in them, and stores of food, oil, and wine. Also in every city *he put* **shields and spears, and made them very strong, having Judah and Benjamin on his side.**

a. **Built cities for defense in Judah**: Stung by the civil war that more than halved his kingdom, Rehoboam set his focus on **defense**, building a series of fortified cities.

i. "The fifteen cities that Ezra lists lie towards Judah's southern and western borders. Their choice seems to have been dictated by threat from Egypt (12:2-4)." (Payne)

b. **In every city he put shields and spears, and made them very strong**: Rehoboam sought to strengthen his kingdom and succeeded to some extent. Yet overall he neglected the spiritual things necessary to strengthen his kingdom.

i. "In these places he laid up stores of provisions, not only to enable *them* to endure a siege; but also that they might be able, from their situation, to supply desolate places." (Clarke)

B. The defection of the priests, Levites, and the godly remnant from Israel to Judah.

1. (13-16) The godly of the northern kingdom migrate to the southern kingdom.

And from all their territories the priests and the Levites who *were* **in all Israel took their stand with him. For the Levites left their common-lands and their possessions and came to Judah and Jerusalem, for Jeroboam and his sons had rejected them from serving as priests to the LORD. Then he appointed for himself priests for the high places, for the demons, and the calf idols which he had made. And after** *the Levites left,* **those from all the tribes of Israel, such as set their heart to seek the LORD God of Israel, came to Jerusalem to sacrifice to the LORD God of their fathers.**

a. **And from all their territories the priests and the Levites who were in all Israel took their stand with him**: This was in response to the state-sponsored idolatry of Jeroboam, the first king of the northern kingdom (1 Kings 12:26-33). These godly servants of the LORD refused to live in a kingdom where worshipping God as He commanded was against the law.

> i. "They would not suffer them to instruct and assist the Israelites in the worship and service of God, nor to go up to Jerusalem to worship in their courses; and these priests would not join with them in the worship of calves, as they were desired and commanded to do; and therefore they willingly forsook all their patrimonies and possessions for God's sake." (Poole)
>
> ii. "He attempted to adapt religion in the interest of the State, and thus destroyed both." (Morgan)

b. **For the Levites left their common-lands and their possessions and came to Judah and Jerusalem**: This meant that since the days of Jeroboam the southern kingdom of Judah was made up not only of the tribes of Judah and Benjamin, but also of a godly remnant from all the ten northern tribes.

> i. Spiritually speaking, Israel was struck twice – by the ungodly religion of Jeroboam and by the departure of the godly and faithful. There were few godly people left in the northern kingdom.
>
> ii. "Viewed even as a stroke of policy, this ejection of the Lord's priests and Levites was a blunder. They went over in a body, almost, to Jeroboam's rival, and thereby 'strengthened the kingdom of Judah.'" (Knapp)
>
> iii. "Note that the laymen *followed* the Levites to Jerusalem…it stresses again the people's unity, with every tribe being represented." (Selman)
>
> iv. This migration of the godly did not end in the days of Jeroboam. "The expression 'Jeroboam and his sons,' i.e., his successors, indicates that migrations by the faithful to Judah was a process that continued down through the years." (Payne)
>
> v. "This remnant of loyal souls, gathered out of all the tribes, left their own country and went to Judah…. Exodus and emigration have very often been the ways of God's advance in the course of time. Such movements have always been sacrificial, but they have been deliverances." (Morgan)

c. **He appointed for himself priests for the high places, for the demons, and the calf idols which he had made**: 1 Kings tells us about the **calf idols**, which were *false representations* of the *true God*. However, we also learn here that Jeroboam established altars **for the demons** (that is, the pagan gods of Canaan).

> i. "So he erected two sorts of high places, some for Baal, and some for the true God, whom he pretended and would be thought to worship in and by the calves." (Poole)

2. (17) The true strength of Judah.

So they strengthened the kingdom of Judah, and made Rehoboam the son of Solomon strong for three years, because they walked in the way of David and Solomon for three years.

> a. **So they strengthened the kingdom of Judah**: This was the true strength of Judah; the godly men and women from the northern kingdom who migrated to the southern kingdom to live there.
>
> b. **Because they walked in the way of David and Solomon for three years**: Sadly, this period did not last longer because of Rehoboam's general bent towards ungodliness.

3. (18-23) The family of Rehoboam.

Then Rehoboam took for himself as wife Mahalath the daughter of Jerimoth the son of David, *and of* Abihail the daughter of Eliah the son of Jesse. And she bore him children: Jeush, Shamariah, and Zaham. After her he took Maachah the granddaughter of Absalom; and she bore him Abijah, Attai, Ziza, and Shelomith. Now Rehoboam loved Maachah the granddaughter of Absalom more than all his wives and his concubines; for he took eighteen wives and sixty concubines, and begot twenty-eight sons and sixty daughters. And Rehoboam appointed Abijah the son of Maachah as chief, *to be* leader among his brothers; for he *intended* to make him king. He dealt wisely, and dispersed some of his sons throughout all the territories of Judah and Benjamin, to every fortified city; and he gave them provisions in abundance. He also sought many wives *for them*.

> a. **For he took eighteen wives and sixty concubines**: Rehoboam obviously did not learn from his father Solomon's error. Though he had far fewer wives and concubines (he was probably less able to support as many), he still had a heart that broke the command of Deuteronomy 17:17.
>
> > i. "By taking 'eighteen wives' Rehoboam willfully disregarded the law of God, both in respect to kingly abuse (Deuteronomy 17:17) and in respect to polygamous marriage...not to mention his disregard of the disastrous precedent set by his father, Solomon, from which he should have learned caution." (Payne)

ii. "He was, however, the son of his father; and, even in the years of peace and prosperity, the animal nature came out in the multiplicity of wives and concubines, until he had practically established, as did his father, a harem on the pattern of the corrupt kings around him." (Morgan)

b. **Rehoboam appointed Abijah the son of Maachah as chief, to be leader among his brothers**: This means that he appointed Abijah to be his successor; the crown prince and perhaps for some period of time co-regent.

i. "Abijah certainly was not the *first-born* of Rehoboam; but as he loved Maachah more than any of his wives, so he preferred her son, probably through his mother's influence." (Clarke)

c. **He dealt wisely, and dispersed some of his sons throughout all the territories of Judah and Benjamin**: This was wise because it kept his many sons apart and less likely to form an alliance against Abijah, who might be considered an illegitimate successor to the throne.

i. "It was true policy to disperse his own sons through the different provinces who were not likely to form any league with Jeroboam against their father." (Clarke)

2 Chronicles 12 – The Chastisement of Rehoboam and Judah

A. Egypt comes against a disobedient kingdom of Judah.

1. (1) The sin of Rehoboam and his people.

Now it came to pass, when Rehoboam had established the kingdom and had strengthened himself, that he forsook the law of the LORD, and all Israel along with him.

> a. **That he forsook the law of the LORD**: Rehoboam did this when he was strong and secure. He trusted in God so long as he felt he needed Him, but he grew *independent* of God instead of more dependent on Him.
>
> > i. 1 Kings 14:21-24 tells us that this forsaking of the law of the LORD went so far as the allowance of *perverted persons in the land*, specifically describing prostitutes associated with the worship of idols. It is possible that, the term *perverted persons* refers to both men and women cultic prostitutes. However, the term was used in Deuteronomy 23:17-18 in distinction to feminine cultic prostitutes.
>
> b. **And all Israel along with him**: The worst part about Rehoboam's sin was that it led the entire kingdom into sin with him.
>
> > i. 1 Kings 14:21-24 describes Judah's apostasy like this: *Judah did evil in the sight of the LORD, and they provoked Him to jealousy with their sins.* These sins *provoked* the LORD to jealousy because they were essentially sins of idolatry. Israel turned their back on the God who loved and redeemed them, and like an unfaithful spouse, they pursued spiritual adultery with idols.

2. (2-4) Egypt attacks a disobedient Judah.

And it happened in the fifth year of King Rehoboam, *that* Shishak king of Egypt came up against Jerusalem, because they had transgressed

against the LORD, with twelve hundred chariots, sixty thousand horsemen, and people without number who came with him out of Egypt; the Lubim and the Sukkiim and the Ethiopians. And he took the fortified cities of Judah and came to Jerusalem.**

> a. **Shishak king of Egypt**: "Known in Egyptian history as Sheshonk I, he was the founder of the Twenty-Second Dynasty and its most energetic Pharaoh. This particular campaign is documented by a list of conquered Palestinian cities that stands to this day carved on the wall of his temple of Amon at Karnak, Thebes." (Payne)

> b. **Because they had transgressed against the LORD**: One might give any number of geopolitical explanations of why the Egyptians attacked the kingdom of Judah at this time. The Chronicler understood that it was really the hand of the LORD in motion because of their disobedience.

>> i. The word **transgressed** (translated *unfaithful* in the NIV) is an important term here. "To be *unfaithful* to God is one of Chronicles' key terms (it never occurs in Samuel and Kings), and its regular occurrence shows Israel's constant estrangement from God.... It involves denying God the worship due to him, usually on a national scale, and is the primary reason given in Chronicles for the exile." (Selman)

> c. **He took the fortified cities of Judah and came to Jerusalem**: This was a serious threat to the entire southern kingdom. It might very well perish in just two generations since David.

3. (5) God's word to Rehoboam and Judah.

Then Shemaiah the prophet came to Rehoboam and the leaders of Judah, who were gathered together in Jerusalem because of Shishak, and said to them, "Thus says the LORD: 'You have forsaken Me, and therefore I also have left you in the hand of Shishak.'"

> a. **Shemaiah the prophet**: This was the same prophet that discouraged Rehoboam from attacking the ten tribes of Israel that had rejected his leadership and formed the northern kingdom of Israel (2 Chronicles 11:1-4). He had the opportunity to speak to all **the leaders of Judah** because they were **gathered** on account of Shishak's invasion.

> b. **You have forsaken Me, and therefore I also have left you in the hand of Shishak**: This was a correction that matched the offense. If Judah insisted on forsaking God, they would find themselves forsaken in the day of their need. The great danger of telling God "Leave me alone" is that someday He may answer that prayer.

B. Repentance and servitude come to Judah.

1. (6) The repentance of Rehoboam and Judah.

So the leaders of Israel and the king humbled themselves; and they said, "The Lord *is* righteous."

> a. **So the leaders of Israel and the king humbled themselves**: This national repentance was initiated by the leaders of the kingdom. Historically, great moves of God's Spirit are seen when *leaders* are zealous about repentance and humility.
>
> b. **The Lord is righteous**: This was the summary of their confession of sin. To recognize that **the Lord is righteous** is also to recognize that we are not. To say this meant they understood that they *deserved* their present misfortune at the hands of Shishak.

2. (7-8) Deliverance with a reminder.

Now when the Lord saw that they humbled themselves, the word of the Lord came to Shemaiah, saying, "They have humbled themselves; *therefore* I will not destroy them, but I will grant them some deliverance. My wrath shall not be poured out on Jerusalem by the hand of Shishak. Nevertheless they will be his servants, that they may distinguish My service from the service of the kingdoms of the nations."

> a. **I will not destroy them, but I will grant them some deliverance**: In response to the repentance of His people, God granted Judah **some deliverance**. He would not allow them to be completely destroyed, but He would allow some difficulty to come to them.
>
> b. **They will be his servants, that they may distinguish My service from the service of the kingdoms of the nations**: When Judah forsook the law of the Lord, it was as if they offered themselves as servants to another master. God will allow them to experience some of the consequences of serving another master.
>
>> i. "They shall be preserved, and serve their enemies, that they may see the difference between the service of God and that of man. While they were pious, they found the service of the Lord to be *perfect freedom*; when they forsook the Lord, they found the fruit to be *perfect bondage*. A sinful life is both expensive and painful." (Clarke)
>>
>> ii. "Know by woeful experience, the worth of my work and wages by the want thereof, and the contrary miseries." (Trapp)

3. (9-12) The "some deliverance" granted to Judah.

So Shishak king of Egypt came up against Jerusalem, and took away the treasures of the house of the Lord and the treasures of the king's house; he took everything. He also carried away the gold shields which

Solomon had made. Then King Rehoboam made bronze shields in their place, and committed *them* to the hands of the captains of the guard, who guarded the doorway of the king's house. And whenever the king entered the house of the Lord, the guard would go and bring them out; then they would take them back into the guardroom. When he humbled himself, the wrath of the Lord turned from him, so as not to destroy *him* completely; and things also went well in Judah.

a. **Took away the treasures of the house of the Lord and the treasures of the king's house**: Solomon left great wealth to his son Rehoboam, both in the temple and in the palace. After only five years, that wealth was largely gone – because Rehoboam and Judah forsook the law of the Lord.

b. **He also carried away the gold shields which Solomon had made**: 1 Kings 10:16-17 mentions these 500 shields, 200 large and 300 small. These shields made beautiful displays in the House of the Forest of Lebanon, but they were of no use in battle. Gold was too heavy and too soft to be used as a metal for effective shields. This was an example of the emphasis of *image* over *substance* that began in the days of Solomon and worsened in the days of Rehoboam.

i. "Rehoboam made in their stead shields of bronze, and with these pathetically tried to keep up former appearances. It is like souls, who, when despoiled of their freshness and power by the enemy, laboriously endeavor to keep up an outward appearance of spiritual prosperity; or, like a fallen church, shorn of its strength, and robbed of its purity, seeking to hide its helplessness, and cover its nakedness, with the tinsel of ritualism, spurious revivalism, union, and anything that promises to give them some appearance." (Knapp)

ii. According to 2016 prices for gold ($1269 an ounce) a large shield would be worth $152,000, meaning about $30 million for the large shields. The small shields would be worth $76,000, meaning about $23 million for the small shields. The total worth of all the shields would be about $53 million invested in gold ceremonial shields – that were now in the hands of the Egyptians.

c. **King Rehoboam made bronze shields in their place**: The replacement of gold with bronze is a perfect picture of the decline under the days of Rehoboam. The dynasty of David went from gold to bronze in five years.

i. "They wished to emphasize how far Rehoboam fell in a mere few years. He had inherited an empire; five years later, master of a small state, he could protect his capital itself only by denuding his palace of its treasures. Solomon's court had despised silver; his son's court had to be content with bronze!" (Payne)

ii. "The picture of Rehoboam's substitution of brass for gold is unutterably pathetic. Yet how often do the people of Jehovah masquerade amid imitations because they have lost the things of pure gold through unfaithfulness and sin." (Morgan)

d. **And committed them to the hands of the captains of the guard**: In the days of Solomon, the gold shields hung on display in the House of the Forest of Lebanon (1 Kings 10:16-17). Under Rehoboam, the replacement bronze shields were kept in a protected guardroom until they were specifically needed for state occasions.

e. **When he humbled himself, the wrath of the Lord turned from him, so as not to destroy him completely**: This great humbling of Rehoboam came *after* he had humbled himself as described in 2 Chronicles 12:6. It shows that God knew there was more humbling to do even after Rehoboam did it himself. Even so, this was God's *favor* and *mercy* to him because both Rehoboam and Judah *deserved* far worse. By the measure of justice alone God had the right **to destroy him completely**.

i. "If God could show favour to a man such as Rehoboam, who typified the attitude which resulted in Judah's eventual collapse, there was always hope for those who humbled themselves before God. Indeed, the interest in the people was surely a direct encouragement to the Chronicler's contemporaries to seek God for themselves." (Selman)

ii. Many in sin humble themselves before God hoping that He will not humble them further. Nevertheless, God knows just how much humbling someone needs, and if more is necessary God will certainly bring it.

f. **Things also went well in Judah**: According to Poole this is literally, "There were *good things*." The idea is either that despite their corruption there was still a remnant of good in Judah and for that reason God held back judgment; or, that despite the terrible loss to the Egyptians there was still a remnant of prosperity in Judah.

4. (13-16) A summary of Rehoboam's reign.

Thus King Rehoboam strengthened himself in Jerusalem and reigned. Now Rehoboam *was* forty-one years old when he became king; and he reigned seventeen years in Jerusalem, the city which the Lord had chosen out of all the tribes of Israel, to put His name there. His mother's name *was* Naamah, an Ammonitess. And he did evil, because he did not prepare his heart to seek the Lord. The acts of Rehoboam, first and last, *are* they not written in the book of Shemaiah the prophet, and of Iddo the seer concerning genealogies? And *there were* wars between

Rehoboam and Jeroboam all their days. So Rehoboam rested with his fathers, and was buried in the City of David. Then Abijah his son reigned in his place.

a. **Thus King Rehoboam strengthened himself in Jerusalem and reigned**: Out of God's mercy, he survived the threat from Shishak and reigned until his natural death.

b. **And he did evil, because he did not prepare his heart to seek the LORD**: This was the root of the problem with Rehoboam. He had even less of a relationship with God than his father Solomon did. At times he did **seek the LORD**, but never with a *prepared heart*.

i. "You see how readily Rehoboam went, first towards God, then towards idols, and then back again, towards God; *he was always ready to shift and change,* he wrought no great reforms in the land; we do not read that, he held a great passover, as Hezekiah did, or that the high places were taken away; but, as soon as Shishak was gone, he felt perfectly content. There was not anything real and permanent in his religion; it did not hold him. He held it sometimes, but it never held him." (Spurgeon)

c. **So Rehoboam rested with his fathers**: The Chronicler seems to give more attention to the life of Rehoboam than the writer of 1 Kings. This may be because Rehoboam is somewhat of a *pattern* and an *encouragement* to the returning exiles to whom the Chronicler first wrote.

i. "Chronicles' over-all view of Rehoboam [has] quite a different feel from Kings. While accepting Rehoboam's very real failings as a leader, Chronicles is keen to demonstrate the value of repentance and the extent of God's mercy." (Selman)

ii. "As the first king of Judah, Rehoboam is an example of God's dealings with David's whole dynasty." (Selman)

iii. Therefore, the following themes are seen in Chronicles' description of Rehoboam:

- Obedience to the prophetic word (2 Chronicles 11:1-4).
- Strengthening the kingdom through building work (2 Chronicles 11:5-12).
- Activities of priests, Levites, and those who seek God (2 Chronicles 11:13-17).
- An expanding royal family (2 Chronicles 11:18-21).
- Humble repentance (2 Chronicles 12:5-12).

2 Chronicles 13 – King Abijah and a Victory for Judah

A. King Abijah speaks to King Jeroboam.

1. (1-3) The two armies gather for war.

In the eighteenth year of King Jeroboam, Abijah became king over Judah. He reigned three years in Jerusalem. His mother's name *was* **Michaiah the daughter of Uriel of Gibeah. And there was war between Abijah and Jeroboam. Abijah set the battle in order with an army of valiant warriors, four hundred thousand choice men. Jeroboam also drew up in battle formation against him with eight hundred thousand choice men, mighty men of valor.**

> a. **In the eighteenth year of King Jeroboam**: This is the only description of the reign of a Judean king that is synchronized with the reign of a contemporary king of Israel. Though the books of 1 and 2 Kings tell the story of both southern and northern kingdoms, 2 Chronicles focuses only on the southern kingdom of Judah. The connection in this verse is probably due to the fact that the events involve Israel as well as Judah.
>
> b. **He reigned three years in Jerusalem**: This son of Rehoboam named Abijah (called Abijam in 1 Kings) only **reigned three years**, showing that God did not bless his reign.
>
> c. **Four hundred thousand choice men…against him with eight hundred thousand choice men**: In this war between the southern kingdom of Judah and the northern kingdom of Israel, there was a clear numerical advantage for the northern kingdom.
>
>> i. "Now it is very possible that there is a *cipher* too much in all these numbers, and that they should stand thus: *Abijah's* army, *forty thousand*; *Jeroboam's eighty thousand; the slain, fifty thousand.*" (Clarke)

ii. On the other hand, "A vast number: but it hath been oft observed and recorded by sacred and profane historians, that in those ancient times there were very numerous armies, and ofttimes very great slaughters; and if this slaughter was more than ordinary, there is nothing strange nor incredible, because the Almighty God fought against the Israelites." (Poole)

2. (4-12) Abijah's appeal to Jeroboam and the army of Israel.

Then Abijah stood on Mount Zemaraim, which *is* in the mountains of Ephraim, and said, "Hear me, Jeroboam and all Israel: Should you not know that the LORD** God of Israel gave the dominion over Israel to David forever, to him and his sons, by a covenant of salt? Yet Jeroboam the son of Nebat, the servant of Solomon the son of David, rose up and rebelled against his lord. Then worthless rogues gathered to him, and strengthened themselves against Rehoboam the son of Solomon, when Rehoboam was young and inexperienced and could not withstand them. And now you think to withstand the kingdom of the L**ORD**, which is in the hand of the sons of David; and you *are* a great multitude, and with you are the gold calves which Jeroboam made for you as gods. Have you not cast out the priests of the L**ORD**, the sons of Aaron, and the Levites, and made for yourselves priests, like the peoples of *other* lands, so that whoever comes to consecrate himself with a young bull and seven rams may be a priest of *things that are* not gods? But as for us, the L**ORD** *is* our God, and we have not forsaken Him; and the priests who minister to the L**ORD** *are* the sons of Aaron, and the Levites *attend* to *their* duties. And they burn to the L**ORD** every morning and every evening burnt sacrifices and sweet incense; *they* also *set* the showbread *in order on* the pure *gold* table, and the lampstand of gold with its lamps to burn every evening; for we keep the command of the L**ORD** our God, but you have forsaken Him. Now look, God Himself is with us as *our* head, and His priests with sounding trumpets to sound the alarm against you. O children of Israel, do not fight against the L**ORD** God of your fathers, for you shall not prosper!"**

a. **The L**ORD** God of Israel gave the dominion over Israel to David forever, to him and his sons, by a covenant of salt**: Abijah's argument is that the dynasty of David is the only legitimate house to rule over the tribes of Israel, including these ten northern tribes that rebelled under Jeroboam.

i. This promise God made to David was called **a covenant of salt**, which meant a *serious* covenant because it was sealed by sacrifice (sacrifices always included salt, Leviticus 2:13). A **covenant of salt** also had the following associations:

- A *pure* covenant (salt stays pure as a chemical compound).
- An *enduring* covenant (salt makes things preserve and endure).
- A *valuable* covenant (salt was expensive).

b. **Yet Jeroboam the son of Nebat, the servant of Solomon the son of David, rose up and rebelled against his lord**: Here King Abijah presents a rather selective view of history. It was true that Jeroboam **rebelled**, but it is also true that Rehoboam was a fool who provoked the northern tribes to rebellion.

i. "It is a strange mixture of misrepresentation and religion. The misrepresentation is in his statement of the reason for the rebellion of Israel, which culminated in the crowning of Jeroboam. He attributed the rebellion to the influence of evil men whom he described as 'sons of Belial.'" (Morgan)

ii. "We need not scrupulously inquire into the lawfulness of this war, for this Abijah, though here he makes a fair flourish, and maintained the better cause, yet was indeed an ungodly man, 1 Kings 15:3, and therefore minded not the satisfaction of his conscience, but only the recovery of his parent's ancient dominions." (Poole)

c. **But as for us, the LORD is our God, and we have not forsaken Him**: Abijah contrasted the rejection of God on behalf of Jeroboam and the people of the northern tribes with the comparative faithfulness of the king and people of Judah.

d. **Do not fight against the LORD God of your fathers, for you shall not prosper!** Abijah brought his sermon to a dramatic finish by challenging the king and people of the northern tribes to recognize that they were really fighting against **the LORD God of** their fathers.

B. God's deliverance for Judah and King Abijah.

1. (13-14) Jeroboam's ambush.

But Jeroboam caused an ambush to go around behind them; so they were in front of Judah, and the ambush *was* behind them. And when Judah looked around, to their surprise the battle line *was* at both front and rear; and they cried out to the LORD, and the priests sounded the trumpets.

a. **Jeroboam caused an ambush to go around behind them**: This was a dishonorable tactic because Jeroboam ambushed while they were negotiating before the battle.

>   i. **The battle line was at both front and rear**: "The point to remember is that our enemies may shut us in on all sides, preventing reinforcements from north, south, east, and west; but no earthly power can ever shut off God from above us…. The way upwards is always kept clear; the ladder which links the beleaguered soul with God and heaven can never be blocked, except by transgression and sin." (Meyer)
>
> b. **And they cried out to the LORD**: When the battle lines unexpectedly changed, the army of Judah knew that a surprise attack from an army twice as large left them in a very dangerous place. The only thing they could do was cry **out to the LORD**.

2. (15-19) Victory for Judah.

Then the men of Judah gave a shout; and as the men of Judah shouted, it happened that God struck Jeroboam and all Israel before Abijah and Judah. And the children of Israel fled before Judah, and God delivered them into their hand. Then Abijah and his people struck them with a great slaughter; so five hundred thousand choice men of Israel fell slain. Thus the children of Israel were subdued at that time; and the children of Judah prevailed, because they relied on the LORD God of their fathers. And Abijah pursued Jeroboam and took cities from him: Bethel with its villages, Jeshanah with its villages, and Ephrain with its villages.

> a. **As the men of Judah shouted, it happened that God struck Jeroboam and all Israel**: They added the shout of faith to their cry to the LORD and **God struck** the army of Israel. We are not told *how* **God struck** them, but God certainly defended His trusting people when they could not defend themselves.
>
>   i. "So 'God routed Jeroboam,' though whether this was through direct supernatural intervention, or through the courage of his embattled people as they saw themselves surrounded by the enemy, is not stated." (Payne)
>
>   ii. "It was a poor business, in that it was a last resort, but it was sincere; and the answer of God was immediate, and complete victory resulted." (Morgan)
>
> b. **The children of Judah prevailed, because they relied on the LORD God of their fathers**: The Chronicler wanted the point to be clear. The reason why Judah defeated Israel, even though they were surprised and outnumbered, was that Judah **relied on the LORD**.
>
>   i. "*Bethel's* capture is an ironic comment on the golden calves' inability to defend their own sanctuary (*cf.* 1 Kings 12:28-33)." (Selman)

3. (20-22) A summary of Abijah's reign.

So Jeroboam did not recover strength again in the days of Abijah; and the LORD struck him, and he died. But Abijah grew mighty, married fourteen wives, and begot twenty-two sons and sixteen daughters. Now the rest of the acts of Abijah, his ways, and his sayings *are* written in the annals of the prophet Iddo.

> a. **Jeroboam did not recover strength again in the days of Abijah**: This ended the ongoing threat from Israel against Judah. Jeroboam was not left strong enough to launch an attack and stayed weak until **the LORD struck him, and he died**.

> b. **But Abijah grew mighty**: The profile of Abijah in 1 Kings 15 is overwhelmingly negative. We read, *he walked in all the sins of his father, which he had done before him; his heart was not loyal to the LORD his God, as was the heart of his father David.* (1 Kings 15:3) Yet the Chronicler says nothing good or bad about the overall reign of Abijah.

>> i. This was because the Chronicler wanted to emphasize the *good* that happened under the reign of Abijah; namely, the great deliverance that came when Judah relied on God. The Chronicler *assumes* the reader knows the material about Abijah in 1 Kings; yet he wanted to show that even a bad man can be shown grace when he relies on the LORD. This would be a great encouragement to the returned exiles to whom the Chronicler first wrote.

>> ii. Yet from our more complete understanding of Abijah's life, we can learn another lesson: *that one great spiritual victory does not make an entire life before God*. One should never trust in a past spiritual accomplishment or season of victory.

>> iii. **The annals of the prophet**: "*Bemidrash*, 'in the commentary;' this, as far as I recollect, is the first place where a *midrash* or *commentary* is mentioned." (Clarke)

2 Chronicles 14 – The Reign of Asa

A. The characteristics of the reign of Asa.

1. (1-6) The blessedness of the reign of King Asa.

So Abijah rested with his fathers, and they buried him in the City of David. Then Asa his son reigned in his place. In his days the land was quiet for ten years. Asa did *what was* good and right in the eyes of the LORD his God, for he removed the altars of the foreign *gods* and the high places, and broke down the *sacred* pillars and cut down the wooden images. He commanded Judah to seek the LORD God of their fathers, and to observe the law and the commandment. He also removed the high places and the incense altars from all the cities of Judah, and the kingdom was quiet under him. And he built fortified cities in Judah, for the land had rest; he had no war in those years, because the LORD had given him rest.

> a. **Asa his son reigned in his place**: This great-grandson of Solomon took the throne of Judah at the end of Jeroboam's reign in Israel, after his father's brief reign.

> b. **Asa did what was good and right in the eyes of the LORD**: As is related in 1 Kings 15:11, Asa was more like his ancestor David in his character as a king than he was like his own father.

> c. **He removed the altars of the foreign gods and the high places**: Asa launched a reform movement that lashed out against both idolatry and officially sanctioned sin.

>> i. 1 Kings 15:12 says that *he banished the perverted persons from the land.* These state-sanctioned homosexual idol-temple prostitutes were introduced into Judah during the reign of Rehoboam (1 Kings 14:24). Asa's father Abijah didn't remove these perversions and idols, but King Asa did.

ii. 1 Kings 15 also tells us that *he removed Maachah his grandmother from being queen mother, because she had made an obscene image of Asherah*. This demonstrated the thoroughness of Asa's reforms. He was able to act righteously even when his family was wrong, in particular his own grandmother (called *Michaiah* in 2 Chronicles 13:2). "It is in a man's own family circle that his faithfulness is put fairly to the test." (Knapp)

d. **He commanded Judah to seek the LORD God of their fathers**: King Asa could not *force* people to seek the LORD and obey him. Yet he could command them with moral force and with his own example.

e. **He also removed the high places**: Interestingly, 1 Kings 15:14 says of the reign of Asa, *but the high places were not removed*. 2 Chronicles 14:3 connects these **high places** with **altars of the foreign gods**. Therefore, Asa removed the high places that were dedicated to idols, but not the ones that were dedicated to the LORD.

f. **The kingdom was quiet under him.... because the LORD had given him rest**: 1 Kings 15:14 tells us that *Asa's heart was loyal to the LORD all his days*. Here we see the blessing he and the kingdom of Judah enjoyed from his loyal heart to God.

i. **He built fortified cities in Judah**: "Though he had no war, yet he provided for it. So did our Queen Elizabeth; and so must every Christian soldier." (Trapp)

2. (7-8) Asa's emphasis on strengthening the nation's defense.

Therefore he said to Judah, "Let us build these cities and make walls around *them*, and towers, gates, and bars, *while* the land *is* yet before us, because we have sought the LORD our God; we have sought *Him*, and He has given us rest on every side." So they built and prospered. And Asa had an army of three hundred thousand from Judah who carried shields and spears, and from Benjamin two hundred and eighty thousand men who carried shields and drew bows; all these *were* mighty men of valor.

a. **So they built and prospered**: The Chronicler includes this account, not previously recorded in 1 Kings, to encourage the people in his own day who had been allowed to rebuild the destroyed city of Jerusalem after its fall to the Babylonians.

B. Deliverance from the Ethiopians.

1. (9-11) The threat from Ethiopia and the cry to God.

Then Zerah the Ethiopian came out against them with an army of a million men and three hundred chariots, and he came to Mareshah. So

Asa went out against him, and they set the troops in battle array in the Valley of Zephathah at Mareshah. And Asa cried out to the LORD his God, and said, "LORD, *it is* nothing for You to help, whether with many or with those who have no power; help us, O LORD our God, for we rest on You, and in Your name we go against this multitude. O LORD, You *are* our God; do not let man prevail against You!"

> a. **Came out against them with an army of a million men and three hundred chariots**: This fearful army obviously posed a great threat to the kingdom of Judah. Even though Judah had an army of 580,000 men (2 Chronicles 14:8), this enemy army was almost twice as large.
>
>> i. Asa could know that God's power was not limited because the army of Judah was smaller, by what God did for Judah under the reign of Abijah, his father (2 Chronicles 13:3).
>>
>> ii. "Zerah himself is most likely to have been a Nubian (= Sudanese) general in the army of Pharaoh Osorkon I (*c*. 924-884 B.C.), Shoshenq I's son and successor (*cf.* 2 Chronicles 12:2ff.)." (Selman)
>
> b. **Asa cried out to the LORD his God**: Asa's prayer showed that he correctly understood that God's power was not enhanced or limited by man's apparent strength or weakness. He recognized that this battle belonged to the LORD and called upon God to defend His honor (**do not let man prevail against You!**).
>
>> i. "Remind God of His entire responsibility." (Meyer)

2. (12-15) God gives Judah victory over the Ethiopians.

So the LORD struck the Ethiopians before Asa and Judah, and the Ethiopians fled. And Asa and the people who *were* with him pursued them to Gerar. So the Ethiopians were overthrown, and they could not recover, for they were broken before the LORD and His army. And they carried away very much spoil. Then they defeated all the cities around Gerar, for the fear of the LORD came upon them; and they plundered all the cities, for there was exceedingly much spoil in them. They also attacked the livestock enclosures, and carried off sheep and camels in abundance, and returned to Jerusalem.

> a. **So the LORD struck the Ethiopians**: God fought on behalf of King Asa and the kingdom of Judah; He fought so effectively that **they were broken before the LORD and His army**.
>
> b. **And they carried away very much spoil**: Not only were the people of God *delivered* from this danger, they were also *enriched* when the LORD fought on their behalf. In this sense, they were more than conquerors in that the LORD did the fighting and they shared in the **spoil**.

i. "The spoil was immense, because the multitude was prodigious, indeed almost incredible; *a million* of men in one place is almost too much for the mind to conceive, but there may be some mistake in the numerals; it is evident from the whole account that the number was vast and the spoil great." (Clarke)

2 Chronicles 15 – Revival and Reform in Judah

A. Azariah brings a warning from God.

1. (1-2) Asa is exhorted to seek God.

Now the Spirit of God came upon Azariah the son of Oded. And he went out to meet Asa, and said to him: "Hear me, Asa, and all Judah and Benjamin. The LORD *is* with you while you are with Him. If you seek Him, He will be found by you; but if you forsake Him, He will forsake you."

>a. **Azariah the son of Oded**: This was one of the lesser-known prophets in the early years of the kingdom of Judah. He came and bravely spoke a word to a king who was flushed with success after the great victory over the Ethiopians.
>
>b. **The LORD is with you while you are with Him**: King Asa and the kingdom of Judah had just enjoyed a significant victory over a mighty army. It would be easy to think that they had a permanent claim to God's favor and blessing. Speaking through the prophet Azariah, God wanted Asa to know the importance of *abiding* in the LORD.
>
>c. **If you seek Him, He will be found by you**: This is an important principle repeated many times in the Bible. The idea is that when we draw near to God, He reveals Himself to us. God does not hide Himself from the seeking heart.
>
>- *You will find Him if you seek Him with all your heart and with all your soul.* (Deuteronomy 4:29)
>- *And you will seek Me and find Me, when you search for Me with all your heart.* (Jeremiah 29:13)
>- *Ask, and it will be given to you; seek, and you will find; knock, and it will be opened to you.* (Matthew 7:7)

i. The converse is also true: **if you forsake Him, He will forsake you**. Ultimately, God gives us what we *want* from Him. God grants to heart that seeks Him what it wants; He also grants the heart that forsakes Him what it desires.

ii. "He revealed an inclusive philosophy of life under the control of God.... The principle is of perpetual application. It represents God as unchanging. All apparent changes on His part are really changes in the attitude of men toward Him. Man with God, finds God with him. Man forsaking God, finds that he is forsaken of God." (Morgan)

2. (3-7) The exhortation in light of the past disobedience of Israel.

"For a long time Israel *has been* without the true God, without a teaching priest, and without law; but when in their trouble they turned to the Lord God of Israel, and sought Him, He was found by them. And in those times *there was* no peace to the one who went out, nor to the one who came in, but great turmoil *was* on all the inhabitants of the lands. So nation was destroyed by nation, and city by city, for God troubled them with every adversity. But you, be strong and do not let your hands be weak, for your work shall be rewarded!"

a. **Without the true God, without a teaching priest, and without law**: The prophet Azariah describes the bad state of Israel in their overconfidence and distance from God. They had rejected God, those who teach them the word of God, and the law itself.

i. **Without a teaching priest** reminds us that the priesthood and the Levites did much more than administer the sacrificial system. They were to be scattered throughout the tribes of Israel to teach the word of God to the people.

ii. "The priests' teaching role was vital to the moral and spiritual quality of national life (*cf. e.g.* Leviticus 10:11; Deuteronomy 33:10; Malachi 2:7; 2 Chronicles 17:7-9), but when it was neglected, the truth about God declined and the fabric of covenant society was undermined." (Selman)

iii. "His words about the 'long time' when 'Israel was without the true God' probably refer to the lawless, and often faithless, days of the Judges (Judges 21:25)." (Payne)

b. **But when in their trouble they turned to the Lord God of Israel, and sought Him, He was found by them**: The Chronicler used this message from the prophet Azariah to remind the people of Israel in his own day (Ezra's days of the return from exile) that even when the people of God were set low because of their disobedience, God would restore them when **they turned to the LORD God of Israel**.

c. **Be strong…for your work shall be rewarded**: In spite of the great trouble that God had visited on His previously disobedient people, King Asa should be encouraged at God's heart for forgiveness and restoration.

i. "This prophecy is unusual in that it is an exposition of earlier parts of the Old Testament though as an example of the speeches in Chronicles it is not untypical. Its style is sermonic, but its prophetic character comes through in the immediacy of its final imperative." (Selman)

B. The reforms of King Asa.

1. (8-9) King Asa cleanses the land and gathers the nation together for worship.

And when Asa heard these words and the prophecy of Oded the prophet, he took courage, and removed the abominable idols from all the land of Judah and Benjamin and from the cities which he had taken in the mountains of Ephraim; and he restored the altar of the LORD that *was* before the vestibule of the LORD. Then he gathered all Judah and Benjamin, and those who dwelt with them from Ephraim, Manasseh, and Simeon, for they came over to him in great numbers from Israel when they saw that the LORD his God was with him.

a. **He took courage, and removed the abominable idols**: This was the good and godly response. Instead of becoming fatalistic or passive, King Asa took action based on the open heart of God to restore and forgive.

i. Some believe that the forgiving nature of God gives one a reason to sin, based on the idea that we can sin now and simply ask forgiveness later. Asa's reaction to the word of the prophet shows the *correct* response to the forgiving nature of God – to respond with a greater love and a greater passion for obedience.

ii. We should notice that this took **courage** for King Asa to do. He had to combat against:

- The entrenched interests in favor of idolatry.
- The unseen spiritual forces in favor of idolatry.
- The example of his predecessors and neighboring tribes to the north in favor of idolatry.
- His own fleshly inclinations in favor of idolatry and compromise.
- The lethargy of compromise and indifference that supports idolatry.

iii. Many well-meaning reformers accomplish little because they lack the **courage** to really stand for their godly convictions.

iv. "What is important is that it touched the entire nation, including the queen mother (15:16), all Judah (14:5), and even the north (15:8-9)." (Selman)

b. **And he restored the altar of the Lord**: King Asa did more than remove the wrong; he also **restored** the right. This is an important part of any reform, and any time of renewal must be more than speaking out against the evil. It must also take positive steps towards the good.

c. **They came over to him in great numbers from Israel when they saw that the Lord his God was with him**: King Asa's bold obedience to God earned the respect of the godly remnant among the apostate northern tribes that made up the kingdom of Israel. They wanted to be part of a committed return to God.

i. The Chronicler recorded these events – not included in the history of King Asa found in 1 Kings – as an encouragement to the returned exiles in his own day. They could believe that if they obeyed God courageously as King Asa did, that God would also gather a faithful remnant to their small number. They could see that courageously obedient believers attract others.

ii. "Chronicles constantly highlights the opportunities for reunification (*cf.* 2 Chronicles 11:13-17; 30:11; 34:6), which always arose in the context of worship rather than as a result of military force (*cf.* 2 Chronicles 11:1-4; 13:8, 13:13-14)." (Selman)

2. (10-15) A public covenant made at Jerusalem.

So they gathered together at Jerusalem in the third month, in the fifteenth year of the reign of Asa. And they offered to the Lord at that time seven hundred bulls and seven thousand sheep from the spoil they had brought. Then they entered into a covenant to seek the Lord God of their fathers with all their heart and with all their soul; and whoever would not seek the Lord God of Israel was to be put to death, whether small or great, whether man or woman. Then they took an oath before the Lord with a loud voice, with shouting and trumpets and rams' horns. And all Judah rejoiced at the oath, for they had sworn with all their heart and sought Him with all their soul; and He was found by them, and the Lord gave them rest all around.

a. **They offered to the Lord at that time seven hundred bulls and seven thousand sheep from the spoil they had brought**: They rightly recognized that their victory came from God, so they gave back to Him from the **spoil** of the victory over the Ethiopians (2 Chronicles 14:12-15).

i. When we recognize that what we have comes from God, it is much easier to give to Him out of what He has given us. A lack of generosity is often rooted in refusing to recognize that God is the ultimate provider and every good and perfect gift comes from Him (James 1:17).

ii. "Such assemblies are typical of a number of kings in Chronicles, including David (1 Chronicles 13:2-5; 15:3; 28:8; 29:1ff), Solomon (2 Chronicles 1:3; 5:6), Jehoshaphat (2 Chronicles 20:5, *etc.*), and especially Hezekiah (*e.g.* 2 Chronicles 29:23; 29:28; 30:2; 30:25)." (Selman)

b. **They entered into a covenant to seek the LORD God of their fathers with all their heart and with all their soul**: After sacrifice, they committed the matter to **a covenant** between them and God. This was after the pattern of the covenant the people of Israel originally made with God at Sinai (Exodus 24:7-8).

i. This covenant was deliberately connected with these past covenants (**to seek the LORD God of their fathers**). This was their way of saying, "LORD God, we want the same relationship with You that our great forefathers enjoyed. We want to be bound to You with the same kind of covenant."

ii. This covenant was supported by the threat of punishment (**whoever would not seek the LORD God of Israel was to be put to death**) and with a public oath (**they took an oath before the LORD with a loud voice**). This combination of a public oath and a promised punishment made the whole community accountable to keep this promise they made. This was a demonstration of the fact that it was a covenant made **with all their heart and with all their soul**. It was not a half-hearted or half-way covenant that no one could be held accountable to.

iii. "Do not think too much of entering into and keeping a covenant with God; but remember that the Lord Jesus, on our behalf, has entered into covenant relation with the Father, and the Father with us in Him. This is the new covenant." (Meyer)

iv. "*Should be put to death*, by virtue of all those laws which command that such persons should be *cut off*, and in pursuance of that law, Deuteronomy 17:2." (Poole)

c. **All Judah rejoiced at the oath**: The seriousness of the covenant became a source of joy for the people. There was a sincere and true joy in being fully committed to God and accountable for that commitment in the community.

d. And He was found by them, and the Lord gave them rest all around: Through the prophet Azariah, God had promised Asa in 2 Chronicles 15:2: *If you seek Him, He will be found by you*. This was the fulfillment of that promise. Not only the king himself, but the nation as a whole **found** the Lord when they sought Him this way.

- They sought Him *together*, having **gathered together at Jerusalem**.
- They sought Him through *sacrifice*, trusting in God's promise of atonement through the blood of an innocent victim.
- They sought Him through *covenant*, made with a view to God's working with His people in the past (**to seek the Lord God of their fathers**).
- They sought Him *completely*, **with all their heart and with all their soul**.
- They sought Him *in an accountable way*, promising punishment upon themselves if they were to forsake this covenant.
- They sought Him *publicly*, having taken a public **oath** together.
- They sought Him *joyfully*, rejoicing in the oath they had taken.

i. Their reward for seeking God in this way was both that they **found** the Lord, and when they found Him, He **gave them rest all around**. Some fear to seek the Lord this diligently because they are afraid that should they really find God, it would be more of a burden than a blessing to them. The Chronicler wanted us to know that when we seek God in this radical way and find Him, the reward is **rest all around**.

3. (16-19) The extension of the reform into the king's own household.

Also he removed Maachah, the mother of Asa the king, from *being* queen mother, because she had made an obscene image of Asherah; and Asa cut down her obscene image, then crushed and burned *it* by the Brook Kidron. But the high places were not removed from Israel. Nevertheless the heart of Asa was loyal all his days. He also brought into the house of God the things that his father had dedicated and that he himself had dedicated: silver and gold and utensils. And there was no war until the thirty-fifth year of the reign of Asa.

a. **Also he removed Maachah the mother of Asa the king, from being queen mother, because she had made an obscene image of Asherah**: This demonstrates the thoroughness of Asa's reforms. He was able to act righteously even when his family was wrong, in particular his own grandmother. "It is in a man's own family circle that his faithfulness is put fairly to the test." (Knapp)

> i. 1 Kings 15:12-15 makes it clearer that **Maachah** was actually the *grandmother* of King Asa. "Maacah was apparently the daughter of Uriel of Gibeah (2 Chronicles 13:2) and Tamar (2 Samuel 14:27), hence the granddaughter of Absalom, David's rebellious son." (Patterson and Austel)

> ii. **An obscene image**: "This image is described as 'obscene' in our English translation, but the Hebrew word is closer in meaning to 'frightening,' 'horrible,' or 'abominable.' Some commentators believe it was some sort of phallic symbol consistent with the fertility cult of Asherah." (Dilday)

> iii. "From the whole, it is pretty evident that the image was a mere *Priapus*, or something of the same nature, and that Maachah had an assembly in the grove where the image was set up, and doubtless worshipped it with the most impure rites. What the Roman *Priapus* was I need not tell the learned reader; and as to the unlearned, it would not profit him to know." (Clarke)

> iv. "The Jews imagine that Maachah repented, and her name became changed into *Michaiah, daughter of Uriel of Gibeah*; and that this was done that there might be no mention of her former name, lest it should be a reproach to her." (Clarke)

b. **But the high places were not removed from Israel**: 2 Chronicles 14:3 says that Asa did remove the high places, but it mentions these high places in connection with *altars of the foreign gods*. Therefore Asa removed the high places that were dedicated to idols, but not the ones that were dedicated to the LORD.

> i. "More probably, however, the addition of *from Israel* (*cf.* 1 Kings 15:14; *cf.* 2 Chronicles 15:8) suggests that the Chronicler distinguished between the high places in Judah (14:3, 5) and those in Israel (15:17)." (Selman)

> ii. "It was also a more extensive removal, 'from the whole land'; for it included areas Asa 'had captured in the hills of Ephraim' during the five years of hostility that had immediately preceded." (Payne)

c. **Nevertheless the heart of Asa was loyal all his days**: Asa's loyal heart was shown in his reforms against idolatry and state-sanctioned perversion, and in his restoration of certain **silver and gold utensils** to the temple.

> i. **There was no war until the thirty-fifth year of the reign of Asa**: "For though there were continual skirmishes between Asa and Baasha

and their people *all their days*, 1 Kings 15:16, yet it did not break forth into an open war till Asa's thirty-fifth year; i.e. till that was ended." (Poole)

2 Chronicles 16 – Asa's Disappointing End

A. A treaty with Syria.

1. (1-3) Asa makes a treaty with Syria to strengthen himself against Israel.

In the thirty-sixth year of the reign of Asa, Baasha king of Israel came up against Judah and built Ramah, that he might let none go out or come in to Asa king of Judah. Then Asa brought silver and gold from the treasuries of the house of the LORD and of the king's house, and sent to Ben-Hadad king of Syria, who dwelt in Damascus, saying, "*Let there be* a treaty between you and me, as there was between my father and your father. See, I have sent you silver and gold; come, break your treaty with Baasha king of Israel, so that he will withdraw from me."

> a. **Baasha king of Israel came up against Judah, and built Ramah, that he might let none go out or come in to Asa king of Judah**: This continues the struggle for dominance between the northern kingdom of Israel and the southern kingdom of Judah. Baasha gained the upper hand in the days of Asa because he effectively blocked a major route into Judah at the city of Ramah. He hoped this military and economic pressure on Judah would force Asa into significant concessions.
>
>> i. "*Baasha's* aim in fortifying *Ramah* was probably to prevent access to Jerusalem for religious or trade reasons. Ramah is usually identified with er-Ram, on the main road just five miles north of Jerusalem." (Selman)
>
> b. **Asa brought silver and gold from the treasuries of the house of the LORD and of the king's house, and sent to Ben-Hadad king of Syria**: Asa used this treasure to buy the favor of Ben-Hadad of Syria so that he would withdraw support from Israel. Apparently, Baasha of Israel could not stand against Judah by himself and he needed the support of Syria.

i. "I will say nothing about what belonged to his own house. He might do as he liked with that so long as he did not spend it upon sin, but he took of the treasure that belonged to the house of the Lord, and gave it to Benhadad to bribe him to break his league with Baasha, and be in league with himself. Thus God was robbed that the unbelieving king might find help in an arm of flesh." (Spurgeon)

c. **Let there be a treaty between you and me, as there was between my father and your father**: Asa was trying to keep the way open for pilgrims from the northern kingdom to come to Jerusalem, and this was a noble goal. His method was completely wrong. He gave treasure from the **house of the Lord** to a pagan king, and he made a **treaty** with that king.

i. Asa seems to have forgotten that his covenant was with God, not with a pagan king. Under the covenant they made with God, the Lord was responsible to protect Judah. Now they invested their *treasure* and their *trust* in a pagan king.

ii. Asa would find that Ben-Hadad and Syria were worse enemies than Israel.

iii. "The power of Ethiopia was broken before him, and Judah's armies returned laden with the spoil. You would not have thought that a man who could perform that grand action would become, a little after, full of unbelief; but the greatest faith of yesterday will not give us confidence for to-day, unless the fresh springs which are in God shall overflow again." (Spurgeon)

iv. "But this was a smaller trouble altogether, and somehow, I fancy, it was because it was a smaller trouble Asa thought that he could manage it very well himself by the help of an arm of flesh. In the case of the invasion by countless hordes of Ethiopians, Asa must have felt that it was of no use calling in Ben-hadad, the king of Syria, or asking any of the nations to help him, for with all their help he would not have been equal to the tremendous struggle. Therefore he was driven to God. But this being a smaller trial, he does not seem to have been so thoroughly divorced from confidence in man." (Spurgeon)

v. "Here good Asa began to decline; which was the worse in him, because in his old age, after so great a victory, and so strict a covenant to cleave close to the Lord." (Trapp)

2. (4-6) The success of Asa's plan.

So Ben-Hadad heeded King Asa, and sent the captains of his armies against the cities of Israel. They attacked Ijon, Dan, Abel Maim, and all the storage cities of Naphtali. Now it happened, when Baasha heard *it*, that he stopped building Ramah and ceased his work. Then King Asa took all Judah, and they carried away the stones and timber of Ramah, which Baasha had used for building; and with them he built Geba and Mizpah.

> a. **So Ben-Hadad heeded King Asa, and sent the captains of his armies against the cities of Israel**: Ben-Hadad was a king and did have some power. Because of the treasure he received from Asa and under the treaty with Asa, he used that power on behalf of Judah.
>
>> i. "*Store cities* is 'Kineroth' in 1 Kings 15:20, which became Genneseret in the post-exilic period (Josephus, *Jewish Wars*, 2.573)." (Selman)
>
> b. **Now it happened, when Baasha heard it, that he stopped building Ramah and ceased his work**: Because of the intervention of the king of Syria, **Baasha** king of Israel stopped his work of building the fortress city of **Ramah** to keep the faithful of Israel from visiting Jerusalem and Judah. We could say that Asa's trust in a pagan king *worked*.
>
>> i. "Now, many people in the world judge actions by their immediate results. If a Christian does a wrong thing, and it prospers, then at once they conclude he was justified in doing it; but, ah! Brethren, this is a poor, blind way of judging the actions of men and the providence of God. Do you not know that there are devil's providences as well as God's providences?" (Spurgeon)
>
>> ii. "Things which appear successful may be in the life of faith most disastrous." (Morgan)

B. God's rebuke to King Asa and the king's response.

1. (7-9) The word from Hanani the Seer.

And at that time Hanani the seer came to Asa king of Judah, and said to him: "Because you have relied on the king of Syria, and have not relied on the LORD your God, therefore the army of the king of Syria has escaped from your hand. Were the Ethiopians and the Lubim not a huge army with very many chariots and horsemen? Yet, because you relied on the LORD, He delivered them into your hand. For the eyes of the LORD run to and fro throughout the whole earth, to show Himself strong on behalf of *those* whose heart *is* loyal to Him. In this you have done foolishly; therefore from now on you shall have wars."

> a. **Hanani the seer**: We don't know much about this prophet, other than his bold word to King Asa here, and that his son was also a prophet who spoke to Baasha the king of Israel (1 Kings 16:1, 16:7) and to Jehoshaphat king of Judah (2 Chronicles 19:2).

b. **Because you have relied on the king of Syria, and have not relied on the LORD your God, therefore the army of the king of Syria has escaped from your hand**: This was a complete surprise to Asa. He believed that the main enemy was *Israel*, because of King Baasha's aggressive building of the Ramah fortress. He succeeded in gaining Syria's help against Baasha and Israel, but he failed to see what God saw: that the bigger enemy was Syria, and God wanted to give him victory over the greater enemy.

i. Compromise blinds us to who our true enemies are and it leads us into alliances with those whom God would rather give us victory over.

c. **Because you relied on the LORD, He delivered them into your hand**: God wanted Asa to remember the great victories of the past. Asa failed to remember that the same God who gave him victory over a greater enemy (**the Ethiopians**) was able to also give him victory over the lesser enemy, Syria.

d. **For the eyes of the LORD run to and fro throughout the whole earth, to show Himself strong on behalf of those whose heart is loyal to Him**: The prophet Hanani's message was clear. God *looks* for ways to defend and show His strength on behalf of those who are committed to Him. Asa's fear that God could not be trusted with the defense of Judah was foolish and wrong; God *wanted* to show His strength on behalf of His trusting people.

i. "The Hebrew word for 'run to and fro' signifieth, not to take a light view, but to search narrowly into the nature and the course of things." (Trapp)

ii. "What an exquisite thought is suggested by the allusion to the eyes of the Lord running to and fro throughout the whole earth! At a glance He takes in our position; not a sorrow, trial, or temptation visits us without exciting his notice and loving sympathy. In all the whole wide earth there is not one spot so lonely, one heart so darkened, as to escape those eyes." (Meyer)

iii. The issue was not the *strength* of God or His *willingness* to use that strength on behalf of His people. The issue was the *loyalty* of the heart of Asa and the people of the kingdom of Judah.

e. **Therefore from now on you shall have wars**: Because of Asa's foolish trust in a pagan king and his rejection of God as their defender, he would bring more **wars** upon himself and the kingdom of Judah.

i. "At one stroke Asa thereby sacrificed the results of his own piety (cf. on 2 Chronicles 15:18) and of God's blessing (2 Chronicles 14:13-14); he induced a pagan ruler to an act of perfidy (2 Chronicles 16:3); precipitated a pattern of Syrian intervention into the affairs of Israel that would have disastrous results throughout the succeeding century (cf. 2 Kings 10:32-33; 12:17-18); and in the most serious deviation of all, he departed from the Lord by placing his primary trust in 'the arm of flesh' (Jeremiah 17:5)." (Payne)

2. (10) Asa rejects the message from Hanani.

Then Asa was angry with the seer, and put him in prison, for *he was enraged at him because of this*. And Asa oppressed *some* of the people at that time.

a. **Then Asa was angry with the seer, and put him in prison**: Instead of taking this word from God to heart and humbling himself, King Asa attacked the messenger. Instead of being humbled he was **enraged**.

i. Asa shows us the tragedy of a man who rules well and seeks the LORD for many years, yet fails in a significant challenge of his faith and then refuses to hear God's correction.

ii. "The precise form of Hanani's punishment is unknown, though he was probably detained in some kind of jail (lit., 'house of stocks'; *cf.* NIV, *prison*; the word for 'prison' in 18:26 is different." (Selman)

b. **And Asa oppressed some of the people at that time**: He struck out against not only Hanani but also against others who were committed to God and could see the error of the king's ways. As a man in compromise and unbelief, the presence of those truly loyal to God was convicting and oppressive to Asa.

3. (11-14) The sad end of the otherwise promising reign of King Asa of Judah.

Note that the acts of Asa, first and last, are indeed written in the book of the kings of Judah and Israel. And in the thirty-ninth year of his reign, Asa became diseased in his feet, and his malady was severe; yet in his disease he did not seek the LORD, but the physicians. So Asa rested with his fathers; he died in the forty-first year of his reign. They buried him in his own tomb, which he had made for himself in the City of David; and they laid him in the bed which was filled with spices and various ingredients prepared in a mixture of ointments. They made a very great burning for him.

a. **Asa became diseased in his feet, and his malady was severe**: This happened after he refused to hear God's word of correction through Hanani the seer. Some think that Asa's foot ailment was gout, "but gout was uncommon in Palestine and ancient Egypt and it is more likely, in view of Asa's age, the severity of the disease and death within two years, to have been a peripheral obstructive vascular disease with ensuing gangrene." (Wiseman)

i. "He had a strong and long fit of the *gout*; this is most likely." (Clarke)

ii. "As he had laid the good prophet by the heels in his bed; to him therefore he should have sought for release; since natural means in this case could do him little good." (Trapp)

b. **Yet in his disease he did not seek the LORD, but the physicians**: The closing chapters of the life of King Asa are discouraging. Here was a man involved in a notable period of trust in God, great victory, and the renewal of God's covenant with His people. All in all, Asa was a good man who did not finish well. The last years of his life were marked by unbelief, hardness against God, oppression of his people, and disease. Age and time do not necessarily make us better; they only do if we continue to follow God in faith.

i. He refused to rely on God in the face of the threat against him from Israel and Syria; he refused to rely on God in His loving correction from Hanani the seer. It is no wonder that he also refused to rely on God regarding his diseased feet at the end of his life. This was a powerful warning to the first readers of the Chronicler, as it is also to us today.

ii. Overall, the Bible is positive about the role of physicians and medical care (Colossians 4:14, Acts 28:9, James 5:14-15, and 1 Timothy 5:23). However, it is never right to seek **the physicians** *instead of* **the LORD**. One may rather trust the LORD and when appropriate, see His hand move through a physician.

iii. "It is not wrong to send for physicians, it is quite right; but it is very wrong to send for physicians in place of crying to God, thus putting the human agency before the divine; besides, it is very probable that these physicians were only heathenish conjurors, necromancers, and pretenders to magical arts, and could not be consulted without implicating the patient in their evil practices." (Spurgeon)

iv. Morgan on Asa: "It is the record of a faulty life, but one in which the deepest thing, that of desire, was right; and so it is the record of a life, the influence of which was a blessing rather than a curse. It is a revealing story."

c. **They made a very great burning for him**: "Such fires were customary for royal funerals (*cf.* Jeremiah 34:5), and were not for cremating the body but as a sign of honour (*cf.* 2 Chronicles 21:19)." (Selman)

i. "He that could drive out that huge army of the Ethiopians, could not drive away death." (Trapp)

2 Chronicles 17 – Features of Jehoshaphat's Reign

A. How King Jehoshaphat pleased God.

1. (1-4) The personal spiritual commitment of King Jehoshaphat.

Then Jehoshaphat his son reigned in his place, and strengthened himself against Israel. And he placed troops in all the fortified cities of Judah, and set garrisons in the land of Judah and in the cities of Ephraim which Asa his father had taken. Now the LORD was with Jehoshaphat, because he walked in the former ways of his father David; he did not seek the Baals, but sought the God of his father, and walked in His commandments and not according to the acts of Israel.

> a. **Then Jehoshaphat his son reigned in his place**: Asa was generally a good king (though he did not finish well) and Jehoshaphat his son followed in his footsteps and **the LORD was with Jehoshaphat, because he walked in the former ways of his father David.**
>
>> i. "*In the first ways*, which David walked in before he fell into those horrid sins of murder and adultery." (Trapp)
>>
>> ii. "Have you never noticed the career of David? What a happy life David's was up to one point!.... But that hour when he walked on the roof of his house, and saw Bathsheba, and gave way to his unholy desires, put an end to the happy days of David…. You recognise him as the same man, but his voice is broken; his music is deep bass, he cannot reach one high note of the scale. From the hour in which he sinned he began to sorrow more and more. So will it be with us if we are not watchful." (Spurgeon)
>
> b. **Strengthened himself against Israel**: Jehoshaphat recognized that the northern kingdom was a danger to Judah militarily, politically, and especially *spiritually*. He therefore strengthened the defenses against this threat and specifically **walked…not according to the acts of Israel.**

i. In his presentation of the history of the kings of Judah, the Chronicler constantly brings the contrast and the challenge before the readers of his day and ours: "Your destiny, as an individual and as a nation, can either be like that of Judah or Israel. You should follow the example of those who **walked...not according to the acts of Israel**."

2. (5-6) The blessing upon his reign.

Therefore the LORD established the kingdom in his hand; and all Judah gave presents to Jehoshaphat, and he had riches and honor in abundance. And his heart took delight in the ways of the LORD; moreover he removed the high places and wooden images from Judah.

a. **Therefore the LORD established the kingdom in his hand**: This was no small accomplishment. In those days kings and kingdoms were fragile and under constant threat. Yet if the descendants of David would seek God first, He promised to take care of their security – and God makes the same promise to His people today (Matthew 6:33).

b. **All Judah gave presents to Jehoshaphat, and he had riches and honor in abundance**: Because Jehoshaphat trusted God, God lifted him up and exalted him as a king. As his **heart took delight in the ways of the LORD**, the LORD gave him the desires of his heart (Psalm 37:4).

c. **Moreover he removed the high places and wooden images from Judah**: 1 Kings 22:43 says that Jehoshaphat *did not* remove the high places. Adam Clarke explains: "In 2 Chronicles 17:6, it is expressly said, that he *did take away the high places*. Allowing that the text is right in 2 Chronicles the two places may be easily recognised. There were *two kinds* of *high places* in the land: 1. Those used for *idolatrous* purposes. 2. Those that were *consecrated to God*, and were used before the temple was built. The former he did take away, the latter he did not."

i. "They may also witness to the deep hold of the Canaanite and syncretic forms of religion on ordinary Israelites. Popular views and practices are often quite different from pronouncements by religious authorities." (Selman)

B. The strength of Jehoshaphat's kingdom.

1. (7-10) The spiritual strength of the kingdom: Jehoshaphat brings the word of God to the people.

Also in the third year of his reign he sent his leaders, Ben-Hail, Obadiah, Zechariah, Nethanel, and Michaiah, to teach in the cities of Judah. And with them *he sent* Levites: Shemaiah, Nethaniah, Zebadiah, Asahel, Shemiramoth, Jehonathan, Adonijah, Tobijah, and Tobadonijah; the

Levites; and with them Elishama and Jehoram, the priests. So they taught in Judah, and *had* the Book of the Law of the LORD with them; they went throughout all the cities of Judah and taught the people. And the fear of the LORD fell on all the kingdoms of the lands that *were* around Judah, so that they did not make war against Jehoshaphat.

a. **To teach in the cities of Judah**: These "teaching priests" have been mentioned by the Chronicler before (2 Chronicles 15:3). They had the important role of bringing the word of God to the people, especially those who lived outside of Jerusalem.

b. **They taught in Judah, and had the Book of the Law of the LORD with them; they went throughout all the cities of Judah and taught the people**: This was the wisest and best policy a security-conscious king of Judah could promote. Because Jehoshaphat sought God first, God sent **fear** upon the neighboring kingdoms, **so that they did not make war against Jehoshaphat**.

i. "By this little band of princes, Levites and priests, sixteen in all, Jehoshaphat did more toward impressing the surrounding nations with a sense of his power than the largest and best-equipped standing army could have secured to him." (Knapp)

ii. "The method adopted was what in these modern times we might describe as the holding of Special Missions throughout the cities of Judah, for the specific purpose of proclaiming and interpreting 'the book of the law of Jehovah.'" (Morgan)

iii. "No better service can be rendered to the nation than that of proclaiming the Word of Jehovah to the people, in cities, towns, villages, and hamlets. By such proclamation the heart of the people may be turned to Jehovah, and so He be enabled to do for them all that is in His heart." (Morgan)

iv. "Thus the nation became thoroughly instructed in their duty to *God*, to the *king*, and to each *other*. They became, therefore, as *one man*; and against a people thus united, on such *principles*, no enemy could be successful." (Clarke)

v. Clarke observed how a similar itinerant ministry in the days of John Wesley and his followers impacted Britain: "Such an itinerant ministry established in these kingdoms for upwards of *fourscore years*, teaching the pure, unadulterated doctrines of the Gospel, with the propriety and necessity of obedience to the laws, has been the principal means, in the hand of God, of preserving the lands from those convulsions and revolutions that have ruined and nearly dissolved the European continent."

vi. "It is said (2 Chronicles 17:2) Jehoshaphat placed forces in all the fenced cities; yet it is not said thereupon that 'the fear of the Lord fell upon the neighbour nations.' But when he had established a preaching ministry in all the cities, then his enemies had a fear, and made no war." (Trapp)

2. (11-19) The international strength of Jehoshaphat's kingdom.

Also *some* of the Philistines brought Jehoshaphat presents and silver as tribute; and the Arabians brought him flocks, seven thousand seven hundred rams and seven thousand seven hundred male goats. So Jehoshaphat became increasingly powerful, and he built fortresses and storage cities in Judah. He had much property in the cities of Judah; and the men of war, mighty men of valor, *were* in Jerusalem. These *are* their numbers, according to their fathers' houses. Of Judah, the captains of thousands: Adnah the captain, and with him three hundred thousand mighty men of valor; and next to him *was* Jehohanan the captain, and with him two hundred and eighty thousand; and next to him *was* Amasiah the son of Zichri, who willingly offered himself to the Lord, and with him two hundred thousand mighty men of valor. Of Benjamin: Eliada a mighty man of valor, and with him two hundred thousand men armed with bow and shield; and next to him *was* Jehozabad, and with him one hundred and eighty thousand prepared for war. These served the king, besides those the king put in the fortified cities throughout all Judah.

a. **Some of the Philistines brought Jehoshaphat presents and silver as tribute; and the Arabians brought him flocks**: Jehoshaphat's commitment to personal and public godliness meant that God exalted his kingdom above the neighboring nations, even as God promised in Deuteronomy 28:1-13.

b. **These served the king**: The true treasure of Jehoshaphat's kingdom was not numbered only in security or material things, but also in the dedicated and courageous men he had surrounding him, these **mighty men of valor**.

i. **Amasiah the son of Zichri, who willingly offered himself to the Lord**: "Amasiah is a man of whom we do not know anything beyond this – he 'willingly offered himself unto the Lord.' There must have been a turning-point in his career, a time when first he knew the grace of God, which wrought such a change in him. There must have been a waking up to the feeling that God deserved his love and his life." (Spurgeon)

ii. Amasiah was a ready servant of the Lord; this is particularly notable because he did it in an otherwise secular calling.

- No one had to press him into service.
- No one had to seek him out for service.
- No one had to look after him once he had begun serving.
- No one had to lead him.

iii. "There is no lawful occupation in which a man cannot thoroughly serve the Lord. It is a great privilege and blessing to be set apart to the work of winning souls; but we must never separate that work from all the rest of the callings of life, as though it alone were sacred, and all the rest were secular and almost sinful. Serve God where you are." (Spurgeon)

2 Chronicles 18 – Jehoshaphat, Ahab, and Micaiah

A. Jehoshaphat goes to Samaria, the capital city of the northern kingdom of Israel.

1. (1) Jehoshaphat's unwise alliance with Ahab.

Jehoshaphat had riches and honor in abundance; and by marriage he allied himself with Ahab.

> a. **Jehoshaphat had riches and honor in abundance**: Because of his personal godliness (2 Chronicles 17:1-4) and public godliness (2 Chronicles 17:7-10), God blessed Jehoshaphat and exalted him among neighboring nations.
>
> b. **By marriage he allied himself with Ahab**: This manner of linking kingdoms by the bond of marriage was common in the ancient world, yet it was an unwise policy for Jehoshaphat. The wisest strategy for the protection of his kingdom was *obedience* instead of compromise with the ungodly King Ahab of Israel and his wife, Queen Jezebel.
>
>> i. 1 Kings 16:29-33 tells us just how bad Ahab was. He introduced the worship of completely new, pagan gods. In his disobedience, Jeroboam (the first king of the kingdom of the northern tribes) said, "I will worship the LORD, but do it my way." Ahab said, "I want to forget about the LORD completely and worship Baal."
>>
>> ii. Ahab was greatly influenced towards wickedness by his Phoenician wife Jezebel. "He was a weak man, the tool of a crafty, unscrupulous, and cruel woman: and some of the worst crimes that have ever been committed have been wrought by weak men, at the instigation of worse - but stronger - spirits than themselves." (Meyer)

2. (2-3) Ahab sets his eyes upon Ramoth-Gilead.

After some years he went down to *visit* Ahab in Samaria; and Ahab killed sheep and oxen in abundance for him and the people who were with him, and persuaded him to go up *with him* to Ramoth Gilead. So Ahab king of Israel said to Jehoshaphat king of Judah, "Will you go with me *against* Ramoth Gilead?" And he answered him, "I *am* as you *are,* and my people as your people; *we will be* with you in the war."

> a. **And persuaded him to go up with him to Ramoth Gilead**: Previously, the king of Syria promised to return certain cities to Israel (1 Kings 20:34) in exchange for leniency after defeat in battle. Apparently this was a city that Ben-Hadad never returned to Israel and it was in a strategically important location.
>
> b. **Will you go with me against Ramoth Gilead?** King Ahab of Israel asked King Jehoshaphat of Judah to help him in this dispute against Syria. This made some sense because Ramoth Gilead was only 40 miles from Jerusalem.

3. (4-8) Jehoshaphat proposes that they seek God in the matter.

Also Jehoshaphat said to the king of Israel, "Please inquire for the word of the LORD today." Then the king of Israel gathered the prophets together, four hundred men, and said to them, "Shall we go to war against Ramoth Gilead, or shall I refrain?" So they said, "Go up, for God will deliver it into the king's hand." But Jehoshaphat said, *"Is there not still a prophet of the* LORD *here, that we may inquire of Him?"* So the king of Israel said to Jehoshaphat, *"There is* still one man by whom we may inquire of the LORD; but I hate him, because he never prophesies good concerning me, but always evil. He *is* Micaiah the son of Imla." And Jehoshaphat said, "Let not the king say such things!" Then the king of Israel called one *of his* officers and said, "Bring Micaiah the son of Imla quickly!"

> a. **Please inquire for the word of the** LORD **today**: Considering the generally adversarial relationship between Ahab and the prophets of Yahweh, this was a bold request of Jehoshaphat to ask of Ahab. It wasn't surprising that Ahab picked prophets who would tell them what they wanted to hear.
>
>> i. "Though Jehoshaphat had already committed himself to the enterprise (2 Chronicles 18:3), and though he went on to disregard the guidance that was given him (2 Chronicles 18:28), he still retained the religion of Yahweh to the extent that he insisted on seeking 'the counsel of the Lord.'" (Payne)

b. **Go up, for God will deliver it into the king's hand**: When Ahab gathered the prophets, they were not faithful prophets of the LORD. These were prophets happy to please their kings, and to tell them what they wanted to hear. Jehoshaphat still wanted to hear from a prophet of Yahweh, the LORD (**Is there not still a prophet of the LORD here, that we may inquire of Him?**).

i. Trapp described this gathering of prophets as, "An ecumenical council."

c. **I hate him, because he never prophesies good concerning me, but always evil**: Ahab hated the messenger because of the message. His real conflict was with God, but he focused his hatred against the prophet Micaiah. Yet he was willing to listen to the king of Judah when he advised that Ahab *should* listen to the prophet Micaiah.

4. (9-11) An object lesson from the unfaithful prophets.

The king of Israel and Jehoshaphat king of Judah, clothed in *their* robes, sat each on his throne; and they sat at a threshing floor at the entrance of the gate of Samaria; and all the prophets prophesied before them. Now Zedekiah the son of Chenaanah had made horns of iron for himself; and he said, "Thus says the LORD: 'With these you shall gore the Syrians until they are destroyed.'" And all the prophets prophesied so, saying, "Go up to Ramoth Gilead and prosper, for the LORD will deliver *it* into the king's hand."

a. **Sat each on his throne, and they sat at a threshing floor at the entrance of the gate of Samaria**: This illustrates the ancient custom of holding court and making decisions at the gates of the city. There were even thrones for high officials to sit on at the gates of the city of Samaria.

b. **Thus says the LORD**: These unfaithful prophets (such as **Zedekiah**) prophesied in the name of the LORD, but they did not prophesy truthfully. Many commentators believe these prophets were *pagan* prophets, perhaps representatives of Asherah or other pagan gods or goddesses. Yet they clearly prophesied in the name of **the LORD**. It is best to regard these *not as pagan prophets*, but unfaithful prophets to the true God.

i. Perhaps these were true followers of Yahweh who were seduced by Ahab's sincere but shallow repentance three years before (1 Kings 21:27-29). After that, they began to align with Ahab uncritically. Three years later they were willing to prophesy lies to Ahab if that was what he wanted to hear.

c. **With these you shall gore the Syrians until they are destroyed**: Zedekiah used a familiar tool of ancient prophets – the object lesson. He used **horns of iron** to illustrate the thrust of two powerful forces, armies that would rout the Syrians. Zedekiah had the agreement of 400 other prophets (**all the prophets prophesied so**).

> i. "Dramas of this kind were a typical method of prophetic revelation (*cf.* Jeremiah 27-28), based on this occasion on the *horns* as a symbol of strength." (Selman)

> ii. This must have been a vivid and entertaining presentation. We can be certain that every eye was on Zedekiah when he used the **horns of iron** to powerfully illustrate the point. It was certainly persuasive to have 400 prophets speak in agreement on one issue. No matter how powerful and persuasive the presentation, *their message was unfaithful.*

5. (12-15) The prophecy of Micaiah, the faithful prophet.

Then the messenger who had gone to call Micaiah spoke to him, saying, "Now listen, the words of the prophets with one accord encourage the king. Therefore please let your word be like *the word of* one of them, and speak encouragement." And Micaiah said, *"As* the Lord lives, whatever my God says, that I will speak." Then he came to the king; and the king said to him, "Micaiah, shall we go to war against Ramoth Gilead, or shall I refrain?" And he said, "Go and prosper, and they shall be delivered into your hand!" So the king said to him, "How many times shall I make you swear that you tell me nothing but the truth in the name of the Lord?"

a. **As the Lord lives, whatever my God says, that I will speak**: The assistant of King Ahab tried to persuade Micaiah to speak in agreement with the 400 other prophets. Micaiah assured him that he would simply repeat what God said to him.

> i. This was a dramatic scene. Micaiah was brought out from prison (1 Kings 22:26 indicates that he came from prison). We see a prophet in rags and chains stand before two kings, ready to speak on behalf of the Lord.

> ii. "This might have daunted the good prophet, but that he had lately seen the Lord sitting upon His throne with all the host of heaven standing by Him, and hence he so boldly looked in the face these two kings in their majesty; for he beheld them as so many mice." (Trapp)

b. **Go and prosper, and they shall be delivered into your hand!** When Micaiah said this, his tone was probably mocking and sarcastic. He said similar *words* to the 400 unfaithful prophets, but delivered a completely different *message.*

c. **How many times shall I make you swear that you tell me nothing but the truth in the name of the LORD?** King Ahab recognized the mocking tone of Micaiah's prophecy and knew it contradicted the message of the 400 prophets. He demanded that Micaiah tell **nothing but the truth** – which Ahab believed and hoped was the message of the 400 other prophets.

6. (16-17) Micaiah speaks the true prophecy from the LORD.

Then he said, "I saw all Israel scattered on the mountains, as sheep that have no shepherd. And the LORD said, 'These have no master. Let each return to his house in peace.'" And the king of Israel said to Jehoshaphat, "Did I not tell you he would not prophesy good concerning me, but evil?"

a. **I saw all Israel scattered on the mountains, as sheep that have no shepherd**: Micaiah was challenged to tell the truth, and now he changed his tone from mocking to serious. He said that not only would Israel be defeated, but also that their leader (**shepherd**) would perish.

b. **Did I not tell you he would not prophesy good concerning me, but evil?** King Ahab said that he wanted the truth – but he couldn't handle the truth. What he didn't consider was that though Micaiah prophesied **evil** towards Ahab, he prophesied *truth*.

i. "Ahab knew in his heart that Micaiah would not fear or flatter him, but only declare the word of Jehovah. This he construed into personal hatred…. Hatred of the messenger of God is clear evidence of willful wickedness." (Morgan)

7. (18-22) Micaiah reveals the inspiration behind the 400 prophets.

Then *Micaiah* said, "Therefore hear the word of the LORD: I saw the LORD sitting on His throne, and all the host of heaven standing on His right hand and His left. And the LORD said, 'Who will persuade Ahab king of Israel to go up, that he may fall at Ramoth Gilead?' So one spoke in this manner, and another spoke in that manner. Then a spirit came forward and stood before the LORD, and said, 'I will persuade him.' The LORD said to him, 'In what way?' So he said, 'I will go out and be a lying spirit in the mouth of all his prophets.' And *the Lord* said, 'You shall persuade *him* and also prevail; go out and do so.' Therefore look! The LORD has put a lying spirit in the mouth of these prophets of yours, and the LORD has declared disaster against you."

a. **I saw the LORD sitting on His throne, and all the host of heaven standing**: King Ahab and others at the court found it hard to explain how one prophet could be right and 400 prophets could be wrong. Here Micaiah explained the message of the 400 prophets. It is possible that this was just a parable, but it is more likely that Micaiah had an accurate prophetic glimpse into the heavenly drama behind these events.

b. On His right hand and His left: Since the **right hand** was the place of favor, this may indicate that God spoke to the *combined* **host of heaven**, both faithful and fallen angelic beings.

> i. Some people forget that Satan and his fellow fallen angels have access to heaven (Job 1:6, Revelation 12:10). There is a well-intentioned but mistaken teaching that *God can allow no evil in His presence*, meaning that Satan and other fallen angels could not be in His presence. These passages show that God *can* allow evil in His presence, though He can have no *fellowship* with evil and one day all evil will be removed from His presence (Revelation 20:14-15).

c. Who will persuade Ahab king of Israel to go up, that he may fall at Ramoth Gilead? God wanted to bring judgment against Ahab, so He asked this group of **the host of heaven** for a volunteer to lead Ahab into battle.

d. I will go out and be a lying spirit in the mouth of all his prophets: Apparently, one of the *fallen* angels volunteered for this task. Since Ahab wanted to be deceived, God would give him what he wanted, using a willing fallen angel who worked through willing unfaithful prophets.

> i. "The Hebrew that underlies the phrase rendered 'a spirit' (came forward) reads literally, 'the (well-known) spirit,' i.e., Satan the tempter (as in Job 1:6-12).... Apparently Micaiah seems to assume among his hearers a working knowledge of the Book of Job." (Payne)

> ii. "This strange incident can only be understood against the background of other Old Testament passages, especially Deuteronomy 13:11 and Ezekiel 14:1-11. both these passages speak of people being enticed by false prophets, in each case as a result of a link with idolatry." (Selman)

8. (23-28) The reaction of the false prophets and Ahab.

Then Zedekiah the son of Chenaanah went near and struck Micaiah on the cheek, and said, "Which way did the spirit from the LORD go from me to speak to you?" And Micaiah said, "Indeed you shall see on that day when you go into an inner chamber to hide!" Then the king of Israel said, "Take Micaiah, and return him to Amon the governor of the city and to Joash the king's son; and say, 'Thus says the king: "Put this *fellow* in prison, and feed him with bread of affliction and water of affliction until I return in peace."'" But Micaiah said, "If you ever return in peace, the LORD has not spoken by me." And he said, "Take heed, all you people!"

a. **Then Zedekiah the son of Chenaanah went near and struck Micaiah on the cheek**: Zedekiah responded the way some do when they are defeated in an argument – he responded with violence.

b. **Put this fellow in prison**: King Ahab responded the way many tyrants do when they are confronted with the truth. Ahab wanted Micaiah imprisoned and deprived (**feed him with bread of affliction and water of affliction**).

i. "The phrase '*bread of affliction and water of affliction*' may be translated 'bread and water of scant measure.'" (Dilday)

c. **If you ever return in peace, the LORD has not spoken by me**: The prophet Micaiah made one final and ultimate appeal. He was willing to be judged by whether his prophecy came to pass or not. Since he knew his words were true, it was fitting for him to cry out as they dragged him back to prison, "**Take heed, all you people!**"

B. The death of King Ahab of Israel.

1. (29) Jehoshaphat and Ahab go into battle.

So the king of Israel and Jehoshaphat the king of Judah went up to Ramoth Gilead. And the king of Israel said to Jehoshaphat, "I will disguise myself and go into battle; but you put on your robes." So the king of Israel disguised himself, and they went into battle.

a. **So the king of Israel and Jehoshaphat the king of Judah went up to Ramoth Gilead**: It is easy to understand why King Ahab of Israel went to this battle; he didn't want to believe that Micaiah's prophecy was true and wanted to courageously oppose it. It is less easy to understand why King Jehoshaphat of Judah went to this battle with Ahab. He should have believed the prophecy of Micaiah and known that the battle would end in disaster and the death of at least Ahab.

i. It may be that Jehoshaphat had a *fatalistic* attitude towards the will of God, figuring that if it all was God's will then there was nothing he or anyone else could do about it.

b. **I will disguise myself and go into battle; but you put on your robes**: Going into the battle, Ahab did not want to be identified as a king and therefore be a special target. He thought this would help protect him against Micaiah's prophecy of doom. It is more difficult to explain why Jehoshaphat agreed to go into the battle as the only clearly identified king. Perhaps he was either not very smart or he had very great faith.

i. "Ahab pretended herein to honour Jehoshaphat, but intended to save himself, and to elude Micaiah's prophecy." (Trapp)

2. (30-34) Jehoshaphat is saved and Ahab dies in battle.

Now the king of Syria had commanded the captains of the chariots who *were* with him, saying, "Fight with no one small or great, but only with the king of Israel." So it was, when the captains of the chariots saw Jehoshaphat, that they said, "It *is* the king of Israel!" Therefore they surrounded him to attack; but Jehoshaphat cried out, and the LORD helped him, and God diverted them from him. For so it was, when the captains of the chariots saw that it was not the king of Israel, that they turned back from pursuing him. Now a certain man drew a bow at random, and struck the king of Israel between the joints of his armor. So he said to the driver of his chariot, "Turn around and take me out of the battle, for I am wounded." The battle increased that day, and the king of Israel propped *himself* up in *his* chariot facing the Syrians until evening; and about the time of sunset he died.

    a. **Fight with no one small or great, but only with the king of Israel**: Ahab's previous mercy to Ben-Hadad (1 Kings 20:31-34) did not win any lasting favor with the rulers of Syria. This strategy of the Syrian army made Ahab's counterstrategy of disguising himself in battle seem very wise.

        i. "Thus doth the unthankful infidel repay the mercy of his late victor… but God had a holy hand in it." (Trapp)

    b. **Jehoshaphat cried out, and the LORD helped him**: Finding himself as the only identifiable king in the battle, Jehoshaphat found himself quickly in danger. He **cried out** to the LORD and was rescued when **they turned back from pursuing him**.

    c. **Now a certain man drew a bow at random, and struck the king of Israel**: This seemed to be pure chance. It was a **certain man**, and he pulled his **bow at random** – but it struck as if it were a sin-seeking missile, hitting right **between the joints of his armor**. God orchestrated the unintended actions of man to result in an exercise of His judgment.

        i. "Probably this man already had shot many arrows, and he went on in his simplicity, little knowing that this particular arrow was to be guided through all the confusion straight to its mark by the unerring knowledge and power of God. Yet so it was." (Morgan)

        ii. "Men may secrete themselves so that other men may never find them; but when the hour of their judgment has come, God takes hold on some ordinary event and makes it the highway on which He comes to carry out His purpose. 'It just happened,' says the man of the world. 'God did it,' says the man of faith." (Morgan)

iii. "And now what joy could Ahab's black soul, ready to depart, have of his ivory house? Who had not rather be a Micaiah in the jail than Ahab in the chariot? Wicked men have the advantage of the way, godly men of the end." (Trapp)

d. **The king of Israel propped himself up in his chariot, facing the Syrians until evening**: Ahab faced the end of his life bravely, dying **propped…up in his chariot** to inspire his troops. When his death became known the battle was over.

i. "It appears that the Israelites and Jews maintained the fight the whole of the day; but when at evening the king died, and this was known, there was a proclamation made, probably with the consent of both Syrians and Israelites, that the war was over." (Clarke)

2 Chronicles 19 – Jehu's Rebuke

A. The goodness of God to Jehoshaphat.

1. (1) He returns safely after the battle.

Then Jehoshaphat the king of Judah returned safely to his house in Jerusalem.

> a. **Then Jehoshaphat the king of Judah returned safely**: This was the mercy of God. Jehoshaphat, clothed in the robes of the king and targeted for death by the army of Syria, should have been killed in battle. Yet he cried out to the LORD and was preserved, returning **safely to his house in Jerusalem**.
>
>> i. "The fact that Jehoshaphat reached home *safely* is significant. It contrasts his fate with Ahab's, and testifies to God's grace given to a person who was almost destroyed by undiscerning folly." (Selman)

2. (2-3) God rebukes Jehoshaphat through Jehu the prophet.

And Jehu the son of Hanani the seer went out to meet him, and said to King Jehoshaphat, "Should you help the wicked and love those who hate the LORD? Therefore the wrath of the LORD *is* upon you. Nevertheless good things are found in you, in that you have removed the wooden images from the land, and have prepared your heart to seek God."

> a. **Jehu the son of Hanani**: His father was a brave prophet, speaking to King Asa. The son Jehu also prophesied to Baasha the king of Israel (1 Kings 16:1, 16:7).
>
> b. **Should you help the wicked and love those who hate the LORD?** Jehu exposed the sin of too much love in Jehoshaphat. He professed to love God, but he also demonstrated love to **those who hate the LORD**. He should never have entered his personal and military alliances with Ahab and the kingdom of Israel.

i. Jehoshaphat should have read and considered Psalm 97:10: *You who love the* LORD, *hate evil!*

ii. "*Love* and *hate* in this context are formal terms for actions within a covenant or treaty relationship rather than emotional feelings, and *help* is a typical Chronicles expression for formal support." (Selman)

c. **Nevertheless good things are found in you**: God did not want Jehoshaphat to be crushed by the rebuke through the words of Jehu, so He included a word of encouragement.

- **That you have removed the wooden images from the land**: God knew that Jehoshaphat did not approve of *all* evil, so He encouraged the king in the places where he did hate evil and refuse compromise.

- **And have prepared your heart to seek God**: Not only did Jehoshaphat seek God, but he also **prepared** his **heart** to do so. This demonstrated the *high priority* Jehoshaphat placed on seeking God.

    i. "And this work of preparing or directing his heart is here ascribed to Jehoshaphat, as elsewhere it is attributed to God, Proverbs 16:1; Philippians 2:13, because it is man's action, but performed by God's grace, preventing, enabling, and inclining him to do it." (Poole)

B. Jehoshaphat's response.

1. (4) Jehoshaphat furthers godliness in the kingdom of Judah.

So Jehoshaphat dwelt at Jerusalem; and he went out again among the people from Beersheba to the mountains of Ephraim, and brought them back to the LORD **God of their fathers.**

a. **So Jehoshaphat dwelt at Jerusalem**: This means that he restricted his adventures abroad. He no longer went to the northern kingdom of Israel and was content to stay where he should.

b. **And brought them back to the** LORD **God of their fathers**: The wording implies that Jehoshaphat did this personally (**he went out again**). This was a wonderful personal work in the cause of godliness on behalf of the king of Judah.

i. "These itinerant campaigns have no real equivalent in the Old Testament, and the prophets, even though they travelled about, were not involved in systematic teaching of the word of God. The nearest parallel is in the New Testament, in Jesus' own itinerant ministry." (Selman)

2. (5-11) The judicial reforms of Jehoshaphat.

Then he set judges in the land throughout all the fortified cities of Judah, city by city, and said to the judges, "Take heed to what you are doing, for you do not judge for man but for the LORD, who *is* with you in the judgment. Now therefore, let the fear of the LORD be upon you; take care and do *it,* for *there is* no iniquity with the LORD our God, no partiality, nor taking of bribes." Moreover in Jerusalem, for the judgment of the LORD and for controversies, Jehoshaphat appointed some of the Levites and priests, and some of the chief fathers of Israel, when they returned to Jerusalem. And he commanded them, saying, "Thus you shall act in the fear of the LORD, faithfully and with a loyal heart: Whatever case comes to you from your brethren who dwell in their cities, whether of bloodshed or offenses against law or commandment, against statutes or ordinances, you shall warn them, lest they trespass against the LORD and wrath come upon you and your brethren. Do this, and you will not be guilty. And take notice: Amariah the chief priest *is* over you in all matters of the LORD; and Zebadiah the son of Ishmael, the ruler of the house of Judah, for all the king's matters; also the Levites *will be* officials before you. Behave courageously, and the LORD will be with the good."

a. **Take heed to what you are doing, for you do not judge for man but for the LORD, who is with you in the judgment**: This was a high and appropriate charge to the judges of Judah. We can understand the interest the Chronicler had in including this material not recorded in 1 or 2 Kings, using the example of Jehoshaphat as an encouragement to the leaders of the rebuilding community of Jerusalem and Judah after the exile.

i. "A very solemn and very necessary caution: judges should feel themselves in the place of God, and judge as those who know they shall be judged for their judgments." (Clarke)

b. **Behave courageously, and the LORD will be with the good**: The prominent theme of courageous obedience is repeated again. It was the job of the judges to **courageously** do what was good, and to then trust that **the LORD will be with the good**.

i. "WITHOUT good and wholesome *laws,* no nation can be prosperous; and vain are the best laws if they be not *judiciously* and *conscientiously* administered." (Clarke)

2 Chronicles 20 – Jehoshaphat's Victory

A. Jehoshaphat's prayer.

1. (1-2) Hostile enemies gather against Judah.

It happened after this *that* the people of Moab with the people of Ammon, and *others* with them besides the Ammonites, came to battle against Jehoshaphat. Then some came and told Jehoshaphat, saying, "A great multitude is coming against you from beyond the sea, from Syria; and they are in Hazazon Tamar" (which *is* En Gedi).

> a. **It happened after this**: This threat to Jehoshaphat and his kingdom happened after his return to seeking God, following his near-death when he allied himself with King Ahab of Israel.
>
> b. **The people of Moab with the people of Ammon, and others with them besides the Ammonites, came to battle against Jehoshaphat**: This **great multitude** was a significant threat against Jehoshaphat, whose last experience on the field of battle was a narrow escape from death.

2. (3-4) The nation gathers to seek God together.

And Jehoshaphat feared, and set himself to seek the Lord, and proclaimed a fast throughout all Judah. So Judah gathered together to ask *help* from the Lord; and from all the cities of Judah they came to seek the Lord.

> a. **And Jehoshaphat feared**: There was certainly a sense in which Jehoshaphat feared the great multitude coming against him. Yet the sense here is that he **feared** the Lord, and was more awed at the power and majesty of God than at the destructive force of his enemies.
>
>> i. "*Jehoshaphat feared*; partly from human frailty, and partly from the remembrance of his own guilt, and the wrath of God denounced against him for it, 2 Chronicles 19:2." (Poole)

b. **And set himself to seek the Lord**: Jehoshaphat set the example by his own personal devotion. He would not call upon the people of Judah to seek the Lord in a way that he did not.

i. This is a recurring theme in 2 Chronicles: the leaders who seek the Lord. We can expect God to do great things when His people, and especially the leaders of His people, seek Him. Others who sought the Lord in 2 Chronicles include:

- The faithful remnant of Israel (2 Chronicles 11:16).
- The people of Judah under King Asa (2 Chronicles 14:4, 15:12-13).
- Jehoshaphat in the early part of his reign (2 Chronicles 19:3).
- King Hezekiah (2 Chronicles 31:21).
- King Josiah (2 Chronicles 34:3).

ii. "His attitude is summed up by the word 'seek', which occurs twice in Hebrew though it is variously translated…. This is a key word in Jehoshaphat's reign, where it has the basic sense of 'worship', but also means to discover God's will. It shows that Jehoshaphat has a higher trust in God than in his military resources." (Selman)

c. **And proclaimed a fast throughout all Judah**: Jehoshaphat called the nation to express their humility and total dependence upon God through a public **fast** – that is, abstaining from all food for a period of time (typically a day or more) and drinking only water.

i. In Mark 9:28-29, Jesus explained that prayer and fasting together were a source of significant spiritual power. It isn't as if prayer and fasting make us more worthy to be blessed or do God's work; it is that prayer and fasting draw us closer to the heart of God, and they put us more in line with His power. Fasting is a powerful expression of our total dependence on Him.

d. **So Judah gathered together to ask help from the Lord**: This showed the Spirit of God at work among His people, prompting them to *respond* to the call issued from their king, Jehoshaphat.

i. "To get this assistance, it was necessary to *seek* it; and to get such *extraordinary* help, they should seek it in an *extraordinary way*; whence he proclaimed a *universal fast*, and all the people came up to Jerusalem to seek the Lord." (Clarke)

3. (5-12) Jehoshaphat leads the assembly in prayer.

Then Jehoshaphat stood in the assembly of Judah and Jerusalem, in the house of the LORD, before the new court, and said: "O LORD God of our fathers, *are* You not God in heaven, and do You *not* rule over all the kingdoms of the nations, and in Your hand *is there not* power and might, so that no one is able to withstand You? *Are* You not our God, *who* drove out the inhabitants of this land before Your people Israel, and gave it to the descendants of Abraham Your friend forever? And they dwell in it, and have built You a sanctuary in it for Your name, saying, 'If disaster comes upon us; sword, judgment, pestilence, or famine; we will stand before this temple and in Your presence (for Your name *is* in this temple), and cry out to You in our affliction, and You will hear and save.' And now, here are the people of Ammon, Moab, and Mount Seir; whom You would not let Israel invade when they came out of the land of Egypt, but they turned from them and did not destroy them; here they are, rewarding us by coming to throw us out of Your possession which You have given us to inherit. O our God, will You not judge them? For we have no power against this great multitude that is coming against us; nor do we know what to do, but our eyes *are* upon You."

> a. **Jehoshaphat stood in the assembly of Judah and Jerusalem**: This large assembly representing the gathered kingdom needed a leader, and the godly Jehoshaphat was the logical one to unite the assembly together in prayer.
>
>> i. Adam Clarke called this "One of the most sensible, pious, correct, and as to its composition, one of the most elegant prayers ever offered under the Old Testament dispensation."
>>
>> ii. "The late renowned Gustavus, king of Sweden, would pray ashipboard, ashore, in the field, in the midst of the battle; as if prayer alone were the surest piece of his whole armour." (Trapp)
>
> b. **Are You not God in heaven, and do You not rule over all the kingdoms of the nations**: Jehoshaphat began his great prayer by recognizing the power of Yahweh over **heaven** and all **kingdoms of the nations**. Other peoples believed in *localized* deities – as if the Moabites had their god, the Philistines their god, the Ammonites their god, and so on. Jehoshaphat recognized that the God of Israel was in fact the God of all **kingdoms**, of all **nations**, of all the earth and indeed of **heaven** itself.
>
> c. **Are You not our God, who drove out the inhabitants of this land before Your people Israel**: Jehoshaphat also prayed recognizing God's great works in the past on behalf of His people. The logic is clear: If God had done great things for His people in the past, He can be prevailed upon to do great things for His people at their moment of great need.

d. **We will stand in this temple and in Your presence**: Jehoshaphat stood on the ground of previous prayer and prior answers to prayer. This echoes the prayer Solomon prayed at the dedication of the temple and it calls upon God to answer not only Jehoshaphat's prayer but Solomon's also (2 Chronicles 6:20-25).

e. **Here are the people of Ammon, Moab, and Mount Seir; whom You would not let Israel invade when they came out of the land of Egypt**: Jehoshaphat prayed with both knowledge and understanding of God's word. He remembered that God did not allow Israel to invade these peoples when they came from Egypt to the Promised Land (Deuteronomy 2:8-9 and 2:19). Since God did not allow Israel to destroy those peoples then, it would be unjust if He allowed them to destroy Judah now. He implicitly prayed that God would not allow His people to suffer as a consequence of their prior obedience.

>i. "I like to plunge my hand into the promises, and then I find myself able to grasp with a grip of determination the mighty faithfulness of God. An omnipotent plea with God is: 'Do as thou hast said.'" (Spurgeon)

f. **For we have no power against this great multitude that is coming against us; nor do we know what to do, but our eyes are upon You**: Here Jehoshaphat – a king standing before his people – openly confessed that he did not have the answer. Their only answer was to trust in God, that His power and goodness would protect Judah when nothing else could.

>i. "The final phrase, *We do not know what to do, but our eyes are upon you*, is one of the most touching expressions of trust in God to be found anywhere in the Bible." (Selman)

>ii. "They said, 'Our eyes are upon thee.' What did they mean by that? They meant, 'Lord, if help does come, it must come from thee. We are looking to thee for it. It cannot come from anywhere else, so we look to thee. But we believe it will come, men will not look for that which they know will not come. We feel sure it will come, but we do not know how, so we are looking; we do not know when, but we are looking. We do not know what thou wouldest have us to do, but as the servant looks to her mistress, so are we looking to thee, Lord. Lord, we are looking.'" (Spurgeon)

B. God answers Jehoshaphat's prayer.

1. (13-15) The promise is given through a prophet.

Now all Judah, with their little ones, their wives, and their children, stood before the LORD. Then the Spirit of the LORD came upon Jahaziel the son of Zechariah, the son of Benaiah, the son of Jeiel, the son of Mattaniah, a Levite of the sons of Asaph, in the midst of the assembly. And he said, "Listen, all you of Judah and you inhabitants of Jerusalem, and you, King Jehoshaphat! Thus says the LORD to you: 'Do not be afraid nor dismayed because of this great multitude, for the battle *is* not yours, but God's.'"

> a. **Now all Judah, with their little ones, their wives, and their children, stood before the LORD**: The sense is that after Jehoshaphat's great prayer, the people stood silently **before the LORD**, waiting upon Him for some sense of direction or encouragement.
>
>> i. "You could have heard the sound even of the wind among the trees at the time, for they were as hushed and as quiet as you were just now. Oh, when you know the Lord means to deliver you, bow your head and just give him the quiet, deep, solemn worship of your spirit." (Spurgeon)
>
> b. **Then the Spirit of the LORD came upon Jahaziel the son of Zechariah… in the midst of the assembly**: Out of this huge group gathered together, the **Spirit of the LORD** came upon one man to speak to the entire **assembly**. This was a spontaneous word of prophecy that came as God's people waited before Him and sought Him.
>
> c. **Do not be afraid nor dismayed because of this great multitude, for the battle is not yours, but God's**: The threat was real – there really was a **great multitude** dedicated to destroying Judah. Yet the command was to **not be afraid nor dismayed**, because **the battle** was God's battle. He would fight on behalf of Judah against this **great multitude**.

2. (16-17) The command to stand and believe.

"'Tomorrow go down against them. They will surely come up by the Ascent of Ziz, and you will find them at the end of the brook before the Wilderness of Jeruel. You will not *need* to fight in this *battle*. Position yourselves, stand still and see the salvation of the LORD, who is with you, O Judah and Jerusalem!' Do not fear or be dismayed; tomorrow go out against them, for the LORD *is* with you."

> a. **Tomorrow go down against them**: This was an important command. One might think that because one might think that because of the promise of 2 Chronicles 20:15, Judah would not even have to show up at the battle and perhaps God wanted them to stay in Jerusalem and pray. Yet, God

wanted them to go out to battle against the enemy and He would use their participation in the battle.

b. **They will surely come up by the Ascent of Ziz**: God knew the plans of the attacking armies precisely and He relayed this information to the king and people of Judah.

c. **You will not need to fight in this battle. Position yourselves, stand still and see the salvation of the LORD**: Judah did not **need to fight in this battle**, yet it did not mean there was *nothing* for them to do. It was a significant step of faith to **position yourselves**, to **stand still**, and to believe that you would **see the salvation of the LORD** in the face of a large attacking army.

d. **Tomorrow go out against them**: There were any number of ways that God *could* have defeated these armies assembled against Judah, but He appointed a way that demanded the participation of faith on behalf of Judah. They had to work in a faith-partnership with God.

3. (18-19) The response of worship and praise.

And Jehoshaphat bowed his head with *his* face to the ground, and all Judah and the inhabitants of Jerusalem bowed before the LORD, worshiping the LORD. Then the Levites of the children of the Kohathites and of the children of the Korahites stood up to praise the LORD God of Israel with voices loud and high.

a. **Bowed before the LORD, worshiping the LORD**: Both king and people knew that the prophetic word through Jahaziel was a true message from God. Receiving it as a word from God, they worshipped the LORD who promised to save His people against this terrible threat. It was a logical response.

i. "They worshipped, but why did they do it? They were not delivered. No, but they were sure they were going to be delivered. Their enemies were not dead. No, they were all alive, but they were sure they would be dead, so they had worship, and their devotion rose from trustful and grateful hearts." (Spurgeon)

b. **Then the Levites of the children of the Kohathites and of the children of the Korahites stood up to praise the LORD God of Israel with voices loud and high**: First they worshipped with the posture of their bodies and hearts; then with song led by the chorus of the Levitical worship leaders.

4. (20-21) The battle is led by singing worshippers.

So they rose early in the morning and went out into the Wilderness of Tekoa; and as they went out, Jehoshaphat stood and said, "Hear me,

O Judah and you inhabitants of Jerusalem: Believe in the LORD your God, and you shall be established; believe His prophets, and you shall prosper." And when he had consulted with the people, he appointed those who should sing to the LORD, and who should praise the beauty of holiness, as they went out before the army and were saying:

"Praise the LORD,
For His mercy *endures* forever."

> a. **So they rose early in the morning and went**: This showed that they really did believe the prophecy from Jahaziel. It was one thing to profess faith among an excited assembly; it was another thing to actually walk out to meet the enemy armies.
>
> b. **Believe in the LORD your God, and you shall be established; believe His prophets, and you shall prosper**: With this exhortation, Jehoshaphat showed that he considered believing the **prophets** of God to be equal to believing **the LORD your God** Himself. This remains true; to believe God's word is to believe God Himself.
>
> c. **And when he had consulted with the people**: Jehoshaphat was wise and good enough to know that since this crisis put **the people** at risk, then **the people** should be **consulted** regarding some of the details, including **those who should sing to the LORD**.
>
>> i. We should not think that at this moment the monarchy of Israel became a democracy. Instead, it fulfilled what it should have always been: a monarchy that was in touch with, and responsive to, the people and their needs and opinions.
>
> d. **Who should praise the beauty of holiness**: God's holiness – His "set-apart-ness" – has a wonderful and distinct **beauty** about it. It is *beautiful* that God is God and not man; that He is more than the greatest man or a super-man. His holy love, grace, justice, and majesty are *beautiful*.
>
> e. **As they went out before the army**: The singers and worshippers *led* the army into this battle. It was clear that Judah expected a battle because they brought the **army**. Yet it was also clear that they expected a supernatural battle because they let the singers and worshippers go **before the army**.
>
>> i. These worshippers obviously took a dangerous step of faith. If the unthinkable happened and God did not intervene, they would be the first ones slaughtered by a merciless enemy. No wonder King Jehoshaphat **consulted with the people** about who these singers and worshippers should be.
>
> f. **And were saying: "Praise the LORD, for His mercy *endures* forever"**: This was the refrain of their song. They did not rest on their own merits or

even the merits of Abraham, Moses, or David. They trusted and rested on the enduring **mercy** of God.

5. (22-30) Victory over the enemy and the plundering of the enemy.

Now when they began to sing and to praise, the Lord set ambushes against the people of Ammon, Moab, and Mount Seir, who had come against Judah; and they were defeated. For the people of Ammon and Moab stood up against the inhabitants of Mount Seir to utterly kill and destroy *them.* **And when they had made an end of the inhabitants of Seir, they helped to destroy one another. So when Judah came to a place overlooking the wilderness, they looked toward the multitude; and there** *were* **their dead bodies, fallen on the earth. No one had escaped. When Jehoshaphat and his people came to take away their spoil, they found among them an abundance of valuables on the dead bodies, and precious jewelry, which they stripped off for themselves, more than they could carry away; and they were three days gathering the spoil because there was so much. And on the fourth day they assembled in the Valley of Berachah, for there they blessed the Lord; therefore the name of that place was called The Valley of Berachah until this day. Then they returned, every man of Judah and Jerusalem, with Jehoshaphat in front of them, to go back to Jerusalem with joy, for the Lord had made them rejoice over their enemies. So they came to Jerusalem, with stringed instruments and harps and trumpets, to the house of the Lord. And the fear of God was on all the kingdoms of** *those* **countries when they heard that the Lord had fought against the enemies of Israel. Then the realm of Jehoshaphat was quiet, for his God gave him rest all around.**

> a. **Now when they began to sing and to praise, the Lord set ambushes against the people…and they were defeated**: Just as God promised, the battle belonged to Him and He won the victory on behalf of Judah. We might say that it was not their **praise** that won the battle, rather it was their faith, yet their **praise** was sure *evidence* of their faith. When one really believes the words and promises of God, they cannot but help to **praise** Him.
>
>> i. "The form of the word for *ambushes* is slightly unusual and really means 'ambushers', and since it is said that God sent them, some have thought that they must be supernatural agents." (Selman)
>
> b. **For the people of Ammon and Moab stood up against the inhabitants of Mount Seir to utterly kill and destroy them**: This describes *how* God **set ambushes** against the enemies of Judah. He prompted them to fight amongst themselves so that they defeated one another, and all Judah had to do was to collect the spoil.

i. "Some understand this ambushment of the holy angels, sent suddenly in upon them to slay them; whereupon they mistaking the matter, and supposing it had been their own companions, flew upon them, and so sheathed their swords in one another's bowels." (Trapp)

c. **So when Judah came to a place overlooking the wilderness, they looked toward the multitude; and there *were* their dead bodies**: It seems that the army of Judah, led by the singing worshippers, never actually engaged the enemy armies. Perhaps God spared them that particular test of faith and by the time they had actually met the enemy armies, they were already **dead**, and **no one had escaped**.

d. **On the fourth day they assembled in the Valley of Berachah, for there they blessed the Lord**: They had assembled together to cry out to God for His deliverance; it was appropriate that they also assemble together to thank God and to bless His name, **for the Lord had made them rejoice over their enemies**.

e. **And the fear of God was on all the kingdoms of those countries when they heard that the Lord had fought against the enemies of Israel**: The victory itself was a warning to the neighboring nations. This gave King Jehoshaphat and his kingdom **rest all around**.

i. We notice that this did not become a *pattern* for warfare in Judah or an invitation to conquest, led by the "invincible army of praise." This was in direct response to a specific word from God; to disobey would have been a sin, but it would have also been a sin to make it a standing pattern for all future warfare in Judah.

ii. The *principle* of God fighting on behalf of His people and the glory of trusting-praise before the battle remained; *how* God wanted His people to participate in the battle would differ from circumstance to circumstance according to the leading of the Holy Spirit in their situation.

iii. Most importantly, we can praise God that Jesus Christ has fought the battle for our salvation and to rescue us from the judgment of God that we so rightly deserved. This makes us *more than conquerors* in Jesus Christ because He fights the battle and defeats our foe, and we share in the spoil (Romans 8:37).

6. (31-37) The close of Jehoshaphat's reign.

So Jehoshaphat was king over Judah. *He was* **thirty-five years old when he became king, and he reigned twenty-five years in Jerusalem. His mother's name** *was* **Azubah the daughter of Shilhi. And he walked in the way of his father Asa, and did not turn aside from it, doing** *what* *was* right in the sight of the LORD. Nevertheless the high places were not taken away, for as yet the people had not directed their hearts to the God of their fathers. Now the rest of the acts of Jehoshaphat, first and last, indeed they *are* written in the book of Jehu the son of Hanani, which *is* mentioned in the book of the kings of Israel. After this Jehoshaphat king of Judah allied himself with Ahaziah king of Israel, who acted very wickedly. And he allied himself with him to make ships to go to Tarshish, and they made the ships in Ezion Geber. But Eliezer the son of Dodavah of Mareshah prophesied against Jehoshaphat, saying, "Because you have allied yourself with Ahaziah, the LORD has destroyed your works." Then the ships were wrecked, so that they were not able to go to Tarshish.

a. **He walked in the way of his father Asa**: Asa was a good king and Jehoshaphat his son followed in his footsteps and did **what was right in the sight of the LORD**.

b. **Nevertheless the high places were not taken away**: Jehoshaphat did not do *everything* he should have as a king. Yet the Chronicler seems to tell us that this was largely because **the people had not directed their hearts to the God of their fathers**. Jehoshaphat was a reformer, but the people would not be thoroughly reformed.

i. "The fault was not in Jehoshaphat, but in the people, who, though they did worship the true God, yet would not be confined to the temple, but for their own conveniency, or from their affection to their ancient customs, chose to worship him in the high places." (Poole)

c. **And he allied himself with him to make ships to go to Tarshish**: 1 Kings 22:48-49 tells us that this initial partnership with **Ahaziah king of Israel** ended in disaster when *the ships were wrecked at Ezion Geber*. It also tells us that after the rebuke from **Eliezer the son of Dodavah**, King Jehoshaphat refused another offer of alliance with Ahaziah. He had learned his lesson and did not add error upon error.

i. "The phrase 'trading ships' interprets a more literal rendering of the Hebrew, i.e., 'ships that could go to Tarshish.' The thought is that these vessels belonged to the class of ships that went to Tarshish; their actual destination was Ophir (cf. on 2 Chronicles 8:18; 1 Kings 22:48)." (Payne)

d. **The LORD has destroyed your works**: This might seem cruel of God, but it was actually mercy. It prevented Jehoshaphat from another ungodly alliance, and yielding to this temptation had hurt him before.

2 Chronicles 21 – Jehoram's Evil Reign

A. The sins of Jehoram.

1. (1-5) The murder of his brothers.

And Jehoshaphat rested with his fathers, and was buried with his fathers in the City of David. Then Jehoram his son reigned in his place. He had brothers, the sons of Jehoshaphat: Azariah, Jehiel, Zechariah, Azaryahu, Michael, and Shephatiah; all these were **the sons of Jehoshaphat king of Israel. Their father gave them great gifts of silver and gold and precious things, with fortified cities in Judah; but he gave the kingdom to Jehoram, because he** was **the firstborn. Now when Jehoram was established over the kingdom of his father, he strengthened himself and killed all his brothers with the sword, and also** others **of the princes of Israel. Jehoram** was **thirty-two years old when he became king, and he reigned eight years in Jerusalem.**

> a. **Then Jehoram his son reigned in his place**: The father of **Jehoram** was the godly King **Jehoshaphat**. Yet one of the worst things Jehoshaphat ever did was arrange the marriage of his son **Jehoram** to Athaliah, the daughter of the evil King Ahab and his wife Jezebel (2 Kings 8:16-18; 8:26).
>
> b. **Their father gave them great gifts...with fortified cities**: Jehoshaphat followed the same wise policy with his sons that Rehoboam had previously followed (2 Chronicles 11:18-23) – to scatter them throughout the kingdom and away from the capital so they would not be a concentrated threat to his one son to succeed him, Jehoram.
>
> > i. "*Jehoshaphat king of Israel*; so he is called, either, 1. Because he was so by right. Or, 2. Because he was king not only of Judah and Benjamin, but of a great number of Israelites, who had come into and settled themselves in his kingdom.... Or, 3. Because all his subjects were Israelites; and therefore he was *king of Israel*, though not *of all Israel*....

Some say *Israel* was foisted into some copies by the transcriber instead of Judah, as it was first written." (Poole)

c. **He strengthened himself and killed all his brothers with the sword, and also others of the princes of Israel**: Despite Jehoshaphat's wise policy of scattering his sons, Jehoram made it a point to murder all his brothers so they would not be any kind of a threat against his reign.

i. "Jehoram's response to God's goodness, however, was to put not only *all his brothers to the sword*, but some of his leading 'officials' as well. 'Made himself strong' therefore, clearly means the violent removal of all other possible claimants to the throne." (Selman)

ii. The wickedness of Jehoram was not a surprise, considering how much he allowed himself to be influenced by the house of Ahab. "Josephus expands on this, indicating that he committed the murders at the prompting of Athaliah." (Dilday)

iii. Perhaps some people thought that the marriage between the royal families of the kingdom of Judah and the kingdom of Israel would lift up the kingdom of Israel spiritually. It didn't work that way. Instead, it brought the kingdom of Judah *down* spiritually.

2. (6-7) Why God showed mercy to Jehoram.

And he walked in the way of the kings of Israel, just as the house of Ahab had done, for he had the daughter of Ahab as a wife; and he did evil in the sight of the Lord. Yet the Lord would not destroy the house of David, because of the covenant that He had made with David, and since He had promised to give a lamp to him and to his sons forever.

a. **He walked in the way of the kings of Israel**: This was not a compliment. While the southern kingdom of Judah had a mixture of godly and wicked kings, the northern kingdom of Israel had nothing but evil, God-rejecting kings.

i. "This was *Athaliah*, daughter of Ahab and Jezebel, who was famous for her impieties and cruelty, as was her most profligate mother. It is likely that she was the principal cause of Jehoram's cruelty and profaneness." (Clarke)

ii. His father Jehoshaphat was a godly man who had a bad and sinful habit of making compromising associations. The worst fruit of this sinful tendency was not evident until after Jehoshaphat's death.

b. **Yet the Lord would not destroy the house of David, because of the covenant that He had made with David**: The implication is that Jehoram's evil was great enough to justify such judgment, but God withheld it out of faithfulness to his ancestor David.

> i. "The *lamp* was more than a symbol of life and of testimony, it reminded the hearer of the covenant (Psalm 132:17, c.f. 2 Chronicles 21:7)." (Wiseman)

> ii. When God first made this promise to David it was not formally called a covenant (1 Chronicles 17, 2 Samuel 7). However, it was divinely called a covenant afterwards (2 Samuel 23:5; Psalm 89:3, 89:34; Psalm 132:11-12). (Payne)

B. The consequences of his sin

1. (8-11) Jehoram's sinful compromise and the revolt of Edom and Libnah.

In his days Edom revolted against Judah's authority, and made a king over themselves. So Jehoram went out with his officers, and all his chariots with him. And he rose by night and attacked the Edomites who had surrounded him and the captains of the chariots. Thus Edom has been in revolt against Judah's authority to this day. At that time Libnah revolted against his rule, because he had forsaken the Lord God of his fathers. Moreover he made high places in the mountains of Judah, and caused the inhabitants of Jerusalem to commit harlotry, and led Judah astray.

> a. **In his days Edom revolted against Judah's authority**: For some time, Edom was essentially a client kingdom to Judah and owed them tribute (taxes). Under the reign of Jehoram, the leaders of Edom sensed weakness in Judah and their opportunity to free themselves.

> > i. "Nothing else is known of trouble in Libnah, a town of uncertain location on Judah's western border not far from Lachish." (Selman)

> > ii. "As long as the kings of Judah remained true to their allegiance to God, they were able to keep in subjection the surrounding nations; but just so soon as they revolted from God these people revolted from them. It was as though power descended into them from the source of all power; and when that link between themselves and God was broken, that between themselves and their subordinates was broken also." (Meyer)

> > iii. This applies to our *passions*; when we are properly submitted to God, our passions are properly submitted to us. When we come out from submission to God, we often find our passions flare up in seemingly overwhelming strength. It also applies to the proper exercise

of authority in any sphere – home, government, church, society – it is safe to submit to those who are already submitted to God.

b. **He rose by night and attacked the Edomites who had surrounded him**: We aren't told the specific outcome of this battle; perhaps it was inconclusive. Yet because of Edom's continued revolt against Judah, it was evident that Judah did not exert itself over Edom and they remained somewhat independent.

c. **Thus Edom has been in revolt against Judah's authority**: This is evidence of the weakness of the kingdom of Jehoram. He thought that the marriage alliance with Ahab and the kingdom of Israel would make Judah stronger, but this act of disobedience only made them weaker – **because he had forsaken the LORD God of his fathers**.

d. **Moreover he made high places**: It was the policy of both his father Jehoshaphat (2 Chronicles 17:6) and his grandfather Asa (2 Chronicles 14:1-5) to work against these **high places**. Jehoram *promoted* them instead.

i. "He is the first Judean king who actually constructed *high places*, among which is probably to be counted a Baal temple in Jerusalem (*cf.* 2 Chronicles 23:17)." (Selman)

e. **And caused the inhabitants of Jerusalem to commit harlotry**: Their idolatry was likened to **harlotry** for two reasons. First, the worship of these pagan sex/fertility gods and goddesses often involved immorality with a pagan priestess or priest. Second, since Israel was obligated to be faithful to God as a wife is obligated to be faithful to her husband, their idolatry was like **harlotry** in a spiritual sense.

2. (12-15) Elijah's letter of rebuke to Jehoram.

And a letter came to him from Elijah the prophet, saying, Thus says the LORD God of your father David: Because you have not walked in the ways of Jehoshaphat your father, or in the ways of Asa king of Judah, but have walked in the way of the kings of Israel, and have made Judah and the inhabitants of Jerusalem to play the harlot like the harlotry of the house of Ahab, and also have killed your brothers, those of your father's household, *who were* better than yourself, behold, the LORD will strike your people with a serious affliction; your children, your wives, and all your possessions; and you *will become* very sick with a disease of your intestines, until your intestines come out by reason of the sickness, day by day.

a. **And a letter came to him from Elijah the prophet**: Elijah's main ministry was to the kings of the northern tribes, the kingdom of Israel.

Yet on occasion God also used him to speak to kings of Judah, this time through **a letter**.

> i. "How could this be, when Elijah was rapt up to heaven in Jehoshaphat's time, 2 Kings 2; 3:11. *Answer*. Either, 1. This was Elisha, or some other prophet called Elijah, because he acted in the spirit and the power of Elijah, for which John the Baptist is also called. Or rather, 2. This was really written by Elijah, who by the Spirit did clearly foresee and foretell the reign and acts of Jehoram." (Poole)
>
> ii. "Elijah may, however, have been gone by the time of the delivery of his letter, so that its sentence of doom could have had the force of a voice coming from the dead." (Payne)

b. **But have walked in the way of the kings of Israel**: This was God's main complaint against Jehoram. He had refused to follow the pattern of his father and grandfather and instead decided to follow the example of his father-in-law Ahab.

c. **Who were better than yourself**: God considered the brothers of Jehoram to be more worthy successors to the throne of Judah than Jehoram himself.

d. **You will become very sick with a disease of your intestines**: God promised this painful ailment would come to Jehoram as a punishment for his sins.

3. (16-17) Further troubles of the reign of Jehoram.

Moreover the LORD stirred up against Jehoram the spirit of the Philistines and the Arabians who *were* near the Ethiopians. And they came up into Judah and invaded it, and carried away all the possessions that were found in the king's house, and also his sons and his wives, so that there was not a son left to him except Jehoahaz, the youngest of his sons.

a. **Moreover the LORD stirred up against Jehoram the spirit of the Philistines and the Arabians**: This was another judgment against Jehoram – to bring enemies against him to trouble his reign.

b. **Also his sons and his wives, so that there was not a son left to him except Jehoahaz, the youngest of his sons**: This was a fitting judgment against Jehoram. In trying to protect his own throne he murdered all his brothers, and eventually found that all **his sons** were taken except one.

> i. "In the outworkings of God's justice, the man who began by massacring his own brothers ended by suffering the loss of his sons and wives." (Payne)

4. (18-20) Jehoram's gruesome end.

After all this the LORD struck him in his intestines with an incurable disease. Then it happened in the course of time, after the end of two years, that his intestines came out because of his sickness; so he died in severe pain. And his people made no burning for him, like the burning for his fathers. He was thirty-two years old when he became king. He reigned in Jerusalem eight years and, to no one's sorrow, departed. However they buried him in the City of David, but not in the tombs of the kings.

> a. **After all this the LORD struck him in his intestines with an incurable disease**: Again, this was a fitting judgment. There was a sense in which Jehoram was rotten spiritually from within; here, God simply caused the physical condition of his body to correspond to the spiritual condition of his soul – **so he died in severe pain**.
>
>> i. "The *Targum* seems to intimate that he had a constipation and inflammation in his bowels; and that at last his bowels gushed out." (Clarke)
>>
>> ii. Apparently he suffered for **two years**. "This was a long while to lie under so intolerable a disease; and yet all this was but a typical hell, a foretaste of eternal torments, unless he repented." (Trapp)
>>
>> iii. "Translation problems have increased the difficulty, and the end may have come suddenly, 'in two days' (*cf.* Keil, Dillard), rather than at the end of the *second year*." (Selman)
>
> b. **And, to no one's sorrow, departed**: This compromising and sinful king was not mourned when he died. "He is one of the most unlovely of all the kings of Judah. 'Exalted by Jehovah,' he was for his wickedness thrust down to a dishonoured grave." (Knapp)
>
>> i. "As he lived wickedly, so he died wishedly." (Trapp)
>>
>> ii. "He was hated while he lived, and neglected when he died; visibly cursed of God, and necessarily execrate by the people whom he had lived only to corrupt and oppress. No *annalist* is mentioned as having taken the pains to write any account of his vile life." (Clarke)
>>
>> iii. "Strange indeed is the human heart. It turns to evil, and pursues it persistently; and yet it never really loves those who lead it in the way of evil.... Love is only inspired by goodness. Men will follow those who lead them in the ways of corruption, but such following is always inspired by evil selfishness, and never by admiration or love." (Morgan)

2 Chronicles 22 – The Evil Reigns of Ahaziah and Athaliah

A. Ahaziah's rise and fall.

1. (1-4) The brief and wicked reign of Ahaziah.

Then the inhabitants of Jerusalem made Ahaziah his youngest son king in his place, for the raiders who came with the Arabians into the camp had killed all the older *sons*. So Ahaziah the son of Jehoram, king of Judah, reigned. Ahaziah *was* forty-two years old when he became king, and he reigned one year in Jerusalem. His mother's name *was* Athaliah the granddaughter of Omri. He also walked in the ways of the house of Ahab, for his mother advised him to do wickedly. Therefore he did evil in the sight of the LORD, like the house of Ahab; for they were his counselors after the death of his father, to his destruction.

    a. **The inhabitants of Jerusalem made Ahaziah his youngest son king in his place**: As will be demonstrated, the son of Jehoram named **Ahaziah** was an unworthy man. Yet the Chronicler explains why the **inhabitants of Jerusalem** made him king – because raiding Arabians **had killed all the older sons**.

        i. "*Men that came with the Arabians*; either, 1. A cruel sort of men who came along with the Arabians, and therefore slew those whom the Arabians had spared, and only carried into captivity. Or, 2. The Philistines, who did accompany the Arabians in this expedition, 2 Chronicles 21:16, who lived near the kingdom of Judah, and therefore thought to make as sure work as they could in destroying all the branches of the royal family." (Poole)

    b. **He reigned one year in Jerusalem**: The short life and reign of Jehoram (he reigned only eight years and died at 40 years of age) should have warned

Ahaziah. His brief reign (**one year**) shows he was even *less* blessed than his father Jehoram.

> i. "Ahaziah succeeded his father, Jehoram, in the critical year 841 B.C. He was not to survive the momentous waves of the political events that were to inundate the ancient Near East in that year. Indeed, in 841 B.C. Shalmaneser III of Assyria (859-824 B.C.) at last was able to break the coalition of western allies with whom he had previously fought a long series of battles (853, 848, 845)." (Patterson and Austel)

> ii. **Forty-two years old**: This is at odds with 2 Kings 8:26 which says that Ahaziah took the throne when 22 years old. "I am satisfied the reading in 2 Chronicles 22:2, is a *mistake*; and that we should read... *twenty-two* instead of *forty-two* years.... Is there a single ancient author of any kind, but particularly those who have written on matters of *history* and *chronology*, whose works have been transmitted to us free of similar errors, owing to the negligence of transcribers?" (Clarke on 2 Kings 8:26)

> iii. "The reading found in the LXX and 2 Kings 8:26 for Ahaziah's age of 'twenty-two years' is to be adopted, rather than the MT's 'forty-two,' which would make him older than his father (cf. 2 Chronicles 21:20)." (Payne)

c. **He also walked in the ways of the house of Ahab, for his mother advised him to do wickedly**: Ahaziah's mother was the wicked **Athaliah**, who was the daughter of Ahab and Jezebel of the northern kingdom of Israel and she was given in marriage to Jehoram, the king of Judah. She brought her influence to bear upon her son and made him more of a son of Ahab and Jezebel than a son of David and his godly descendants.

> i. Through her control of her son and her subsequent reign as queen (2 Chronicles 22:10-12), **Athaliah** exercised great power in Judah.

> ii. "During both reigns, therefore, Ahab's dynasty was in effective control of Judah. The unity of Judah and Israel is eloquently symbolized by the names of their kings. No other Israelite king was called Jehoram or Ahaziah, yet both names are used of successive contemporary rulers in Judah and Israel." (Selman)

2. (5-9) Ahaziah falls in judgment along with Ahab's house by Jehu in Israel.

He also followed their advice, and went with Jehoram the son of Ahab king of Israel to war against Hazael king of Syria at Ramoth Gilead; and the Syrians wounded Joram. Then he returned to Jezreel to recover from the wounds which he had received at Ramah, when he fought against Hazael king of Syria. And Azariah the son of Jehoram, king of

Judah, went down to see Jehoram the son of Ahab in Jezreel, because he was sick. His going to Joram was God's occasion for Ahaziah's downfall; for when he arrived, he went out with Jehoram against Jehu the son of Nimshi, whom the LORD had anointed to cut off the house of Ahab. And it happened, when Jehu was executing judgment on the house of Ahab, and found the princes of Judah and the sons of Ahaziah's brothers who served Ahaziah, that he killed them. Then he searched for Ahaziah; and they caught him (he was hiding in Samaria), and brought him to Jehu. When they had killed him, they buried him, "because," they said, "he is the son of Jehoshaphat, who sought the LORD with all his heart." So the house of Ahaziah had no one to assume power over the kingdom.

a. **Went with Jehoram the son of Ahab king of Israel to war against Hazael king of Syria**: Ahaziah's close association with the wicked house of Ahab developed into a war alliance with Israel against Syria. His connection with his mother's family (she was a daughter of Ahab and Jezebel, 2 Kings 8:18) was so strong and sympathetic that he paid a visit to the injured and sick King of Israel (**Jehoram**).

b. **Then he searched for Ahaziah; and they caught him**: Jehu is one of the more interesting men of the Old Testament. God raised him up to bring judgment against the dynasty of Omri that ruled the northern kingdom of Israel (2 Kings 9:1-26). In the course of fulfilling that divine commission, he also came against **Ahaziah**, king of Judah.

i. Jehu had no direct command or commission from God to bring judgment upon the king of Judah, but he did anyway. Consciously or unconsciously, he was guided by God and he killed Ahaziah.

ii. **And the sons of Ahaziah's brothers**: "The Hebrew calls them 'sons of the brothers of Ahaziah', but, since his actual brothers were dead (2 Chronicles 21:17; 22:1) and their sons were probably no more than children, they are best regarded as 'kinsmen.'" (Selman)

c. **When they had killed him**: Ahaziah was happy to associate himself with the northern kingdom of Israel and their wicked kings. Therefore he died in the same judgment that came upon the king of Israel through Jehu.

i. Ahaziah was also a blood relative of Ahab (Ahab was his grandfather), therefore making him liable under the judgment that came upon Ahab and his descendants. "By failing to separate himself from Jehoram, he made himself liable to suffer the same punishment that God had previously announced against Ahab's house which he had chosen Hazael and Jehu to carry out." (Selman)

ii. 2 Kings 9:1-26 also records the reign of Ahaziah and his inglorious end at the hands of Jehu. The reconciliation of the details of the death of Ahaziah between 2 Chronicles 22 and 2 Kings 9 is complicated, but definitely possible. Adam Clarke – among other commentators – carefully works out the details.

iii. "The final movements of Ahaziah are difficult to trace but may perhaps be reconstructed as follows: he fled south from Jezreel so as to hide in Samaria. He was brought to Jehu, who fatally wounded him near Ibleam (between Jezreel and Samaria); he fled by chariot northwest to Megiddo, where he died (2 Kings 9:27); and his body was carried by Ahaziah's servants to Jerusalem (2 Kings 9:28), where they buried him." (Payne)

d. **They buried him**: When Ahaziah was killed in battle, they gave him a dignified burial – not for his own sake, but only because his ancestor Jehoshaphat was a godly man.

B. The reign of Queen Athaliah.

1. (10) The evil Queen Athaliah reigns over Judah.

Now when Athaliah the mother of Ahaziah saw that her son was dead, she arose and destroyed all the royal heirs of the house of Judah.

a. **When Athaliah the mother of Ahaziah saw that her son was dead**: She used the occasion of her son's death to take power for *herself*, and she *reigned over the land* for six years (2 Kings 11:1-3).

i. We remember that Athaliah was the daughter of Ahab and Jezebel, and was given to Jehoram, king of Judah as a bride. She was a bad influence on both her husband (King Jehoram of Judah) and her son (King Ahaziah of Judah).

b. **And destroyed all the royal heirs**: Athaliah was from the family of Ahab, and Jehu had completely destroyed all of Ahab's descendants in Israel. Now, after Jehu's coup, Athaliah tried to save something for Ahab's family by trying to eliminate the house of David in Judah.

i. "However, no evil anger is sufficient to frustrate divine purpose, and against the wickedness of one woman God set the compassion of another." (Morgan)

ii. Years before, the king of Judah – Jehoshaphat – married his son to this daughter of Ahab and Jezebel, hoping to make an alliance with those wicked and apostate leaders. "And this was the fruit of Jehoshaphat's marrying his son to a daughter of that idolatrous and wicked house of Ahab, even the extirpation of all his posterity but one." (Poole)

iii. "No character in history, sacred or secular, stands out blacker or more hideous than this daughter-in-law of the godly Jehoshaphat." (Knapp)

2. (11-12) God uses Jehoshabeath to preserve the royal line of David.

But Jehoshabeath, the daughter of the king, took Joash the son of Ahaziah, and stole him away from among the king's sons who were being murdered, and put him and his nurse in a bedroom. So Jehoshabeath, the daughter of King Jehoram, the wife of Jehoiada the priest (for she was the sister of Ahaziah), hid him from Athaliah so that she did not kill him. And he was hidden with them in the house of God for six years, while Athaliah reigned over the land.

a. **But Jehoshabeath**: This little-known woman (known as *Jehosheba* in 2 Kings 11:2) had an important place in God's plan of the ages. Through her courage and ingenuity, she preserved the royal line of David through which the Messiah would come. Evil people like Athaliah will begin their work, **but** God can always raise up a **Jehoshabeath**.

i. "This incident is really a tale of two women." (Selman)

ii. "Thus evil always breaks down. It is extremely clever, it calculates on all the changes, and seems to leave no unguarded place; but with unvarying regularity it fails somewhere to cover up its tracks, or to insure its victory." (Morgan)

iii. **She was the sister of Ahaziah**: "It is not likely that Jehosheba was the daughter of *Athaliah*; she was a sister, we find, to Ahaziah the son of Athaliah, but probably by a different mother." (Clarke)

b. **He was hidden with them in the house of God for six years**: Though Ahaziah was a bad king who made evil alliances, he was still a descendant of David and the successor of his royal line. For the sake of David, God remembered His promise and spared this one young survivor to the massacre of Athaliah. The line of David was almost extinguished and continued only in the presence of a small boy named **Joash**, but God preserved that flickering flame.

i. "Josephus (*Antiquities* 9.7.1) says that the *bedroom* where the child and his nurse hid was a room where spare furniture and mattresses were stored." (Wiseman)

ii. Like the boy Samuel, Joash grew up in the temple. Like Samuel, he probably found little ways to help the priests, whatever could be done without attracting too much attention.

iii. "Nothing but the miraculous intervention of the divine providence could have saved the line of David at this time, and preserved the prophecy relative to the Messiah. The whole truth of that prophecy, and the salvation of the world, appeared to be now suspended on the brittle thread of the life of an *infant* of a year old, (see 2 Chronicles 24:1,) to destroy whom was the interest of the reigning power! But God can save by few as well as by many. He had purposed, and vain were the counter-exertions of earth and hell." (Clarke)

iv. "There are hours in human history when it seems as though evil were almost all powerful. It entrenches itself in great strength; it builds up great ramparts; it inaugurates policies of the utmost craft and cleverness. It seems to be able to bind together a kingdom which is invincible. All this is false seeming. There is no finality, no security, in the apparent might of iniquity." (Morgan)

2 Chronicles 23 – Jehoiada and the Crowning of Joash

A. The plan is put into practice.

1. (1-7) Jehoiada and his plan to restore Joash to the throne of Judah.

In the seventh year Jehoiada strengthened himself, *and made a* **covenant with the captains of hundreds: Azariah the son of Jeroham, Ishmael the son of Jehohanan, Azariah the son of Obed, Maaseiah the son of Adaiah, and Elishaphat the son of Zichri. And they went throughout Judah and gathered the Levites from all the cities of Judah, and the chief fathers of Israel, and they came to Jerusalem. Then all the assembly made a covenant with the king in the house of God. And he said to them, "Behold, the king's son shall reign, as the L**ORD** has said of the sons of David. This** *is* **what you shall do: One-third of you entering on the Sabbath, of the priests and the Levites,** *shall be* **keeping watch over the doors; one-third** *shall be* **at the king's house; and one-third at the Gate of the Foundation. All the people** *shall be* **in the courts of the house of the L**ORD**. But let no one come into the house of the L**ORD** except the priests and those of the Levites who serve. They may go in, for they** *are* **holy; but all the people shall keep the watch of the L**ORD**. And the Levites shall surround the king on all sides, every man with his weapons in his hand; and whoever comes into the house, let him be put to death. You are to be with the king when he comes in and when he goes out."**

> a. **Jehoiada strengthened himself, and made a covenant with the captains**: Jehoiada was a godly man who was concerned with restoring the throne of David to the line of David, and taking it away from this daughter of Ahab and Jezebel. He was also the husband of Jehoshabeath, the woman who hid the young boy Joash and protected him from Athaliah's massacre.

i. "The easiest thing for Jehoiada would have been to shut himself up in the temple, and leave things to take their course. The noblest thing was to come forth, and boldly confront the rampant evil of his time." (Meyer)

ii. "The world is full of Athaliahs, and it is not befitting that the Jehoiadas should remain at their holy rites and services if there is a paramount need for action in the world's battlefield, in the strife against wrong." (Meyer)

b. **Then all the assembly made a covenant with the king in the house of God**: From the *place* where the oath was made and the *context* of the oath, we learn that the worship of the true God was not dead in Judah. These **captains** could respond to their responsibility before the LORD.

c. **Behold, the king's son shall reign**: This was a dramatic moment. For six years everyone believed there were no more surviving heirs of David's royal line and there was no legitimate ruler to displace the wicked Athaliah. The secret had to be secure because **the king's son** would be immediately killed if his existence was revealed. The **captains** must have been shocked by the sight of this six-year-old heir to the throne.

i. One reason Athaliah was able to reign for six years was that *no one knew any alternative*. Many people live under the reign of Satan because they don't really know there is a legitimate king ready to take reign in their lives.

d. **This is what you shall do**: Jehoiada had a plan to depose the wicked Queen Athaliah and to replace her with the boy king. These leaders needed to follow his plan carefully, and to do it **on the Sabbath**. Jehoiada chose the Sabbath for the day of the coup, because that was the day when the guards changed their shifts and they could assemble two groups of guards at the temple at the same time without attracting attention.

i. "It was a weighty work he went about, and therefore he took the wisest course, the fittest time; on the Sabbath, when the congregation met; and in the temple, wither Athaliah and her courtiers seldom came." (Trapp)

2. (8-11) Joash is crowned king.

So the Levites and all Judah did according to all that Jehoiada the priest commanded. And each man took his men who were to be on duty on the Sabbath, with those who were going *off duty* on the Sabbath; for Jehoiada the priest had not dismissed the divisions. And Jehoiada the priest gave to the captains of hundreds the spears and the large and small shields which *had belonged* to King David, that *were* in the

temple of God. Then he set all the people, every man with his weapon in his hand, from the right side of the temple to the left side of the temple, along by the altar and by the temple, all around the king. And they brought out the king's son, put the crown on him, *gave him* the Testimony, and made him king. Then Jehoiada and his sons anointed him, and said, *"Long* live the king!"

a. **So the Levites and all Judah did according to all that Jehoiada the priest commanded**: This was an important plan that had to be followed carefully. Athaliah was a powerful enemy and many had a vested interest in her corrupt reign.

b. **The spears and the large and small shields which had belonged to King David, that were in the temple of God**: These men were equipped with weapons dating from the days of King David. It was fitting for these soldiers, who would set the heir of David's royal line back on the throne of Judah, to use these weapons which had belonged to King David.

c. **And they brought out the king's son**: First the **king's son** had to be *revealed*. No one could support him, and he could not take his rightful throne, until he was **brought out** before the people.

d. **Put the crown on him**: Next, the **king's son** had to be *crowned*. This was the public and official recognition of him as king.

e. **Gave him the Testimony**: The **king's son** had to come *with the word of God*. Joash appeared before the people holding the scrolls of God's word.

> i. Deuteronomy 17:18 says that the king should have his own copy of the Scriptures. "This is the basis for the British custom of presenting the monarch with a copy of the Bible during the coronation service." (Wiseman)

f. **And made him king**: The **king's son** had to be received. He had the royal right to impose his reign, but he instead allowed his rule to be received.

g. **Anointed him**: The **king's son** could never fulfill his office without a divine anointing.

h. **And said, "Long live the king!"** The **king's son** received praise once he was recognized as their king.

> i. We can and should follow the same pattern in our reception of Jesus Christ, the *true* **king's son**.

> ii. "Is not the spiritual condition of too many children of God represented by the condition of the Temple, during the early years of the life of Joash? The king was within its precincts, the rightful heir of the crown and defender of the worship of Jehovah: but as a matter

of fact, the crown was on the head of the usurper Athaliah, who was exercising a cruel and sanguinary tyranny. The king was limited to a chamber, and the majority of the priests, with all the people, had not even heard of his existence. There needs to be an anointing, an enthroning, a determination that He shall exercise his power over the entire Temple of our Being." (Meyer)

B. Athaliah's demise.

1. (12-13) Her distress upon discovering the plot against her.

Now when Athaliah heard the noise of the people running and praising the king, she came to the people *in* the temple of the LORD. When she looked, there was the king standing by his pillar at the entrance; and the leaders and the trumpeters *were* by the king. All the people of the land were rejoicing and blowing trumpets, also the singers with musical instruments, and those who led in praise. So Athaliah tore her clothes and said, "Treason! Treason!"

> a. **When she looked, there was the king**: For the usurper queen mother this was a horrifying sight. For six years she ruled because she believed there were no legitimate claimants to the throne of David. Now she sees that one son of Ahaziah – Joash, *her own grandson* – escaped her murderous intent.
>
> b. **All the people of the land were rejoicing**: They were obviously weary of the wicked reign of Athaliah.
>
> c. **Treason! Treason!** The charge was not unfounded. This was treason against her government, but it was a well-founded and godly treason against a tyrannical, wicked ruler.

2. (14-15) She and her supporters are executed

And Jehoiada the priest brought out the captains of hundreds who were set over the army, and said to them, "Take her outside under guard, and slay with the sword whoever follows her." For the priest had said, "Do not kill her in the house of the LORD." So they seized her; and she went by way of the entrance of the Horse Gate *into* the king's house, and they killed her there.

> a. **Take her outside under guard, and slay with the sword whoever follows her**: This was both righteous and prudent. It was a just sentence against this woman who had murdered so many, and prudent precautions were taken so she could not mount a resistance.
>
> b. **Do not kill her in the house of the LORD**: As a priest, Jehoiada had a great concern for the sanctity and reputation of the temple. Yet in the place where horses entered, **they killed her there**.

i. "Her own treason against the true and abiding King of the nation was defeated. Thus, sooner or later, and in ways equally dramatic, the moment arrives when those who plot and plan against Heaven and righteousness, find themselves looking at the evidences of the triumph of God and of goodness over all their wickedness." (Morgan)

C. The reforms of Jehoiada the priest.

1. (16-17) Jehoiada makes a covenant.

Then Jehoiada made a covenant between himself, the people, and the king, that they should be the Lord's people. And all the people went to the temple of Baal, and tore it down. They broke in pieces its altars and images, and killed Mattan the priest of Baal before the altars.

a. **A covenant between himself, the people, and the king**: This shows that God intends that both kings and citizens have mutual obligations towards the other. Neither have absolute rights over or against the other.

i. "Along with Jehoiada's political revolution came a corresponding religious revival – that king, priest, and citizenry would together 'be the Lord's people.'" (Payne)

ii. "The climax is not Joash's coronation but a covenant renewing the nation's relationship with God." (Selman)

b. **That they should be the Lord's people**: The covenant was between the Lord and the king and the people. They re-committed themselves to honor, obey, and serve God.

c. **And all the people went to the temple of Baal, and tore it down**: In 2 Kings 10 Jehu supervised the destruction of the temple of Baal in Samaria. Here the temple of Baal in Jerusalem was destroyed, and appropriately destroyed by **the people**.

i. They didn't stop at destroying the building itself; they went on to destroy both the sacred objects dedicated to Baal and to kill **Mattan the priest of Baal**. "The execution of 'Mattan the priest of Baal' carried out the requirement of God's Word directed against those who should lead others into false religion (Deuteronomy 13:5-10)." (Payne)

2. (18-21) Jehoiada restores the proper plans of worship and service.

Also Jehoiada appointed the oversight of the house of the Lord to the hand of the priests, the Levites, whom David had assigned in the house of the Lord, to offer the burnt offerings of the Lord, as *it is* written in the Law of Moses, with rejoicing and with singing, *as it was established* by David. And he set the gatekeepers at the gates of the house of the Lord, so that no one *who was* in any way unclean should enter. Then he

took the captains of hundreds, the nobles, the governors of the people, and all the people of the land, and brought the king down from the house of the LORD; and they went through the Upper Gate to the king's house, and set the king on the throne of the kingdom. So all the people of the land rejoiced; and the city was quiet, for they had slain Athaliah with the sword.

a. **Whom David had assigned…as it is written in the Law of Moses**: The priest Jehoiada was careful to reinstitute these practices and customs according to *Biblical* patterns, based on what God had revealed to **David** and **Moses**.

i. **So that no one who was in any way unclean should enter**: "Oh that we also had store of such porters, to keep out the unclean from holy ordinances!" (Trapp)

b. **And set the king on the throne of the kingdom**: After more than six dark years, now the rightful king of Judah once again ruled over his grateful people. No wonder, **the people of the land rejoiced**.

i. "The people's *rejoicing* augmented the joy of temple worship, and sounded a note unheard since the days of Jehoshaphat (2 Chronicles 20:27). That the city was *quiet* was a sign of God's blessing, which often followed special acts of faith and obedience (*cf.* 1 Chronicles 4:40; 22:9; 2 Chronicles 13:22; 14:4-5; 20:30)." (Selman)

2 Chronicles 24 – The Rise and Fall of Joash

A. Joash repairs the temple.

1. (1-3) Joash's forty year reign.

Joash *was* seven years old when he became king, and he reigned forty years in Jerusalem. His mother's name *was* Zibiah of Beersheba. Joash did *what was* right in the sight of the LORD all the days of Jehoiada the priest. And Jehoiada took two wives for him, and he had sons and daughters.

> a. **He reigned forty years in Jerusalem**: This was a long and mostly blessed reign. **Joash** (also called *Jehoash* in 2 Kings 12, simply a variant spelling) fell short of full commitment and complete godliness, but he did advance the cause of God in the kingdom of Judah.
>
>> i. "The number of wives and children shows God restoring the years the locusts had eaten." (Selman)
>
> b. **Joash did what was right in the sight of the LORD all the days of Jehoiada the priest**: This implies that when Jehoiada died, Joash no longer did what was right in the sight of the LORD. This chapter will document that Joash turned to idolatry when Jehoiada died, and judgment followed.

2. (4-7) The need and the heart to repair the temple.

Now it happened after this *that* Joash set his heart on repairing the house of the LORD. Then he gathered the priests and the Levites, and said to them, "Go out to the cities of Judah, and gather from all Israel money to repair the house of your God from year to year, and see that you do it quickly." However the Levites did not do it quickly. So the king called Jehoiada the chief *priest*, and said to him, "Why have you not required the Levites to bring in from Judah and from Jerusalem the collection, *according to the commandment* of Moses the servant of the LORD and of the assembly of Israel, for the tabernacle of witness?" For

the sons of Athaliah, that wicked woman, had broken into the house of God, and had also presented all the dedicated things of the house of the LORD to the Baals.

>a. **Joash set his heart on repairing the house of the LORD**: This indicated the godly concern that Joash had regarding the condition of the temple. He knew that a prosperous and secure kingdom mattered little if the things of God were neglected or despised.
>
>>i. He also knew that the condition of the temple was a valid measurement of the heart and passion of the people of God for the things of God. The temple was not God, but neglect and despising of the temple reflected neglect and despising of God.
>
>b. **Go out to the cities of Judah, and gather from all Israel money to repair the house of your God**: There was not enough money in the royal treasury to underwrite this project. Therefore the king commanded the Levites in Judah's outer cities to collect money and bring it back for the project in Jerusalem.
>
>c. **However the Levites did not do it quickly**: For some reason the **Levites** did not share the same passion as King Joash did for the condition of the temple. Perhaps they felt that the townspeople of the outer towns would not embrace and support this work. Nevertheless, Joash held them to account and got the work moving.
>
>>i. "'But the Levites did not act at once,' both because of natural inertia (still true even of Christian workers), and because of the priestly demands that seem to have exhausted the normal revenues on current operations and their own support." (Payne)
>
>d. **For the sons of Athaliah, that wicked woman, had broken into the house of God**: This explains *why* the temple was in such disrepair. It wasn't just normal wear and tear usage; it was a deliberate campaign against the temple and the worship of the true God prompted by **Athaliah** and her **sons**.

3. (8-14) The temple is repaired and worship is resumed.

Then at the king's command they made a chest, and set it outside at the gate of the house of the LORD. And they made a proclamation throughout Judah and Jerusalem to bring to the LORD the collection *that* Moses the servant of God *had imposed* on Israel in the wilderness. Then all the leaders and all the people rejoiced, brought their contributions, and put *them* into the chest until all had given. So it was, at that time, when the chest was brought to the king's official by the hand of the Levites, and when they saw that *there was* much money, that the king's scribe

and the high priest's officer came and emptied the chest, and took it and returned it to its place. Thus they did day by day, and gathered money in abundance. The king and Jehoiada gave it to those who did the work of the service of the house of the LORD; and they hired masons and carpenters to repair the house of the LORD, and also those who worked in iron and bronze to restore the house of the LORD. So the workmen labored, and the work was completed by them; they restored the house of God to its original condition and reinforced it. When they had finished, they brought the rest of the money before the king and Jehoiada; they made from it articles for the house of the LORD, articles for serving and offering, spoons and vessels of gold and silver. And they offered burnt offerings in the house of the LORD continually all the days of Jehoiada.

> a. **They made a chest, and set it outside at the gate of the house of the LORD**: Under the direction of King Joash, the priests gave the people the opportunity to give. Even willing givers should be given an opportunity.
>
>> i. "Then he placed a collection chest in a strategic location on the right side of the altar, giving the repair project a high priority and a corresponding high visibility." (Dilday, 2 Kings 12)
>>
>> ii. 2 Kings 12:6-13 indicates that part of the problem was poor and wasteful administration. Therefore King Joash got to the heart of the problem and through Jehoiada the priest, he implemented a system where the money would be set aside, saved, and then wisely spent for the repair and refurbishing of the temple.
>
> b. **To bring to the LORD the collection that Moses the servant of God had imposed on Israel in the wilderness**: This brings to mind the offering that Moses received to build the tabernacle in Exodus 35. That was a divinely inspired plan to receive freely made offerings from the people of Israel.
>
>> i. "The tax itself was based on the half-shekel tax for the *Tent*, though it was also renewed by Nehemiah (Nehemiah 10:32)." (Selman)
>>
>> ii. It is possible for God to cause the money and materials to just appear by a miracle. Yet He chooses to almost always fund His work through the willing gifts of His people. He works this way because we need to be a giving people.
>>
>> iii. This idea is echoed in 2 Corinthians 9:7: *So let each one give as he purposes in his heart, not grudgingly or of necessity; for God loves a cheerful giver.*
>
> c. **Thus they did day by day, and gathered money in abundance**: Through the careful and diligent administration of these freely given gifts,

an **abundance** of money was gathered for the work. God cares not only that His people give generously, but also that their gifts be diligently and carefully administered.

d. **So the workmen labored, and the work was completed by them**: God's blessing was clearly on the work, but He would not do the work *for* them. So the king and the priest wisely hired the right kind of workers and paid them directly, so that money would not be lost or wasted on administration.

> i. "When the people were assured that the money would really be used for the purpose for which it was given, they responded generously and so similar arrangements were continued by Josiah (2 Kings 22:3-7)." (Wiseman)

e. **They brought the rest of the money before the king and Jehoiada**: The people were so generous, and the administration was so wise and honest, that there was an *excess* of money for the restoration project, money which was given to supply new **articles for the house of the LORD**. This was wonderful evidence of both God's blessing and man's generosity and wise stewardship.

> i. These replaced "what had been taken away, partly by the Arabian plunderers, and partly by Athaliah's sacrilegious sons." (Trapp)

> ii. In all likelihood, this generous giving was somewhat of a surprise. "Which he thought would not be any great sum, because of the great iniquity and impiety which yet had reigned for many years, and yet continued in the generality of the people of the land, the Levites not excepted, as the last clause of this verse shows." (Poole)

4. (15-16) The death of Jehoiada.

But Jehoiada grew old and was full of days, and he died; *he was* **one hundred and thirty years old when he died. And they buried him in the City of David among the kings, because he had done good in Israel, both toward God and His house.**

> a. **He was one hundred and thirty years old when he died**: This unusually long life for this influential priest was evidence of both God's blessing upon his godly life, and God's mercy towards King Joash and Judah. When Joash was no longer under the influence of Jehoiada, he took a definite turn for the worse, and in His mercy God delayed this as long as possible.

> b. **They buried him in the City of David among the kings, because he had done good in Israel**: The measure of his influence is indicated by the honored burial place they gave Jehoiada. The **good** he did in Israel was especially **toward God and His house**.

i. "See the influence of one man. One man can sway a state. One man can check sin. One man can be the head of a host who shall serve God, and honor his name." (Spurgeon)

B. The apostasy of Joash.

1. (17-19) Joash is influenced to do evil.

Now after the death of Jehoiada the leaders of Judah came and bowed down to the king. And the king listened to them. Therefore they left the house of the LORD God of their fathers, and served wooden images and idols; and wrath came upon Judah and Jerusalem because of their trespass. Yet He sent prophets to them, to bring them back to the LORD; and they testified against them, but they would not listen.

a. **The leaders of Judah came and bowed down to the king. And the king listened to them**: Joash seems to have been a fundamentally weak man; he did good when he was under the influence of the godly Jehoiada, but he did evil when he was under the influence of these **leaders of Judah**, who led them into idolatry.

i. "In most fawning and flattering manner did these court parasites present themselves before him…persuading him that during the days of Jehoiada he had been a king without a kingdom, a lord without a dominion, a subject to his subjects." (Trapp)

ii. "Do you not see those gentlemen coming, bowing and scraping a hundred times before they get up to him? They 'made obeisance to the king.' Jehoiada had not often made much obeisance to him; he had treated him with due respect as his king, but he had also spoken to him honestly and faithfully." (Spurgeon)

iii. "That they might not be confined to unnecessary and troublesome journeys in coming to Jerusalem to worship, but might have the liberty which their forefathers enjoyed of worshipping God in the high places; which liberty, when once they had obtained, they knew they could then worship idols without observation or disturbance, which was the thing at which they aimed." (Poole)

iv. "All that Joash had done was to give his heart to Jehoiada, not to Jehovah. It is very easy to be outwardly religious by giving your heart to your mother, or your father, or your aunt, or your uncle, or some good person who helps you to do what is right. You are doing all this out of love to them, which is at best but a very secondary motive. God says, 'My son, give me thine heart.'" (Spurgeon)

b. **Therefore they left the house of the LORD God of their fathers**: They only felt free to worship idols *after* they had forsaken the house of God. It showed both the shallowness of their commitment to God and the preservative effect of their prior attendance.

    i. "Let our church-forsakers chew on this: let them see what good patriots they are." (Trapp)

c. **Yet He sent prophets to them, to bring them back to the LORD; and they testified against them, but they would not listen**: This second sin was greater than the initial sins of weakness and idolatry. Joash would not listen to God's **prophets** or the correction they brought to him.

2. (20-22) Zechariah's message to Joash and his death.

Then the Spirit of God came upon Zechariah the son of Jehoiada the priest, who stood above the people, and said to them, "Thus says God: 'Why do you transgress the commandments of the LORD, so that you cannot prosper? Because you have forsaken the LORD, He also has forsaken you.'" So they conspired against him, and at the command of the king they stoned him with stones in the court of the house of the LORD. Thus Joash the king did not remember the kindness which Jehoiada his father had done to him, but killed his son; and as he died, he said, "The LORD look on *it*, and repay!"

a. **The Spirit of God came upon Zechariah the son of Jehoiada the priest, who stood above the people**: This prophet, the son of the influential priest, had a position of leadership as a priest. The phrase **stood above the people** probably indicates that he was a leading priest, one who pronounced the priestly benediction over the assembly of Israel.

    i. The description of the **Spirit of God** coming upon Zechariah is significant. "Therefore God pronounced judgment through a prophesying priest, Jehoiada's son *Zechariah*, whom the *Spirit of God* 'clothed'…. Two of the three Old Testament examples of this distinctive expression occur in Chronicles (*cf.* Judges 6:34; 1 Chronicles 12:18)." (Selman)

    ii. "As we put on a cloak or dress, so does the Spirit of God, as it were, hide Himself in those who surrender themselves to Him, so that it is not they who speak and act, but He within them…. Remember the cloth or leather must yield itself easily to the movements of its wearer, and not less pliable and supple must we be to the Spirit of God." (Meyer)

b. **Because you have forsaken the LORD, He also has forsaken you**: The Chronicler includes this aspect of the account – not included in the 2

Kings record – especially because this principle was relevant to the returned exiles in the days Chronicles was written. They needed to remember the principle *draw near to God and He will draw near to you* (James 4:8), and the *inverse* of that principle.

c. **So they conspired against him, and at the command of the king they stoned him**: Both the leaders and the common people **conspired** to murder Zechariah. They not only rejected his message; they also silenced the prophet who spoke with the words of conviction.

> i. "What a most wretched and contemptible man was this, who could imbrue his hands in the blood of a prophet of God, and the son of the man who had saved him from being murdered, and raised him to the throne! Alas, alas!" (Clarke)

d. **The LORD look on it, and repay!** Zechariah's dying words were a plea to God, asking *Him* to **repay** according to His justice. It is the perfect prayer of the persecuted, leaving all vengeance in the hand and wisdom of God.

> i. "Zechariah is not looking for personal revenge but asking God to act in keeping with his declared principles of justice." (Selman)

> ii. "And so he did; for, at the end of that year, the Syrians came against Judah, destroyed all the princes of the people, sent their spoils to Damascus; and Joash, the murderer of the prophet, the son of his benefactor, was himself murdered by his own servants. Here was a most signal display of the divine retribution." (Clarke)

> iii. This whole evil tragedy is filled with ironies.
>
> - The people did not listen to the command of the LORD, but they did listen to the evil command of King Joash.
> - Joash answered the kindness of Jehoiada to him with cruelty to the son of Jehoiada.
> - Zechariah was murdered in the same place where his father Jehoiada had anointed Joash king (2 Chronicles 23:10-11).

3. (23-24) God brings judgment on Judah and Joash through the Syrians

So it happened in the spring of the year *that* the army of Syria came up against him; and they came to Judah and Jerusalem, and destroyed all the leaders of the people from among the people, and sent all their spoil to the king of Damascus. For the army of the Syrians came with a small company of men; but the LORD delivered a very great army into their hand, because they had forsaken the LORD God of their fathers. So they executed judgment against Joash.

a. **The army of Syria came up…and destroyed all the leaders of the people**: The leaders who were an unwise and ungodly influence upon Joash were the same leaders who were **destroyed** and had their **spoil** plundered.

b. **The army of the Syrians came with a small company of men; but the LORD delivered a very great army into their hand**: Under the judgment of God, the small army of the Syrians overcame the **very great army** of Judah.

i. God promised that His obedient people would be blessed with success far beyond their numbers (Leviticus 26:8), and that when disobedient, they would suffer disproportionate defeat (Leviticus 26:17, 26:37).

4. (25-27) A wounded Joash is assassinated by his servants.

And when they had withdrawn from him (for they left him severely wounded), his own servants conspired against him because of the blood of the sons of Jehoiada the priest, and killed him on his bed. So he died. And they buried him in the City of David, but they did not bury him in the tombs of the kings. These are the ones who conspired against him: Zabad the son of Shimeath the Ammonitess, and Jehozabad the son of Shimrith the Moabitess. Now *concerning* **his sons, and the many oracles about him, and the repairing of the house of God, indeed they** *are* **written in the annals of the book of the kings. Then Amaziah his son reigned in his place.**

a. **His own servants conspired against him**: This is startling, and shows that the blessing of God had long before vanished from the compromised king, who began so well but failed to finish well.

i. They were prompted to assassinate Joash **because of the blood of the sons of Jehoiada the priest**. Yet there may also have been the fact of the recent defeat by Syria. "The murder of Joash by his *officials* or servants implies that it may have been the result of disaffection following the defeat by Hazael." (Wiseman)

ii. "So disobedience brings its own bitter reward, and what God's people sow they always, in some way or another, reap. Joash abundantly deserved his inglorious and terrible end." (Knapp)

iii. "Thus ended a reign full of promise and hope in the beginning, but profligate, cruel, and ruinous in the end. Never was the hand of God's justice more signally stretched out against an apostate king and faithless people, than at this time." (Clarke)

iv. "The 'many prophecies' about Joash probably refer to such prophetic threatenings as are noted in 2 Chronicles 24:19-20." (Payne)

b. **They are written in the annals of the book of the kings**: There is no record of repentance on Joash's part. He never came back to, or fulfilled, his bright early promise.

i. "The fact that he was not honoured by a place in the royal cemetery (in contrast to Jehoiada) is important in Chronicles." (Selman)

ii. "Yes, and there are some whose hearts are not right towards God, who nevertheless are very zealous about the externals of divine worship. It is a much easier thing to build a temple for God than it is to be a temple for God; and it is a much more common thing for persons to show zeal in repairing temples than in reforming their own manners." (Spurgeon)

iii. "There was a want of principle in Joash, and it is of that I want to warn all our friends. Do not, I pray you, be satisfied with the practice of piety without the principles of piety. It is not enough to have a correct creed; you must have a renewed heart. It is not sufficient to have an ornate ritual; you must have a holy life, and to be holy you must be renewed by the Holy Spirit. If this change is not wrought in you by the Holy Ghost, you who yield so readily to good will yield just as quickly to evil." (Spurgeon)

iv. "The study of the story of Joash offers a striking illustration of how a weak man is easily influenced. It emphasises the need of strong individual character, which can only be created by direct dealing with God." (Morgan)

v. "However valuable the influence of a good man may be, it remains true that if a man has nothing more to lean on than that, if it should fail, collapse is almost inevitable. All foundations fail, save one." (Morgan)

2 Chronicles 25 – The Reign of Amaziah

A. His victory over Edom.

1. (1-2) The limited good of the reign of Amaziah.

Amaziah *was* twenty-five years old *when* he became king, and he reigned twenty-nine years in Jerusalem. His mother's name *was* Jehoaddan of Jerusalem. And he did *what was* right in the sight of the LORD, but not with a loyal heart.

> a. **He did what was right in the sight of the LORD**: Amaziah, son of the great reformer Joash, continued the generally godly reign began by his father.
>
>> i. "He made a good beginning in thus adhering closely to the law. Happy would it have been for him and for his kingdom had he continued as he began." (Knapp)
>
> b. **But not with a loyal heart**: Compared to Joash, Amaziah faithfully continued his policies. Yet some of those policies permitted compromises, such as the allowing of continued sacrifices and incense offerings *on the high places* (2 Kings 14:1-4). Compared to David – the greatest human king to reign over the people of God – Amaziah did not match up favorably (2 Kings 14:1-4).
>
>> i. "The root idea of the Hebrew word translated 'perfect' [**loyal** in the NKJV] is being whole, complete. Imperfection of heart consists in incomplete surrender. Some chamber of the temple is retained for selfish purposes. What it was in the case of Amaziah we are not told, but the fact remains that notwithstanding the general direction of his life…the whole heart was not set on doing the will of God." (Morgan)

2. (3-4) An example of Amaziah's obedience.

Now it happened, as soon as the kingdom was established for him, that he executed his servants who had murdered his father the king. However he did not execute their children, but *did* as *it is* written in the Law in the Book of Moses, where the LORD commanded, saying, "The fathers shall not be put to death for their children, nor shall the children be put to death for their fathers; but a person shall die for his own sin."

> a. **He executed his servants who had murdered his father the king**: This was both just and in the best interest of Amaziah. It was good for him to eliminate those who found the assassination of the king a reasonable way to change the kingdom.
>
>> i. It also fulfilled God's command to punish murderers with execution, first given in Genesis 9:5-7.
>
> b. **He did not execute their children, but did as it is written in the Law of the Book of Moses**: It was the standard practice of the ancient world to execute not only the guilty party in such a murder but also their family. Amaziah went against the conventional practice of his day and obeyed the word of God instead (Deuteronomy 24:16).
>
>> i. "Wherein he showed some faith and courage, that he would obey this command of God, though it was very hazardous to himself, such persons being likely to seek revenge for their father's death." (Poole)

3. (5-8) Preparations for battle against Edom.

Moreover Amaziah gathered Judah together and set over them captains of thousands and captains of hundreds, according to *their* fathers' houses, throughout all Judah and Benjamin; and he numbered them from twenty years old and above, and found them to be three hundred thousand choice *men, able* to go to war, who could handle spear and shield. He also hired one hundred thousand mighty men of valor from Israel for one hundred talents of silver. But a man of God came to him, saying, "O king, do not let the army of Israel go with you, for the LORD *is* not with Israel; *not with* any of the children of Ephraim. But if you go, be gone! Be strong in battle! *Even so,* God shall make you fall before the enemy; for God has power to help and to overthrow."

> a. **He also hired one hundred thousand mighty men of valor from Israel**: In assembling an army (that would eventually fight against Edom), Amaziah **hired** mercenary troops from the northern tribes of Israel. This was a common practice in the ancient world.
>
> b. **O king, do not let the army of Israel go with you, for the LORD is not with Israel**: This anonymous prophet warned King Amaziah to not use the Israelite troops that he had hired. Going further, he warned him that if he

should go to battle using these Israelite troops, **God shall make you fall before the enemy**.

> i. Even though it made military sense for Amaziah to hire and use these troops, according to the word from God, it made no spiritual sense. This is because **God has power to help and to overthrow**. To fight *with* God is to receive His **help**; to fight *against* Him is to have God **overthrow** you.

4. (9) Amaziah's question and the answer from the prophet.

Then Amaziah said to the man of God, "But what *shall we* do about the hundred talents which I have given to the troops of Israel?" And the man of God answered, "The LORD is able to give you much more than this."

> a. **But what shall we do about the hundred talents which I have given to the troops of Israel?** Amaziah heard and understood the word of God from His messenger. Yet his question was familiar: "How much will it cost me to be obedient?" This is not necessarily a bad question to ask if we are willing to be persuaded by the LORD's answer.

> b. **The LORD is able to give you much more than this**: The prophet wisely answered Amaziah. Whatever obedience costs, it is always ultimately cheaper than disobedience.

>> i. "But you say that you have already entered into so close an alliance that you cannot draw back. You have invested your capital, you have gone to great expenditure. Yet it will be better to forfeit these than Him." (Meyer)

5. (10-13) Amaziah's obedience and the victory over Edom.

So Amaziah discharged the troops that had come to him from Ephraim, to go back home. Therefore their anger was greatly aroused against Judah, and they returned home in great anger. Then Amaziah strengthened himself, and leading his people, he went to the Valley of Salt and killed ten thousand of the people of Seir. Also the children of Judah took captive ten thousand alive, brought them to the top of the rock, and cast them down from the top of the rock, so that they all were dashed in pieces. But as for the soldiers of the army which Amaziah had discharged, so that they would not go with him to battle, they raided the cities of Judah from Samaria to Beth Horon, killed three thousand in them, and took much spoil.

> a. **So Amaziah discharged the troops that had come to him from Ephraim, to go back home**: He had paid them as promised, trusting that

God was able to return to him *much more*, and he sent them home in faith, trusting God to both protect and provide.

> i. This **greatly aroused** the dismissed army against Judah, probably because they counted on the anticipated plunder as additional income.
>
> ii. "The Israelites' *great rage*, repeated in Hebrew for emphasis, shows further why the Lord is not with them." (Selman)

b. **Amaziah strengthened himself, and leading his people, he went to the Valley of Salt and killed ten thousand of the people of Seir**: Walking in obedience to God, Amaziah saw the victory God promised. The Edomites, who had apparently rebelled against Judah's authority, were defeated.

> i. "His victory is definite enough, though it is achieved without any acknowledgment of God's help and with excessive violence." (Selman)

c. **They raided the cities of Judah from Samaria to Beth Horon, killed three thousand in them, and took much spoil**: This shows the wickedness of the dismissed Israelite soldiers and their hunger for plunder and **spoil**. They were determined to enrich themselves through conquest, beyond their soldier's wages.

> i. "Because they were both disgraced by this rejection, and disappointed of that prey and spoil which they hoped to gain, whereas now they were sent away empty; for the one hundred talents probably were given to their officers only to raise men for this service; that sum being otherwise too small to be distributed into so many hands." (Poole)
>
> ii. "The soldiers of Israel committed depredations on their way back. This was the result of the folly and sin of Amaziah's proposal. We may be forgiven, and delivered, and yet there will be after-consequences which will follow us from some ill-considered act. Sin may be forgiven, but its secondary results are sometimes very bitter." (Meyer)

B. Amaziah's sin and the judgment against him.

1. (14-16) Amaziah's strange idolatry and arrogance.

Now it was so, after Amaziah came from the slaughter of the Edomites, that he brought the gods of the people of Seir, set them up *to be* his gods, and bowed down before them and burned incense to them. Therefore the anger of the Lord was aroused against Amaziah, and He sent him a prophet who said to him, "Why have you sought the gods of the people, which could not rescue their own people from your hand?" So it was, as he talked with him, that *the king* said to him, "Have we made you the king's counselor? Cease! Why should you be killed?" Then the prophet

ceased, and said, "I know that God has determined to destroy you, because you have done this and have not heeded my advice."

> a. **He brought the gods of the people of Seir, set them up to be his gods, and bowed down before them**: This action of Amaziah shows the deep foolishness of idolatry. These **gods of the people of Seir** were unable to defend or help the Edomites, yet he worshipped them. God sent a prophet to make this point clear to King Amaziah.
>
>> i. "Amaziah's achievement seems to bring out the worst in him. Whereas he had previously made some response to God, now he turns to idolatry, persecution, revenge, intransigence, pride, and apostasy." (Selman)
>
> b. **Have we made you the king's counselor? Cease!** The king arrogantly silenced the prophet, yet he pronounced a final word of judgment against Amaziah.
>
>> i. This was a rejection of God's mercy to Amaziah. God was kind to send him a correcting prophet "When he might have sent him to hell with a thunderbolt; as the patientest man upon earth would have done likely, had he been in God's place and power." (Trapp)

2. (17-20) The king of Israel warns the king of Judah.

Now Amaziah king of Judah asked advice and sent to Joash the son of Jehoahaz, the son of Jehu, king of Israel, saying, "Come, let us face one another *in battle*." And Joash king of Israel sent to Amaziah king of Judah, saying, "The thistle that *was* in Lebanon sent to the cedar that was in Lebanon, saying, 'Give your daughter to my son as wife'; and a wild beast that *was* in Lebanon passed by and trampled the thistle. Indeed you say that you have defeated the Edomites, and your heart is lifted up to boast. Stay at home now; why should you meddle with trouble, that you should fall; you and Judah with you?" But Amaziah would not heed, for it *came* from God, that He might give them into the hand *of their enemies*, because they sought the gods of Edom.

> a. **Come, let us face one another in battle**: Proud from his success against Edom, Amaziah decided to make war against the northern kingdom of Israel, no doubt in retaliation for the plundering attacks by the dismissed mercenaries of Israel (2 Chronicles 25:5-16).
>
>> i. He had reason to believe he would be successful. He had recently assembled a 300,000 man army that killed 20,000 men in a victory over Edom (2 Chronicles 25:5, 11-12). King Joash (Jehoahaz) of Israel seemed very weak, having only 50 horsemen, 10 chariots, and 10,000 foot soldiers after being defeated by the Syrians (2 Kings 13:7).

b. **The thistle that was in Lebanon**: The reply of Joash king of Israel was both wise and diplomatic. With this little story and its application, he counseled Amaziah to glory in his previous victory over Edom but then to **stay at home**.

> i. "The thistle, imagining himself to be equal with the cedar, presumptuously suggested a marriage alliance between them. The difference between the two was made obvious when a wild beast passed through and crushed the thistle underfoot. Of course the beast was powerless to injure the cedar." (Dilday)

c. **Why should you meddle with trouble so that you fall; you and Judah with you?** Amaziah should have listened to this word from Jehoash, but he didn't. He provoked a fight he should have avoided, and did not consider either the likelihood of success or the effect his defeat would have on the whole kingdom of Judah.

d. **It came from God, that He might give them into the hand of their enemies, because they sought the gods of Edom**: Because of Amaziah's foolish embrace of idolatry, God allowed him to enter into a foolish war with Israel. Foolish idols led him into foolish choices, and the wise God in heaven allowed him to experience the effect of these choices.

> i. "*It came of God*, who gave him up to his own error and passion, in order to his ruin." (Poole)

3. (21-24) Proud King Amaziah is defeated by Israel.

So Joash king of Israel went out; and he and Amaziah king of Judah faced one another at Beth Shemesh, which *belongs* to Judah. And Judah was defeated by Israel, and every man fled to his tent. Then Joash the king of Israel captured Amaziah king of Judah, the son of Joash, the son of Jehoahaz, at Beth Shemesh; and he brought him to Jerusalem, and broke down the wall of Jerusalem from the Gate of Ephraim to the Corner Gate; four hundred cubits. And *he took* all the gold and silver, all the articles that were found in the house of God with Obed-Edom, the treasures of the king's house, and hostages, and returned to Samaria.

a. **Israel captured Amaziah king of Judah**: Because of his foolish attack against Israel, Amaziah *lost his freedom* and for a time became a prisoner of the king of Israel.

> i. "His name means 'strength of Jah'; but we read, 'he strengthened *himself* (2 Chronicles 25:11); his character of self-sufficiency thus belying his name – a thing not uncommon in our day." (Knapp)

b. **Broke down the wall of Jerusalem**: Because of his foolish attack against Israel, Amaziah *saw the defenses of Jerusalem broken down*. Not only did they lose the battle at Beth Shemesh, but they were also in a weaker position to face future attacks.

c. **And he took all the gold and silver**: Because of his foolish attack against Israel, Amaziah *lost the treasure of the people of God*. It wasn't just a loss of his *personal* wealth (**the treasures of the king's house**), but also of the **gold and silver** of God's people. Amaziah didn't have the wisdom to see how losing this battle would hurt others as well as himself.

> i. This even extended to **hostages** who were taken from Jerusalem to Samaria. The decision to attack Israel was his alone, but the price paid for the foolish attack was paid by the whole kingdom of Judah. It is a sober warning to all leaders, to consider how their foolish decisions affect many other people.

> ii. "The quarrel of Amaziah was certainly *just*, yet he was put to the rout; he did *meddle to his hurt; he fell*, and *Judah fell with him*, as Jehoash had said." (Clarke)

4. (25-28) He is hated and killed by his own subjects.

Amaziah the son of Joash, king of Judah, lived fifteen years after the death of Joash the son of Jehoahaz, king of Israel. Now the rest of the acts of Amaziah, from first to last, indeed *are* they not written in the book of the kings of Judah and Israel? After the time that Amaziah turned away from following the Lord, they made a conspiracy against him in Jerusalem, and he fled to Lachish; but they sent after him to Lachish and killed him there. Then they brought him on horses and buried him with his fathers in the City of Judah.

a. **They made a conspiracy against him in Jerusalem**: The embarrassing loss against Israel undermined Amaziah's support among the leaders of Judah.

> i. He lived **fifteen years** after the death of Jehoash (which probably prompted his release from imprisonment in Israel), "But it was a kind of a lifeless life.... He lay all the while under the hatred and contempt of his subjects." (Trapp)

> ii. "At a preliminary stage his sixteen-year-old son Uzziah was elevated to coregency – and to actual rule – in 790 B.C." (Payne)

b. **He fled to Lachish; but they sent after him to Lachish and killed him there**: Amaziah tried but was unable to escape the conspirators. He was assassinated, just like his father was (2 Kings 12:20-21).

i. "Lachish was the first of the cities of Judah to adopt the idolatries of the kingdom of Israel ('the beginning of the sin to the daughter of Zion: for the transgressions of Israel were found in thee,' Micah 1:13), and it was natural for the idolatrous Amaziah to seek an asylum there." (Knapp)

ii. 'He no doubt became very unpopular after having lost the battle with the Israelites; the consequence of which was the dismantling of Jerusalem, and the seizure of the royal treasures, with several other evils. It is likely that the last *fifteen* years of his reign were greatly embittered: so that, finding the royal city to be no place of *safety*, he endeavoured to secure himself at Lachish; but all in vain, for thither his murderers pursued him; and he who forsook the Lord was forsaken by every friend, perished in his gainsaying, and came to an untimely end." (Clarke)

2 Chronicles 26 – The Reign of Uzziah

A. The years of blessing and strength.

1. (1-5) The overview of Uzziah's reign.

Now all the people of Judah took Uzziah, who *was* sixteen years old, and made him king instead of his father Amaziah. He built Elath and restored it to Judah, after the king rested with his fathers. Uzziah *was* sixteen years old when he became king, and he reigned fifty-two years in Jerusalem. His mother's name was Jecholiah of Jerusalem. And he did *what was* right in the sight of the Lord, according to all that his father Amaziah had done. He sought God in the days of Zechariah, who had understanding in the visions of God; and as long as he sought the Lord, God made him prosper.

> a. **He did what was right in the sight of the Lord**: The reign of Uzziah was largely characterized by the good he did **in the sight of the Lord**. His godliness was rewarded with a long reign of 52 years.
>
>> i. Uzziah came to the throne in a difficult era: "Following the tragic events that brought King Amaziah's reign to an end, Jerusalem was in disarray, a major section of its protective wall destroyed, its temple and palace emptied of their treasures, and some of its inhabitants taken away to Israel as hostages." (Dilday)
>>
>> ii. Knapp suggests that Uzziah became king in an unusual manner: "He seems to have come by the throne, not in the way of ordinary succession, but by the direct choice of the people. The princes had been destroyed by the Syrians toward the close of his grandfather Joash's reign (2 Chronicles 24:23), leaving the people a free hand."
>>
>> iii. **Now all the people of Judah took Uzziah**: "The idea that the king could be chosen by the will of the people was never entirely lost in Judah." (Selman)

b. **As long as he sought the LORD, God made him prosper**: This generally mixed review of Uzziah's reign is also indicated by 2 Kings 15:1-4, which tells us that Uzziah (also called *Azariah* in 2 Kings) did not remove the *high places*, traditional places of sacrifice to the LORD and sometimes doorways to idolatry.

i. "The two names are best understood as variants arising from the interchangeability of two closely related Hebrew roots." (Selman)

2. (6-15) The strength, security, and fame of Uzziah's reign.

Now he went out and made war against the Philistines, and broke down the wall of Gath, the wall of Jabneh, and the wall of Ashdod; and he built cities *around* **Ashdod and among the Philistines. God helped him against the Philistines, against the Arabians who lived in Gur Baal, and against the Meunites. Also the Ammonites brought tribute to Uzziah. His fame spread as far as the entrance of Egypt, for he became exceedingly strong. And Uzziah built towers in Jerusalem at the Corner Gate, at the Valley Gate, and at the corner buttress of the wall; then he fortified them. Also he built towers in the desert. He dug many wells, for he had much livestock, both in the lowlands and in the plains;** *he also had* **farmers and vinedressers in the mountains and in Carmel, for he loved the soil. Moreover Uzziah had an army of fighting men who went out to war by companies, according to the number on their roll as prepared by Jeiel the scribe and Maaseiah the officer, under the hand of Hananiah,** *one* **of the king's captains. The total number of chief officers of the mighty men of valor** *was* **two thousand six hundred. And under their authority** *was* **an army of three hundred and seven thousand five hundred, that made war with mighty power, to help the king against the enemy. Then Uzziah prepared for them, for the entire army, shields, spears, helmets, body armor, bows, and slings** *to cast* **stones. And he made devices in Jerusalem, invented by skillful men, to be on the towers and the corners, to shoot arrows and large stones. So his fame spread far and wide, for he was marvelously helped till he became strong.**

a. **He went out and made war against the Philistines**: Uzziah was active in opposing the ancient enemies of the Israelites. The Philistines may also have been active against Judah in the not too distant past, perhaps being among those *who came with the Arabians* and massacred many of the royal family of David (2 Chronicles 22:1).

i. With this heart to make war against their ancient enemies, no wonder that **God helped him against the Philistines**.

ii. "The Philistines lost two of their major cities, *Gath* and *Ashdod* as well as *Jabneh*. The latter was formerly Jabneel of Judah (Joshua

15:11) and later became Jamnia where the Sanhedrin was re-formed after Jerusalem's destruction in A.D. 70." (Selman)

b. **The Ammonites brought tribute to Uzziah**: This was another example of the strength of Uzziah's kingdom. He exacted **tribute** from the **Ammonites**, which was like a tax that recognized their lower place under Judah.

c. **His fame spread.... he built towers.... He dug many wells.... Uzziah had an army.... he made devices in Jerusalem**: Uzziah was a remarkable king, who had a broad interest in the improvement of his kingdom. Because of his many achievements, it was fitting that his **fame spread** among other nations.

i. "The reality of Uzziah's 'towers of the desert' (of arid southern Judah) has been validated by the discovery of an eighth-century tower at Qumran." (Payne)

ii. "Repairs in Jerusalem were necessitated by the damage incurred during the previous reign (note the specific mention of the *Corner Gate* in 2 Chronicles 25:23) and possibly by an earthquake (Amos 1:1; Zechariah 14:5)." (Selman)

iii. One unique description of Uzziah is that **he loved the soil**. This shows that he had a mind and a heart for more than technology and fame; he also had an interest in practical matters and things that benefited the majority of his people.

iv. "This is a perfection in a king: on husbandry every state depends. Let their trade or commerce be what they may, there can be no true national prosperity if agriculture do not prosper; for the king himself is served by the field." (Clarke)

d. **He made devices in Jerusalem, invented by skillful men, to be on the towers and the corners, to shoot arrows and large stones**: There is some debate and even controversy as to whether these were *defensive* or *offensive* inventions. If it does describe the invention of catapults, it is a remarkable thing that Uzziah and his men invented such things more than two hundred years before archaeological evidence suggests.

i. "His (literally) 'inventions' were probably protective shields or screens on city walls enabling archers and others to operate in comparative safety." (Selman)

ii. Yet Clarke quotes a Targum at 2 Chronicles 26:15: "He made in Jerusalem ingenious instruments, and little hollow towers, to stand upon the towers and upon the bastions, for the shooting of arrows, and projecting of great stones."

iii. "This is the very first intimation on record of any warlike engines for the *attack* or *defence* of besieged places; and this account is long prior to any thing of the kind among either the Greeks or the Romans…. The *Jews* alone were the inventors of such engines; and the invention took place in the reign of Uzziah, about *eight hundred* years before the Christian era. It is no wonder that, in the consequence of this, *his name spread far abroad*, and struck terror into his enemies." (Clarke)

e. **For he was marvelously helped till he became strong**: At the end of this extended section praising and promoting the goodness of Uzziah's reign, we read this ominous word. At some point in his success, he began to turn from God's help and began to trust in his own strength.

i. "The chief reason for Uzziah's success is God's *help*. This is a special word in Chronicles (*cf. e.g.* 1 Chronicles 12:19; 2 Chronicles 14:11; 25:8) whose meaning is equivalent in the New Testament to the enabling work of the Holy Spirit (*cf.* Romans 8:26; 2 Timothy 1:14; *cf.* Acts 26:22; 1 Thessalonians 2:2)." (Selman)

B. Uzziah's sin and punishment.

1. (16) The proud heart of Uzziah.

But when he was strong his heart was lifted up, to *his* destruction, for he transgressed against the LORD his God by entering the temple of the LORD to burn incense on the altar of incense.

a. **When he was strong his heart was lifted up, to his destruction**: Uzziah is a prominent example of a man who handled adversity better than success.

i. "The history of men affords persistent witness to the subtle perils which are created by prosperity. More men are blasted by it than by adversity…. Prosperity always puts the soul in danger of pride, of the heart lifted up; and pride ever goeth before destruction, and a haughty spirit before a fall." (Morgan)

ii. "God cannot trust some of us with prosperity and success, because our nature could not stand them. We must tug at the oar, instead of spreading the sail, because we have not enough ballast." (Meyer)

b. **He transgressed against the LORD his God by entering the temple of the LORD to burn incense on the altar**: Azariah violated what had become a general principle in God's dealing with Israel: that no king should also be a priest, and that the offices of prophet, priest, and king should not be combined in one man – *until* the Messiah, who fulfilled all three offices.

i. "Uzziah is *unfaithful* (2 Chronicles 26:16, 18). This is the most important expression for sin in Chronicles, and it can bring down a dynasty (1 Chronicles 10:13) or take a nation into exile (1 Chronicles 5:25; 9:1; 2 Chronicles 33:19; 36:14). The term has not appeared since Rehoboam's time (2 Chronicles 12:2) but now will become a regular theme to the end of the book." (Selman)

ii. "Uzziah's problem was that he was not content with the authority God had given him and wanted to add more priestly functions to his royal power. Absolute power, however, has no place in God's kingdom." (Selman)

2. (17-21) Confrontation and a fitting punishment.

So Azariah the priest went in after him, and with him were eighty priests of the LORD; valiant men. And they withstood King Uzziah, and said to him, *"It is* not for you, Uzziah, to burn incense to the LORD, but for the priests, the sons of Aaron, who are consecrated to burn incense. Get out of the sanctuary, for you have trespassed! You *shall have* no honor from the LORD God." Then Uzziah became furious; and he *had* a censer in his hand to burn incense. And while he was angry with the priests, leprosy broke out on his forehead, before the priests in the house of the LORD, beside the incense altar. And Azariah the chief priest and all the priests looked at him, and there, on his forehead, he *was* leprous; so they thrust him out of that place. Indeed he also hurried to get out, because the LORD had struck him. King Uzziah was a leper until the day of his death. He dwelt in an isolated house, because he was a leper; for he was cut off from the house of the LORD. Then Jotham his son *was* over the king's house, judging the people of the land.

a. **So Azariah the priest went in after him**: It took courage to confront a king, an heir of King David, a commander of the armies of Judah. Yet Azariah the priest knew that King Uzziah's crime was so great that it justified this confrontation.

b. **It is not for you, Uzziah, to burn incense to the LORD, but for the priests**: Azariah simply called Uzziah to recognize this long-standing principle. God clearly declared that only the descendants of Aaron could come to Him as priests (excepting the priesthood according to Melchizedek, which priesthood Jesus belonged to).

c. **Then Uzziah became furious.... leprosy broke out on his forehead**: With his head full of pride and fury, Uzziah began to see leprosy break out upon his head. No doubt he first saw the problem in the faces of the horrified priests who looked at the leprosy as it first appeared on his face.

i. "*The leprosy even rose up in his forehead*; so as he could not hide his shame; though it is probable it was also in the rest of his body." (Poole)

ii. "Despite the seriousness of what Uzziah had done, God still does not act until Uzziah becomes 'enraged', an emphatic word occurring twice in verse 19. God's righteous anger only breaks out against human rebellious anger." (Selman)

d. **Indeed he also hurried to get out, because the LORD had struck him**: Uzziah would not listen to the Biblical commands and customs that forbade him to enter the temple and offer incense. He would not listen to the rebuke and warning from the priests. Yet he did listen to the judgment of God against him, and he finally **hurried to get out**.

e. **King Uzziah was a leper until the day of his death**: Uzziah came into the temple as an arrogant king, and he left as a humbled leper and stayed that way for the remainder of his life. He could not even go into the outer courts of the temple which were once open to him as to other worshippers (**he was cut off from the house of the LORD**). In overstepping this boundary, he found his freedom more restricted than ever before.

i. "It was a fearful stroke from God. Death was the actual penalty enjoined by the law for his crime (Numbers 18:7), and leprosy was really that – a living death, prolonged and intensified." (Knapp)

ii. "He who could not content himself with God's allowance, but usurped the priest's place and office, is now deprived of the privilege of the meanest of his people, a just and most suitable judgment." (Poole)

3. (22-23) The death and burial of King Uzziah.

Now the rest of the acts of Uzziah, from first to last, the prophet Isaiah the son of Amoz wrote. So Uzziah rested with his fathers, and they buried him with his fathers in the field of burial which *belonged* to the kings, for they said, "He is a leper." Then Jotham his son reigned in his place.

a. **The rest of the acts of Uzziah, from first to last, the prophet Isaiah the son of Amoz wrote**: This connection between Isaiah and Uzziah is noted in Isaiah 6:1, when the death of the king contributed to the call of the prophet: *In the year that King Uzziah died, I saw the Lord sitting on a throne* (Isaiah 6:1).

i. It is important to consider the reign of Uzziah in totality:

- He began his reign at only 16 years of age.
- He reigned for 52 years.

- Overall, he was a good and strong king who led Israel to many military victories and who was an energetic builder and visionary.
- Despite all this, Uzziah had a tragic end.

ii. Therefore, when Isaiah wrote that he was called *in the year King Uzziah died*, he said a lot. It is to say, "In the year a great and wise king died." But it is also to say, "In the year a great and wise king who had a tragic end died." Isaiah had great reason to be discouraged and disillusioned at the death of King Uzziah, because a great king had passed away, and because his life ended tragically. Yet despite it all, he saw the enthroned LORD God who was greater than any earthly king.

b. **For they said, "He is a leper"**: This is a sad and somewhat unfortunate summation of a mostly great king of Judah, yet it shows the great expense and tragedy of not finishing well, and that late mistakes and scandals can color a whole lifetime or career.

i. "This is the last of three successive reigns which concludes with a period of disobedience and disaster, and it seems that nothing is able to prevent Judah and their kings sliding into sin and judgment. Idolatry, rejection of the prophets, violence, and pride repeat themselves with devastating regularity." (Selman)

ii. "Though Uzziah's pride did not cause the exile, it is an excellent illustration of why the exile eventually came about. From now on, Judah's end is definitely in sight." (Selman)

iii. "Reference to a separate burial place may be confirmed by an ossuary inscription of the Hasmonean period: 'Here were brought the bones of Uzziah, king of Judah, and not to be moved.'" (Selman)

iv. "I have lived long enough to observe that the greatest faults that are ever committed by professedly Christian men are not committed by young people. Most painful is it, to me to remember that the worst cases of backsliding and apostasy that I have ever seen, in this church, have been by old men and middle-aged men, – not by young people; for, somehow or other, the young people, if they are truly taught of God, know their weakness, and so they cry to God for help; but it often happens that more experienced people begin to think that they are not likely to fall into the faults and follies of the young; and I care not how old a man may be – even if seven centuries had passed over his head:, – if he began to trust in himself, he would be a fool, and soon he would have a grievous fall." (Spurgeon)

2 Chronicles 27 – Jotham's Godly Reign

A. The good reign of King Jotham.

1. (1-2) An overview of the reign of Jotham.

Jotham *was* twenty-five years old when he became king, and he reigned sixteen years in Jerusalem. His mother's name *was* Jerushah the daughter of Zadok. And he did *what was* right in the sight of the LORD, according to all that his father Uzziah had done (although he did not enter the temple of the LORD). But still the people acted corruptly.

    a. **And he did what was right in the sight of the LORD**: Jotham was another king of Judah who was generally good. This stands in strong contrast to the evil done by the contemporary kings of Israel. Among the kings of Judah, there were good and godly kings.

    b. **According to all that his father Uzziah had done**: The pattern is seen in both the kingdoms of Israel and Judah, where the son reigns as his father had before him. While this is not concretely predetermined, certainly this is a principle that shows us the great influence that a father has on a son.

        i. Yet, **he did not enter the temple of the LORD**. "He regarded his father's sin rather as a beacon to warn him away from that rock on which Uzziah's life had been wrecked." (Spurgeon)

        ii. "It is a great, mercy for us, when we have seen others *sin,* if we use their shipwrecks as beacons for ourselves. What fascination should there be in sin?" (Spurgeon)

    c. **But still the people acted corruptly**: The word **still** is important, because it tells us that this corruption did not begin with the reign of Jotham, but continued from the days of his predecessor, Uzziah. Though he had a bad end, the personal character of Uzziah was generally godly. Yet it seems that he was, in general, more godly than the common people.

i. Payne says of Uzziah and the kings of Israel that reigned in his days, "Below the surface prosperity that was enjoyed by both kingdoms at this time, the contemporary preaching of Hosea and Amos indicates the presence of serious moral and spiritual decay."

ii. "Though Isaiah, Hosea, Micah, and other holy prophets then living showed them their sin. To this day, people will not leave their old evil customs, though never so much preached down." (Trapp)

2. (3-6) The accomplishments of Jotham.

He built the Upper Gate of the house of the Lord, and he built extensively on the wall of Ophel. Moreover he built cities in the mountains of Judah, and in the forests he built fortresses and towers. He also fought with the king of the Ammonites and defeated them. And the people of Ammon gave him in that year one hundred talents of silver, ten thousand kors of wheat, and ten thousand of barley. The people of Ammon paid this to him in the second and third years also. So Jotham became mighty, because he prepared his ways before the Lord his God.

a. **He built the Upper Gate of the house of the Lord**: This was always a positive sign in Judah. When kings and leaders were concerned about the **house of the Lord**, it reflected some measure of spiritual revival.

i. In particular, it seems that Jotham rebuilt the *link* between the temple and the palace. "He wished free access from his own house to that of the Lord. He would strengthen the link between the two houses – keep his line of communication open (to use a military figure) with the source of his supplies of strength and wisdom. This is one of the secrets of his prosperity and power." (Knapp)

ii. His father Uzziah misunderstood the link between the royal house and the house of God, demanding priestly authority (2 Chronicles 26:16-21). Many kings before him wanted *no link* between the royal house and the house of God. Jotham understood that he was a king and not a priest, yet he wanted a good, open link between the palace and the temple.

b. **Moreover he built cities in the mountains of Judah, and in the forests he built fortresses and towers**: Jotham extended his concern to build Judah beyond Jerusalem and the temple. This made his kingdom strong and able to subdue neighboring peoples such as the **Ammonites**.

i. "He also turned his attention to urban planning, construction cities in the highlands of Judah that, together with a system of towers and fortification in the wooded areas, could serve both economic and military purposes." (Patterson and Austel)

ii. "The tribute was substantial, something over three tons of *silver* and approximately *ten thousand* donkey loads of *barley*." (Selman)

c. **So Jotham became mighty, because he prepared his ways before the LORD his God**. The building of this link between the palace and the temple was one of the chief ways that he prepared his way before the LORD. "That high gate between the palace and the temple was better than a Chinese wall around his kingdom. It is in communion with God that real prosperity and power is found." (Knapp)

i. "While there was no definite national reform during his reign, he seems to have gone quietly forward along true lines, and his strength is attributed to the fact that he ordered his ways before Jehovah his God." (Morgan)

ii. "*Jotham must have been a man of prayer*. He could not have prepared his ways thus anywhere except at the mercy-seat. He must have been in the habit of taking his daily troubles to his God, and of seeking guidance from him in his daily difficulties, and of blessing him for his daily mercies. He must have been in constant communion with his God, or else he could not have ordered his ways aright before him." (Spurgeon)

iii. "Jotham is the only one of all the Hebrew kings, from Saul down, against whom God has nothing bad to record. In this his character is in beautiful accord with his name, *Jehovah-perfect*." (Knapp)

iv. "I do not remember ever meeting one who really walked with God who did not make orderliness one of the first principles of life.... They are the habits of the soul that walks before God, and which is accustomed to think of Him as seeing in secret, and considering all our ways." (Meyer)

3. (7-9) The summary of his reign.

Now the rest of the acts of Jotham, and all his wars and his ways, indeed they *are* written in the book of the kings of Israel and Judah. He was twenty-five years old when he became king, and he reigned sixteen years in Jerusalem. So Jotham rested with his fathers, and they buried him in the City of David. Then Ahaz his son reigned in his place.

a. **All his wars and his ways**: 2 Kings 15:37 tells us, *In those days the LORD began to send Rezin king of Syria and Pekah the son of Remaliah*. Under the inspiration of the Holy Spirit, the writer of 2 Kings tells us that it was the hand of the *LORD* that sent these foreign rulers who troubled Judah.

i. "During Jotham's reign, the combined forces of King Rezin of Syria and King Pekah of Israel began their invasion of Judah, but the full impact of these military assaults was not felt until Jotham's son became king." (Dilday)

ii. "The reference to 'all' Jotham's wars suggests that prior to the Ammonite campaign, for which as king he had sole responsibility, he may have served as field commander for the alliance that was conceived by his quarantined father, Uzziah." (Payne)

b. **So Jotham rested with his fathers**: After the stories of the three previous kings, each of whom started well but finished poorly, it is somewhat of a relief to read of a king who did not have such a disappointing end.

2 Chronicles 28 – The Evil Reign of Ahaz

A. The sin of Ahaz and the punishment of Ahaz.

1. (1-4) Ahaz rejects God and embraces idols.

Ahaz *was* twenty years old when he became king, and he reigned sixteen years in Jerusalem; and he did not do *what was* right in the sight of the LORD, as his father David *had done*. For he walked in the ways of the kings of Israel, and made molded images for the Baals. He burned incense in the Valley of the Son of Hinnom, and burned his children in the fire, according to the abominations of the nations whom the LORD had cast out before the children of Israel. And he sacrificed and burned incense on the high places, on the hills, and under every green tree.

a. **He did not do what was right in the sight of the LORD**: This briefly describes the reign of perhaps the worst king of Judah. Whereas many previous kings fell short in some area or another, of Ahaz it is simply said that **he did not do what was right in the sight of the LORD**.

b. **As his father David had done**: Ahaz had plenty of good examples, both immediately in his father Jotham and historically in his ancestor **David**. Ahaz rejected these godly examples and walked in his own way.

c. **He walked in the ways of the kings of Israel**: Ahaz not only rejected the godly heritage of David, he embraced the ungodly ways of the kings of the northern kingdom of Israel. The southern kingdom of Judah had a mixture of godly and ungodly kings; the northern kingdom of Judah had *only* ungodly kings, and Ahaz followed *their* pattern.

i. "This is the first instance where Judah imitates Israel's apostasy." (Wiseman)

ii. Micah 7:2-7 is a good description of the depravity of the times of Ahaz and the reaction of the godly remnant to it.

d. **And burned his children in the fire**: This describes Ahaz's participation in the worship of Molech. The pagan god (or, *demon*, more accurately) Molech was worshipped by heating a metal statue representing the god until it was red hot, then placing a living infant on the outstretched hands of the statue, while beating drums drowned out the screams of the child until it burned to death.

> i. In Leviticus 20:1-5, God pronounced the death sentence against all who worshipped Molech, saying: *I will set My face against that man, and will cut him off from his people, because he has given some of his descendants to Molech, to defile My sanctuary and profane My holy name* (Leviticus 20:3).
>
> ii. Sadly, even a man as great as Solomon at least sanctioned the worship of Molech and built a temple to this idol (1 Kings 11:7). One of the great crimes of the northern tribes of Israel was their worship of Molech, leading to the Assyrian captivity (2 Kings 17:17). King Manasseh of Judah gave his son to Molech (2 Kings 21:6). Up to the days of King Josiah of Judah, Molech worship continued, because he destroyed a place of worship to that idol (2 Kings 23:10).
>
> iii. "The 'Valley of (the son of) Hinnom' descended eastward below the southern edge of the city of Jerusalem; and it became noted as the scene of Judah's most revolting pagan practices (2 Chronicles 33:6). It was later defiled by King Josiah and converted into a place of refuse for the city (2 Kings 23:10); thus the perpetual fires of 'Gehenna' became descriptive of hell itself (Mark 9:43)." (Payne)

e. **According to the abominations of the nations whom the LORD had cast out before the children of Israel**: The Canaanite nations that occupied Canaan before the time of Joshua also practiced this terrible form of human and child sacrifice. God would bring judgment upon Judah for their continued practice of these sins.

> i. This reminds us that the war against the Canaanites in the Book of Joshua – as terrible and complete as it was – was *not* a racial war. God's judgment did not come upon the Canaanites through the armies of Israel because of their *race*, but because of their *sin*. If Israel insisted on walking in the same sins, God would bring similar judgment upon them.

2. (5-8) A great slaughter and captivity of many from Judah.

Therefore the LORD his God delivered him into the hand of the king of Syria. They defeated him, and carried away a great multitude of them as captives, and brought *them* to Damascus. Then he was also

delivered into the hand of the king of Israel, who defeated him with a great slaughter. For Pekah the son of Remaliah killed one hundred and twenty thousand in Judah in one day, all valiant men, because they had forsaken the LORD God of their fathers. Zichri, a mighty man of Ephraim, killed Maaseiah the king's son, Azrikam the officer over the house, and Elkanah *who was* second to the king. And the children of Israel carried away captive of their brethren two hundred thousand women, sons, and daughters; and they also took away much spoil from them, and brought the spoil to Samaria.

a. **Therefore the LORD his God delivered him into the hand of the king of Syria**: 2 Kings 16:5-6 tells us more about the confederation of Israel and Syria in this attack against Judah. This was part of King Pekah of Israel's anti-Assyria policy. He thought that with Judah defeated, Syria and Israel together could more effectively resist the resurgent power of the Assyrian Empire.

i. Isaiah 7 makes it clear that the goal of this attack was to dethrone Ahaz and set up a Syrian king over Judah, a certain *son of Tabeal* (Isaiah 7:6).

ii. **The LORD his God**: "God was *his* God, though not by covenant and grace, and special relation, which Ahaz had renounced, yet by his sovereign dominion over him; for God did not forfeit his right by Ahaz's denying of it." (Poole)

b. **Who defeated him with a great slaughter**: The loss of 120,000 Judean soldiers and 200,000 civilian hostages in these battles with Israel and Syria meant that it was a dark time for Judah, and it looked as if the dynasty of David would soon be extinguished, as so many dynasties in the northern kingdom of Israel had ended.

3. (9-15) The prophet's rebuke to Israel is heeded

But a prophet of the LORD was there, whose name *was* Oded; and he went out before the army that came to Samaria, and said to them: "Look, because the LORD God of your fathers was angry with Judah, He has delivered them into your hand; but you have killed them in a rage *that* reaches up to heaven. And now you propose to force the children of Judah and Jerusalem to be your male and female slaves; *but are* you not also guilty before the LORD your God? Now hear me, therefore, and return the captives, whom you have taken captive from your brethren, for the fierce wrath of the LORD *is* upon you." Then some of the heads of the children of Ephraim, Azariah the son of Johanan, Berechiah the son of Meshillemoth, Jehizkiah the son of Shallum, and Amasa the son of Hadlai, stood up against those who came from the

war, and said to them, "You shall not bring the captives here, for we *already* have offended the LORD. You intend to add to our sins and to our guilt; for our guilt is great, and *there is* fierce wrath against Israel." So the armed men left the captives and the spoil before the leaders and all the assembly. Then the men who were designated by name rose up and took the captives, and from the spoil they clothed all who were naked among them, dressed them and gave them sandals, gave them food and drink, and anointed them; and they let all the feeble ones ride on donkeys. So they brought them to their brethren at Jericho, the city of palm trees. Then they returned to Samaria.

a. **A prophet of the LORD was there, whose name was Oded**: This brave prophet went with the 200,000 captives taken from the conquered southern kingdom to the northern kingdom of Israel, to make the leaders of Israel conscious of this crime against their fellow tribes.

b. **You shall not bring captives here, for we *already* have offended the LORD**: Remarkably, the leaders of Israel responded to the message from Oded and recognized their own sin and guilt. They cared for the captives from the spoil of battle and sent them back to Judah.

i. "Here we have the picture of a good preacher. Oded teacheth, reproveth, exhorteth, turneth himself into all shapes, of spirit and of speech, that he may work upon his hearers; and he had his desire." (Trapp)

ii. "To this beautiful speech nothing can be added by the best comment; it is simple, humane, pious, and overwhelmingly convincing: no wonder it produced the effect mentioned here. That there was much of humanity in the heads of the children of *Ephraim* who joined with the prophet on this occasion, 2 Chronicles 28:15 sufficiently proves." (Clarke)

B. The decline and fall of King Ahaz.

1. (16-21) Ahaz puts his trust in the kings of Assyria instead of the LORD.

At the same time King Ahaz sent to the kings of Assyria to help him. For again the Edomites had come, attacked Judah, and carried away captives. The Philistines also had invaded the cities of the lowland and of the South of Judah, and had taken Beth Shemesh, Aijalon, Gederoth, Sochoh with its villages, Timnah with its villages, and Gimzo with its villages; and they dwelt there. For the LORD brought Judah low because of Ahaz king of Israel, for he had encouraged moral decline in Judah and had been continually unfaithful to the LORD. Also Tiglath-Pileser king of Assyria came to him and distressed him, and did not assist him.

For Ahaz took part *of the treasures* from the house of the LORD, from the house of the king, and from the leaders, and he gave *it* to the king of Assyria; but he did not help him.

> a. **At the same time King Ahaz sent to the kings of Assyria to help him**: This was because, as 2 Kings 16 explains, the combined armies of Israel and Syria had not only overcome many cities of Judah, but were at the time laying siege against Jerusalem. 2 Kings 16:5 says, *they besieged Ahaz but could not overcome him.* To his shame in this time of crisis, Ahaz looked to **the kings of Assyria** instead of the LORD.
>
>> i. Before Ahaz did this, Isaiah offered him a sign for assurance of God's help in the struggle against the combined armies of Israel and Syria (Isaiah 7:1-12). "This was a fair offer to a foul sinner" (Trapp), but Ahaz refused under the excuse of not wanting to test God, when instead he really wanted to trust in the king of Assyria.
>>
>> ii. The prophecy of Isaiah 7 – including the announcement of the *Immanuel* sign – came from Isaiah to King Ahaz during this joint Israeli and Syrian invasion (also apparently with the help of **the Edomites** and the **Philistines**) Yet for the sake of David, God did not allow this disastrous attack on Judah to prevail. He would not allow this Satanic plot against the Messianic dynasty of David to succeed.
>>
>> iii. The kings of Israel and Syria thought of themselves as burning torches, come to destroy Judah and the dynasty of David. God said they were just like burnt-out smoking sticks, who would not ultimately do much damage (Isaiah 7:4).
>>
>> iv. Through Isaiah's message to Ahaz, he assured the wicked king – who did not really listen – "There should be a remnant left to return to the land; and the virgin should bear a son, so there should not fail a king upon the throne of David. The dynasty could never be destroyed, for of Immanuel's kingdom there shall be no end." (Knapp)
>>
>> v. "*The kings of Assyria*, i.e. the king; the plural number for the singular." (Poole)
>
> b. **For the LORD brought Judah low because of Ahaz king of Israel**: This was both because of the personal ungodliness of Ahaz and because of the poor example he was to others (**he had encouraged moral decline in Judah**).
>
>> i. An example of his personal decline was his appeal to the Assyrian king, to whom he said, *I am your servant and your son. Come up and save me* (2 Kings 16:7). Ahaz surrendered to one enemy in order to

defeat another. He refused to trust in the God of Israel and instead submitted himself and his kingdom to an enemy of Israel.

ii. "The address 'I am your servant and your son' clearly places Ahaz as the petitioning vassal and shows he was trusting in Assyria rather than in the LORD, against the advice of Isaiah (Isaiah 7:10-16; *cf.* Exodus 23:22)." (Wiseman)

c. **For Ahaz took part of the treasures from the house of the LORD…but he did not help him**: Essentially, Ahaz made Judah a subject kingdom to Assyria. Ahaz now took his orders from the Assyrian king, sacrificing the independence of the kingdom of Judah. Worse yet, **he did not help him**. It was useless.

i. We can only wonder what blessing might have come if Ahaz would have surrendered and sacrificed to the LORD with the same energy and whole heart that he surrendered to the Assyrian king.

ii. "How different was his great ancestor David! 'In my distress,' he says, 'I called upon the Lord, and cried unto my God' (Psalm 18:6). Even his wicked grandson Manasseh sought the Lord his God 'when he was in affliction.' But Ahaz seemed determined to fill up the measure of his sins." (Knapp)

2. (22-27) The apostasy and end of King Ahaz.

Now in the time of his distress King Ahaz became increasingly unfaithful to the LORD. This *is that* King Ahaz. For he sacrificed to the gods of Damascus which had defeated him, saying, "Because the gods of the kings of Syria help them, I will sacrifice to them that they may help me." But they were the ruin of him and of all Israel. So Ahaz gathered the articles of the house of God, cut in pieces the articles of the house of God, shut up the doors of the house of the LORD, and made for himself altars in every corner of Jerusalem. And in every single city of Judah he made high places to burn incense to other gods, and provoked to anger the LORD God of his fathers. Now the rest of his acts and all his ways, from first to last, indeed they *are* written in the book of the kings of Judah and Israel. So Ahaz rested with his fathers, and they buried him in the city, in Jerusalem; but they did not bring him into the tombs of the kings of Israel. Then Hezekiah his son reigned in his place.

a. **In the time of his distress King Ahaz became increasingly unfaithful to the LORD**: Times of trial and distress do not necessarily drive people closer to God. Sometimes people allow such distresses to drive them *away* from God. Ahaz was notable among that type, so much so that the Chronicler noted, **That is that King Ahaz.**

i. "These hammers of the Most High did but beat upon cold iron." (Trapp)

ii. "Ahaz also 'behaved without restraint' and was *most unfaithful*. The former expression really means to favour licence rather than true liberty, while the latter is a typical term in Chronicles for failing to give God his due." (Selman)

iii. "The evil of his character is supremely demonstrated in that calamities seemed not to have the effect, as they so often had among his predecessors, of rousing him to consciousness of his sin." (Morgan)

iv. **This is that King Ahaz**: "A black mark is put against his name, to show how greatly guilty he was. Those who rebel against divine checks, and will not be held in by the providence of God, are to be written down in capital letters as great sinners. They sin with emphasis who sin against the chastising rod." (Spurgeon)

b. **For he sacrificed to the gods of Damascus which had defeated him**: 2 Kings 16 tells us that this happened after a visit that Ahaz made to Damascus. He returned from the visit and made a new altar after the pattern of what he saw in Damascus and he took their forms, their style, and their gods. Sadly, he even received the help of Urijah the priest.

i. 2 Kings 16 also tells us that Ahaz served as a priest at the altar of his own design. Since he created his own place of worship, it also made sense that he would disregard God's command that a king must not serve as a priest (Numbers 18:7).

ii. Ahaz's grandfather Azariah (Uzziah) dared to enter the temple and serve God as a priest (2 Chronicles 26). Yet at least Azariah *falsely* worshipped the *true God*. Ahaz *falsely* worshipped a *false god* of his own creation. "Uzziah for so doing was smitten with leprosy; but Ahaz of a far worse disease, an incurable hardness of heart." (Trapp)

c. **Cut in pieces the articles of the house of God, shut up the doors of the house of the LORD**: Ahaz could not bring in his pagan, corrupt innovations without *also* removing what had stood before at the temple. This was an ungodly exchange, taking away the good and putting in the bad. Collectively, all these things served to *discourage* the worship of the true God at the temple of God.

i. "He caused the Divine worship to be totally suspended; and they continued shut till the beginning of the reign of Hezekiah, one of whose first acts was to reopen them, and thus to restore the Divine worship." (Clarke)

ii. "Ahaz's appropriation of the panels and bases from the sacred furniture does not seem to be for the purpose of sending a further gift to Tiglath-pileser but rather for deemphasizing their importance in the worship services. Perhaps he planned to reuse them in some other decorative way. At any rate death overtook him before his attention could be turned to them. They are mentioned among the several items that were carried away in the later Babylonian despoiling of Jerusalem (2 Kings 25:13-14; Jeremiah 27:19-20; 52:17-23)." (Patterson and Austel)

iii. We remember that *all this took place at the temple Solomon built unto the* LORD. The mere *location* did not make it true worship. Sometimes idols are worshipped at a house that was once dedicated to the true God.

d. **And in every single city of Judah he made high places to burn incense to other gods**: During these changes, Ahaz shut down the operation of the temple and established small pagan altars all around Judah.

i. "It would seem as though the light of truth were absolutely extinguished. It was not so, however, for it is likely that throughout the whole reigns of Jotham and Ahaz, Isaiah was uttering his message, and that during the reign of Ahaz Micah also was delivering the word of God." (Morgan)

e. **Now the rest of his acts and all his ways**: So ended the reign of perhaps the worst king of Judah. Micah – who prophesied during the reign of Ahaz – describes the man who works to *successfully do evil with both hands* (Micah 7:3). The idea is that the man pursues evil with all his effort, *with both hands*. He may very well have had King Ahaz in mind.

i. "He died a natural death, though he was so detestable a miscreant. God putteth off the punishment of many wicked wretches till the other world." (Trapp)

ii. "Ahaz was evil by choice, persistent in evil in spite of calamity, blasphemously rebellious notwithstanding the direct warnings of the prophet of God. This attitude of the king made the darkness all the denser." (Morgan)

2 Chronicles 29 – Hezekiah and the Cleansing of the Temple

A. The cleansing of the temple.

1. (1-2) The general assessment of his reign.

Hezekiah became king *when he was* twenty-five years old, and he reigned twenty-nine years in Jerusalem. His mother's name *was* Abijah the daughter of Zechariah. And he did *what was* right in the sight of the Lord, according to all that his father David had done.

> a. **Hezekiah became king when he was twenty-five years old**: Hezekiah came to the throne of Judah at the very end of the kingdom of Israel. Three years after the start of his reign the Assyrian armies set siege to Samaria, and three years after that the northern kingdom was conquered.
>
>> i. The sad fate of the northern kingdom was a valuable lesson to Hezekiah. He saw first-hand what happened when the people of God rejected their God and His word, and worshipped other gods.
>
> b. **He reigned twenty-nine years in Jerusalem**: Hezekiah was one of the better kings of Judah, and thus had a long and mostly blessed reign. No doubt his mother **Abijah** was a godly and important influence on his life.
>
>> i. "His mother was Abijah, the daughter of Zechariah, probably the person mentioned by the prophet Isaiah (Isaiah 8:2) as a 'faithful witness.' This possible friendship of his mother for the prophet, combined with the certainty that up to this time he had been under the influence of Isaiah's ministry, may account for Hezekiah's action on coming to the throne." (Morgan)
>
> c. **He did what was right in the sight of the Lord**: Hezekiah was one of Judah's most zealous reformers, even prohibiting worship on *the high*

places (2 Kings 18:4). These were popular altars for sacrifice set up as the worshipper desired, not according to God's direction.

> i. "God was never happy about this practice, but none of the other good kings ever found the courage to forbid it. Hezekiah did." (Dilday)
>
> ii. 2 Kings 18:5-6 makes this remarkable statement about Hezekiah: *He trusted in the LORD God of Israel, so that after him was none like him among all the kings of Judah, nor who were before him. For he held fast to the LORD; he did not depart from following Him, but kept His commandments, which the LORD had commanded Moses.*

2. (3-11) Hezekiah exhorts the cleansing and restoration of the temple.

In the first year of his reign, in the first month, he opened the doors of the house of the LORD and repaired them. Then he brought in the priests and the Levites, and gathered them in the East Square, and said to them: "Hear me, Levites! Now sanctify yourselves, sanctify the house of the LORD God of your fathers, and carry out the rubbish from the holy *place.* **For our fathers have trespassed and done evil in the eyes of the LORD our God; they have forsaken Him, have turned their faces away from the dwelling place of the LORD, and turned** *their* **backs** *on Him.* **They have also shut up the doors of the vestibule, put out the lamps, and have not burned incense or offered burnt offerings in the holy** *place* **to the God of Israel. Therefore the wrath of the LORD fell upon Judah and Jerusalem, and He has given them up to trouble, to desolation, and to jeering, as you see with your eyes. For indeed, because of this our fathers have fallen by the sword; and our sons, our daughters, and our wives** *are* **in captivity. Now** *it is* **in my heart to make a covenant with the LORD God of Israel, that His fierce wrath may turn away from us. My sons, do not be negligent now, for the LORD has chosen you to stand before Him, to serve Him, and that you should minister to Him and burn incense."**

> a. **Sanctify yourselves, sanctify the house of the LORD God of your fathers, and carry out the rubbish from the holy place**: Tragically, the condition of both the Levites and the temple was so bad that they seemed incapable of reforming themselves without this push from King Hezekiah.
>
> b. **Have turned their faces away…and turned their backs on Him**: They had failed because they gave God their **back** instead of their **face**. One might say that in every opportunity to encounter God, we have the choice to turn either our **back** or our **face** to God.
>
> > i. Poole suggests that the idea of turning the back to God could also be understood literally, because according to 2 Kings 16, in the days

of Ahaz the altar was moved and its replacement was directed to the east, in the manner of pagan altars instead of toward the west as God commanded. The idea was therefore that under this dangerous innovation, one had to literally turn his back to the temple and the ark of God to stand before the altar.

c. **They have also shut up the doors of the vestibule, put out the lamps, and have not burned incense or offered burnt offerings**: This happened in the days of Ahaz, the father of Hezekiah (2 Chronicles 28:24). Hezekiah knew that it was time to open up the temple again, both to clean it out and so that it could operate as intended.

d. **Therefore the wrath of the Lord fell upon Judah and Jerusalem**: In a remarkable way, Hezekiah recognized that the calamities that had come to Judah came *because of their disobedience*. It takes a wise and godly person to admit this, and to act appropriately.

i. "He made no attempt to blame on God the calamities which had overtaken the nation." (Morgan)

e. **My sons, do not be negligent now, for the Lord has chosen you to stand before Him, to serve Him**: This call to courage from Hezekiah to the priests and Levites was focused on their sense of *calling* (**the Lord has chosen you**). Getting back to a focus upon their calling and their central purpose (to serve and honor God) was essential, and this exhortation demonstrates that they had lost this focus.

i. Hezekiah set the example in this devoted service to God, in that he even destroyed a notable artifact from the Exodus – the bronze serpent of Moses known as *Nehushtan* – when it became an idol (2 Kings 18:4).

3. (12-19) Cleansing the temple.

Then these Levites arose: Mahath the son of Amasai and Joel the son of Azariah, of the sons of the Kohathites; of the sons of Merari, Kish the son of Abdi and Azariah the son of Jehallelel; of the Gershonites, Joah the son of Zimmah and Eden the son of Joah; of the sons of Elizaphan, Shimri and Jeiel; of the sons of Asaph, Zechariah and Mattaniah; of the sons of Heman, Jehiel and Shimei; and of the sons of Jeduthun, Shemaiah and Uzziel. And they gathered their brethren, sanctified themselves, and went according to the commandment of the king, at the words of the Lord, to cleanse the house of the Lord. Then the priests went into the inner part of the house of the Lord to cleanse *it*, and brought out all the debris that they found in the temple of the Lord to the court of the house of the Lord. And the Levites took *it* out and

carried *it* to the Brook Kidron. Now they began to sanctify on the first *day* of the first month, and on the eighth day of the month they came to the vestibule of the LORD. So they sanctified the house of the LORD in eight days, and on the sixteenth day of the first month they finished. Then they went in to King Hezekiah and said, "We have cleansed all the house of the LORD, the altar of burnt offerings with all its articles, and the table of the showbread with all its articles. Moreover all the articles which King Ahaz in his reign had cast aside in his transgression we have prepared and sanctified; and there they *are,* before the altar of the LORD."

a. **Then these Levites arose**: These were men who *had* been complicit in the neglect and disgrace of the temple. Yet the Chronicler rightly noted these men by name, because when they were exhorted by King Hezekiah to do what was right in cleansing and restoring the temple, *they did it.*

b. **On the sixteenth day of the first month they finished**: This relates the staggering extent of the prior damage to the temple, in that it took 16 days to simply carry out the rubbish that had accumulated in the temple, including even **the inner part of the house of the LORD.**

c. **All the articles which King Ahaz in his reign had cast aside in his transgression we have prepared and sanctified; and there they are**: After the first step of removing the problem, now they could put back what had been taken out during the reign of Ahaz (2 Chronicles 28:24 and 2 Kings 16:17-18).

B. The restoration of worship.

1. (20-27) Sacrifice and worship are organized again.

Then King Hezekiah rose early, gathered the rulers of the city, and went up to the house of the LORD. And they brought seven bulls, seven rams, seven lambs, and seven male goats for a sin offering for the kingdom, for the sanctuary, and for Judah. Then he commanded the priests, the sons of Aaron, to offer *them* on the altar of the LORD. So they killed the bulls, and the priests received the blood and sprinkled *it* on the altar. Likewise they killed the rams and sprinkled the blood on the altar. They also killed the lambs and sprinkled the blood on the altar. Then they brought out the male goats *for* the sin offering before the king and the assembly, and they laid their hands on them. And the priests killed them; and they presented their blood on the altar as a sin offering to make an atonement for all Israel, for the king commanded *that* the burnt offering and the sin offering *be made* for all Israel. And he stationed the Levites in the house of the LORD with cymbals, with

stringed instruments, and with harps, according to the commandment of David, of Gad the king's seer, and of Nathan the prophet; for thus *was* the commandment of the LORD by his prophets. The Levites stood with the instruments of David, and the priests with the trumpets. Then Hezekiah commanded *them* to offer the burnt offering on the altar. And when the burnt offering began, the song of the LORD *also* began, with the trumpets and with the instruments of David king of Israel.

a. **Then he commanded the priests, the sons of Aaron, to offer them on the altar of the LORD**: In his bold restoration of the service of the temple, Hezekiah was not so foolish as to overstep the Biblical and traditional commands and to offer these sacrifices himself. His great-grandfather Uzziah did this to his own judgment (2 Chronicles 26:16-23).

i. "The whole enterprise is characterized by a concern to do everything as God required, especially as the king's command was regarded as 'the words of the LORD' (2 Chronicles 29:15)." (Selman)

ii. "For the assembly to lay their hands on the goats of the sin offering was to designate these as substitutes for their own lives and to transfer their sins to the animal victims.... The goats thus served as types of Christ's death in the sinner's stead (2 Corinthians 5:21)." (Payne)

iii. The diligence of Hezekiah was evident in that he **rose early** to do these things. "His zeal for God's glory made his obedience prompt and present, ready and speedy. He could not rest until he had reformed." (Trapp)

iv. It was also shown in offering *more* than the law commanded. "This was more than the law required; see Leviticus 4:13, etc. It ordered *one calf* or *ox* for the sins of the *people*, and *one he-goat* for the sins of the *prince*; but Hezekiah here offers many more." (Clarke)

b. **And when the burnt offering began, the song of the LORD also began**: In his arrangement of this restoration of temple service, Hezekiah was careful to include both *offering* and *worship*. Each honored God in important ways.

i. "The Hebrew that lies behind the phrase 'singing to the LORD' is literally 'the song of the LORD' (NASB), which suggests a specific writing, i.e., perhaps including the canonical Psalms that were then available for use in worship." (Payne)

ii. Hezekiah was wise in making worship such a priority. "Every human being's first priority should be to acknowledge God's worth. That, for example, is how the ten commandments begin (Exodus 20:3-6), it is the reason for Jesus' obedient death on the cross, and it is the chief characteristic of the community in heaven (Revelation 4:1-5:14; 22:1-9)." (Selman)

2. (28-30) The assembly of Judah joins in the worship and recognition of sacrificial offerings.

So all the assembly worshiped, the singers sang, and the trumpeters sounded; all *this continued* until the burnt offering was finished. And when they had finished offering, the king and all who were present with him bowed and worshiped. Moreover King Hezekiah and the leaders commanded the Levites to sing praise to the LORD with the words of David and of Asaph the seer. So they sang praises with gladness, and they bowed their heads and worshiped.

a. **So all the assembly worshipped, the singers sang, and the trumpeters sounded**: Each person played their part in this large, communal honoring of God.

i. "This chapter contains a parable of the cleansing of the heart, meant to be a temple for God; but the doors of prayer are unopened, the lamps of testimony unlit, the burnt-offerings of self-sacrifice neglected." (Meyer)

ii. "You tell me that you cannot sing the Lord's song; then I know you have gone into the strange land of backsliding. You acknowledge that for some time now you have taken no delight in God or his service; then I am sure that the temple is badly in need of renovation." (Meyer)

iii. "The music of your life is still, because you are out of accord with the will of God; but when by surrender and consecration there is unison, your heart will be filled with songs without words, and love like an ocean in the fullness of her strength." (Meyer)

iv. The description of instruments in this passage is compelling evidence that they should be used today in worshipping God, but not all are convinced of this. "Away with such portentous baubles from the worship of that infinite Spirit who requires his followers to worship him *in spirit and in truth*, for to no such worship are those instruments friendly." (Clarke)

b. **King Hezekiah and the leaders commanded the Levites to sing praise to the LORD with the words of David and of Asaph the seer**: They worshipped God with the best words they could find – the words of the great psalms of praise written by David and others.

3. (31-36) Thank and fellowship offerings and the resulting joy.

Then Hezekiah answered and said, "Now *that* you have consecrated yourselves to the LORD, come near, and bring sacrifices and thank offerings into the house of the LORD." So the assembly brought in sacrifices and thank offerings, and as many as were of a willing heart *brought* burnt offerings. And the number of the burnt offerings which the assembly brought was seventy bulls, one hundred rams, *and* two hundred lambs; all these *were* for a burnt offering to the LORD. The consecrated things *were* six hundred bulls and three thousand sheep. But the priests were too few, so that they could not skin all the burnt offerings; therefore their brethren the Levites helped them until the work was ended and until the *other* priests had sanctified themselves, for the Levites were more diligent in sanctifying themselves than the priests. Also the burnt offerings *were* in abundance, with the fat of the peace offerings and *with* the drink offerings for *every* burnt offering. So the service of the house of the LORD was set in order. Then Hezekiah and all the people rejoiced that God had prepared the people, since the events took place so suddenly.

a. **Now that you have consecrated yourselves to the LORD, come near, and bring sacrifices and thank offerings into the house of the LORD**: Once they had properly sacrificed and cleansed the temple and their own hearts before the LORD, *now* the **assembly** was invited to come and bring their personal offerings. One of the great purposes of the temple – as a place for the personal sacrifice and worship of the believer – was now restored.

i. "Sacrifices and offerings are only acceptable when those offering them are themselves consecrated to Jehovah." (Morgan)

ii. "Sacrifice for sin in both the Old Testament and the New is the springboard for the sacrifice of praise (Colossians 3:15-16; Hebrews 13:15) and for the fellowship or communion meal (1 Corinthians 11:23-26)." (Selman)

b. **The priests were too few, so that they could not skin all the burnt offerings**: The pent-up desire of the people to sacrifice and honor God through sacrifices was so great that when they were given the opportunity the priests were overwhelmed.

i. Wisely, **their brethren the Levites helped them until the work was ended**. This was a good example of temporarily suspending a commandment out of godly necessity.

ii. It was also fitting on this occasion because **the Levites were more diligent in their sanctifying themselves than the priests**. "For the truest faith is often found among the humble; and throughout history 'professional' religious leaders have too often been among those least willing to submit to Christ and to the Word." (Payne)

c. **Hezekiah and all the people rejoiced that God had prepared the people**: The remarkable response of the assembly was proof that **God had prepared the people**. There could never be such a response unless God was at work among His people, and this was evidence of such a work.

i. "It was, as a very great, so a sudden change, that the people, who but the other day were so ready to comply with wicked Ahaz in his idolatrous and impious prescriptions, were now so free and forward in God's service; whereby it plainly appeared to be the work of the Almighty God changing their hearts by his Holy Spirit." (Poole)

ii. "Two consequences followed from these offerings. The first was to acknowledge that only God had made it all possible (2 Chronicles 29:36; cf. 1 Corinthians 12:3; Ephesians 2:18). The second was that everyone *rejoiced* (2 Chronicles 29:36), in complete contrast with the situation with which they had begun." (Selman)

2 Chronicles 30 – Hezekiah's Passover

A. The letter of invitation.

1. (1-5) The tribes of Israel are invited to celebrate the Passover.

And Hezekiah sent to all Israel and Judah, and also wrote letters to Ephraim and Manasseh, that they should come to the house of the LORD at Jerusalem, to keep the Passover to the LORD God of Israel. For the king and his leaders and all the assembly in Jerusalem had agreed to keep the Passover in the second month. For they could not keep it at the regular time, because a sufficient number of priests had not consecrated themselves, nor had the people gathered together at Jerusalem. And the matter pleased the king and all the assembly. So they resolved to make a proclamation throughout all Israel, from Beersheba to Dan, that they should come to keep the Passover to the LORD God of Israel at Jerusalem, since they had not done *it* for a long *time* in the *prescribed* manner.

a. **Hezekiah sent to all Israel and Judah**: The timing of this invitation is somewhat hard to precisely determine. It seems to have happened when Israel was defeated and prostrate under Assyria, yet perhaps before the kingdom as a whole had been depopulated through exile. Therefore this invitation actually went out to the remnant that had, up to this point, escaped exile (2 Chronicles 30:6).

i. "In all probability, this Passover was observed before the final passing of the northern kingdom into captivity." (Morgan)

ii. "Any such compliance had been prohibited during the two centuries that had followed Jeroboam's division of the Solomonic empire (2 Chronicles 30:5, 26; 1 Kings 12:27-28). But now King Hoshea's capital in Samaria was subject to Assyrian siege (2 Chronicles 30:6; 2 Kings 17:5), and the northern ruler was powerless to interfere." (Payne)

b. **To keep the Passover**: This great feast celebrated the great and glorious deliverance of God on Israel's behalf in the days of the Exodus (Exodus 12). It was a deliberate, emblematic reminder of the central act of redemption in the Old Testament (the deliverance from slavery in Egypt).

> i. Communion is likewise an emblematic reminder of the central act of redemption of the New Testament (and the Bible as a whole). The long neglect of Passover among the tribes of Israel would be like a church that had not celebrated the Lord's Table in a long, long time.
>
> ii. "Jesus is the ultimate Passover lamb, who by his own body and blood established a new covenant (*cf.* Luke 22:14-20). Just as Hezekiah's congregation were cleansed and healed, Christians are made clean by their Passover sacrifice, except that Jesus' sacrifice is the ultimate and unrepeatable Passover." (Selman)

c. **Had agreed to keep the Passover in the second month**: Normally, Passover was kept in the first month (Numbers 9:1-5). However, there were special circumstances under which Passover could be kept in the **second month** (Numbers 9:5-14). Because **they could not keep it at the regular time**, here, under Hezekiah, they kept it in the **second month**.

> i. "Hezekiah therefore, and his counsellors, thought that they might extend that to the *people at large*, because of the delay necessarily occasioned by the cleansing of the temple, which was granted to *individuals* in such cases as the above, and the result showed that they had not mistaken the mind of the Lord upon the subject." (Clarke)

d. **Since they had not done it for a long time**: Even though Passover was one of the three feasts that deserved special emphasis (Exodus 23:14-17), it had not been celebrated **for a long time**. Hezekiah was dedicated to righting this wrong.

2. (6-9) The letter to the tribes.

Then the runners went throughout all Israel and Judah with the letters from the king and his leaders, and spoke according to the command of the king: "Children of Israel, return to the LORD God of Abraham, Isaac, and Israel; then He will return to the remnant of you who have escaped from the hand of the kings of Assyria. And do not be like your fathers and your brethren, who trespassed against the LORD God of their fathers, so that He gave them up to desolation, as you see. Now do not be stiff-necked, as your fathers *were, but* yield yourselves to the LORD; and enter His sanctuary, which He has sanctified forever, and serve the LORD your God, that the fierceness of His wrath may turn away from you. For if you return to the LORD, your brethren and your children

will be treated **with compassion by those who lead them captive, so that they may come back to this land; for the L**ORD **your God** *is* **gracious and merciful, and will not turn** *His* **face from you if you return to Him."**

a. **Children of Israel, return to the** LORD **God of Abraham, Isaac, and Israel**: The northern kingdom of Israel had fallen and all that remained after the exile to the Assyrians was **the remnant of you who have escaped**. Yet Hezekiah still believed in the concept of the **Children of Israel**, those of the tribes of Israel descended from the great patriarchs.

i. In the history of the divided kingdoms there were some attempts to reunify by force, but these came to nothing. "In comparison with previous failures, this incident shows that the only really effective approach to unity has to be based on the principle of faithful worship." (Selman)

ii. "The good of our brethren in other kingdoms must also be minded." (Trapp)

b. **Do not be stiff-necked, as your fathers were**: This was especially relevant as the letter went to the remnant of the northern kingdom. Generally speaking, they had neglected the Jerusalem Passover for a long time.

i. "Hezekiah knew that the poor remnant of Israel were in great affliction: he therefore presseth them to repentance, whereby men return to God, as by sin they run from him.... Hezekiah thought it was good striking while the iron was hot." (Trapp)

c. **For if you return to the** LORD: The letter of invitation promised two things if the remnant of Israel would **return to the** LORD and obediently celebrate this Passover in Jerusalem. First, under God's blessing it would go well with those already taken **captive** by the Assyrians. Second, God would restore the northern kingdom and allow them to **come back to this land**.

i. These promises were based on an eternal principle of God's character: that He **will not turn His face from you if you return to Him**. God promises to draw near to those who draw near to Him.

3. (10-12) The reaction to the letter in Israel and Judah.

So the runners passed from city to city through the country of Ephraim and Manasseh, as far as Zebulun; but they laughed at them and mocked them. Nevertheless some from Asher, Manasseh, and Zebulun humbled themselves and came to Jerusalem. Also the hand of God was on Judah to give them singleness of heart to obey the command of the king and the leaders, at the word of the LORD**.**

a. **But they laughed at them and mocked them**: Mostly, the reception among the remnant of the northern kingdom was not warm. Reflecting the same attitude of heart that brought the kingdom as a whole into exile, the people of the northern kingdom **laughed at** and **mocked** the messengers who invited them to this great Passover in Jerusalem.

i. We note there was no rational argument against the invitation; it was all opposed with simple laughter and mocking. For the frivolous and simple-minded, these replace serious thought.

ii. "Josephus saith that these Israelites thus invited slew both the messengers and those prophets also that exhorted them to go up." (Trapp)

b. **Nevertheless some from Asher, Manasseh, and Zebulun humbled themselves and came to Jerusalem**: Happily, there was a remnant of the remnant that responded to the message and came from the former northern kingdom.

i. "Far more northerners participated than previously, and the recent fall of the northern kingdom in 722 B.C. meant that Jerusalem now offered the only alternative for corporate worship of the Lord." (Selman)

c. **The hand of God was on Judah**: The response among the peoples and villages of Judah was entirely different. God gave **them singleness of heart to obey the command** of the Lord and their king.

B. The Passover celebrated.

1. (13-17) Preparations and sacrifices made.

Now many people, a very great assembly, gathered at Jerusalem to keep the Feast of Unleavened Bread in the second month. They arose and took away the altars that *were* **in Jerusalem, and they took away all the incense altars and cast** *them* **into the Brook Kidron. Then they slaughtered the Passover** *lambs* **on the fourteenth** *day* **of the second month. The priests and the Levites were ashamed, and sanctified themselves, and brought the burnt offerings to the house of the Lord. They stood in their place according to their custom, according to the Law of Moses the man of God; the priests sprinkled the blood** *received* **from the hand of the Levites. For** *there were* **many in the assembly who had not sanctified themselves; therefore the Levites had charge of the slaughter of the Passover** *lambs* **for everyone** *who was* **not clean, to sanctify** *them* **to the Lord.**

a. **Many people, a very great assembly**: This was the greatest assembly gathered for a Passover in generations. Not only had the Passover been neglected in Judah for many years, but this Passover also included those from the remnant of the northern tribes who responded to the invitation.

b. **They arose and took away the altars that were in Jerusalem**: These were either altars to pagan gods or unauthorized altars to the true God. Both were prohibited, and as a demonstration of preparation for this great Passover, the city was cleansed of all idolatrous or unauthorized worship.

i. "So must we also first cast the baggage into the brook, and then come to the Lord's supper." (Trapp)

c. **Then they slaughtered the Passover lambs on the fourteenth day of the second month**: This shows the Passover being celebrated according to the Scriptural commands (allowing for the celebration of Passover in the second month according to Numbers 9:5-14). They took care to honor and obey in their celebration of this important feast.

2. (18-20) God is merciful to the ignorant worshippers.

For a multitude of the people, many from Ephraim, Manasseh, Issachar, and Zebulun, had not cleansed themselves, yet they ate the Passover contrary to what was written. But Hezekiah prayed for them, saying, "May the good Lord provide atonement for everyone *who* prepares his heart to seek God, the Lord God of his fathers, though *he is* not *cleansed according to the purification of the sanctuary.*" And the Lord listened to Hezekiah and healed the people.

a. **For a multitude of the people…had not cleansed themselves**: This **multitude** seems to have mostly come from the remnant of the northern tribes, who would naturally be ignorant about how to properly prepare for Passover.

i. "It was a motley crowd which assembled, and multitudes of the people were utterly ignorant of the Divine arrangements for preparation. Hezekiah's tenderness was manifested in the pity he felt for these people, and in the prayer he offered on their behalf." (Morgan)

ii. "This largeness of heart is always characteristic of men who are really in fellowship with God, for it is in harmony with the heart of God." (Morgan)

b. **Yet they ate the Passover contrary to what was written**: We would expect that this would result in a great punishment or judgment against them. Instead, **Hezekiah prayed for them**, asking **the good Lord to provide atonement**. In response, **the Lord listened to Hezekiah and healed the people**.

i. This shows the wonderful and warm mercy of God. By the letter of the command, the people deserved judgment for their disobedience. Yet God showed His mercy and goodness to those who had prepared their **heart to seek God**, though in ignorance they did not do it all according to the commandments.

ii. "Unaccustomed to temple usage, strangers to the temple rites, they had participated in the festivities of this great Passover without submitting first to the necessary ablutions. Their heart was prepared to seek God, they were proud of the great past, they desired to stand right with the Lord God of their fathers; but they were sadly ignorant and careless. The only thing to be done was to pray that their ignorance and negligence might be forgiven." (Meyer)

iii. "You may not understand doctrine, creed, or rite; but be sure to seek God. No splendid ceremonial nor rigorous etiquette can intercept the seeking soul." (Meyer)

iv. Their pattern of preparing to receive the Passover is instructive for those who come to the communion table, especially those who feel unworthy to partake of communion.

- They forgot their differences and came together as one people.
- They removed their idols.
- They prepared their hearts.
- Their sins and ignorance were confessed.
- They prayed.

3. (21-22) Worship, teaching, and fellowship.

So the children of Israel who were present at Jerusalem kept the Feast of Unleavened Bread seven days with great gladness; and the Levites and the priests praised the Lord day by day, *singing* to the Lord, accompanied by loud instruments. And Hezekiah gave encouragement to all the Levites who taught the good knowledge of the Lord; and they ate throughout the feast seven days, offering peace offerings and making confession to the Lord God of their fathers.

a. **So the children of Israel who were present at Jerusalem**: There was special **gladness** for these who had come from the northern tribes. They had never before experienced such obedient and joyful worship, where they **praised the Lord day by day, singing to the Lord**.

b. **All the Levites who taught the good knowledge of the Lord**: The gathering at this Passover was not only given to worship, but also to teaching. This was helpful and good at all times; one might say it was *urgently needed* with the presence of the northern tribes.

i. This remnant of the remnant of the northern tribes came to God in ignorance, and in His mercy God received them (2 Chronicles 30:18-20). Yet God didn't want to *leave* them in ignorance, so He used the Levites **who taught the good knowledge of the LORD**.

ii. "It is a fine and expressive character given of these men. 'They taught the good knowledge of God to the people.' This is the great work, or should be so, of every Christian minister. They should convey that knowledge of God to the people by which they may be saved; that is, *the good knowledge of the Lord*." (Clarke)

c. **They ate throughout the feast seven days, offering peace offerings and making confession**: The third component to their gathering was *fellowship*. They shared the same food, the same relationship with God (demonstrated by the **peace offerings**) and the same need for Him (demonstrated by their **confession** of sin).

i. "*Making confession*: either, 1. Confessing their sins; which work was to accompany many of their sacrifices; of which see Leviticus 5:5; 16:21. Or rather, 2. Confessing God's goodness, or praising of God, which oft goes under this name, as 1 Chronicles 16:8, 24, which also seems to be more proper work for this season of joy." (Poole)

4. (23-27) The resulting joy and answered prayer.

Then the whole assembly agreed to keep *the feast* another seven days, and they kept it *another* seven days with gladness. For Hezekiah king of Judah gave to the assembly a thousand bulls and seven thousand sheep, and the leaders gave to the assembly a thousand bulls and ten thousand sheep; and a great number of priests sanctified themselves. The whole assembly of Judah rejoiced, also the priests and Levites, all the assembly that came from Israel, the sojourners who came from the land of Israel, and those who dwelt in Judah. So there was great joy in Jerusalem, for since the time of Solomon the son of David, king of Israel, *there had* been nothing like this in Jerusalem. Then the priests, the Levites, arose and blessed the people, and their voice was heard; and their prayer came *up* to His holy dwelling place, to heaven.

a. **The whole assembly agreed to keep the feast another seven days**: This was a remarkable and wonderful response to their experience of worship, teaching, and fellowship. They *wanted* to make the necessary sacrifices to continue the feast for another week, and they did it **with gladness**.

i. There is no indication in the text that they offered more Passover lambs or continued eating unleavened bread, which belonged to the specific seasons of these feasts. The emphasis is on their continuation of worship, teaching, and fellowship.

ii. This was substantially supported by King Hezekiah. "*A thousand bullocks and seven thousand sheep;* which generosity is the more considerable, because it was in the beginning of his reign, when he found the royal exchequer exhausted and empty; and when he had been at great expense about the cleansing and refitting of the temple, and making preparations for this great feast." (Poole)

b. **Since the time of Solomon the son of David, king of Israel, there had been nothing like this in Jerusalem**: Since those days there had not been a Passover in Jerusalem so widely and enthusiastically celebrated.

c. **The priests, the Levites, arose and blessed the people**: According to Numbers 6:22-27, it was the duty of the priests to bless the people with these words: *The LORD bless you and keep you; the LORD make His face shine upon you, and be gracious to you; the LORD lift up His countenance upon you, and give you peace.* As the priests obeyed this command, **their voice was heard**, even **to heaven** and the people were indeed blessed.

i. "The phrase 'the priests and the Levites' may here be rendered as 'the Levitical priests,' since it was the priests whom Moses had authorized 'to bless the people.'" (Payne)

2 Chronicles 31 – Provision for the Priests

A. The aftermath of Hezekiah's Passover.

1. (1) The work against idolatry.

Now when all this was finished, all Israel who were present went out to the cities of Judah and broke the sacred pillars in pieces, cut down the wooden images, and threw down the high places and the altars; from all Judah, Benjamin, Ephraim, and Manasseh; until they had utterly destroyed them all. Then all the children of Israel returned to their own cities, every man to his possession.

> a. **All Israel who were present went out to the cities of Judah and broke the sacred pillars**: After the glorious double-length Passover celebration, the people renounced all idolatry in the strongest terms possible.
>
>> i. "Hezekiah's previous emphasis on removing the paraphernalia of idol worship (*cf.* 2 Chronicles 29:15-19; 30:14; also 2 Kings 18:22) now became a popular movement." (Selman)
>
> b. **From all Judah, Benjamin, Ephraim, and Manasseh**: This shows how broad the work was, including not only the kingdom of Judah but also substantial portions of the territory of the northern tribes.
>
>> i. This reformation "was not only carried on through *Judah*, but they carried it into *Israel*; whether through a transport of religious zeal, or whether with the *consent* of Hoshea the Israelitish king, we cannot tell." (Clarke)

2. (2-3) The restoration and support of the regular priestly work.

And Hezekiah appointed the divisions of the priests and the Levites according to their divisions, each man according to his service, the priests and Levites for burnt offerings and peace offerings, to serve, to give thanks, and to praise in the gates of the camp of the LORD. The

king also *appointed* a portion of his possessions for the burnt offerings: for the morning and evening burnt offerings, the burnt offerings for the Sabbaths and the New Moons and the set feasts, as *it is* written in the Law of the Lord.

> a. **And Hezekiah appointed the divisions of the priests and the Levites according to their divisions**: Hezekiah did not allow the recent Passover celebration to be a one-time event. He followed up by the organization and institution of the regular priestly service.
>
>> i. "The Hebrew for Hezekiah's assigning the priests to divisions is definite: he 'appointed THE divisions of the priests.' He reestablished the twenty-four rotating courses that had been set up by David (1 Chronicles 25) to insure orderly worship." (Payne)
>
> b. **For burnt offerings…to serve…to give thanks…and to praise in the gates**: This shows some of the duties of the **priests and the Levites**. Their work included the administration of the sacrifices, general service, and worship.
>
>> i. **In the gates of the camp of the Lord**: "Of the temple, fitly compared to a camp, for the watch and the ward there kept by the priests, and for the convention of the people thither, as to their rendezvous, to pray, which is the chief service of our spiritual warfare." (Trapp)
>
> c. **The king also appointed a portion of his possessions**: King Hezekiah was so committed to the restoration of the proper priestly service that he personally supported their work with a **portion of his possessions**.

3. (4-5) The tithe is commanded and brought.

Moreover he commanded the people who dwelt in Jerusalem to contribute support for the priests and the Levites, that they might devote themselves to the Law of the Lord. As soon as the commandment was circulated, the children of Israel brought in abundance the firstfruits of grain and wine, oil and honey, and of all the produce of the field; and they brought in abundantly the tithe of everything.

> a. **Moreover he commanded the people who dwelt in Jerusalem to contribute support for the priests and the Levites**: King Hezekiah did not present this as an *option* for the people of Judah. They were **commanded** to fulfill their obligations under the Law of Moses to support the priesthood through their tithes (Numbers 18:21-24).
>
>> i. As God said in Numbers 18:21, *I have given the children of Levi all the tithes in Israel.* God commanded the tithes (a giving of ten percent of one's income) be given to the Levites for their support. This establishes

the principle that the tithes *belong* to God (He said *I have given*, so they are His to give), but He gave them to the Levites.

ii. When an Israelite failed to give their tithe, they were not robbing the Levite – though the money ended up with them. They were robbing God (Malachi 3:8-10), because God received the tithe from the giver, and He gave it to the Levite.

iii. Some today think the tithe, since it went to support the Levites (who were, in a sense, government workers in ancient Israel), is covered by government taxes of today, and that the free-will giving mentioned in the Old Testament answers to the New Testament emphasis on giving. We can say that the New Testament nowhere specifically commands tithing, but it certainly does speak of it in a positive light, if it is done with a right heart (Luke 11:42).

iv. It is also important to understand that tithing is not a principle dependent on the Mosaic Law; as Hebrews 7:5-9 explains, tithing was practiced and honored by God before the Law of Moses.

v. What the New Testament does speak with great clarity on is the principle of giving; that giving should be regular, planned, proportional, and private (1 Corinthians 16:1-4); that it must be generous, freely given, and cheerful (2 Corinthians 9).

vi. Since the New Testament doesn't emphasize tithing, it need not be strictly applied by Christians (though some Christians do argue against tithing on the basis of self-interest); but since giving is to be proportional, we should be giving *some* percentage – and ten percent is a good benchmark – and starting place! For some to give ten percent is nowhere near enough; for others, at their present time, five percent may be a massive step of faith.

vii. If our question is, "How little can I give and still be pleasing to God?" our heart isn't in the right place at all. We should have the attitude of some early Christians, who essentially said: "We're not under the tithe – we can give *more*!" Giving and financial management is a *spiritual* issue, not just a financial one (Luke 16:11).

b. **That they might devote themselves to the Law of the LORD**: This reminds us of another duty of the Levites, beyond what was mentioned in 2 Chronicles 31:2 – the study and teaching of **the Law of the LORD**. The support of the Levites through the tithes of the people enabled this.

i. This is much the same principle as what Paul wrote in 1 Timothy 5:17-18: *Let the elders who rule well be counted worthy of double honor, especially those who labor in the word and doctrine. For the Scripture* says, *"You shall not muzzle an ox while it treads out the grain,"* and, *"The laborer is worthy of his wages."*

c. **As soon as the commandment was circulated…they brought in abundantly the tithe of everything**: The response of the people was impressive. Instead of thinking of reasons why this command did not apply to them or excuses to relieve themselves of the obligation, **they brought in abundantly the tithe of everything**.

i. "The *firstfruits* were the priests prerogative (Numbers 18:12-13), but the *tithe*, whether of crops and fruit or the herds was presented to the Levites (Numbers 18:21; *cf.* Leviticus 27:30-33)." (Selman)

B. The distribution and blessing of the tithe.

1. (6-10) The reception of the tithes.

And the children of Israel and Judah, who dwelt in the cities of Judah, brought the tithe of oxen and sheep; also the tithe of holy things which were consecrated to the LORD their God they laid in heaps. In the third month they began laying them in heaps, and they finished in the seventh month. And when Hezekiah and the leaders came and saw the heaps, they blessed the LORD and His people Israel. Then Hezekiah questioned the priests and the Levites concerning the heaps. And Azariah the chief priest, from the house of Zadok, answered him and said, "Since *the people* began to bring the offerings into the house of the LORD, we have had enough to eat and have plenty left, for the LORD has blessed His people; and what is left *is* this great abundance."

a. **In the third month they began laying them in heaps**: The giving of tithes was so abundant that it took four months to simply receive all the gifts. No wonder Hezekiah and the leaders **blessed the LORD and His people Israel** when they saw the evidence of generous giving.

i. "*They blessed the Lord*; both for giving such plentiful provisions to his land in this year, and for giving his people such liberal and pious hearts towards this good work." (Poole)

ii. Their happiness was not only because it meant that there would be plenty for the priests and Levites, it also showed that the Spirit of God was working powerfully in the people of Israel.

iii. **The tithe of holy things**: "The *tithe of the holy* or *dedicated things* probably refers to gifts made by the Levites to the priest from what they themselves had received." (Selman)

b. **Since the people began to bring the offerings into the house of the LORD, we have had enough to eat and have plenty left**: The priests and Levites had long been neglected, and now they had plenty.

2. (11-19) The administration of the tithes.

Now Hezekiah commanded *them* to prepare rooms in the house of the LORD, and they prepared them. Then they faithfully brought in the offerings, the tithes, and the dedicated things; Cononiah the Levite had charge of them, and Shimei his brother *was* the next. Jehiel, Azaziah, Nahath, Asahel, Jerimoth, Jozabad, Eliel, Ismachiah, Mahath, and Benaiah *were* overseers under the hand of Cononiah and Shimei his brother, at the commandment of Hezekiah the king and Azariah the ruler of the house of God. Kore the son of Imnah the Levite, the keeper of the East Gate, *was* over the freewill offerings to God, to distribute the offerings of the LORD and the most holy things. And under him *were* Eden, Miniamin, Jeshua, Shemaiah, Amariah, and Shecaniah, *his* faithful assistants in the cities of the priests, to distribute allotments to their brethren by divisions, to the great as well as the small. Besides those males from three years old and up who were written in the genealogy, they distributed to everyone who entered the house of the LORD his daily portion for the work of his service, by his division, and to the priests who were written in the genealogy according to their father's house, and to the Levites from twenty years old and up according to their work, by their divisions, and to all who were written in the genealogy; their little ones and their wives, their sons and daughters, the whole company of them; for in their faithfulness they sanctified themselves in holiness. Also for the sons of Aaron the priests, *who were* in the fields of the common-lands of their cities, in every single city, *there were* men who were designated by name to distribute portions to all the males among the priests and to all who were listed by genealogies among the Levites.

a. **Hezekiah commanded them to prepare rooms in the house of the LORD**: King Hezekiah was wise enough to know that it was important to properly manage the generous gifts of God's people. They were concerned to do everything **faithfully**, out of respect to both God and His people who generously gave.

b. **Cononiah the Levite had charge of them**: Hezekiah put faithful men in positions of responsibility and accountability over these tithes. The king knew that faithful administration is promoted when people are accountable as **overseers**.

i. "Good planning and the implementation of adequate supporting structures provide a framework in which wholehearted and meaningful worship can take place. Hezekiah therefore prepared storerooms to receive the gifts, and various officials were appointed to collect and distribute them." (Selman)

c. **They distributed to everyone who entered the house of the LORD his daily portion for the work of his service**: The tithes were used to support those who did the **work** of ministry to the LORD and His people (and of course, to support their families as well).

i. "This is alleged as a reason why their wives and children were provided for out of the holy things, because they sequestered themselves from worldly affairs, by which they might otherwise have provided for their families, and entirely devoted themselves to holy administrations." (Poole)

ii. "Moses had ordered that the Levites should not begin their labour till they were *thirty* years of age: but David changed this order, and obliged them to begin at *twenty*." (Clarke)

3. (20-21) Hezekiah's godliness and prosperity.

Thus Hezekiah did throughout all Judah, and he did what *was* good and right and true before the LORD his God. And in every work that he began in the service of the house of God, in the law and in the commandment, to seek his God, he did *it* with all his heart. So he prospered.

a. **He did what was good and right and true before the LORD his God**: Hezekiah's godliness was exemplary among the kings of Judah. His concern was not primarily for political power or prestige, but for what was **good and right and true before the LORD**. Additionally, when he did something **he did it with all his heart**.

i. "Hezekiah finished his task because he *sought* God *wholeheartedly*. In this, he complied with David's advice (*cf.* 1 Chronicles 22:19; 28:9) and followed the pattern of other kings (*cf.* 2 Chronicles 15:17; 22:9; *cf.* 2 Chronicles 11:16; 19:3)." (Selman)

ii. "In every respect he was a thoroughly excellent man, saw his duty to God and to his people, and performed it with becoming zeal and diligence. May God ever send such *kings* to the nations of the world; and may the *people* who are blessed with such be duly obedient to them, and thankful to the God who sends them!" (Clarke)

b. **So he prospered**: His prosperity was evidence of the blessing of God, especially in connection with his own generosity and wise stewardship.

i. "These words reveal his purpose, his method, and the result; and form a revelation of abiding value to all who are called upon to perform Divine service in any form. His purpose was 'to seek his God'; and the expression is exactly equivalent to that with which we are familiar: 'Seek ye first His kingdom.' His method was that of complete devotion, 'with all his heart.' The result was that of prosperity, that is, of success in the very work which was attempted." (Morgan)

2 Chronicles 32 – God Protects Jerusalem

A. God protects Jerusalem from the Assyrians.

1. (1) Sennacherib's attack.

After these deeds of faithfulness, Sennacherib king of Assyria came and entered Judah; he encamped against the fortified cities, thinking to win them over to himself.

> a. **After these deeds of faithfulness**: Our tendency is to think that when we are genuinely faithful to God we will be immune from attack. The experience of Hezekiah and countless other men and women of God tell us otherwise.
>
>> i. "It would seem to be a strange answer of God to the faithfulness of His child, that a strong foe should at the moment invade the kingdom; and yet how often the experience of the people of God is of this nature." (Morgan)
>>
>> ii. Adam Clarke had another perspective: "God did not permit the pious prince to be *disturbed* till he had completed the reformation which he had begun."
>
> b. **Sennacherib king of Assyria came and entered Judah**: This was part of his larger campaign in the region, including the conquest of the northern tribes organized as the kingdom of Israel.
>
>> i. We might say that the Chronicler is not telling us the complete story here. He does not include what we learn from 2 Kings 18:13-16, that Hezekiah unwisely and unsuccessfully tried to satisfy Sennacherib with gold and treasures from the temple. It didn't work, and after conquering nearly all the **fortified cities** of Judah, the king of Assyria prepared to set a siege against Jerusalem.

ii. "He clearly expects the reader to be familiar with 2 Kings 18-20, but, whereas the Chronicler normally adapts sections of earlier Scripture, here everything has been amplified and summarized in order to concentrate on the theme of Yahweh's supremacy." (Selman)

2. (2-8) Hezekiah prepares against the coming attack and siege of the Assyrians.

And when Hezekiah saw that Sennacherib had come, and that his purpose was to make war against Jerusalem, he consulted with his leaders and commanders to stop the water from the springs which *were* **outside the city; and they helped him. Thus many people gathered together who stopped all the springs and the brook that ran through the land, saying, "Why should the kings of Assyria come and find much water?" And he strengthened himself, built up all the wall that was broken, raised** *it* **up to the towers, and** *built* **another wall outside; also he repaired the Millo** *in* **the City of David, and made weapons and shields in abundance. Then he set military captains over the people, gathered them together to him in the open square of the city gate, and gave them encouragement, saying, "Be strong and courageous; do not be afraid nor dismayed before the king of Assyria, nor before all the multitude that** *is* **with him; for** *there are* **more with us than with him. With him** *is* **an arm of flesh; but with us** *is* **the LORD our God, to help us and to fight our battles." And the people were strengthened by the words of Hezekiah king of Judah.**

a. **To stop the water from the springs outside the city**: This was done in preparation for the coming siege, and possibly in connection with the tunnel that Hezekiah directed to be cut to keep the water supply secure within the city (2 Chronicles 32:30).

i. "Jerusalem's water supply was vulnerable to any attack, since it was totally dependent on two springs, Gihon in the Kidron valley and En-Rogel two miles to the south." (Selman)

ii. "No doubt the Assyrian army suffered much through this, as a Christian army did eighteen hundred years after this. When the crusaders came, in A.D. 1099, to besiege Jerusalem, the people of the city stopped up the wells, so that the Christian army was reduced to the greatest necessities and distress." (Clarke)

b. **He strengthened himself, built up all the wall that was broken, raised it up to the towers**: This and the other preparations reflect how serious the threat was and how diligent Hezekiah was to defend Jerusalem and Judah.

i. "Part of a *wall* which could well be Hezekiah's has been uncovered on the western hill. At seven metres thick, it is the thickest Iron Age wall known in Palestine, and was presumably designed to withstand powerful Assyrian battering rams." (Selman)

c. **Be strong and courageous; do not be afraid nor dismayed**: Hezekiah understood that the defense of Israel did not depend only on walls and towers and shields and water supplies; it also depended on the strength, courage, and determination of their soldiers.

i. **For there are more with us than with him**: "We have more power than they have. (These words he quotes from the prophet Elisha, 2 Kings 6:16.) This was soon proved to be true by the slaughter made by the angel of the Lord in the Assyrian camp." (Clarke)

ii. **But with us is the LORD our God**: "The import of 'Immanuel,' by which name Christ now began to be known amongst them." (Trapp)

3. (9-19) Sennacherib's propaganda campaign.

After this Sennacherib king of Assyria sent his servants to Jerusalem (but he and all the forces with him *laid siege* **against Lachish), to Hezekiah king of Judah, and to all Judah who** *were* **in Jerusalem, saying, "Thus says Sennacherib king of Assyria: 'In what do you trust, that you remain under siege in Jerusalem? Does not Hezekiah persuade you to give yourselves over to die by famine and by thirst, saying, "The LORD our God will deliver us from the hand of the king of Assyria"? Has not the same Hezekiah taken away His high places and His altars, and commanded Judah and Jerusalem, saying, "You shall worship before one altar and burn incense on it"? Do you not know what I and my fathers have done to all the peoples of** *other* **lands? Were the gods of the nations of those lands in any way able to deliver their lands out of my hand? Who** *was there* **among all the gods of those nations that my fathers utterly destroyed that could deliver his people from my hand, that your God should be able to deliver you from my hand? Now therefore, do not let Hezekiah deceive you or persuade you like this, and do not believe him; for no god of any nation or kingdom was able to deliver his people from my hand or the hand of my fathers. How much less will your God deliver you from my hand?'" Furthermore, his servants spoke against the LORD God and against His servant Hezekiah. He also wrote letters to revile the LORD God of Israel, and to speak against Him, saying, "As the gods of the nations of** *other* **lands have not delivered their people from my hand, so the God of Hezekiah will not deliver His people from my hand." Then they called out with a loud voice in Hebrew to the people of Jerusalem who** *were* **on the wall, to frighten them and trouble them, that they might take the city. And they spoke against the God of**

Jerusalem, as against the gods of the people of the earth; the work of men's hands.

a. **Sennacherib king of Assyria sent his servants to Jerusalem**: While the bulk of his army was busy at **Lachish**, Sennacherib sent some men to Jerusalem to prepare for the siege, especially with psychological combat.

i. The mention of **Lachish** is important historically. Lachish was thirty miles south-west of Jerusalem. Archaeologists have discovered a pit there with the remains of about 1,500 casualties of Sennacherib's attack. In the British Museum, you can see the Assyrian carving depicting their siege of the city of Lachish, which was an important fortress city of Judah.

ii. "An interesting wall relief taken from the excavation of Sennacherib's royal palace in Nineveh is preserved in the British Museum. It portrays the Assyrian king on a portable throne in his military camp outside Lachish. Prisoners of war are marching by on foot, and all the booty from the city is being displayed on ox-wagons." (Dilday)

b. **In what do you trust, that you remain under siege in Jerusalem?** These servants of Sennacherib (known as *the Tartan, the Rabsaris, and the Rabshakeh* in 2 Kings 18:17) tried to shake the trust Hezekiah and the people of Jerusalem had in the LORD.

i. We might wish that Hezekiah trusted in the LORD, and that this is what the Assyrians mocked. Instead, Hezekiah put his hope in an alliance with Egypt, and the Assyrians wanted him to lose confidence in that alliance.

ii. It was a great temptation for Hezekiah during this time to make a defensive alliance with Egypt, which seemed to be the only nation strong enough to protect Judah against the mighty Assyrians. As a prophet, Isaiah did everything he could to discourage Hezekiah and the leaders of Judah from putting their trust in Egypt (Isaiah 19:11-17, 20:1-6, 30:1-7). The LORD wanted Judah to trust Him instead of Egypt.

c. **Has not the same Hezekiah taken away His high places and His altars**: The Assyrian accuser knew that King Hezekiah had implemented broad reforms in Judah, including the removal of the *high places* (2 Kings 18:3-4). Yet in the Assyrian's thinking, Hezekiah's reforms had really *displeased* God, so he should not expect help from the LORD God of Israel. The Assyrian would say, "Look at all the places there used to be where people would worship the LORD God of Israel. Now, since Hezekiah came in, there is only one place. More is always better, so the Lord God of Israel must be pretty sore at Hezekiah!"

> i. The enemy of our souls has an amazing way of discouraging our obedience. If Hezekiah was not careful, this argument of the Assyrian would start to make sense, when really it was demonic logic through and through.
>
> ii. "The theological misunderstanding shown by the field commander at this point argues for the authenticity of the speech, which many critics have dubbed a free creation by the author of the narrative." (Grogan, Isaiah Commentary)

> d. **Do you not know what I and my fathers have done to all the peoples of other lands?** The Assyrian's speech was intended to *destroy their trust in God*. His message was simple and brilliant in its Satanic logic: "The gods of other nations have not been able to protect them against us. Your God is just like one of them, and can't protect you either."
>
> > i. For anyone who had the spiritual understanding to see it, Judah could have started planning the victory party right then, when the Assyrian wrote **so the God of Hezekiah will not deliver His people from my hand**. It was one thing to speak against Judah, its people and leaders. It was another thing altogether to mock the Lord God of Israel this way, and count Him as "just another god."

4. (20-23) Hezekiah's prayer and victory.

Now because of this King Hezekiah and the prophet Isaiah, the son of Amoz, prayed and cried out to heaven. Then the Lord sent an angel who cut down every mighty man of valor, leader, and captain in the camp of the king of Assyria. So he returned shamefaced to his own land. And when he had gone into the temple of his god, some of his own offspring struck him down with the sword there. Thus the Lord saved Hezekiah and the inhabitants of Jerusalem from the hand of Sennacherib the king of Assyria, and from the hand of all *others*, and guided them on every side. And many brought gifts to the Lord at Jerusalem, and presents to Hezekiah king of Judah, so that he was exalted in the sight of all nations thereafter.

> a. **King Hezekiah and the prophet Isaiah, the son of Amoz, prayed and cried out to heaven**: We learn more about this powerful and beautiful prayer in 2 Kings 19:1-5. Hezekiah and Isaiah went into the House of the Lord and prayed humbly and passionately, and God heard from heaven.
>
> > i. "It was the indignity done to Jehovah that stirred these two holy men to the heart.... Oh that we were possessed with a similar zeal for

God, so that we might look at sin as it affects Him, and lament over the awful wrongs which are continually being perpetrated against his holy, loving nature! What an argument this would give us in prayer!" (Meyer)

ii. Isaiah the prophet brought assurance of the answer to this prayer to Hezekiah in 2 Kings 19:6-7.

b. **And the L**ORD **sent an angel who cut down every mighty man of valor**: With a simple and powerful strike, God destroyed this mighty army in one night. 185,000 died at the hand of the angel of the LORD (2 Kings 19:35). Against all odds, and against every expectation except the expectation of faith, the Assyrian army was turned back without having even shot an arrow into Jerusalem. The unstoppable was stopped, the undefeated was defeated.

i. The prophet Hosea made this same prediction: *Yet I will have mercy on the house of Judah, will save them by the* LORD *their God, and will not save them by bow, nor by sword or battle, by horses or horsemen.* (Hosea 1:7)

ii. "Herodotus, the Greek historian, recorded that one night Sennacherib's army camp was infested with mice (or rats) that destroyed the arrows and shield-thongs of the soldiers. He probably got this tradition from Egyptian sources, and it could well be a somewhat garbled version of the event recorded here." (Grogan)

iii. Some have speculated that there was a natural means that the angel used. "This has been thought to be a bacillary dysentery which had a three-day incubation period." (Wiseman)

iv. "There was never a more conspicuous and glorious deliverance than when the angel of God wrought for Israel against Assyria." (Meyer)

v. "This event ranks, in fact, with Israel's crossing of the Red Sea as one of the two greatest examples of the Lord's intervention to save his people." (Payne)

c. **So he returned shamefaced to his own land**: The shame seems to have left his face rather quickly. After this retreat from Judah, Sennacherib commissioned a record, which is preserved in the spectacular Annals of Sennacherib (the Taylor Prism), which can be seen in the British Museum. It shows how full of pride Sennacherib's heart still was, even if he could not claim he conquered Jerusalem.

i. "I attacked Hezekiah of Judah who had not subjected himself to me, and took forty-six fortresses, forts and small cities. I carried away captive 200,150 people, big and small, both male and female, a multitude of horses, young bulls, asses, camels, and oxen. Hezekiah himself I locked up in Jerusalem like a bird in its cage. I put up banks against the city. I separated his cities whose inhabitants I had taken prisoners from his realm and gave them to Mitiniti, king of Ashdod, Padi, king of Ekron, and Zilbel, king of Gaza and thus diminished his country. And I added another tax to the one imposed on him earlier." (Cited in Bultema, commentary on Isaiah)

ii. "The Biblical account concludes with the much debated statement that the Assyrian army was struck down in some way during the night with considerable loss of life, following which the siege was called off.... The Assyrian Annals tacitly agree with the Biblical version by making no claim that Jerusalem was taken, only describing tribute from Hezekiah." (T.C. Mitchell, *The Bible in the British Museum*)

iii. "God spared *Sennacherib*, not in mercy, but in wrath, reserving to him a more dreadful and shameful death by the hands of his own children." (Poole)

d. **And when he had gone into the temple of his god, some of his own offspring struck him down with the sword there**: Some 20 years after he returned, his own sons killed him. Perhaps Sennacherib thought he had escaped the judgment of God, but he hadn't. He met the bitter end of death at the end of swords held by his own sons.

i. An old Jewish legend – and nothing more than a legend – says how it was that Sennacherib's sons came to kill him. Sennacherib was troubled at how God seemed to bless the Jews so much, and tried to find out why. Someone told him it was because Abraham had loved God so much that he was willing to sacrifice his son to the LORD. Sennacherib thought he would be even more favored by God, and decided to kill two of his sons in sacrifice to the LORD, becoming even more blessed than Abraham and his descendants. But his two sons learned of the plan, and killed him before he could kill them, thus fulfilling the word of the LORD.

ii. **He was exalted in the sight of all nations thereafter**: "They saw that God was his *friend*, and would undertake for him; and they did not wish to have such a man for their *enemy*." (Clarke)

B. The remainder of Hezekiah's reign.

1. (24-26) Hezekiah is humbled and God relents.

In those days Hezekiah was sick and near death, and he prayed to the LORD; and He spoke to him and gave him a sign. But Hezekiah did not

repay according to the favor *shown* him, for his heart was lifted up; therefore wrath was looming over him and over Judah and Jerusalem. **Then Hezekiah humbled himself for the pride of his heart, he and the inhabitants of Jerusalem, so that the wrath of the LORD did not come upon them in the days of Hezekiah.**

> a. **In those days**: This happened at the time of the Assyrian invasion of Judah because Jerusalem had not been delivered from the Assyrian threat yet (2 Kings 20:6). The events of this chapter are also recorded in Isaiah 38.
>
>> i. "Interpreters agree that the events described in chapters 38 and 39 preceded the invasion of 701 B.C..... Many date these events in 703 B.C., but the evidence more strongly suggests a date of about 712 B.C." (Wolf, commentary on Isaiah)
>
> b. **Was sick and near death**: We are not told how Hezekiah became sick. It may have been through something obvious to all, or it may have been through something known only to God. However Hezekiah became sick, it was certainly permitted by the LORD.
>
> c. **He spoke to him and gave him a sign**: This sign – the sign of the retreating sundial – is recorded in 2 Kings 20:8-11.
>
> d. **Hezekiah did not repay according to the favor shown him**: Sadly, Hezekiah did not receive this miracle with the gratitude that he should have. Yet he did humble **himself for the pride of his heart**, and was saved a greater judgment.
>
>> i. "All which probably raised in him too great an opinion of himself, as if these things were done, if not by his power, yet, at least, for his piety and virtues. And instead of walking humbly with God, and giving the glory all entirely to him, he took the honour to himself, and vaingloriously showed his riches and precious treasures to the Babylonish ambassadors." (Poole)

2. (27-33) The summation of the reign of Hezekiah.

Hezekiah had very great riches and honor. And he made himself treasuries for silver, for gold, for precious stones, for spices, for shields, and for all kinds of desirable items; storehouses for the harvest of grain, wine, and oil; and stalls for all kinds of livestock, and folds for flocks. Moreover he provided cities for himself, and possessions of flocks and herds in abundance; for God had given him very much property. This same Hezekiah also stopped the water outlet of Upper Gihon, and brought the water by tunnel to the west side of the City of David. Hezekiah prospered in all his works. However, *regarding* **the ambassadors of the princes of Babylon, whom they sent to him to inquire**

about the wonder that was *done* in the land, God withdrew from him, in order to test him, that He might know all *that was* in his heart. Now the rest of the acts of Hezekiah, and his goodness, indeed they *are* written in the vision of Isaiah the prophet, the son of Amoz, *and* in the book of the kings of Judah and Israel. So Hezekiah rested with his fathers, and they buried him in the upper tombs of the sons of David; and all Judah and the inhabitants of Jerusalem honored him at his death. Then Manasseh his son reigned in his place.

a. **Hezekiah had very great riches and honor.... God had given him very much property**: Hezekiah often generously used these great riches for good (2 Chronicles 31:3), but sometimes he managed his and the kingdom's wealth foolishly (2 Kings 20:12-21).

b. **Brought the water by tunnel to the west side of the City of David**: This tunnel was an amazing engineering feat. He built an aqueduct to insure fresh water inside the city walls even during sieges. It was more than 650 yards long through solid rock, begun on each end and meeting in the middle. It can still be seen today and it empties into the pool of Siloam.

i. "This tunnel, found in 1880, was cut for 643 metres to cover a direct distance of 332 metres to enable the defenders to fetch water within the protective walls even during a siege." (Wiseman)

ii. "An inscription in cursive Hebrew of the early eighth century B.C. details the work: 'When (the tunnel) was driven through while (the quarrymen were swinging their) axes, each man towards the other and, while there was still 3 cubits to be cut through (there was heard) the voice of a man calling to his fellow, for there was a crevice (?) on the right…and when the tunnel was (finally) driven through, the quarrymen hewed each towards the others, axe against axe. Then the waters flowed from the Spring to the Pool for 1,200 cubits and the height of the rock above the head(s) of the quarrymen was 100 cubits.'" (Wiseman)

c. **However, regarding the ambassadors of the princes of Babylon**: This unfortunate chapter in the life of Hezekiah is recorded in 2 Kings 20:12-21. He was flattered by the visit of the ambassadors from this up-and-coming world power, and showed them the riches of the kingdom – riches which they later took by siege and war.

i. "It was not *spiritual* pride, as with his great-grandfather Uzziah; but *worldly* pride – 'the pride of life,' we might say. It was *his* precious things, *his* armor, *his* treasures, *his* house, *his* dominion, etc., that he showed the ambassadors from Babylon." (Knapp)

ii. In this case Hezekiah faced – and failed under – a temptation common to many, especially those in ministry – the temptation of success. Many men who stand strong against the temptations of failure and weakness fail under the temptations of success and strength.

d. **So Hezekiah rested with his fathers**: There is no doubt that Hezekiah started out as a godly king, and overall his reign was one of outstanding godliness. Yet his beginning was much better than his end; Hezekiah did not finish well. God gave Hezekiah the gift of 15 more years of life (2 Kings 20:6), but the added years did not make him a better or a more godly man.

i. Time or age doesn't necessarily make us any better. Consider that time does nothing but pass away. We sometimes say, "time will tell," "time will heal," or "time will bring out the potential in me." But time will do nothing of the sort! Time will only come and go. It is only how we *use* time that matters. Hezekiah didn't make good use of the extra time the LORD gave him.

ii. "Hezekiah was buried on the sloping hill where the tombs of David's descendants were cut (2 Chronicles 32:33). This was because the royal Iron Age burial caves north of the city were full by this time and hereafter no Judean king was buried in the rock-hewn caves there." (Wiseman)

iii. "Notwithstanding the lapses of the latter days, the reign was most remarkable, especially when it is remembered how fearful was the condition into which the nation had come at this time." (Morgan)

2 Chronicles 33 – The Reigns of Manasseh and Amon

A. The reign of Manasseh, son of Hezekiah.

1. (1-2) A summary of the reign of Manasseh, a 55-year rule of evil.

Manasseh *was* twelve years old when he became king, and he reigned fifty-five years in Jerusalem. But he did evil in the sight of the LORD, according to the abominations of the nations whom the LORD had cast out before the children of Israel.

a. **Manasseh was twelve years old when he became king**: This means that he was born in the *last fifteen years* of Hezekiah's life, the *additional* fifteen years that Hezekiah prayed for (2 Kings 20:6). Those additional fifteen years brought Judah one of its worst kings.

i. "Had this good king been able to foresee the wickedness of his unworthy son, he would doubtless have no desire to recover from his sickness. Better by far die childless than beget a son such as Manasseh proved to be." (Knapp)

b. **And he reigned fifty-five years in Jerusalem**: This was both a remarkably long and a remarkably evil reign. A long career or longevity is not necessarily evidence of the blessing and approval of God.

i. "He was a son of David, but he was the very reverse of that king, who was always faithful in his loyalty to the one and only God of Israel. David's blood was in his veins, but David's ways were not in his heart. He was a wild, degenerate shoot of a noble vine." (Spurgeon)

c. **According to the abominations of the nations whom the LORD had cast out before**: Manasseh imitated the sins of both the Canaanites and the Israelites of the northern kingdom (2 Kings 16:3). Since God brought judgment on these groups for their sin, casting them out of their land, then similar judgment against an unrepentant Judah should be expected.

2. (3-9) The specific sins of Manasseh.

For he rebuilt the high places which Hezekiah his father had broken down; he raised up altars for the Baals, and made wooden images; and he worshiped all the host of heaven and served them. He also built altars in the house of the LORD, of which the LORD had said, "In Jerusalem shall My name be forever." And he built altars for all the host of heaven in the two courts of the house of the LORD. Also he caused his sons to pass through the fire in the Valley of the Son of Hinnom; he practiced soothsaying, used witchcraft and sorcery, and consulted mediums and spiritists. He did much evil in the sight of the LORD, to provoke Him to anger. He even set a carved image, the idol which he had made, in the house of God, of which God had said to David and to Solomon his son, "In this house and in Jerusalem, which I have chosen out of all the tribes of Israel, I will put My name forever; and I will not again remove the foot of Israel from the land which I have appointed for your fathers; only if they are careful to do all that I have commanded them, according to the whole law and the statutes and the ordinances by the hand of Moses." So Manasseh seduced Judah and the inhabitants of Jerusalem to do more evil than the nations whom the LORD had destroyed before the children of Israel.

a. **He rebuilt the high places which Hezekiah his father had broken down**: Manasseh opposed the reforms of his father Hezekiah and he brought Judah back into terrible idolatry.

i. This shows us that repentance and reform and revival are not permanent standing conditions. What is accomplished at one time can be opposed and turned back at another time.

b. **He raised up altars for the Baals, and made wooden images**: Manasseh did not want to imitate his godly father. Instead, he imitated one of the very worst kings of Israel: Ahab. He embraced the same state-sponsored worship of Baal and Asherah (honored with **a carved image**) that marked the reign of Ahab.

c. **He also built altars in the house of the LORD**: It was bad enough for Manasseh to allow this idol worship into Judah. Worse, he corrupted the worship of the true God at the temple, and made the temple a place of idol altars, including those dedicated to his cult of astrological worship (**he built altars for all the host of heaven**).

d. **He built altars for all the host of heaven in the two courts of the house of the LORD**: Manasseh did not only bring back old forms of idolatry; he also brought new forms of idolatry to Judah. At this time the Babylonian Empire was rising in influence, and they had a special attraction to astrological worship. Manasseh probably imitated this.

i. "The king's apostate worship of 'the starry host' had evil precedents going as far back as the time of Moses (Deuteronomy 4:19; Acts 7:42), but such practices were a particular sin of Assyro-Babylonians, with their addiction to astrology." (Payne)

ii. "But this Manasseh sought out for himself unusual and outlandish sins. Bad as Ahab was, he had not worshipped the host of heaven. That was an Assyrian worship, and this man must need import from Assyria and Babylonia worship that was quite new." (Spurgeon)

e. **He caused his sons to pass through the fire**: Manasseh sacrificed his own son to the Canaanite god Molech, who was worshipped with the burning of children.

f. **Practiced soothsaying, used witchcraft and sorcery, and consulted mediums and spiritists**: Manasseh invited direct Satanic influence by his approval and introduction of these occult arts.

i. "The Hebrew word for 'spiritists' is *yiddeoni*, by etymology, 'a knowing one.' It referred originally to ghosts, who were supposed to possess superhuman knowledge; but it came to be applied to those who claimed power to summon them forth, i.e., to witches." (Payne)

g. **He even set a carved image, the idol which he had made, in the house of God**: The Chronicler seems too polite to say it, but 2 Kings 21:7 tells us that this **idol** was Asherah, the Canaanite goddess of fertility. This god was worshipped through ritual prostitution. This means that Manasseh made the temple into an idolatrous brothel, dedicated to Asherah.

i. "From the whole it is evident that Asherah was no other than *Venus*; the nature of whose worship is plain enough from the mention of *whoremongers* and *prostitutes*." (Clarke)

ii. "Manasseh *repeated these sins and exaggerated them each time*. After one forbidden idol had been enshrined, he set up another yet more foul, and after building altars in the courts of the temple, he ventured further.... Thus he piled up his transgressions and multiplied his provocations." (Spurgeon)

h. **Manasseh seduced Judah and the inhabitants of Jerusalem to do more evil than the nations whom the LORD had destroyed**: 2 Kings 21:9 tells us what the attitude of the people was: *they paid no attention*.

This described the basic attitude of the people of Judah during the 55-year reign of Manasseh. They *paid no attention* to the generous promises of God, promising protection to His obedient people. In addition, they were willingly **seduced** by Manasseh's wickedness and were attracted **to do more evil**.

> i. "He did all he could to pervert the national character, and totally destroy the worship of the true God; and he succeeded." (Clarke)
>
> ii. "How superficial had been the nation's compliance with Hezekiah's reforms! Without a strong spiritual leader, the sinful people quickly turned to their own evil machinations. The judgment of God could not be far away." (Patterson and Austel)
>
> iii. This was a transformation of the culture from something generally honoring God to a culture that glorified idolatry and immorality. In general we can say this happened because the people *wanted* it to happen. They didn't care about the direction of their culture.

B. Manasseh's repentance.

1. (10-11) God chastises of Manasseh.

And the LORD spoke to Manasseh and his people, but they would not listen. Therefore the LORD brought upon them the captains of the army of the king of Assyria, who took Manasseh with hooks, bound him with bronze *fetters*, and carried him off to Babylon.

> a. **And the LORD spoke to Manasseh and his people**: This was the great mercy of God. He was under no obligation to warn or correct them; God would have been completely justified in exercising judgment immediately. Instead, **the LORD spoke to Manasseh and his people**.
>
> > i. 2 Kings 21:10-15 tells more about these specific warnings of the prophets.
>
> b. **But they would not listen**: Despite God's gracious warnings, neither the king nor the people would **listen**. God found more compelling ways to speak to the rulers and people of Judah.
>
> > i. 2 Kings 21:16 tells us of the terrible extent of Manasseh's sin: *Moreover Manasseh shed very much innocent blood, till he had filled Jerusalem from one end to another, besides his sin by which he made Judah sin, in doing evil in the sight of the LORD.*
> >
> > ii. "We cannot vouch for the tradition that the prophet Isaiah was put to death by him by being sawn in sunder, but terrible as is the legend, it is not at all improbable." (Spurgeon)

c. **Therefore the LORD brought upon them the captains of the army of the king of Assyria:** God allowed Manasseh to be taken and carried away as a captive, after the pattern of his own sinful bondage.

> i. "God sent him into the dungeon to repent; as he did David into the depths, and Jonah into the whale's belly to pray. Adversity hath whipt many a soul to heaven, which otherwise prosperity had coached to hell." (Trapp)

> ii. "No mention is made of Manasseh's exile in Assyrian sources, even though Manasseh appears in the annals of Esarhaddon (680-669 B.C.) and Ahsurbanipal (668-626 B.C.) as a rather unwilling vassal forced to provide supplies for Assyria's building and military enterprises. It is quite possible that he rebelled against these impositions at some point." (Selman)

> iii. "Manasseh's presence in *Babylon* is not surprising, since Assyria had had a long interest in Babylon, which was under the direct control for the whole of Esarhaddon's reign and after Shamash-shum-unkin's demise." (Selman)

2. (12-13) The remarkable repentance of Manasseh.

Now when he was in affliction, he implored the LORD his God, and humbled himself greatly before the God of his fathers, and prayed to Him; and He received his entreaty, heard his supplication, and brought him back to Jerusalem into his kingdom. Then Manasseh knew that the LORD *was* God.

a. **When he was in affliction, he implored the LORD his God**: Manasseh was not the first one (and not the last) to turn back to God after a severe season of **affliction**. It has been said that God speaks to us in our pleasures and he shouts to us in our pains. Manasseh finally listened to God's shouting through **affliction**.

> i. "The Assyrians were notoriously a fierce people, and Manasseh, having provoked them, felt all the degradation, scorn, and cruelty which anger could invent. He who had trusted idols was made a slave to an idolatrous people; he who had shed blood very much was now in daily jeopardy of the shedding of his own; he who had insulted the Lord must now be continually insulted himself." (Spurgeon)

b. **And humbled himself greatly before the God of his fathers**: The word **humbled** reminds us that the essence of Manasseh's sin was *pride*. The phrase **God of his fathers** reminds us that Manasseh returned to the godly heritage he received from his father Hezekiah.

i. This is a wonderful example of the principle, *Train up a child in the way he should go, and when he is old he will not depart from it* (Proverbs 22:6). Manasseh was raised by a godly father, yet he lived in defiance of his father's faith for most of his life. Nevertheless, at the end of his days he truly repented and served God.

c. **He received his entreaty, heard his supplication, and brought him back to Jerusalem into his kingdom**: God graciously restored the late-repenting Manasseh. This gracious response to Manasseh was the final step in his return to the LORD (**Then Manasseh knew that the LORD was God**).

i. "He was convinced by his own experience of God's power, justice, and goodness, that Jehovah alone was the true God, and not those idols which he had worshipped, by which he had received great hurt, and no good." (Poole)

ii. "Manasseh's repentance was evidently the chief subject in the mind of the chronicler, and while his sins are painted faithfully and revealed in all their hideousness, all becomes but background which flings into relief Manasseh's genuine penitence and the ready and gracious response to God." (Morgan)

iii. In his sermon, *The Old Testament "Prodigal,"* Spurgeon imagined what it would be like for the remnant of believers in Jerusalem to hear that Manasseh was returning from Babylon. They had a brief pause in the persecution they had suffered from the evil king, and at least a slow-down in the official promotion of idolatry. Now to hear he was coming back must have driven them to their knees, asking God to have mercy on them once again. Imagine their surprise when they found that King Manasseh returned a repentant, converted man!

iv. "Oh! I do not wonder at Manasseh's sin one half so much as I wonder at God's mercy." (Spurgeon)

3. (14-17) The late deeds of Manasseh.

After this he built a wall outside the City of David on the west side of Gihon, in the valley, as far as the entrance of the Fish Gate; and *it* enclosed Ophel, and he raised it to a very great height. Then he put military captains in all the fortified cities of Judah. He took away the foreign gods and the idol from the house of the LORD, and all the altars that he had built in the mount of the house of the LORD and in Jerusalem; and he cast *them* out of the city. He also repaired the altar of the LORD, sacrificed peace offerings and thank offerings on it, and commanded Judah to serve the LORD God of Israel. Nevertheless the people still sacrificed on the high places, *but* only to the LORD their God.

a. **After this he built a wall**: Before he was humbled and repentant, Manasseh didn't care very much for the defense of Judah and Jerusalem. Now, with a more godly perspective, he cared deeply about the security of God's people and the kingdom of Judah.

> i. "This was probably a weak place that he fortified; or a part of the wall which the Assyrians had broken down, which he now rebuilt." (Clarke)

b. **He took away the foreign gods and the idol from the house of the LORD**: Before he was humbled and repentant, Manasseh *promoted* the worship of idols. Now, he destroyed idols and promoted the worship of the true God of Israel alone; he even **commanded Judah to serve the LORD God of Israel**.

> i. "Manasseh's religious reforms represented a direct reversal of earlier policies (vv. 2-9), since each of the items removed in verse 15 is mentioned in verses 3, 7." (Selman)

> ii. "Turn to Him with brokenness of soul, and He will not only forgive, but bring you out again; and give you, as He did Manasseh, an opportunity of undoing some of those evil things which have marred your past." (Meyer)

c. **Nevertheless the people still sacrificed on the high places, but only to the LORD their God**: This reminds us of the distinction between two different kinds of **high places**. Some were altars to pagan idols; others were unauthorized altars to the true God. Manasseh stopped all the pagan worship in Judah, but unauthorized (that is, outside the temple) worship of the God of Israel continued.

> i. "Half a century of paganism could not be counteracted by half-a-dozen years of reform." (Payne)

> ii. "While repentance of personal sin brings ready forgiveness, the influence of the sin is terribly likely to abide." (Morgan)

4. (18-20) Manasseh's death and burial.

Now the rest of the acts of Manasseh, his prayer to his God, and the words of the seers who spoke to him in the name of the LORD God of Israel, indeed they *are written* in the book of the kings of Israel. Also his prayer and *how God* received his entreaty, and all his sin and trespass, and the sites where he built high places and set up wooden images and carved images, before he was humbled, indeed they *are* written among the sayings of Hozai. So Manasseh rested with his fathers, and they buried him in his own house. Then his son Amon reigned in his place.

a. **The rest of the acts of Manasseh**: The Chronicler must refer to documents that have more information than the 2 Kings text. 2 Kings does not mention the repentance of Manasseh, and does not tell us anything about his reign substantially different than what we read in 2 Chronicles.

i. "Manasseh illustrates one of the central themes of Chronicles, that God can fulfill his promise of restoration in 2 Chronicles 7:12-16 to the repentant even in the most extreme circumstances." (Selman)

ii. "As for despair, it is damnable. While the story of Manasseh stands on record, no mortal hath a just excuse to perish in despair; no one is justified in saying, 'God will never forgive me.' Read over again the history of Manasseh; see to what lengths of sin he went, to what extravagant heights of evil he climbed; and then say to yourself, 'Did sovereign mercy reach him? Then it can also reach me.'" (Spurgeon)

b. **So Manasseh rested with his fathers**: Manasseh was a remarkably bad and evil king, yet at the end of his days he truly repented and served God. In this way, we can say that it was very true that **Manasseh rested with his fathers**.

i. "Manasseh's conversion helps to explain a longstanding problem in Kings, namely, why the exile did not fall in Manasseh's reign if his sins were really so serious." (Selman)

ii. Yet, his repentance was too late to change the nation. "The widespread revolts during the reign of Ashurbanipal, which occurred from 652-648 B.C., may provide the occasion for Manasseh's summons to Babylon and imprisonment. If so, his subsequent release and reform were apparently far too late to have much of an effect on the obdurately backslidden people." (Patterson and Austel)

iii. It was also not soon enough to change the *destiny* of the kingdom. "Years later, when Jerusalem fell to the Babylonians, the writer would blame Judah's punishment on the sins of Manasseh (2 Kings 24:3-4)." (Dilday)

iv. Manasseh "more than any other single person was responsible for the final destruction of the kingdom of Judah (2 Kings 23:26; 24:3; Jeremiah 15:4)." (Payne)

C. The reign of Amon, son of Manasseh.

1. (21-23) A two-year, evil reign

Amon *was* twenty-two years old when he became king, and he reigned two years in Jerusalem. But he did evil in the sight of the Lord, as his father Manasseh had done; for Amon sacrificed to all the carved images

which his father Manasseh had made, and served them. And he did not humble himself before the LORD, as his father Manasseh had humbled himself; but Amon trespassed more and more.

> a. **He reigned two years in Jerusalem**: This unusually short reign is an indication that the blessing of God was *not* upon the reign of Amon.
>
> b. **And he did evil in the sight of the LORD, as his father Manasseh had done.... he did not humble himself before the LORD, as his father Manasseh had**: Amon sinned as Manasseh had sinned, without having the repentance that Manasseh had. It is likely that one of the greatest sorrows to the repentant Manasseh was that his sons, and others who were influenced by his sin, did not also repent.
>
>> i. "There is not one bright spot in this king's character to relieve the darkness of his life's brief record." (Knapp)
>>
>> ii. "Glycas saith that Amon hardened himself in sin by his father's example, who took his swing in sin, and yet at length repented. So, thought he, will I do; wherefore he was soon sent out of the world for his presumption, dying in his sins, as 2 Chronicles 33:23." (Trapp)
>>
>> iii. "Manasseh and Amon in their contrasting ways show that a fatalistic attitude in the face of God's judgment is quite unjustified." (Selman)

2. (24-25) The assassination of Amon.

Then his servants conspired against him, and killed him in his own house. But the people of the land executed all those who had conspired against King Amon. Then the people of the land made his son Josiah king in his place.

> a. **His servants conspired against him, and killed him in his own house**: This story of conspiracy and assassination seems to belong among the kings of *Israel*, not Judah. Yet when the kings and people of Judah began to imitate the sins of their conquered northern neighbors, they slipped into the same chaos and anarchy that marked the last period of Israel's history.
>
>> i. "Although the Scriptures give no reason for the conspiracy, its cause may lie within the tangled web of revolts that Asurbanipal suppressed from 642-639 and that caused him to turn his attention to the west.... Amon's death may thus reflect a power struggle between those who wished to remain loyal to the Assyrian crown and those who aspired to link Judah's fortunes to the rising star of Psammetik I (664-609) of Egypt's Twenty-Sixth Dynasty." (Patterson and Austel)
>
> b. **But the people of the land executed all those who had conspired against King Amon**: This was a hopeful sign. Up to this point, the people

of Judah had largely tolerated some 57 years of utterly wicked kings who led the nation in evil. Now it seems that they wanted righteousness and justice instead of the evil they had lived with for so long.

i. In some way, it could be said that the people of Judah had these wicked kings for more than 50 years because *that is what they wanted*. God gave them the leaders they wanted and deserved. Now, as the people of the kingdom turned towards godliness, God gave them a better king.

c. **Then the people of the land made his son Josiah king in his place**: Though king Amon was assassinated, God did not yet allow Judah to slip into the same pit of anarchy that Israel had sunk into. Because of the righteous action of **the people of the land**, there was no change of *dynasty*, and the rightful heir to the throne of David became king.

i. "The only positive contribution Amon made to the history of Judah was to produce one of the best kings to reign on the throne of Jerusalem." (Dilday)

2 Chronicles 34 – Josiah and the Book of the Law

A. The beginnings of Josiah's reforms.

1. (1-2) A summary of the reign of Josiah, the son of Amon.

Josiah *was* eight years old when he became king, and he reigned thirty-one years in Jerusalem. And he did *what was* right in the sight of the LORD, and walked in the ways of his father David; *he* did *not* turn aside to the right hand or to the left.

> a. **Josiah was eight years old when he became king**: Unusually, this young boy came to the throne at **eight years** of age. This was because of the assassination of his father.
>
>> i. "At last, after more than three hundred years, the prophecy of 'the man of God out of Judah' is fulfilled (1 Kings 13:2)." (Knapp)
>
> b. **He did what was right in the sight of the LORD**: This was true of Josiah at this young age, but it is really more intended as a general description of his reign rather than a description of him at eight years of age.

2. (3-7) Josiah against idolatry in Judah and the former kingdom of Israel.

For in the eighth year of his reign, while he was still young, he began to seek the God of his father David; and in the twelfth year he began to purge Judah and Jerusalem of the high places, the wooden images, the carved images, and the molded images. They broke down the altars of the Baals in his presence, and the incense altars which *were* above them he cut down; and the wooden images, the carved images, and the molded images he broke in pieces, and made dust of them and scattered *it* on the graves of those who had sacrificed to them. He also burned the bones of the priests on their altars, and cleansed Judah and Jerusalem. And *so he did* in the cities of Manasseh, Ephraim, and Simeon, as far as Naphtali and all around, with axes. When he had broken down the altars and the wooden images, had beaten the carved images into

powder, and cut down all the incense altars throughout all the land of Israel, he returned to Jerusalem.

a. **He began to purge Judah and Jerusalem of the high places, the wooden images, the carved images, and the molded images**: The worship of this great variety of idols was entrenched after the reign of Amon. The late reforms of Manasseh helped against this trend, but since the short but wicked reign of Amon, there was much idolatry in the land.

i. The variety of idols described shows *how deep* idolatry was in Judah. There were idols dedicated to **Baal** and to *Asherah* (2 Kings 23:4) and to *all the host of heaven* (2 Kings 23:5) in the *very temple itself* (2 Kings 23:4). From the 2 Kings account, it seems that Josiah began the cleansing reforms at the center and worked outwards.

ii. "'Seeking' in Chronicles describes the habit of looking to God in every situation, and also the attitude which God looks for in those who pray (2 Chronicles 7:14; 30:19)." (Selman)

iii. **In the twelfth year**: Payne connects this with "a particular time of chaos that occurred throughout the ancient Near East and that was precipitated by an invasion from the north of barbaric, nomadic horsemen known as the Scythians (628-626 B.C.).... Their incursions wrought terror among complacent Jews (Jeremiah 6:22-24; Zephaniah 1:12)."

iv. "Five or six several words are here used, to show how he mawled them, and made mortar of them, as we say; such was his holy indignation, zeal, and revenge." (Trapp)

b. **He also burned the bones of the priests on their altars**: Josiah did this both to carry out the prescribed punishment of idolatrous priests in Israel *and* to defile these pagan altars.

i. Josiah's reforms did not only remove sinful *things*, but also the sinful *people* that promoted and permitted these sinful things. The idols that filled the temple did not get there or stay there on their own – there were **priests** who were responsible for these sinful practices.

ii. Any thorough reformation cannot only deal with sinful things; it must also deal with sinful people. If sinful people are not dealt with, they will quickly bring back the sinful things that were righteously removed.

c. **And so he did in the cities of Manasseh, Ephraim, and Simeon.... throughout all the land of Israel**: Since the kingdom of Israel had been conquered by the Assyrian Empire and was in the process of being depopulated as a result of exile, Josiah could extend his reforms there also.

i. "*Even unto Naphtali*; which was in the utmost and northern borders of the kingdom of Israel. For it must be remembered that the ten tribes were now gone into captivity; and those who were come in their stead were weak and few, and not able to withstand the power of Josiah." (Poole)

3. (8-13) The restoration of the temple.

In the eighteenth year of his reign, when he had purged the land and the temple, he sent Shaphan the son of Azaliah, Maaseiah the governor of the city, and Joah the son of Joahaz the recorder, to repair the house of the LORD his God. When they came to Hilkiah the high priest, they delivered the money that was brought into the house of God, which the Levites who kept the doors had gathered from the hand of Manasseh and Ephraim, from all the remnant of Israel, from all Judah and Benjamin, and *which* they had brought back to Jerusalem. Then they put *it* in the hand of the foremen who had the oversight of the house of the LORD; and they gave it to the workmen who worked in the house of the LORD, to repair and restore the house. They gave *it* to the craftsmen and builders to buy hewn stone and timber for beams, and to floor the houses which the kings of Judah had destroyed. And the men did the work faithfully. Their overseers *were* Jahath and Obadiah the Levites, of the sons of Merari, and Zechariah and Meshullam, of the sons of the Kohathites, to supervise. *Others of* the Levites, all of whom were skillful with instruments of music, *were* over the burden bearers and *were* overseers of all who did work in any kind of service. And *some* of the Levites *were* scribes, officers, and gatekeepers.

a. **In the eighteenth year of his reign**: After his energetic campaign to cleanse the land of Judah and Israel of idolatry, then Josiah put his efforts towards restoring the neglected temple, much as his predecessor Hezekiah had done (2 Chronicles 29).

i. "The Chronicler (2 Chronicles 34-35) appears to present a two-stage sequence of events: (i) the purification of religious practices in Judah, Jerusalem and Naphtali in Josiah's twelfth year, and (ii) a continuing reformation stimulated by the discovery of the Book of the Law in the eighteenth year. But this may be a presentation to fit in with the Chronicler's particular emphases." (Wiseman)

ii. "If Josiah had not yet seen a copy of this book, (which is not impossible,) yet there was so much of the law left in the minds and memories of the people, as might easily persuade and direct him to all that he did till this time." (Poole)

iii. It is possible that Josiah was motivated to rebuild the temple after hearing (or remembering) that this was what King Jehoash did many years before (2 Kings 12).

b. Then they put it in the hand of the foremen who had oversight of the house of the Lord: Josiah understood that the work of repair and rebuilding the temple needed organization and funding. He paid attention to both of these needs when he gave **Hilkiah** oversight over this restoration work of the temple. As a result, **the men did the work faithfully**.

i. According to Jeremiah 1:1-2, the prophet Jeremiah was the son of this particular priest **Hilkiah**. Jeremiah began his ministry during the reign of King Josiah.

4. (14-17) The discovery of the Book of the Law.

Now when they brought out the money that was brought into the house of the Lord, Hilkiah the priest found the Book of the Law of the Lord *given* by Moses. Then Hilkiah answered and said to Shaphan the scribe, "I have found the Book of the Law in the house of the Lord." And Hilkiah gave the book to Shaphan. So Shaphan carried the book to the king, bringing the king word, saying, "All that was committed to your servants they are doing. And they have gathered the money that was found in the house of the Lord, and have delivered it into the hand of the overseers and the workmen."

a. **Hilkiah the priest found the Book of the Law of the Lord**: According to Deuteronomy 31:24-27, there was to be a copy of *this Book of the Law* beside the ark of the covenant, beginning in the days of Moses. The word of God was *with* Israel, but it was greatly *neglected* in those days.

i. "'The Book,' however, seems to have become misplaced during the apostate administrations of the previous kings, Manasseh and Amon, under whom the ark had been moved about (2 Chronicles 35:3)." (Payne)

ii. "Hilkiah's personal announcement, '*I have found the Book of the Law*', stands out sharply.... Secretary Shaphan confirms that the find took place in the context of the workers' faithfulness." (Selman)

iii. "Though a close connection between Josiah's scroll and Deuteronomy had been accepted for a long time, the implications of this for the origins of Deuteronomy are much more uncertain, since neither Kings or Chronicles provides direct evidence for the thesis, advocated repeatedly since 1805, that the scroll was composed as part of a Deuteronomic reform movement." (Selman)

iv. "Was this the *autograph* of Moses? It is very probable that it was; for in the parallel place, 2 Chronicles 34:14, it is said to be the book of *the law of the Lord by Moses*. It is supposed to be that part of Deuteronomy, (Deuteronomy 28-30, and 31,) which contains the renewing of the covenant in the plains of Moab, and which contains the most terrible invectives against the corrupters of God's word and worship." (Clarke)

b. **Shaphan carried the book to the king**: Here the word of God spreads. It had been forgotten and regarded as nothing more than an old, dusty book. Now it was found, read, and spread. We should expect some measure of spiritual revival and renewal to follow.

i. Throughout the history of God's people, when the word of God is recovered and spread, then spiritual revival follows. It can begin as simply as it did in the days of Josiah, with one man finding and reading and believing and spreading the Book.

ii. Another example of this in history is the story of Peter Waldo and his followers, sometimes known as Waldenses. Waldo was a rich merchant who gave up his business to radically follow Jesus. He hired two priests to translate the New Testament into the common language and using this, he began to teach others. He taught in the streets or wherever he could find someone to listen. Many common people came to hear him and started to radically follow Jesus Christ. He taught them the text of the New Testament in the common language and was rebuked by church officials for doing so. He ignored the rebuke and continued to teach, eventually sending his followers out two by two into villages and market places, to teach and explain the scriptures. The scriptures were memorized by the Waldenses, and it was not unusual for their ministers to memorize the entire New Testament and large sections of the Old Testament. The word of God – when found, read, believed, and spread – has this kind of transforming power.

5. (18-21) King Josiah hears the word of God.

Then Shaphan the scribe told the king, saying, "Hilkiah the priest has given me a book." And Shaphan read it before the king. Thus it happened, when the king heard the words of the Law, that he tore his clothes. Then the king commanded Hilkiah, Ahikam the son of Shaphan, Abdon the son of Micah, Shaphan the scribe, and Asaiah a servant of the king, saying, "Go, inquire of the Lord for me, and for those who are left in Israel and Judah, concerning the words of the book that is found; for great *is* the wrath of the Lord that is poured out on us, because our fathers have not kept the word of the Lord, to do according to all that is written in this book."

a. **When the king heard the words of the Law**: The hearing of God's word did a spiritual work in King Josiah. It was not merely the transmission of information; the hearing of God's word had an impact of spiritual power on Josiah.

i. "A medieval Archbishop of Canterbury…assumed that Josiah listened to the whole book at one sitting: 'What a contrast to our present-day kings and magnates! If once a year they hear the word of God preached, they find it nauseating and leave the church before the end of the sermon'." (Selman)

b. **He tore his clothes**: The tearing of clothing was a traditional expression of horror and astonishment. In the strongest way possible, Josiah showed his grief on his own account and on account of the nation. This was an expression of deep conviction of sin, and a good thing.

i. Revival and spiritual awakening are marked by such expressions of the conviction of sin. Dr. J. Edwin Orr, in *The Second Evangelical Awakening in Britain*, recounted some examples from the great movement that impacted Britain and the world in 1859-1861:

ii. This conviction of sin is the special work of the Holy Spirit, even as Jesus said in John 16:8: "And when He has come, He will convict the world of sin."

c. **Go, inquire of the LORD for me**: It wasn't that King Josiah knew nothing of God or how to seek Him. It was that he was so under the conviction of sin that he did not know what to do next.

d. **For great is the wrath of the LORD that is poured out on us**: Josiah knew that the kingdom of Judah deserved *judgment* from God. He could not hear the word of God and respond to the Spirit of God without seriously confronting the sin of his kingdom.

6. (22-28) God speaks to King Josiah.

So Hilkiah and those the king *had appointed* went to Huldah the prophetess, the wife of Shallum the son of Tokhath, the son of Hasrah, keeper of the wardrobe. (She dwelt in Jerusalem in the Second Quarter.) And they spoke to her to that *effect*. Then she answered them, "Thus says the LORD God of Israel, 'Tell the man who sent you to Me, "Thus says the LORD: 'Behold, I will bring calamity on this place and on its inhabitants, all the curses that are written in the book which they have read before the king of Judah, because they have forsaken Me and burned incense to other gods, that they might provoke Me to anger with all the works of their hands. Therefore My wrath will be poured out on this place, and not be quenched.'"' But as for the king of Judah, who

sent you to inquire of the LORD, in this manner you shall speak to him, 'Thus says the LORD God of Israel: *"Concerning* the words which you have heard; because your heart was tender, and you humbled yourself before God when you heard His words against this place and against its inhabitants, and you humbled yourself before Me, and you tore your clothes and wept before Me, I also have heard *you,"* says the LORD. Surely I will gather you to your fathers, and you shall be gathered to your grave in peace; and your eyes shall not see all the calamity which I will bring on this place and its inhabitants.""'" So they brought back word to the king.

> a. **Huldah the prophetess**: We know little of this woman other than this mention here (and the similar account recorded in 2 Kings 22:14). With the apparent approval of King Josiah, Hilkiah the priest consulted this woman for spiritual guidance. It wasn't because of her own wisdom and spirituality, but that she was recognized as a **prophetess** and could reveal the heart and mind of God.
>
>> i. There were certainly other prophets in Judah. "Though the contemporary prophet Jeremiah is not mentioned, he commended Josiah (Jeremiah 22:15-16) and the prophet Zephaniah (1:1) was at work in this reign." (Wiseman) Yet for some reason – perhaps spiritual, perhaps practical – they chose to consult **Huldah the prophetess**.
>>
>> ii. "We find from this, and we have many facts in all ages to corroborate it, that a pontiff, a pope, a bishop, or a priest, may, in some cases, not possess the true knowledge of God; and that a simple *woman*, possessing the life of God in her soul, may have more knowledge of the divine testimonies than many of those whose office it is to explain and enforce them." (Clarke)
>
> b. **I will bring calamity on this place and on its inhabitants**: Josiah knew that Judah deserved judgment, and that judgment would indeed come. Judah and its leaders had acted against the LORD for too long, and would not genuinely repent so as to avoid eventual judgment.
>
> c. **All the curses that are written in the book**: God's word was true, even in its promises of judgment. God's faithfulness is demonstrated as much by His judgment upon the wicked as it is by His mercy upon the repentant.
>
>> i. "Josiah went on with the work of reformation, even when he knew that nationally it was foredoomed to failure.... She distinctly told him that there would be no true repentance on the part of the people, and therefore that judgment was inevitable. It was *then* that the heroic strength of Josiah manifested itself, in that he went on with his work.... No pathway of service is more difficult than that of bearing

witness to God, in word and in work, in the midst of conditions which are unresponsive." (Morgan)

d. **Because your heart was tender**: Josiah's heart was tender in two ways. First, it was **tender** to the word of God and was able to receive the convicting voice of the Holy Spirit. Second, it was **tender** to the message of judgment from Huldah in the previous verses.

i. **You humbled yourself before God when you heard His words**: "Have you ever noticed the difference between being humble and being humbled? Many persons are humbled who are not humble at all.... It is a voluntary humiliation of soul which is inculcated by the example of Josiah, and may the Spirit of God make us willing in the day of his power, that we may willingly humble ourselves before God." (Spurgeon)

e. **You shall be gathered to your grave in peace**: Though Josiah died in battle, there are at least three ways that this was true.

- He died before the great spiritual disaster and exile came to Judah.
- He was gathered to the spirits of his fathers, who were in peace.
- He died in God's favor, though by the hand of an enemy.

i. "Though Josiah died in violent circumstances (2 Chronicles 35:20-24), this does not invalidate God's promise which really means that the exile would not take place during Josiah's lifetime." (Selman)

f. **Your eyes shall not see all the calamity which I will bring on this place**: This was God's mercy to Josiah. His own godliness and tender heart could not stop the eventual judgment of God, but it could delay it. Inevitable judgment is sometimes delayed because of the tender hearts of the people of God.

i. God delayed judgment even in the case of Ahab, who responded to a word of warning with a kind of repentance (1 Kings 21:25-29).

B. The honest repentance of King Josiah and the people of Judah.

1. (29-30) Josiah reads the word of God to the leaders of Judah.

Then the king sent and gathered all the elders of Judah and Jerusalem. The king went up to the house of the Lord, with all the men of Judah and the inhabitants of Jerusalem; the priests and the Levites, and all the people, great and small. And he read in their hearing all the words of the Book of the Covenant which had been found in the house of the Lord.

a. **The king sent and gathered all the elders of Judah**: Josiah heard the promise of both eventual judgment and the immediate delay of judgment. He did not respond with indifference or simple contentment that he would not see the judgment in his day. He wanted to get the kingdom right with God, and he knew that he could not do it all by himself – he needed **all the elders of Judah** to join in broken repentance with him.

b. **And he read in their hearing all the words of the Book**: The king did this himself. He was so concerned that the nation would hear the word of God that **he read** it to them himself.

> i. "It is especially interesting that he regards the written form of God's word as superior to inherited tradition and is willing to pay the cost of correcting his priorities." (Selman)

2. (31-33) The covenant is renewed.

Then the king stood in his place and made a covenant before the LORD, to follow the LORD, and to keep His commandments and His testimonies and His statutes with all his heart and all his soul, to perform the words of the covenant that were written in this book. And he made all who were present in Jerusalem and Benjamin take a stand. So the inhabitants of Jerusalem did according to the covenant of God, the God of their fathers. Thus Josiah removed all the abominations from all the country that *belonged* **to the children of Israel, and made all who were present in Israel diligently serve the LORD their God. All his days they did not depart from following the LORD God of their fathers.**

a. **The king stood in his place and made a covenant before the LORD, to follow the LORD**: King Josiah stood before the people and publicly declared his commitment to obey the word of God to the very best of his ability (**with all his heart and all his soul**).

> i. "*[He] made a covenant* is literally '[he] cut a covenant,' which goes back to the practice of cutting the carcass of an animal and separating the parts so the contracting parties could seal their agreement by walking between them (cf. Genesis 15:17; Jeremiah 34:18)." (Dilday)

b. **And he made all who were present…take a stand**: It wasn't enough for the king himself to do it and to offer his example to the people. They had to *follow* by taking a **stand** for the covenant themselves. This showed that the work of God's Spirit went beyond the king and the leaders and extended to the people also.

> i. "It is likely that he caused them all to *arise* when he read the terms of the covenant, and thus testify their approbation of the covenant itself, and their resolution to observe it faithfully and perseveringly." (Clarke)

ii. "The ceremony compares with the basic Mizpah covenant (1 Samuel 8:11-17; 10:25) and the renewal of the covenant at Shechem (Joshua 24), both of which marked turning points in Jewish history." (Wiseman)

c. **All his days they did not depart from following the LORD God of their fathers**: The work of King Josiah had a lasting effect among the people of Judah. They stayed faithful to God during his reign.

2 Chronicles 35 – Josiah's Passover

A. Josiah's great Passover.

1. (1-6) Josiah directs the priests and the Levites for the Passover.

Now Josiah kept a Passover to the LORD in Jerusalem, and they slaughtered the Passover *lambs* on the fourteenth *day* of the first month. And he set the priests in their duties and encouraged them for the service of the house of the LORD. Then he said to the Levites who taught all Israel, who were holy to the LORD: "Put the holy ark in the house which Solomon the son of David, king of Israel, built. *It shall* no longer *be* a burden on *your* shoulders. Now serve the LORD your God and His people Israel. Prepare *yourselves* according to your fathers' houses, according to your divisions, following the written instruction of David king of Israel and the written instruction of Solomon his son. And stand in the holy *place* according to the divisions of the fathers' houses of your brethren the *lay* people, and *according to* the division of the father's house of the Levites. So slaughter the Passover *offerings*, consecrate yourselves, and prepare *them* for your brethren, that *they* may do according to the word of the LORD by the hand of Moses."

a. **They slaughtered the Passover lambs on the fourteenth day of the first month**: The previous Passover of note was in the days of Hezekiah (2 Chronicles 30:1-3). That Passover had to be celebrated in the second month, but Josiah was able to keep this great Passover at the appointed time in the **first month** (Numbers 9:1-5).

b. **He set the priests in their duties and encouraged them for the service**: Josiah understood that it would take an enormous amount of planning and work to properly conduct this Passover. The priests needed to be both **set** and **encouraged** for this.

i. "The first thing is to get every man into his proper place; the next thing is for every man to have a good spirit in his present place, so as to occupy it worthily." (Spurgeon)

c. **Put the holy ark in the house which Solomon the son of David, king of Israel, built**: Under Josiah's direction, Hilkiah the priest recently had found the copy of the Law of Moses in the temple. Now we learn that under the apostate administrations of the previous kings, Manasseh and Amon, apparently the **holy ark** had also been removed from the temple. Now, King Josiah directed that it be returned to its rightful place.

i. **It shall no longer be a burden on your shoulders** indicates that the ark was not at "rest" in the holy place of the temple. The time was long overdue to return it to its rest.

ii. "The Hebrews tell us, that the priests in those idolatrous times had carried the holy ark out of the temple – that it might not stand there among those heathenish idols – and conveyed it to the house of Shallum, who was uncle to the prophet Jeremiah, and husband to the prophetess Huldah." (Trapp)

d. **So slaughter the Passover offerings**: One of the main features of the Passover was the sacrifice of a lamb for each household (Exodus 12:43-49). This meant a substantial amount of work for the priests.

2. (7-9) Lambs provided for the Passover sacrifice.

Then Josiah gave the *lay* people lambs and young goats from the flock, all for Passover *offerings* for all who were present, to the number of thirty thousand, as well as three thousand cattle; these *were* from the king's possessions. And his leaders gave willingly to the people, to the priests, and to the Levites. Hilkiah, Zechariah, and Jehiel, rulers of the house of God, gave to the priests for the Passover *offerings* two thousand six hundred *from the flock*, and three hundred cattle. Also Conaniah, his brothers Shemaiah and Nethanel, and Hashabiah and Jeiel and Jozabad, chief of the Levites, gave to the Levites for Passover *offerings* five thousand *from the flock* and five hundred cattle.

a. **Josiah gave the lay people lambs and young goats from the flock**: This was staggering generosity on the part of King Josiah. He provided **thirty thousand** lambs or goats for the Passover sacrifice, as well as **three thousand cattle**. It shows how passionate King Josiah was to have a proper Passover celebration, that he was willing to bear the expense.

i. "The total number of offerings is more than double that at Hezekiah's Passover (2 Chronicles 30:24), a further indication of the greater generosity and significance of this occasion." (Selman)

b. **And his leaders gave willingly to the people**: As is often the custom, the generosity of the leader (King Josiah) prompted the generosity of others.

3. (10-14) The slaughter of the Passover lambs and the sacrificial meal.

So the service was prepared, and the priests stood in their places, and the Levites in their divisions, according to the king's command. And they slaughtered the Passover *offerings;* and the priests sprinkled *the blood* with their hands, while the Levites skinned *the animals*. Then they removed the burnt offerings that *they* might give them to the divisions of the fathers' houses of the *lay* people, to offer to the LORD, as *it is* written in the Book of Moses. And so *they did* with the cattle. Also they roasted the Passover *offerings* with fire according to the ordinance; but the *other* holy *offerings* they boiled in pots, in caldrons, and in pans, and divided *them* quickly among all the *lay* people. Then afterward they prepared portions for themselves and for the priests, because the priests, the sons of Aaron, *were busy* in offering burnt offerings and fat until night; therefore the Levites prepared portions for themselves and for the priests, the sons of Aaron.

a. **So the service was prepared**: "*The service was arranged* is a rare but significant phrase occurring additionally in the Old Testament only at 2 Chronicles 8:16; 29:35, meaning that everything had been done as God required." (Selman)

b. **And they slaughtered the Passover offerings**: It seems that on this Passover the sacrifices were all directly made by the priests themselves. They did not allow the head of each household to perform the sacrifice individually.

i. "In contrast to Hezekiah's practice and the implications of the Pentateuchal law (Deuteronomy 16:5-6; 2 Chronicles 30:17), the Levites slaughtered all the Passover lambs." (Selman)

ii. Clarke had a different suggestion: "The *people* themselves might slay their own paschal lambs, and then present the *blood* to the *priests*, that they might *sprinkle* it before the altar; and the *Levites* flayed them, and made them ready for dressing."

c. **They roasted the Passover offerings with fire according to the ordinance**: This was the second aspect of the Passover celebration – a festive meal enjoyed by the entire nation, household by household.

i. **They roasted the Passover offerings with fire**, "To set forth Christ roasted for us in the fire of his Father's fierce wrath." (Trapp)

ii. "While the flocks of sheep and goats provided for the paschal lambs, the cattle must have served for peace offerings, for feasting throughout the days of Unleavened Bread that followed the Passover." (Payne)

d. **Then afterward they prepared portions for themselves and for the priests**: This was the correct order. First the people were served, and then the **priests** and the Levite leaders.

4. (15-19) The greatness of Josiah's Passover.

And the singers, the sons of Asaph, *were* in their places, according to the command of David, Asaph, Heman, and Jeduthun the king's seer. Also the gatekeepers were at each gate; they did not have to leave their position, because their brethren the Levites prepared portions for them. So all the service of the LORD was prepared the same day, to keep the Passover and to offer burnt offerings on the altar of the LORD, according to the command of King Josiah. And the children of Israel who were present kept the Passover at that time, and the Feast of Unleavened Bread for seven days. There had been no Passover kept in Israel like that since the days of Samuel the prophet; and none of the kings of Israel had kept such a Passover as Josiah kept, with the priests and the Levites, all Judah and Israel who were present, and the inhabitants of Jerusalem. In the eighteenth year of the reign of Josiah this Passover was kept.

a. **The singers, the sons of Asaph, were in their places**: There was nothing in the Law of Moses directing singing or a communal worship service at the celebration of Passover. Josiah therefore went beyond the commandment to make this an especially meaningful and memorable occasion.

b. **Also the gatekeepers were at each gate; they did not have to leave their position**: This shows that Josiah was mindful of the security and the strength of the kingdom even during this great celebration. Every guard stayed ready and on duty, and **the Levites prepared portions** for the grateful **gatekeepers**.

c. **So all the service of the LORD was prepared the same day**: Because of the remarkable planning, organization, and hard work of the king, the priests, and the Levites, this massive amount of sacrifice and festive meals were all **prepared the same day**. They did this not out of some strange compulsion, but in trying to be obedient to the command of Moses for the day on which to observe Passover (Numbers 9:1-5).

d. **There had been no Passover kept in Israel like that since the days of Samuel the prophet**: This celebration of Passover was so significant that one had to go back *before* the time of David and Solomon to find a keeping of Passover that was so well organized and joyfully conducted.

> i. This Passover was remarkable for several reasons.
>
> - It was remarkable in the magnitude of its celebration, including even the remnant of the north who came to celebrate it in Jerusalem. "'All Judah and Israel' includes people from north and south, implying a larger attendance than at Hezekiah's Passover (*cf.* 2 Chronicles 30:25)." (Selman)
> - It was remarkable in its strict obedience to the Law of Moses
> - It was remarkable in the way it shined amidst these dark years in Judah's history.
>
> ii. "No, not Hezekiah; for at his passover the congregation was not so great, nor so well prepared; nor were the Levites and singers so well marshalled, nor the sacrifices so many." (Trapp)
>
> iii. "Josiah's passover was so vast and rare a success because of the large amount of previous preparation, as is described in this chapter." (Meyer)

B. The death of King Josiah.

1. (20-22) Josiah disregards God's warning and goes to war.

After all this, when Josiah had prepared the temple, Necho king of Egypt came up to fight against Carchemish by the Euphrates; and Josiah went out against him. But he sent messengers to him, saying, "What have I to do with you, king of Judah? *I have* **not** *come* **against you this day, but against the house with which I have war; for God commanded me to make haste. Refrain** *from meddling with* **God, who** *is* **with me, lest He destroy you." Nevertheless Josiah would not turn his face from him, but disguised himself so that he might fight with him, and did not heed the words of Necho from the mouth of God. So he came to fight in the Valley of Megiddo.**

> a. **Necho king of Egypt came up to fight against Carchemish**: This was part of the geopolitical struggle between the declining Assyrian Empire and the emerging Babylonian Empire. The Assyrians made an alliance with the Egyptians to protect against the growing power of the Babylonians.
>
> b. **King Josiah went out against him**: Sadly, Josiah disregarded what was actually good counsel from Necho when he said **What have I to do with you, king of Judah? I have not come against you this day**. Josiah stubbornly refused to hear this warning (which was actually from God).

i. Josiah was in sin because his attack against Egypt was in support of the Assyrian Empire, and he had no business supporting the Assyrian Empire. "The only reason for doing so must have been some supposed political advantage. Against that kind of action the prophets were constantly warning the kings. A word claiming to be from God, forbidding what was already forbidden, had a weight of moral appeal almost amounting to certainty." (Morgan)

ii. Interestingly, Necho himself said, "**for God has commanded me to make haste. Refrain from meddling with God, who is with me, lest He destroy you.**" It is unlikely that Necho understood and meant that he was in fact an agent of the God of Israel; he probably said and understood this in terms of his own gods and his own incorrect understanding of God. Nevertheless, it was an unknowing divine prophecy, much as the words of Caiaphas regarding the death of Jesus (John 11:49-52).

iii. "Yet, methinks, he ought so far to have regarded it, as to have inquired the mind of God about it; which he neglected to do, and therefore he cannot be wholly excused, and is here taxed for it." (Poole)

iv. "How Josiah was supposed to recognize God's guidance is not specified, though sanctified common sense would have been a perfectly adequate response." (Selman)

v. "Such a story must, to say the least, give us pause, and make us enquire as to how far we are ever justified in refusing to consider a word which is claimed as a divine message, even when it comes from sources from which we should least expect to receive it." (Morgan)

c. **Nevertheless Josiah would not turn his face from him**: Josiah thought he could escape the prediction of Necho by disguising himself in battle – yet he was still shot by archers and died. This was a sad end to one of the great kings of Judah.

i. "It was not of faith, else why 'disguise' himself? There is no record of any prayer before the battle, as in the case of so many of his godly ancestors; and this rash act of Josiah seems unaccountable." (Knapp)

ii. "The exact place of the battle seems to have been *Hadadrimmon*, in the valley of Megiddo, for there Zechariah tells us, chapter 12:11, was the great mourning for Josiah." (Clarke)

iii. "The reality of the contest at 'Megiddo' has received archaeological confirmation from the ruins of the site's Stratum II." (Payne)

2. (23-25) Josiah's death and burial

And the archers shot King Josiah; and the king said to his servants, "Take me away, for I am severely wounded." His servants therefore took him out of that chariot and put him in the second chariot that he had, and they brought him to Jerusalem. So he died, and was buried in *one of* **the tombs of his fathers. And all Judah and Jerusalem mourned for Josiah. Jeremiah also lamented for Josiah. And to this day all the singing men and the singing women speak of Josiah in their lamentations. They made it a custom in Israel; and indeed they** *are* **written in the Laments.**

> a. **And the archers shot King Josiah**: Though he was disguised, he was still wounded and killed. We can admire the bravery of Josiah, but not his stubborn insistence on disregarding the warnings from God and going into battle.
>
> > i. "He repented at his death, no doubt, of his rashness." (Trapp)
> >
> > ii. "The manner of Josiah's demise is also interpreted ironically by being paralleled with Ahab's demise (*cf.* 2 Chronicles 18:29-34). The links are quite explicit, for each king *disguised himself*, *archers* delivered the fatal blow, and each king admitted *I am wounded*, and was propped up in a *chariot* before he died. The ultimate irony is that despite Josiah's previous record, he died in the same way as someone who was known to 'hate the LORD' (2 Chronicles 19:2)." (Selman)
>
> b. **And to this day all the singing men and the singing women speak of Josiah in their lamentations**: Zechariah 12:11 tells us a bit of this great mourning, using it as a comparison to the great mourning that will come upon the Jewish people when they turn to their once-rejected Messiah: *In that day there shall be a great mourning in Jerusalem, like the mourning at Hadad Rimmon in the plain of Megiddo.*
>
> > i. "These dirges are then said to be 'written in the Laments' – a book that is no longer extant and which is not to be confused with the prophet's later laments over Josiah's sons (Jeremiah 22:10, 20-30) or over Jerusalem's fall (Lamentations)." (Payne)
> >
> > ii. "Far from being embarrassed by Huldah's prophecy, therefore, the Chronicler is at pains to stress that God kept his promises about Josiah's peaceful burial and the exile's continuing delay despite Josiah's stupidity and violent death." (Selman)

3. (26-27) The summary of the reign of good King Josiah.

Now the rest of the acts of Josiah and his goodness, according to *what was* **written in the Law of the LORD, and his deeds from first to last, indeed they** *are* **written in the book of the kings of Israel and Judah.**

a. **The rest of the acts of Josiah and his goodness**: It seems that Josiah's reign was remembered with special fondness; perhaps because he ended up being the *last* good king of Judah.

i. Yet, the people of the kingdom turned against God very quickly after the reign of Josiah. "Josiah had evidently made himself greatly beloved by them, and the probability is that the reforms he instituted were based on that love rather than on the people's real return to devotion to God." (Morgan)

ii. "Even so, Josiah's passing removed the last obstacle to the coming catastrophe." (Selman)

b. **According to what was written in the Law of the Lord**: This is what made Josiah such a good king and a good man. He had a great interest in, and obedience to, **what was written in the Law of the Lord**.

2 Chronicles 36 – The Fall of Jerusalem

A. The last four kings of Judah.

1. (1-4) The short reign of King Jehoahaz.

Then the people of the land took Jehoahaz the son of Josiah, and made him king in his father's place in Jerusalem. Jehoahaz *was* twenty-three years old when he became king, and he reigned three months in Jerusalem. Now the king of Egypt deposed him at Jerusalem; and he imposed on the land a tribute of one hundred talents of silver and a talent of gold. Then the king of Egypt made *Jehoahaz's* brother Eliakim king over Judah and Jerusalem, and changed his name to Jehoiakim. And Necho took Jehoahaz his brother and carried him off to Egypt.

> a. **Then the people of the land took Jehoahaz the son of Josiah, and made him king in his father's place**: This son of Josiah was made king by will of the people. The name **Jehoahaz** means "the Lord has seized," and was possibly a throne name for this son of Josiah. His given name seems to have been Shallum (Jeremiah 22:11, 1 Chronicles 3:15).
>
>> i. "The regular succession to the throne of Judah ceased with the lamented Josiah. Jehoahaz was not the eldest son of the late king. Johanan and Jehoiakim were both older than he (1 Chronicles 3:15). He was made king by popular choice: it was the preference of the multitude, not the appointment of God." (Knapp)
>>
>> ii. "It seems that after Necho had discomfited Josiah, he proceeded immediately against *Charchemish*, and in the interim, Josiah dying of his wounds, the people made his son king." (Clarke)
>>
>> iii. "His name is omitted from among those of our Lord's ancestors in Matthew 1...which may imply that God did not recognize Jehoahaz, the people's choice, as being in a true sense the successor." (Knapp)

iv. 2 Kings 23:32 tells us, *he did evil in the sight of the LORD*. The reforms of King Josiah were wonderful, but they were not a long-lasting revival. His own son Jehoahaz did not follow in his godly ways.

b. **Necho took Jehoahaz his brother and carried him off to Egypt**: After the defeat of King Josiah in battle, Pharaoh was able to dominate Judah and make it effectively a vassal kingdom and a buffer against the growing Babylonian Empire. He **imposed on the land a tribute** and put on the throne of Judah a puppet king, a brother of Jehoahaz (**Eliakim**, renamed **Jehoiakim**).

2. (5-8) The reign and captivity of Jehoiakim.

Jehoiakim *was* twenty-five years old when he became king, and he reigned eleven years in Jerusalem. And he did evil in the sight of the LORD his God. Nebuchadnezzar king of Babylon came up against him, and bound him in bronze *fetters* to carry him off to Babylon. Nebuchadnezzar also carried off *some* of the articles from the house of the LORD to Babylon, and put them in his temple at Babylon. Now the rest of the acts of Jehoiakim, the abominations which he did, and what was found against him, indeed they *are* written in the book of the kings of Israel and Judah. Then Jehoiachin his son reigned in his place.

a. **Jehoiakim was twenty-five years old when he became king**: Jehoiakim was nothing more than a puppet king presiding over a vassal kingdom under the Egyptians. He imposed heavy taxes on the people and paid the money to the Egyptians, as required (2 Kings 23:35).

i. "Necho had placed him there as a viceroy, simply to *raise* and *collect his taxes*." (Clarke)

ii. "Yet at the same time Jehoiakim was wasting resources on the construction of a new palace by forced labour (Jeremiah 22:13-19)." (Wiseman)

b. **He did evil in the sight of the LORD**: Jehoiakim, like his brother Jehoahaz, did not follow the godly example of his father Josiah.

i. Jeremiah 36:22-24 describes the great ungodliness of Jehoiakim – how he even burned a scroll of God's word. In response to this, Jeremiah received this message from God: *And you shall say to Jehoiakim king of Judah, "Thus says the LORD: 'You have burned this scroll, saying, "Why have you written in it that the king of Babylon will certainly come and destroy this land, and cause man and beast to cease from here?"' Therefore thus says the LORD concerning Jehoiakim king of Judah: 'He shall have no one to sit on the throne of David, and his dead body shall be cast out to the heat of the day and the frost of the night.'"* (Jeremiah 36:29-30)

ii. "To all his former evils he added this, that he slew Urijah the prophet (Jeremiah 26:20, 23)." (Trapp)

c. **Nebuchadnezzar king of Babylon came up**: Nebuchadnezzar, king of the Babylonian Empire, was concerned with Judah because of its strategic position in relation to the empires of Egypt and Assyria. Therefore it was important to him to conquer Judah and make it a subject kingdom, securely loyal to Babylon.

i. Nebuchadnezzar came against Jerusalem because the Pharaoh of Egypt invaded Babylon. In response the young prince Nebuchadnezzar defeated the Egyptians at Carchemish, and then he pursued their fleeing army all the way down to the Sinai. Along the way (or on the way back), he subdued Jerusalem, which had been loyal to the Pharaoh of Egypt.

ii. This happened in 605 B.C. and it was the first (but not the last) encounter between Nebuchadnezzar and Jehoiakim. There would be two later invasions (597 and 587 B.C.).

iii. This specific attack is documented by the Babylonian Chronicles, a collection of tablets discovered as early as 1887, held in the British Museum. In them, Nebuchadnezzar's 605 B.C. presence in Judah is documented and clarified. When the Babylonian chronicles were finally published in 1956, they gave us first-rate, detailed political and military information about the first 10 years of Nebuchadnezzar's reign. L.W. King prepared these tablets in 1919; he then died, and they were neglected for four decades.

iv. Excavations also document the victory of Nebuchadnezzar over the Egyptians at Carchemish in May or June of 605 B.C. Archaeologists found evidence of battle, vast quantities of arrowheads, layers of ash, and a shield of a Greek mercenary fighting for the Egyptians.

v. This campaign of Nebuchadnezzar was interrupted suddenly when he heard of his father's death and raced back to Babylon to secure his succession to the throne. He traveled about 500 miles in two weeks – remarkable speed for travel in that day. Nebuchadnezzar only had the time to take a few choice captives (such as Daniel), a few treasures and a promise of submission from Jehoiakim.

d. **Bound him in bronze fetters to carry him off to Babylon**: According to 2 Kings 24:1-7 this happened because Jehoiakim rebelled against Nebuchadnezzar. God did not bless this rebellion because though Jehoiakim was a patriot of the kingdom of Judah, he was not a man submitted to God. These sins were among those things that were **found against him**.

i. 2 Chronicles 36:6 tells us that Nebuchadnezzar intended to take Jehoiakim to Babylon, bound in bronze fetters. Yet Jeremiah 22:19 tells us that he would be disgracefully buried outside of Jerusalem.

ii. "The closing formulae make no reference to the burial of Jehoiakim, whose death occurred about December 598 before the first capture of Jerusalem by Nebuchadnezzar. 2 Chronicles 36:7 implies that he was taken to Babylon, but Jeremiah 22:19 tells how he was thrown unmourned outside Jerusalem, perhaps by a pro-Babylonian group who gave him the unceremonial burial of 'an ass'." (Wiseman)

iii. "2 Chronicles 36:6 states that Nebuchadnezzar 'bound him in fetters, to carry him to Babylon.' It does not say he *was* taken there. He may have been released after promising subjection to his conqueror." (Knapp)

3. (9-10) The reign of Jehoiachin and his recall to Babylon.

Jehoiachin *was* eight years old when he became king, and he reigned in Jerusalem three months and ten days. And he did evil in the sight of the Lord. At the turn of the year King Nebuchadnezzar summoned *him* and took him to Babylon, with the costly articles from the house of the Lord, and made Zedekiah, *Jehoiakim's* brother, king over Judah and Jerusalem.

a. **Jehoiachin was eight years old when he became king**: 2 Kings 24:8 tells us that *Jehoiachin was eighteen years old when he became king*. The difference between these two accounts is probably due to the error of a copyist in Chronicles.

i. "2 Chronicles 36:9 makes him eight years old at the beginning of his reign.... But some Hebrew MSS., Syriac, and Arabic, read 'eighteen' in Chronicles' so 'eight' must be an error of transcription." (Knapp)

ii. Jehoiachin "Was probably the throne-name of Jeconiah, abbreviated also to Coniah." (Wiseman)

b. **And he did evil in the sight of the Lord**: He carried on in the tradition of the wicked kings of Judah.

i. "Jeremiah said of Jehoiakim, (Jehoiachin's father) 'He shall have none to sit upon the throne of David' (Jeremiah 36:30). The word 'sit' here means to '*firmly* sit,' or 'dwell'; and Jehoiachin's short three months' reign was not that surely. And Zedekiah, Jehoiachin's successor, was Jehoiakim's *brother*, not his son." (Knapp)

ii. "That he was a grievous offender against God, we learn from Jeremiah 22:24, which the reader may consult; and in the man's punishment, see his crimes." (Clarke)

c. **King Nebuchadnezzar summoned him and took him to Babylon**: The previous king of Judah (Jehoiakim) led a rebellion against Nebuchadnezzar. Now the king of Babylon came with his armies against Jerusalem, and Jehoiachin hoped to appease Nebuchadnezzar by submitting himself, his family, and his leaders to the Babylonian king. God allowed Jehoiachin to be taken as a bound captive back to Babylon.

i. "His presence in Babylon is attested by tablets listing oil and barley supplies to him, his family and five sons in 592-569 B.C. and naming him as 'Yaukin king of the Judeans.'" (Wiseman)

d. **With costly articles from the house of the Lord**: On this second attack against Jerusalem, Nebuchadnezzar took whatever valuables remained in the temple or in the royal palaces of Jerusalem.

i. "The fall of Jerusalem didn't come about in one cataclysmic battle; it occurred in stages." (Dilday)

- Nebuchadnezzar's initial subjugation of the city about 605 B.C.
- The destruction by Nebuchadnezzar's marauding bands, 601 to 598 B.C.
- The siege and fall of Jerusalem under Nebuchadnezzar's main army on 16 March, 597 B.C.
- Nebuchadnezzar's return to completely destroy and depopulate Jerusalem in the summer of 586 B.C.

4. (11-14) The reign of Zedekiah and his rebellion against Babylon.

Zedekiah *was* twenty-one years old when he became king, and he reigned eleven years in Jerusalem. He did evil in the sight of the Lord his God, *and* did not humble himself before Jeremiah the prophet, *who spoke* from the mouth of the Lord. And he also rebelled against King Nebuchadnezzar, who had made him swear *an oath* by God; but he stiffened his neck and hardened his heart against turning to the Lord God of Israel. Moreover all the leaders of the priests and the people transgressed more and more, *according* to all the abominations of the nations, and defiled the house of the Lord which He had consecrated in Jerusalem.

a. **Zedekiah was twenty-one years old when he became king**: Since Nebuchadnezzar had completely humbled Judah, he put a king on the throne whom he thought would submit to Babylon. He chose this uncle of Jehoiachin, who was also a brother to Jehoiakim.

> i. "This king (597-587 B.C.) inherited a much reduced Judah, for the Negeb was lost (Jeremiah 13:18-19) and the land weakened by the loss of its experienced personnel. There were both a pro-Egyptian element and false prophets among the survivors (Jeremiah 28-29; 38:5)." (Wiseman)
>
> ii. 2 Kings 24:17 tells us that the name of **Zedekiah** was originally *Mattaniah*. The name **Zedekiah** means, *The Lord is Righteous*. The righteous judgment of God would soon be seen against Judah.

b. **He did evil in the sight of the LORD**: His evil was especially shown in that he **did not humble himself before Jeremiah the prophet**. Instead of listening to Jeremiah or other messengers of God he instead mocked and disregarded the message.

> i. "Zedekiah first disregarded Jeremiah's messages (Jeremiah 34:1-10); he came in time to direct his inquiries to this same prophet (Jeremiah 21); and he finally pled with him for help (Jeremiah 37). But at no point did he sincerely submit to the requirements of the Lord that Jeremiah transmitted to him." (Payne)

c. **He also rebelled against King Nebuchadnezzar**: Jeremiah tells us that there were many false prophets in those days who preached a message of victory and triumph to Zedekiah, and he believed them instead of Jeremiah and other godly prophets like him. Therefore, he **rebelled against King Nebuchadnezzar**.

> i. For example, Jeremiah 32:1-5 tells us that Jeremiah clearly told Zedekiah that he would not succeed in his rebellion against Babylon. Zedekiah arrested Jeremiah and imprisoned him for this, but the prophet steadfastly stayed faithful to the message God gave him.
>
> ii. "Through acts of infidelity toward his imperial master, he unwisely touched off the final revolt that brought down the vengeance of the Babylonians on Judah and Jerusalem; and thus both the state and the city were destroyed." (Payne)

d. **Moreover all the leaders of the priests and the people transgressed more and more**: These last kings of Judah were all wicked and deserving of judgment, but they were not alone in their sin and rejection of God. The **leaders**, the **priests**, and the **people** also **transgressed more and more**, pushing both God and Nebuchadnezzar to the limit.

B. The fall of Jerusalem and the Babylonian exile.

1. (15-16) The rejection of the message and the messengers.

And the Lord God of their fathers sent *warnings* to them by His messengers, rising up early and sending *them*, because He had compassion on His people and on His dwelling place. But they mocked the messengers of God, despised His words, and scoffed at His prophets, until the wrath of the Lord arose against His people, till *there was* no remedy.

a. **The Lord God of their fathers sent warnings to them**: God, great in mercy to His people, sent many warnings but these warnings were rejected. The greatness of His **compassion** towards His people is shown by the expression **rising up early and sending them**.

i. "What a touching and graphic phrase! How did God yearn over that sinful and rebellious city! Like a man who has had a sleepless night of anxiety for his friend or child, and rises with the dawn to send a servant on a message of inquiry, or a message of love. How eager is God for men's salvation." (Meyer)

b. **They mocked…despised…scoffed**: This tragic triple rejection of God's message and messengers sealed the doom of Judah. They rejected the message until **there was no remedy** and nothing could turn back the judgment of God.

i. "Three complaints are made in particular, that they were unfaithful, defiled the temple, and laughed at the prophets. All three are frequent themes throughout Chronicles, and it is as if the entire message of Chronicles were being summed up." (Selman)

ii. "*Till there was no remedy*; because the people would not repent, and God would not pardon them." (Poole)

iii. "Men's sins put thunderbolts into God's hands." (Trapp)

iv. "The cataclysm which has been threatened since Ahaz (2 Chronicles 28:9, 13, 25; 29:8, 10; 30:8) has been held back only because of the faith and repentance of individual leaders (*cf.* 2 Chronicles 29:10; 30:8-9; 32:25-26; 33:6; 34:21, 25). Now there is *no remedy*, a chilling phrase meaning literally 'no healing'. It implies the cancellation of God's promise to heal his land and that therefore even prayer will be utterly useless." (Selman)

2. (17-19) Jerusalem is despoiled and given over to destruction.

Therefore He brought against them the king of the Chaldeans, who killed their young men with the sword in the house of their sanctuary, and had no compassion on young man or virgin, on the aged or the

weak; He gave *them* all into his hand. And all the articles from the house of God, great and small, the treasures of the house of the Lord, and the treasures of the king and of his leaders, all *these* he took to Babylon. Then they burned the house of God, broke down the wall of Jerusalem, burned all its palaces with fire, and destroyed all its precious possessions.

a. **He brought against them the king of the Chaldeans**: Having rejected the message and the messengers of His *compassion* (2 Chronicles 36:15), God turned Judah over to a leader and a people who had no **compassion** upon their people.

i. "The end comes remarkably swiftly, like a bird of prey suddenly swooping down after circling repeatedly over its victim.... The final collapse under Zedekiah is therefore merely the final stage in a process that has long been inevitable." (Selman)

b. **He gave them all into his hand.... all the articles from the house of God.... all its palaces...all its precious possessions**: The emphasis is on the complete nature of the destruction the Babylonians brought to Jerusalem and its people. Nothing was spared and all was destroyed.

i. "The over-all impression is of unrelieved destruction. 'All, every' is used fivefold in verses 17-19, which together with *young* and *old, large and small*, and finally (literally), 'to destruction' confirms that there was no respite, no escape." (Selman)

c. **Then they burned the house of God**: This was the end of Solomon's great temple. Solomon's great temple was now a ruin. It would stay a ruin for many years until it was rebuilt in a humble form by the returning exiles in the days of Ezra.

i. "The Talmud declares that when the Babylonians entered the temple, they held a two-day feast there to desecrate it; then, on the third day, they set fire to the building. The Talmud adds that the fire burned throughout that day and the next." (Dilday)

ii. "Thus the temple was destroyed in the *eleventh* year of Zedekiah, the *nineteenth* of Nebuchadnezzar, the *first* of the XLVIIIth Olympiad, in the *one hundred and sixtieth* current year of the era of Nabonassar, *four hundred and twenty-four* years *three* months and *eight* days from the time in which Solomon laid its foundation stone." (Clarke)

d. **Broke down the wall of Jerusalem**: The walls of Jerusalem – the physical security of the city – were now destroyed. Jerusalem was no longer a place of safety and security. The walls would remain a ruin until they were rebuilt by the returning exiles in the days of Nehemiah.

i. "Thus, ends the history of a people the most fickle, the most ungrateful, and perhaps on the whole the most sinful, that ever existed on the face of the earth. But what a display does all this give of the power, justice, mercy, and long-suffering of the Lord! There was no people like this people, and no God like their God." (Clarke)

ii. "In the end, the exile came not because Israel sinned, but because they spurned God's offers of reconciliation." (Selman)

3. (20-21) The seventy-year Babylonian captivity.

And those who escaped from the sword he carried away to Babylon, where they became servants to him and his sons until the rule of the kingdom of Persia, to fulfill the word of the LORD by the mouth of Jeremiah, until the land had enjoyed her Sabbaths. As long as she lay desolate she kept Sabbath, to fulfill seventy years.

a. **Those who escaped from the sword he carried away to Babylon**: This was the third major wave of captivity, taking the remaining people except for the *poor of the land* (2 Kings 25:12).

i. "Of the prominent men of Jerusalem, only Jeremiah and Gedaliah were left behind (2 Kings 25:22; cf. Jeremiah 39:11-14). Jeremiah's stand on the Babylonian issue was doubtless well-known." (Dilday)

b. **Where they became servants to him and his sons**: One fulfillment of this was the taking of Daniel and his companions into captivity. Daniel was one *of the king's descendants* taken into the palace of the king of Babylon (Daniel 1:1-4).

i. "The exiles came 'to Babylon' where 'they became servants'; and yet, after an initial period of discouragement (Psalm 137) and oppressive service (cf. Isaiah 14:2-3), at least some Jews gained favor and status (2 Kings 25:27-30; Daniel 1:19; 2:49; 6:3)." (Payne)

c. **Until the rule of the kingdom of Persia**: The Persians (together with the Medes) conquered the Babylonians in 539 B.C. and the Jewish people were only allowed to return to their native lands *after* the Persians came to power.

i. The ancient Greek historian Herodotus relates that the Persian King Cyrus conquered Babylon by diverting the flow of the Euphrates into a nearby swamp. This lowered the level of the river so his troops marched through the water and under the river-gates. They still would not have been able to enter *had not the bronze gates of the inner walls been left inexplicably unlocked*. This was exactly what God predicted in Isaiah 44:28-45:7 and Jeremiah 51:57-58. *God opened the gates of the city of Babylon for Cyrus*, and put it in writing 200 years before it happened.

d. **To fulfill the word of the LORD by the mouth of Jeremiah, until the land had enjoyed her Sabbaths**: God had commanded Israel to observe a Sabbath for the land, allowing it to rest every seven years (Exodus 23:10-11). The people of Judah had denied the land its Sabbaths over a period of some 490 years, meaning that they "owed" the land 70 Sabbaths, and **to fulfill seventy years** God took the years back during the Babylonian exile.

> i. This was promised to a disobedient Israel hundreds of years before: *Then the land shall enjoy its sabbaths as long as it lies desolate and you are in your enemies' land; then the land shall rest and enjoy its sabbaths. As long as it lies desolate it shall rest; for the time it did not rest on your sabbaths when you dwelt in it.* (Leviticus 26:34-35)
>
> ii. Jeremiah spoke of the 70 years of exile in two places: Jeremiah 25:11-13 and Jeremiah 29:10.

4. (22-23) Cyrus allows the Jewish people to return to Jerusalem.

Now in the first year of Cyrus king of Persia, that the word of the LORD by the mouth of Jeremiah might be fulfilled, the LORD stirred up the spirit of Cyrus king of Persia, so that he made a proclamation throughout all his kingdom, and also *put it* in writing, saying, Thus says Cyrus king of Persia: All the kingdoms of the earth the LORD God of heaven has given me. And He has commanded me to build Him a house at Jerusalem which is in Judah. Who *is* among you of all His people? May the LORD his God *be* with him, and let him go up!

a. **Now in the first year of Cyrus king of Persia**: God gave the Persian king a sense of urgency about this, and the relief from exile was granted the very **first year** of his reign as **the LORD stirred up** his **spirit**.

> i. Cyrus made a decree giving Ezra and the Babylonian captives the right to return to Jerusalem and rebuild the temple in 538 B.C. (Ezra 1:1-4 and Ezra 5:13-17).
>
> ii. "Cyrus's policy of cooperating with local religions and of encouraging the return of exiles has received explicit archaeological confirmation from the inscriptions of the king himself (cf. especially the famous 'Cyrus Cylinder')." (Payne)

b. **All the kingdoms of the earth the LORD God of heaven has given me**: This remarkable recognition of God's hand upon his life may be connected with the remarkable prophecies regarding Cyrus in Isaiah 44:28-45:4.

c. **He has commanded me to build Him a house at Jerusalem**: The command of Cyrus not only allowed the return of the exiled people, but also a rebuilding of the destroyed temple.

i. "'To build him a house' is a deliberate echo of the central promise of the Davidic covenant (*cf.* 1 Chronicles 17:11-12; 22:10; 28:6; 2 Chronicles 6:9-10). Cyrus of course is thinking only of the house in *Jerusalem*, but in the Chronicler's thought this phrase is inevitably connected with both houses of the Davidic covenant, the dynasty as well as the temple." (Selman)

d. **Who is among you of all His people? May the LORD his God be with him, and let him go up!** The Books of 1 and 2 Chronicles end with this wonderful and remarkable encouragement to return and rebuild Jerusalem. This was the necessary and helpful encouragement to the first readers of Chronicles, letting them see their connection with God's broader plan of the ages.

i. Sadly, only a small percentage decided to return from exile; but those who did needed the encouragement to know they were making a valuable contribution to God's work.

ii. "Unlike the Book of Kings, with its central message of stern moral judgments, Chronicles exists essentially as a book of hope, grounded on the grace of our sovereign Lord.... [Chronicles shows that] History is a process, not of disintegration, but of sifting, of selection, and of development." (Payne)

iii. "In the end, therefore, the end is also a fresh start. God's promises continue through the exile, on through his own generation and into the future." (Selman)

1 and 2 Chronicles – Bibliography

Clarke, Adam *The Holy Bible, Containing the Old and New Testaments, with A Commentary and Critical Notes, Volume II – Joshua to Esther* (New York: Eaton and Mains, 1827?)

Meyer, F.B. *Our Daily Homily* (Westwood, New Jersey: Revell, 1966)

Morgan, G. Campbell *Searchlights from the Word* (New York: Revell, 1926)

Payne, J. Barton, "1 & 2 Chronicles" *The Expositor's Bible Commentary, Volume 4* (Grand Rapids, Michigan: Zondervan, 1992)

Poole, Matthew *A Commentary on the Holy Bible, Volume 1* (London, Banner of Truth Trust, 1968)

Selman, Martin J. *1 Chronicles, An Introduction and Commentary* (Leicester, England: Inter-Varsity Press, 1994)

Selman, Martin J. *2 Chronicles, An Introduction and Commentary* (Leicester, England: Inter-Varsity Press, 1994)

Spurgeon, Charles Haddon *The New Park Street Pulpit, Volumes 1-6* and *The Metropolitan Tabernacle Pulpit, Volumes 7-63* (Pasadena, Texas: Pilgrim Publications, 1990)

Trapp, John *A Commentary on the Old and New Testaments, Volume 1 – Genesis to Second Chronicles* (Eureka, California: Tanski Publications, 1997)

Wilkenson, Bruce *The Prayer of Jabez* (Sisters, Oregon: Multnomah Publishers, 2000)

As the years pass, I love the work of studying, learning, and teaching the Bible more than ever. I'm so grateful that God is faithful to meet me in His Word.

Once again, I am tremendously grateful to Alison Turner for her proofreading and editorial suggestions, especially with a challenging manuscript. Alison, thank you so much!

Thanks to Brian Procedo for the cover design and the graphics work.

Most especially, thanks to my wife Inga-Lill. She is my loved and valued partner in life and in service to God and His people.

David Guzik

David Guzik's Bible commentary is regularly used and trusted by many thousands who want to know the Bible better. Pastors, teachers, class leaders, and everyday Christians find his commentary helpful for their own understanding and explanation of the Bible. David and his wife Inga-Lill live in Santa Barbara, California.

You can email David at
david@enduringword.com

For more resources by David Guzik,
go to www.enduringword.com

www.ingramcontent.com/pod-product-compliance
Lightning Source LLC
Chambersburg PA
CBHW031611160426
43196CB00006B/93